CRISIS AND CHANGE IN THE JAPANESE FINANCIAL SYSTEM

Innovations in Financial Markets and Institutions

Editor:

Mark Flannery
University of Florida

Other books in the series:

Cummins, J. David and Santomero, Anthony M.:
Changes in the Life Insurance Industry: Efficiency, Technology and Risk Management
Barron, J.M., and Staten, M.E.:
Credit Life Insurance: A Re-Examination of Policy and Practice
Cottrell, A.F., Lawlor, M.S., Wood, J.H.:
The Causes and Costs of Depository Institution Failures
Anderson, S., Beard, T.R., Born, J.:
Initial Public Offerings: Findings and Theories
Anderson, S., and Born, J.:
Closed-End Investment Companies
Kaufman, G.:
Banking Structures in Major Countries
England, C.:
Governing Banking's Future
Hancock, D.:
A Theory of Production for the Financial Firm
Gup, B.:
Bank Mergers: Current Issues and Perspectives

CRISIS AND CHANGE IN THE JAPANESE FINANCIAL SYSTEM

edited by

Takeo Hoshi
University of California, San Diego

Hugh Patrick
Columbia University

KLUWER ACADEMIC PUBLISHERS
Boston / Dordrecht / London

Distributors for North, Central and South America:
Kluwer Academic Publishers
101 Philip Drive
Assinippi Park
Norwell, Massachusetts 02061 USA
Telephone (781) 871-6600
Fax (781) 681-9045
E-Mail <kluwer@wkap.com>

Distributors for all other countries:
Kluwer Academic Publishers Group
Distribution Centre
Post Office Box 322
3300 AH Dordrecht, THE NETHERLANDS
Telephone 31 78 6392 392
Fax 31 78 6546 474
E-Mail <services@wkap.nl>

Electronic Services <http://www.wkap.nl>

Library of Congress Cataloging-in-Publication Data

Crisis and change in the Japanese financial system / edited by Takeo Hoshi, Hugh Patrick.
p.cm. --(Innovations in financial markets and institutions)
Includes bibliographical references.
ISBN 0-7923-7783-4 (acid-free paper)
1.Finance--Japan.2.Financial institutions--Japan. I.Hoshi, Takeo. II.Patrick, Hugh T. III. Series.

HG187.J3 C75 2000
332'.0952--dc21

00-020395

Printed on acid-free paper.

Printed in the United States of America

TABLE OF CONTENTS

Contributors...vii

Preface...xi

1. **The Japanese Financial System: An Introductory Overview**
Takeo Hoshi and Hugh Patrick...1

PART I THE ORIGINS OF JAPAN'S BANKING CRISIS

2. **What Caused Japan's Banking Crisis?**
Thomas F Cargill...37

3. **Causes of Japan's Banking Problems in the 1990s**
Kazuo Ueda...59

PART II RESPONDING TO CRISIS

4. **The Stagnant Japanese Economy in the 1990s: The Need for Financial Supervision to Restore Sustained Growth**
Takatoshi Ito...85

5. **The Reorganization of Japan's Financial Bureaucracy: The Politics of Bureaucratic Structure and Blame Avoidance**
Nobuhiro Hiwatari...109

6. **The Disposal of Bad Loans in Japan: The Case of the CCPC**
Frank Packer...137

7. **Bank Lending in Japan: Its Determinants and Macroeconomic Implications**
Kazuo Ogawa and Shin-Ichi Kitasaka...159

8. **The Postal Savings System, Fiscal Investment and Loan Program, and Modernization of Japan's Financial System**
Thomas F Cargill and Naoyuki Yoshino...201

PART III FINANCIAL STRUCTURE CHANGE AND THE BIG BANG

9. **The Big Bang: Idea and Reality**
Akiyoshi Horiuchi....................233

10. **The Big Bang in Japanese Securities Markets**
Shoichi Royama....................253

11. **Japan's Financial Big Bang: Its Impact on the Legal System and Corporate Governance**
Hideki Kanda....................277

12. **Big Bang Deregulation and Japanese Corporate Governance: A Survey of the Issues**
Michael S Gibson....................291

Subject Index....................315

THE CONTRIBUTORS

Editors

Takeo Hoshi is Associate Professor at the Graduate School of International Relations and Pacific Studies (IR/PS) at the University of California, San Diego, where he has been on the faculty since 1988. In 1997–98 he was Tokio Marine & Fire Visiting Associate Professor on the Faculty of Economics at Osaka University. He has recently been appointed Editor of the *Journal of the Japanese and International Economies,* after being Associate Editor since 1993. He received a Bachelor of Arts in Social Sciences from the University of Tokyo in 1983, and a Ph.D. in Economics from Massachusetts Institute of Technology in 1988.

Hugh Patrick is R. D. Calkins Professor of International Business at Columbia Business School. He is Director of the Center on Japanese Economy and Business, and also serves as Co-Director of the University's APEC Study Center. He is Chair of the International Steering Committee of the Pacific Trade and Development (PAFTAD) conference series. He received his B.A. from Yale University in 1951 and M.A. degrees in Japanese Studies (1955) and Economics (1957) and his Ph.D. in Economics (1960) from the University of Michigan.

Authors

Thomas F. Cargill is Professor of Economics at the University of Nevada at Reno. He is a member of the Advisory Council of the Korean Economic Institute of America in Washington, D.C. He has been a Visiting Scholar and Researcher at the Bank of Japan (1984, 1994), the Japanese Ministry of Finance (1987), the Japanese Ministry of Posts and Telecommunications (1992), and Keio University (1997). He received a B.S. in Economics from the University of San Francisco in 1964 and a Ph.D. in Economics from the University of California, Davis in 1968.

Michael S. Gibson is an Economist in the Trading Risk Analysis Section, Division of Research and Statistics of the Board of Governors of the Federal Reserve System, Washington, D.C. where he does research in empirical finance. In addition to working at the Fed, he was on the faculty of the University of

Chicago Graduate School of Business for two years. He earned his B.A. in Economics from Stanford University (1988) and his Ph.D. in Economics from MIT (1993).

Nobuhiro Hiwatari is Professor of Contemporary Japanese Politics at the Institute of Social Science, University of Tokyo, where he has been teaching since 1993. He has also taught Japanese political economy at the University of California, Berkeley (1996–97) and Columbia University (1998–99) and was a Visiting Scholar at Harvard University and Cambridge University (St. John's College). He has a Ph.D. from the University of California (1989) and Doctorate of Laws from the University of Tokyo (1990).

Akiyoshi Horiuchi is Dean of the Center for International Research on the Japanese Economy and Professor in the Department of Economics at the University of Tokyo, where he has been on the faculty since 1984. Previously he was on the faculty at the Institute of Economic Research, Hitotsubashi University and the Department of Economics, Yokohama National University.

Takatoshi Ito is serving as Deputy Vice Minister for International Affairs in the Ministry of Finance, currently on leave from Hitotsubashi University, where he is Professor at the Institute of Economic Research. Previously he was Senior Advisor in the Research Department of the International Monetary Fund in Washington, D.C., Professor of Economics at the University of Minnesota between 1979 and 1988, and a Visiting Professor at Harvard University from 1992 to 1994. Professor Ito received a B.A. and M.A. in Economics from Hitotsubashi University in 1973 and 1975, and a Ph.D. in Economics from Harvard University in 1979.

Hideki Kanda is Professor of Law at the University of Tokyo. His main areas of specialization include commercial law, corporate law, banking and securities regulation. He served as Visiting Professor of Law at the University of Chicago Law School in 1989, 1991 and 1993, and as Visiting Professor at Harvard Law School in 1996. Professor Kanda received an LL.B. from the University of Tokyo (1977).

Kazuo Ogawa is Professor of the Institute of Social and Economic Research at Osaka University. In 1998–99 he was a Visiting Scholar at the Department of Economics, University of California, San Diego. Previously he taught at Kobe and Kyoto Universities, and served as Chief Research Economist at the Economic Research Institute of the Economic Planning Agency. In 1986–87, he was a Visiting Scholar at the Department of Economics, Yale University. Professor Ogawa received his B.A. and M.A. in Economics from Kobe University and a Ph.D. in Economics from the University of Pennsylvania.

Frank Packer is a Senior Economist in the Capital Markets Function of the Federal Reserve Bank of New York. Dr. Packer is a member of the Basel working group on credit ratings, which reports to the Bank for International Settlements (BIS). Dr. Packer has also been a Fulbright Scholar at the University of Tokyo and a Visiting Scholar at the Bank of Japan. He received a B.A. in History and Economics from Harvard University in 1981, an M.B.A. from the University of Chicago Graduate School of Business in 1985, and a Ph.D. in Economics and Finance from Columbia University's Graduate School of Business in 1993.

Shoichi Royama is President of Takaoka National College in Japan. Previously he was Professor at the Osaka School of International Public Policy at Osaka University, where he taught from 1969. His public activities include membership in The Forum for Policy Innovations; the Board of Directors, Osaka Securities Exchange; Member (Vice Chairman), Council on Finance, Ministry of Finance, Japan; Board of Auditors, The Asia and Oceania Foundation, The Daiwa Bank; Board of Directors, The Ishii Securities Market Research Foundation; and Board of Directors, The Japan Securities Research Institute. He was on the Securities and Exchange Council of the Ministry of Finance; the Council of The Suntory Foundation; and Board of Directors, The Matsushita International Foundation. Professor Royama received his B.A. and M.A. in Economics from Tokyo University in 1963 and 1965, and a Doctorate of Economics from Osaka University in 1982.

Kazuo Ueda has been a Member of the Policy Board of the Bank of Japan since April 1998. Previously he was a Professor (from 1993) and an Assistant Professor (from 1989) at the University of Tokyo, as well as Assistant Professor at Osaka University (from 1982) and British Columbia University (from 1980). He received his B.S. in Mathematics from the University of Tokyo in 1974 and his Ph.D. in Economics from MIT in 1980.

Naoyuki Yoshino is Professor of Economics at Keio University where he has been on the faculty since 1990. Previously he was an Associate Professor in the Graduate School of Policy Science at Saitama University in Japan (1982–90), and an Assistant Professor at the State University of New York at Buffalo (1979–81). He is a member of the Asset Management Council of the Ministry of Finance Trust Fund Bureau. He has been a Visiting Scholar at the Institute of Post and Telecommunications, the Ministry of Finance, and the Bank of Japan. He has served on numerous government councils, ministries and/or agencies, including most recently membership on the financial reform council under former Prime Minister Kiichi Miyazawa. Professor Yoshino received an M.A. in Economics from Tohoku University in 1975 and a Ph.D. in Economics from Johns Hopkins University in 1979.

PREFACE

As it enters the 21st century, the Japanese financial system is undergoing a major transformation, a process accelerated by a sense of impending crises. The banking system, dominated by large banks, has been suffering from serious problems with nonperforming loans since the bursting of the stock market and urban real estate bubbles at the beginning of the 1990s. Delay by regulatory authorities and the banks themselves made matters worse and led to a banking crisis in late 1997 and early 1998. Not expecting this, the Japanese government in late 1996 inaugurated a Big Bang of comprehensive financial deregulation designed to create "free, fair, and open financial markets." In late 1998 and early 1999 the government finally embarked on a major reform of the banking system, including making available some ¥60 trillion ($500 billion at 120 yen/dollar) of government funds. The Ministry of Finance (MOF), which had dominated the Japanese financial system and policy for most of the postwar period, has been deprived of most of the regulatory power it once possessed. Japanese financial institutions now seem to care more about ratings given by private agencies and other indicators in financial markets than in guidance by the MOF. The changes underway are profound.

The purpose of this book is to describe, analyze, and evaluate this process. The chapters address various issues relating to the transition of the Japanese financial system from a bank-centered and relationship-based system to a market-based and competitive system. Questions taken up include: Why did Japanese banks get into such serious trouble? Why has the MOF lost its immense power? How will the financial deregulation of the Big Bang further change the Japanese financial system, including the huge government financial institutions and postal savings? What are some broader implications of the transition?[1]

The book is divided into three parts. Part I considers the origins of Japan's banking crisis. Part II focuses on five particularly important areas of major actual and potential changes. Part III addresses the Big Bang and its effects and potential systemic externalities.

Inevitably this project owes much to many people. Our first debt of gratitude is to the authors, all distinguished and very busy specialists on various aspects of Japanese finance. Preliminary versions of most of these chapters were presented at the conference "The Japanese Financial System: Restructuring for the Future" held at Columbia University in October 1998. That conference was the catalyst for this project and volume. The authors have responded very constructively to the detailed comments in the process by which their chapters went through several revisions. They and we thank the assigned discussants at the conference: Professors Mitsuhiro Fukao, Yasushi Hamao, Edward Kane, Anil Kashyap, Randall Kroszner, Allan Meltzer, David Weinstein, and Mr Jeffrey Young. Charles Calomiris, Montrone Professor of Private Enterprise at the Columbia Business School, was instrumental with Takeo Hoshi in planning, organizing, and running the October 1998 conference; he merits our special thanks.

This project was not financially inexpensive, due mainly to travel and editing costs. It was funded by various Columbia Business School research-support organizations: the Jerome Chazen Institute of International Business; Center for International Business Education; and the corporate sponsors of the Center on Japanese Economy and Business, in particular Sumitomo Corporation of America, Sanwa Bank, Saga Corporation, Kikkoman, Takata Corporation, Bank of Tokyo-Mitsubishi, Tokyo Electric Power, Chase Manhattan Bank, Sumitomo Chemical, Mitsui Marine and Fire, Mitsubishi Trust and Banking Corporation, Fuji Xerox, Higa Industries, Mitsui and Company (USA), Tsuchiya, and the Japan Chamber of Commerce and Industry of New York. Without their financial support this project would not have been possible.

The publication process takes considerably more effort and meticulous and thoughtful care than is generally recognized. We thank particularly Larry Meissner, who worked intensively with us in editing the chapters; and Yvonne Thurman, Center Program Officer, who managed the entire project process, including communications with authors and preparation of the final versions of the chapters. Our thanks go also to Stephanie Giorgio, who worked closely with the editors in typing the Introduction; to Sally Sztrecska, who formatted and prepared the manuscript for camera-ready publication; and to Elizabeth Murry, Business Publisher at Kluwer Academic Publishers.

Finally, we thank each other. It has been educational and fun working together.

Takeo Hoshi
Hugh Patrick
October 1999

NOTE

1 We both also have been engaged in research on a number of these issues. For our analysis and views, which support and are complementary to those by the authors here, see Hoshi and Kashyap (1999) and Patrick (1998).

REFERENCES

Hoshi, Takeo and Anil Kashyap. 1999. "The Japanese Banking Crisis: Where did it come from and how will it end?" NBER Macroeconomics Annual 1999. MIT Press.

Patrick, Hugh. 1998 Oct. "Japan's Economic Misery: What's Next?" Eldon D Foote Lecture in International Business. University of Alberta.

ERRATA

Crisis and Change In The Japanese Financial System

Edited by Takeo Hoshi and Hugh Patrick

ISBN: 0-7923-7783-4

The publisher regrets that an error appeared in the first chapter in the first printing of this book. Below please find the corrected text.

Chapter 1

THE JAPANESE FINANCIAL SYSTEM: AN INTRODUCTORY OVERVIEW

Takeo Hoshi
University of California, San Diego

and

Hugh Patrick
Columbia Business School

The 1990s have been a time of crisis and change in the Japanese financial system. The crisis did not emerge all of a sudden. It developed in part because of policy mistakes, including years of regulatory forbearance in the face of serious problems with nonperforming loans. The crisis also was a consequence of changes in the system—some internally generated, others imposed by changes in the global environment; some needed, others undesired or unintended. The change also did not happen all of a sudden: for some 20 years the system has been evolving and developing, in response both to market forces and to the gradual and lopsided process of financial deregulation. This book describes, analyzes, and evaluates the crisis and the changes and considers the issues the Japanese financial system faces as it enters the 21st century.

We argue that the crisis is over in the sense that the underlying problems are now being addressed, or at least acknowledged, that a systemic banking crisis has been averted. The solutions will take time, but Japan's financial system—and its economy—are not going to collapse. As for change, the Big Bang is the important penultimate step of the deregulation process. The magnitude of the transformation is remarkable. During most of the postwar period, Japan's financial system was characterized by the dominance of bank financing, close relations between banks and their corporate clients, and heavy regulation by the government. That is now becoming what seems to be the opposite: a system where financial institutions compete in capital and other financial markets without heavy intervention from the government.

As general background for the chapters that follow, this introduction provides a brief survey of the postwar financial system in Japan and indicates the particular relevance of each of the other chapters. This is followed by an over-

Chapter 1

THE JAPANESE FINANCIAL SYSTEM: AN INTRODUCTORY OVERVIEW

Takeo Hoshi
University of California, San Diego

and

Hugh Patrick
Columbia Business School

We argue that the crisis is over in the sense that the underlying problems are now being addressed, or at least acknowledged, such that a systemic banking crisis has been averted. The crisis did not emerge all of a sudden. It developed in part because of policy mistakes, including years of regulatory forbearance in the face of serious problems with nonperforming loans. The crisis also was a consequence of changes in the system—some internally generated, others imposed by changes in the global environment; some needed, others undesired or unintended. The change also did not happen all of a sudden: for some 20 years the system has been evolving and developing, in response both to market forces and to the gradual and lopsided process of financial deregulation. This book describes, analyzes, and evaluates the crisis and the changes and considers the issues the Japanese financial system faces as it enters the 21st century.

We argue that the crisis is over in the sense that the underlying problems are now being addressed, or at least acknowledged, that a systemic banking crisis has been averted. The solutions will take time, but Japan's financial system—and its economy—are not going to collapse. As for change, the Big Bang is the important penultimate step of the deregulation process. The magnitude of the transformation is remarkable. During most of the postwar period, Japan's financial system was characterized by the dominance of bank financing, close relations between banks and their corporate clients, and heavy regulation by the government. That is now becoming what seems to be the opposite: a system where financial institutions compete in capital and other financial markets without heavy intervention from the government.

As general background for the chapters that follow, this introduction provides a brief survey of the postwar financial system in Japan and indicates the particular relevance of each of the other chapters. This is followed by an overview of those chapters. Each author provides further analyses and greater detail on specific topics and issues from a perspective and approach that enriches the book.

Neither the presumably successful completion of the Big Bang program by 31 March 2001 nor the 1998–99 banking system reforms will complete the process of financial deregulation fully, or alone establish a competitive, effective, and efficient financial system. All chapter authors allude, often explicitly and in some detail, to remaining problems and issues. We conclude this introductory chapter by considering five sets of ongoing difficulties.

TRANSFORMATION OF THE BANK-CENTERED FINANCIAL SYSTEM

The postwar Japanese financial system was shaped under heavy regulation. Until the early 1990s, many interest rates remained under tight control. International flows of financial assets also were heavily regulated. The financial industry was highly segmented and each category of financial institution was prohibited from expanding into the territory of the others. The system has been well described in a number of studies, including Suzuki (1986 and 1987), Cargill and Royama (1988), and Aoki and Patrick (1994).

Tables 1.1, 1.2, and 1.3 show various categories of financial institutions in Japan and their assets and deposits as of 1970, 1989, and 1998, which are selected to reflect the period before financial deregulation, the peak of asset prices boom in the 1980s, and the most recent period for which comprehensive data are available. As discussed below, boundaries between some categories have become blurred. Until the 1980s, however, separation of business by different category of financial institutions was strictly enforced.

There are two types of commercial banks in Japan: city banks and regional banks. Together they are called ordinary banks; both are primarily in the business of collecting deposits and making loans. City banks have their headquarters in major cities (usually, Tokyo or Osaka), make loans to large corporate customers, and (in principle) operate nationwide. Even though their number is small, they hold a large market share. Regional banks have their headquarters in smaller cities and deal with customers in their regions. Both city and regional banks traditionally focused on short-term lending.

Long-term lending was reserved for long-term credit banks and trust banks. Long-term credit banks raised funds by issuing financial debentures rather than taking deposits, and made long-term loans to large customers. Their debentures were bought by other banks, which were allowed to use the debentures as collateral to borrow funds from the Bank of Japan, as well as by wealthy individuals and the government's Trust Fund Bureau.

TABLE 1.1. Assets and Deposits of Financial Institutions, 1970 Year-end (in billion yen and percents)

Category	Total Deposits ¥[1]	Deposit Share %	Total Assets ¥[2]	Number[3]
City banks	24,298	33.8	36,889	15
Long-term credit banks	809	1.1	6,548	3
Trust banks	1,701	2.4	2,514	7
Regional banks	14,500	20.2	17,215	61
Sogo banks	6,366	8.9	7,627	72
Shinkin banks	7,740	10.8	9,429	502
Credit co-ops	1,978	2.8	2,150	532
Labor co-ops	358	0.5	395	46
Agricultural co-ops	6,187	8.6	7,115	6015
Fisheries co-ops	227	0.3	423	1596
Securities companies	—	—	1,296	247
Life insurance companies	—	—	5,570	20
Non-life insurance companies	—	—	1,354	21
Postal life and annuity	—	—	2,411	20,551
Postal savings	7,744	10.8	—	20,551
Government institutions[4]	—	—	7,692	10

1. In addition to deposits, city banks collected funds by issuing ¥126 billion of debentures and long-term credit banks issued ¥4,640 billion of debentures.
2. For credit cooperatives, labor cooperatives, agricultural cooperatives, fisheries cooperatives, and securities companies, total assets are calculated as the sum of major assets, and hence can be slightly less than the actual amount. For government financial institutions, includes only loans and discounts.
3. As of 31 December 1970, except for life insurance companies and non-life insurance companies, which are for 31 March 1971. For postal life and annuity and for postal savings the number is the number of post offices.
4. Government financial institutions include Japan Development Bank; Export-Import Bank of Japan; People's Finance Corp; Housing Loan Corp; Agriculture, Forestry and Fisheries Finance Corp; Small Business Finance Corp; Hokkaido and Tohoku Development Corp; Small Business Credit Insurance Corp; Local Public Enterprise Finance Corp; and Medical Care Facilities Finance Corp.
Source: Bank of Japan, *Economic Statistics Annual*, 1971 and 1997.

The primary business of trust banks was to make long-term loans to large firms using money entrusted by many small investors. For a long time, there were seven trust banks. (In addition, three commercial banks were allowed to do trust business using their own trust accounts. The trust accounts in commercial banks are not included in the numbers in Tables 1.1 to 1.3.) After deregulation allowed securities companies to set up trust-bank subsidiaries from April 1, 1993, the number had increased to 33 by 1997, including some foreign entrants.

TABLE 1.2. Assets and Deposits of Financial Institutions, 1989 Year-end (in billion yen and percents)

Category	Total Deposits ¥[1]	Deposit Share %	Total Assets ¥[2]	Number[3]
City banks	195,456	24.1	328,311	13
Long-term credit banks	7,923	1.0	69,841	3
Trust banks	13,599	1.7	51,113	7
Regional banks	135,969	16.8	164,516	64
Sogo banks	52,555	6.5	62,660	68
Shinkin banks	74,279	9.2	87,413	454
Credit co-ops	18,999	2.3	21,089	414
Labor co-ops	6,675	0.8	6,788	47
Agricultural co-ops	51,459	6.4	54,166	3722
Fisheries co-ops	1,903	0.2	2,750	1674
Securities companies	—	—	38,711	210
Life insurance companies	—	—	116,160	25
Non-life insurance companies	—	—	23,767	24
Postal life and annuity	—	—	44,776	23,408
Postal savings	134,572	16.6	—	23,408
Government institutions[4]	—	—	83,722	11
Overseas branches of Japanese banks	113,072	14.0	175,577	272
Foreign banks	4,462	0.6	23,280	82

1. In addition to deposits, city banks collected funds by issuing ¥10,960 billion of debentures and long-term credit banks issued ¥40,391 billion of debentures.
2. For credit cooperatives, labor cooperatives, agricultural cooperatives, fisheries cooperatives, and securities companies, total assets are calculated as the sum of major assets, and hence can be slightly less than the actual amount. For government financial institutions, includes only loans and discounts.
3. As of 31 December 1989, except for life insurance companies and non-life insurance companies, which are for 31 March 1990. For postal life and annuity and for postal savings the entry is the number of post offices.
4. Government financial institutions include, in addition to the 10 listed in Table 1.1, note 4, the Okinawa Development Finance Corp.
Source: Bank of Japan, *Economic Statistics Annual*, 1990 and 1997.

A number of foreign banks (93 in 1997) have branches or representative offices in Japan, but the size of this category is very small. Their share of deposits was less than 1% in 1997. Until 1983 the Bank of Japan did not even report data about foreign banks in its statistics annual.

City banks, long-term credit banks, trust banks, and to some extent regional banks catered to larger corporate customers. There was another group of financial institutions focused on lending to small business. *Sogo* banks (called re-

TABLE 1.3. Assets and Deposits of Financial Institutions: 1998 Year End

Category	Number	Total Assets (¥ billion)	Total Deposits (¥ billion) Share (%) in parentheses
City Banks	9	371,017	212,273 (21.7)
Long-term Credit Banks	3	69,744	8,087 (0.8)
Trust Banks	33	64,810	27,083 (2.8)
Regional Banks	64	199,975	171,947 (17.6)
Regional Banks II	61	73,101	63,985 (6.5)
Overseas Branches of Japanese Banks	397	85,687	29,458 (3.0)
Foreign Banks	89	59,019	8,228 (0.8)
Shinkin Banks	396	115,529	102,363 (10.5)
Credit Cooperatives	326	22,593	20,739 (2.1)
Labor Cooperatives	41	11,576	11,008 (1.1)
Agricultural Cooperatives	1,724	71,977	69,950 (7.2)
Fisheries Cooperatives	986	2,041	1,571 (0.2)
Securities Companies	217	27,158	
Life Insurance Companies	45	192,608	
Non-life Insurance Companies	33	30,940	
Postal Life Insurance and Postal Annuity	24,638	109,557	
Postal Savings	24,638		251,413 (25.7)
Government Financial Institutions	11	147,728	

Source: Bank of Japan, *Economic Statistics Monthly*, March 1999, Japanese Bankers Association, *Japanese Banks 1999*, Bank of Japan, *Economic Statistics Annul*, 1997.

Notes: The assets and deposits numbers are as of the end of December 1998. The numbers of institutions are as of the end of March 1999. The number for overseas branches of Japanese banks is at the end of December 1995. For postal life insurance and postal annuity and postal savings, the number for the column "Number" indicates the number of post offices as of the end of March, 1997. In addition to the deposits, city banks collected funds by issuing ¥5,112 billion of bank debentures and long-term credit banks issued ¥31,260 billion of bank debentures. For credit cooperatives, labor cooperatives, agricultural cooperatives, fisheries cooperatives, and securities companies, total assets are calculated as the sum of major assets, and hence can be slightly less than the actual amount. Government financial institutions include The Japan Development Bank, The Export-Import Bank of Japan, The People's Finance Corporation, The Housing Loan Corporation, The Agriculture, Forestry and Fisheries Finance Corporation, The Small Business Finance Corporation, The Hokkaido and Tohoku Development Corporation, The Small Business Credit Insurance Corporation, The Local Public Enterprise Finance Corporation, The Medical Care Facilities Finance Corporation, and The Okinawa Development Finance Corporation. For government financial institutions, the number in "Total Assets" includes loans and discounts only.

gional banks II after 1989), *shinkin* banks, and credit cooperatives are in this group, as well as some government financial institutions (including the Small Business Finance Corporation and the People's Finance Corporation). *Sogo* banks do the same sort of business as city banks and regional banks, except for restriction on loans to large customers (which were less than 20% of their total loans as of 1986, for example). In 1989 *sogo* banks were forced to convert into ordinary banks and they now comprise the category regional banks II, sometimes referred to as second-tier regional banks.

Shinkin banks and credit cooperatives primarily collect deposits from, and make loans to, members. *Shinkin*, but not co-ops, are allowed to have extensive branch networks to collect deposits from non-members. Agricultural cooperatives, fisheries cooperatives, and labor cooperatives are other specialized cooperative financial institutions which cater to their members. Labor cooperatives and fisheries cooperatives are quite small, but the collective size of agricultural cooperatives is substantial. Their deposits are roughly equal to those of the regional banks II.

Deposit-taking financial institutions, which include all the private sector financial institutions discussed so far, were prohibited from conducting security business or insurance business. Security businesses, such as brokerage and underwriting securities, were reserved for security companies, and the insurance business is still reserved for insurance companies. Insurance is further categorized into life insurance and casualty insurance. Until the late 1990s, non-life insurers were prohibited from selling life insurance policies and life insurers were prohibited from selling casualty insurance policies.

An important feature of the Japanese financial system is the large amount of funds channeled through government financial institutions. Postal savings collect deposits at more than 20,000 post offices throughout Japan. As of 1998, the size of postal savings exceeded the total deposits at city banks and accounted for more than a quarter of all deposits. Post offices also sell life insurance and annuities. In 1998, assets in postal life insurance accounts were more than a half of the combined total assets of all private life insurance companies.

Postal savings and postal life insurance are important sources of funds for the government's fiscal investment and loan program (FILP), which is administered by the Trust Fund Bureau of the Ministry of Finance (MOF). It allocates its funds to government financial institutions, purchase of central and local government bonds, and various central government special projects through government financial institutions. As indicated by the assets shown in Tables 1.1, 1.2, and 1.3, the amount of loans by government financial institutions is substantial. In 1998, for example, their loan amount exceeded the combined total assets of long-term credit banks and trust banks, and reached almost 40% of the total assets of city banks. (Thomas Cargill and Naoyuki Yoshino analyze the postal savings system in Chapter 8.)

Main Banks

Banks played the dominant role in the postwar Japanese financial system. Capital markets, especially for corporate debentures and commercial paper, were underdeveloped, due in large part to MOF's restrictive regulatory framework. Long-term credit banks and trust banks specialized in long-term financing of corporations, complementing the city banks' focus on short-term lending. Together they formed the core of the main bank system, treated in detail in Aoki and Patrick (1994).

Aoki, Patrick, and Sheard (1994) define the main bank system as "a nexus of relationships" that consists of three elements.

The first is a multitude of relationships between a firm and its main bank. The main bank typically is the largest lender, but the close relationship extends well beyond lending. A main bank is usually one of the largest shareholders of a firm and sometimes provides management assistance. When a firm is in financial trouble, its main bank often puts together a "rescue" operation, which includes dispatch of directors as well as fresh loans, and tries to rescue the firm from financial distress. For healthy firms, other services provided by the main bank become relatively more important. When a firm issues bonds, the main bank often serves as trustee of the collateral or as the guarantor (see Campbell and Hamao 1994). Many firms also concentrate their transaction and settlement accounts at their main banks.

For many large firms, the main bank relationship is an important part of a broader alliance called *keiretsu* (see Gerlach 1992), which is the grouping of major firms across diverse industry sectors. Each keiretsu has a bank as a core member, and member firms are related through borrowing from that bank, mutual shareholdings, personnel exchange, trade in intermediate products, and other group activities. Even though the overlap between the main bank relationship and keiretsu relationships is large, it is also important to note that some firms that are not part of a keiretsu have close relationship with a main bank and that some large keiretsu firms (such as Toyota) are quite independent from any bank.

The second element is "a unique reciprocal relationship among major banks", modeled by Sheard (1994a). Although the typical Japanese firm borrows from many lenders, the main bank plays the dominant role in monitoring the firm and intervening in the event of financial distress. In this sense, the other creditors "delegate" monitoring to the main bank. Through such cooperation, the banks can avoid duplication of monitoring efforts.

The third element is the government regulation that supports the system. As Ueda (1994) argues, heavy regulation imposed by MOF protected the banking sector not only from competition within the sector but also from competition from capital markets. This made it easy for banks to agree on the reciprocal arrangements described above. The rents created by regulation provided an extra incentive for banks to continue behaving as a good main bank by rescuing troubled customers

The government protected the banks mainly to maintain the stability of the financial system. As Patrick (1971) points out, the financial panic of 1927 had a major impact on the regulatory approach to banking, which previously had allowed easy entry, extensive competition, and bank failures. Regulators subsequently gave the highest priority to stability, and this stance was inherited and maintained by postwar regulators, which of course meant their power was immense.

An extreme version of the pursuit of stability in banking is the so-called convoy system, which allows no banks to fail. All banks were supposed to grow at about the same rate, and maintain their relative position. When, on occasion, a small, weak bank becomes nearly insolvent, MOF arranged a merger with a stronger bank. Although protection of the banking sector originally was motivated by concern for stability, it also promoted the main bank system.

In addition to the reduction of monitoring costs through reciprocal delegation described above, the main bank system was beneficial in reducing certain problems in corporate finance and in improving corporate governance. For example, as Hoshi, Kashyap and, Scharfstein (1991) found, investment by keiretsu firms, which have strong main bank relationships, is not very sensitive to the amount of their internal funds, suggesting that the main bank system mitigates informational and incentive problem that otherwise would give rise to a financing constraint. Rescue operations also are beneficial because they prevent inefficient closures of financially distressed but economically solvent corporations. Hoshi, Kashyap, and Scharfstein (1990) found that firms with strong main bank ties recover from financial distress more quickly than those without such ties.

Sheard (1989) focuses on the disciplinary aspect of rescue operations. During a rescue, the management that has led the company into financial trouble often is replaced by new management. In this sense, the main bank system fills the role of disciplining management that hostile takeovers play in the United States.

We can identify some potential problems of the main bank system. Most of these can be traced to the heavy regulation that supported it. For example, by suppressing capital markets, regulation penalized established firms that would have been able to raise funds more cheaply from capital markets than by borrowing from banks. Too much dependence on banks can also lead to too little risk-taking because banks are primarily debt holders and do not gain from upside risk. Government protection of banks, especially the convoy system, promoted inefficiencies in the banking sector. Because the convoy system made sure no bank lagged far behind the others, it ended up discouraging innovation and encouraging herding. For example, MOF restricted creation of new financial instruments until all banks were able to participate in them.

Change

Japan's bank-centered financial system started to change gradually in the late 1970s. The process has not been smooth, and it has created substantial tensions and problems. Subsequent chapters deal with those tensions and problems, and delve into the future of the Japanese financial system. Formally, the specific changes usually have involved "deregulation" or "liberalization" of the rules or procedures governing the financial system, but "change" as used here is a broader term.

The impetus for change came from a dramatic shift in the pattern of financial flows in Japan caused by the slowing of economic growth in the mid-1970s, and the economy shifted from ex-ante excess private investment demand to ex-ante excess private saving. The corporate sector reduced its financial deficit and the government sector widened its financial deficit. Moderate growth diminished expectations by corporations and hurt investment demand. Retained earnings from the rapid growth period meant many corporations had accumulated substantial internal capital, and this further reduced corporate demand for external funds. At the same time, slowed growth reduced tax revenue just when the government had committed to expand its social welfare expenditures. This forced the government to rely on bonds to finance sizable deficits. Thus, the financial surplus in the household sector, which traditionally had funded the mainly corporate sector's deficit, was now used to finance the government deficit as well.

In the rapid growth era the government had maintained a balanced budget policy, and the amount of government debt outstanding was very small. When, in the mid-1970s, the government started issuing large amounts of debt every year, the traditional practice of forcing major banks to buy low-yield government bonds became unsustainable. When the amount of bond issue was small, the banks had not objected to purchasing them, mainly because the Bank of Japan bought the bonds from them a year or so later in order to meet its money supply growth targets. With increased amounts of government bond issue, the Bank of Japan could not continue this practice without risking high inflation.

The government's need to develop primary and secondary markets for its bonds started the process of financial deregulation, but it was soon expanded into other markets. International capital controls were lifted so that Japanese corporations and investors could have access to foreign markets and foreign corporations and investors could have access to Japanese markets. Interest rates regulation started to be relaxed. The segmentation of financial institutions by business lines gradually became less pronounced. Development of capital markets (combined with the relaxation of international capital controls) gave large Japanese corporations important alternatives to bank financing.

The process of deregulation has been very slow. For example, regulation of deposit rates was completely lifted only in 1994. Banks and security firms were allowed partial entry to each other's business only in 1993. Corporate bond issuance became open to all corporations only in 1996. The Big Bang, announced in late 1996 and due to be completed by the end of fiscal 2000 (31 March 2001), has as its objective the establishment of free, fair, open and competitive financial markets. It is discussed in more detail by Horiuchi (Chapter 9) and Royama (Chapter 10).

Deregulation of financing choices for large firms was faster than in other areas. During the 1980s many large firms obtained access to foreign as well as domestic bond markets. As a result, large firms had reduced their dependence on banks substantially by the end of the 1980s. (Large firms are defined here as those listed firms with total assets of more than ¥120 billion at 1990 prices.) Thus, as many large firms depended less on their main banks, an important foundation of the main bank system was significantly eroded. The share of bank debt to total assets for large manufacturing firms was around 35% in the 1970s, but quickly declined in the 1980s and fell below 15% by the 1990s (Figure 1.1).

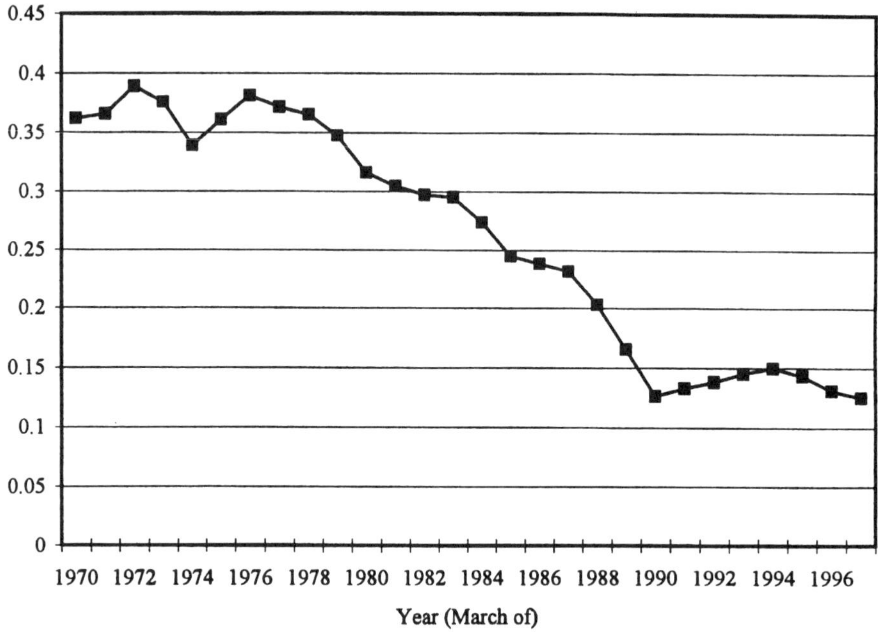

Source: Authors' calculation using Japan Development Bank Database.

Note: The figure shows the (weighted) average ratio of total bank loans to total assets for large manufacturing firms in Japan for the most recent accounting year ended in the last 12 months. Large firms here are defined to be those listed firms with total assets more than 120 billion yen in 1990 prices.

FIGURE 1.1. Bank debt to total assets ratio: large manufacturing firms.

When the large banks started to lose their large clients in the late 1980s, they began lending to small and medium firms with which they previously had not had a close relationship. Buying government bonds instead of lending was not an attractive option because the government aggressively reduced its large budget deficit in the late 1980s. Small- and medium-firm loans collateralized by real estate looked especially attractive because of the land price boom in the late 1980s; moreover real estate had long been correctly considered the safest form of collateral.

BANKING PROBLEMS IN THE 1990s

With hindsight, many people recognize the asset prices boom in Japan in the late 1980s was a bubble. As one would expect of a bubble, it collapsed. In Japan's case, it burst suddenly and hard. From 1985 to the end of 1989, the peak of the bubble in the stock market, the Nikkei 225 index increased 237%. Then, within three years, the index gave up more than 80% of that gain. Similarly, from 1985 to 1991, the peak of the bubble in the land market, the land price index for the six largest cities increased 207%. By 1997 commercial real estate prices had dropped to only 20–30% of their peak. As of mid-1999, land prices in the six cities were still declining.

With the bubble's bursting, the Japanese economy slumped into the long stagnation of the 1990s. The growth rate of real GDP plunged to 1.5% (the annual average from 1990 to 1994) compared with a 5.5% average in the previous four years. To counter this stagnation, the government had to give up its policy goal of a balanced budget, which had just been achieved in fiscal 1991. Fiscal conservatism, however, continued to dominate macroeconomic policy making, and monetary policy was the main policy tool for expansion, as had been the case in the 1980s. Between 1991 and 1993, the Bank of Japan cut its discount rate seven times, going from 6.0% to 1.75%. By 1994, however, it was clear that the expansionary monetary policy was not sufficient to end the stagnation. In the fiscal 1994 budget, the government reinstated the issue of deficit bonds. The economy began to recover and the growth rate improved to 5.1% by 1996. It appeared recovery was well on track.

However, encouraged by the recovery, the government in early 1997 quickly and strongly changed its fiscal policy from ease to restraint, reverting once again to fiscal conservatism. A temporary income tax reduction was ended, and co-payments for the national health insurance system were raised. The consumption tax rate was increased from 3% to 5%. The government revenue increases amounted to about two percentage points of GDP. The first quarter of 1997 showed phenomenal growth—thanks to an increase of expenditures for consumer durables to avoid the higher consumption tax rate implemented on

1 April—but then economic conditions deteriorated quickly. By the fourth quarter of 1997, economic growth was negative. Japan went into its longest recession in the postwar period as the economy recorded negative growth for five consecutive quarters. In the first quarter of 1999 GDP suddenly shot up at a reported 8.1% annual rate, led by a very high rate of government investment attributable to the late 1998 supplementary fiscal-stimulus package, but also showing surprising, if modest, increases in private consumption and business investment. Better-than-expected economic performance in the second quarter, which many analysts had initially projected to be a strongly negative "payback" for the surprising first quarter, suggests that Japan's recession has ended in 1999 and recovery has begun. However, recovery will probably be slow and gradual, and concerns remain that demand will not be sufficient to sustain growth in 2000.

The *Jûsen* Problem

When real estate prices started to fall in the early 1990s, many property-related loans made by Japanese banks began to turn sour, and the economy's stagnation added to an increasing level of nonperforming loans. The problems of the financial system first surfaced as the troubles at housing loan companies, the *jûsen*. Because we believe the *jûsen* case was the important overture to the Japanese banking crisis, we consider it here in some detail; it is considered in more detail in Ito (Chapter 4) and Hiwatari (Chapter 5). (For an even more detailed analysis of the debacle, see Milhaupt and Miller (1997).)

Jûsen were non-bank financial institutions set up by banks in the early 1970s to engage in home mortgage loans. A huge movement of people from rural Japan to cities accompanied rapid economic growth in the 1960s, creating high demand for housing in urban areas and hence demand for housing finance. Large banks, busy servicing their large corporate customers' demand for funds, were not interested in home mortgages. However, with the guidance and encouragement of MOF, banks created seven *jûsen*. In the 1980s, as deregulation allowed large companies to wean themselves away from bank financing, banks (including the *jûsen* founders) started to enter the home mortgage business. *Jûsen*, no longer able to compete effectively in their original niche, dramatically increased lending to real estate companies. *Jûsen* found themselves competing with banks that were both their founders and an important source of funds. A higher cost of funds inevitably made *jûsen* loan portfolios riskier than those of banks. Worse, many high-risk loans were "introduced" (for finders fees) to *jûsen* by founder banks, which themselves would not lend for such projects.

Agricultural credit cooperatives were another important class of lenders to *jûsen* as the co-ops had excess funds due to increasing deposits by members (farmers) selling land during the land price boom and falling loan demand for farm investment. The importance of agricultural credit co-op loans to *jûsen* substantially increased after MOF administrative guidance in March 1990 discouraged banks (but not co-ops) from increasing loans made to non-bank financial institutions, including *jûsen*.

When the bubbles collapsed, *jûsen* ended up with an enormous and increasing amount of nonperforming loans. In 1991, this was estimated to be ¥4.6 trillion, or 38% of total loans by *jûsen*. A rescue package was put together by creditors under MOF guidance in 1991. The founder banks forgave some loans and reduced interest rates on the remainder, and non-founder lenders promised to continue to lend to the *jûsen*. In return, the *jûsen* were supposed to make cost-cutting efforts. (This package resembles the stylized rescue operation for troubled industrial corporations discussed, for example, in Sheard (1994b).) The founder banks were the main banks of troubled *jûsen* and were to play the leading role in the rescue.

By 1993 it was clear that the initial package would not work. The economy continued to do poorly, land prices continued to decline, and the financial health of *jûsen* continued to deteriorate. Sanwa Bank, one of the founder banks of the *jûsen* Nippon Housing Loan Corporation (NHLC), proposed a plan to divide NHLC into good-loan and bad-loan companies. The good-loan part would continue the business, while the bad-loan part would go through a court-supervised liquidation. MOF rejected the plan: it would not allow Sanwa to deviate from the logic of main-bank rescue.

Instead MOF revised the restructuring plan: the interest rate on loans by founder banks was reduced to zero, the rate on loans from other banks was reduced to 2.5%, and the rate on loans from agricultural credit co-ops was reduced to 4.5%. Under the assumption that land prices would stop falling, and in fact would increase by 25% in the following 10 years, the plan was deemed sufficient to revive the *jûsen*.

The assumptions behind the restructuring plan of 1993 turned out to be too optimistic. By 1995, 75% of *jûsen* loans were nonperforming and 60% were deemed completely unrecoverable. Leverage (the debt to equity ratio) was astonishingly more than 150. Four years of forbearance by MOF had significantly worsened the situation. By 1995, it was clear that the *jûsen* could not be saved. The question was who would pay for the losses—hitherto hidden—that would be revealed by liquidation. The debate became highly political, as Hiwatari discusses (Chapter 5).

At the heart of the debate was whether "lender-liability" or "founder-liability" should prevail in allocating losses. Lender liability is the logic behind pro-rata allocation of losses among creditors, which is often used in a court-supervised liquidation. Founder liability is the logic behind the main bank system, which allocates disproportionately larger losses to founder banks (the main banks). The final result was a compromise, modified founder-liability, which forced founder banks to shoulder ¥3.5 trillion of losses, other banks ¥1.7 trillion, agricultural credit cooperatives ¥530 billion, and taxpayers ¥680 billion. Thus, the *jûsen* case was the first episode that deviated from the traditional norm of the main bank rescue and convoy system, and that required government funds.

The agricultural credit cooperatives often are criticized for having benefited disproportionately from public funds and having argued bitterly against bearing any losses at all (because they had worked under the norm of the main bank and convoy systems, believing they had Ministry of Finance guarantees), but their behavior does not seem that irresponsible or opportunistic. For a useful discussion of this implicit government encouragement for agricultural credit cooperatives to make loans to *jûsen*, see Milhaupt (1999).

The *jûsen* crisis was just the first of a sequence of major difficulties the Japanese financial system experienced in the 1990s. During the summer of 1995, in the midst of Diet discussion on *jûsen* resolution, bad loans led to the failure of Hyogo Bank (largest among regional banks II) and two large credit unions (Cosmo and Kizu). The financial markets began to suspect that other banks in Japan also suffered from severe bad loans problem. Under the convoy system, even healthy banks would suffer from the cost of bailing out weak institutions, so foreign banks started to charge higher rates on their interbank loans to all Japanese banks. The emergence of this "Japan premium" in the summer of 1995 increased the cost of funds for Japanese financial institutions and further eroded their profitability. The Japan premium had almost disappeared by the end of 1995, but reemerged in late 1997 as the banking problem developed into a full-blown crisis. Repeated assurances of bank health by the Japanese government did not help reduce the premium unless the announcement was accompanied by concrete actions to deal with the bad loan problem (Peek and Rosengren 1999).

Two-Pronged Policy

Government policy toward the financial system during the 1990s can be understood as a two-pronged approach: accommodation and reform. The government responded to emerging failures and near insolvencies of banks in a nonsystematic way. Measures taken were most often well within the convoy system. For example, when Toho Sogo Bank became an early victim of the post-bubble stagnation, the government had Iyo Bank absorb it, effective 1 April 1992, with subsidies from the Deposit Insurance Corporation (DIC). When Toyo Shinkin Bank failed, it was merged with Sanwa Bank in October 1992. Even after the *jûsen* resolution jeopardized continuation of the convoy system, MOF used a convoy-like arrangement to resurrect failed Hyogo Bank as Midori Bank in April 1996. The shareholders of Midori Bank were large city banks and the Bank of Japan, which provided fresh capital under MOF guidance. When Taiheiyo Bank failed in April 1996, its business was transferred to Wakashio Bank, which was set up by Sakura Bank with financial assistance from DIC. However, when Hanwa Bank failed later that year, it was simply liquidated.

The formula of making other banks assist a weak bank financially was applied to prop up ailing Nippon Credit Bank in early 1997. (Such a formula is called *hougacho* (subscription list) implying that MOF solicits banks for funds to prop up a weak bank.) In October 1997, four weak regional banks were merged into two banks under MOF guidance and financial assistance from DIC. As in the *jûsen* case, the government hoped the land prices would start increasing again before the nonperforming loan problems affected large banks. Such a turn-around, however, never happened.

Even as the nonperforming loan problem was mounting, the process of financial deregulation not only continued, it accelerated. The momentum for deregulation reached a peak when the economy showed signs of recovery in 1996. In late 1996, Prime Minister Hashimoto announced a plan to complete deregulation of the Japanese financial system by 2001. This has become known as the Japanese Big Bang.

In May 1997 the Foreign Exchange Act was revised, with implementation from 1 April 1998. This reform abolished most of the international capital controls that had remained after an extensive liberalization in 1980. This was followed by proposals by each of three Ministry of Finance councils: Financial System Research Council, Securities and Exchange Council, and Insurance Council. Published in June 1997, the proposals describe the contents of the Big Bang in each area (see Horiuchi, Chapter 9).

As discussed below, problems in the Japanese financial system developed into a crisis in late 1997. Most of the Big Bang plans, however, have been implemented as initially planned. When the Big Bang program is fully implemented, the transformation of the Japanese financial system from a bank-centered system to a market-centered system will be close to complete.

Two reforms undermining the convoy system passed the Diet in 1996. First, the government decided to move financial supervision and examination out of MOF to a newly created Financial Supervisory Agency (FSA). Second, reform of the Banking Act introduced Prompt Corrective Action (PCA). Both changes were scheduled to be introduced in 1998. Under PCA, regulators are required to intervene quickly at poorly capitalized banks, a significant deviation from the discretionary policy of the convoy system. These reforms were considered part of long-run institution building to prepare for the new market-based financial system. When the Diet deliberated them, there was no intention of using the new institutions to address the current problems of the financial system. The government hoped the nonperforming loan problem would have disappeared by the time the new institutions become operative.

MOF hung on to the two-pronged approach of trying to complete the deregulation program while maintaining financial sector stability using the convoy system until late 1997, when it started to crumble. When Japan went into a serious recession in 1997, that exacerbated the banking problems. The crisis reached a peak in November 1997. The month began with Sanyo Securities, a mid-size security firm famous for having the world's largest trading floor (built during the bubble) filing for bankruptcy protection. This was the first postwar default in the overnight interbank loan market, a shocking event. Then Hokkaido Takushoku Bank, a city bank whose plan to merge with Hokkaido Bank, a regional bank, had just faltered, faced serious trouble securing liquidity in interbank loan markets, and had to close. This was the first case of a major bank failure in postwar Japan. A week later, Yamaichi Securities, one of the Big Four security houses, was reported (correctly) to have huge undisclosed losses and collapsed. Before the month ended, Tokuyo City Bank, a regional bank, also failed.

These events generated a crisis mentality in the government, and eventually led to creation of a framework that allows a systematic resolution of the banking crisis. However, the process was far from straightforward.

Following the crisis in November, the government quickly made an arrangement with the Bank of Japan and the Deposit Insurance Corporation to put up as much as ¥30 trillion of public funds to deal with the banking crisis. Of this, ¥17 trillion was for the protection of depositors of failed financial institutions and the remaining ¥13 trillion was to inject capital into under-capitalized but presumably healthy banks. The decision to use public funds was a significant departure from the traditional approach based on the convoy system. Recall that in the *jûsen* case, the fight over using less than ¥0.7 trillion deadlocked the Diet for many days.

However, the government and banks were not exactly ready to recognize the bad loan problems and resolve the crisis once and for all, using public funds if necessary. Thus, in January 1998, the government introduced two options in the accounting standards which meant banks could make their books look better than they really were. First, banks were allowed to evaluate their shareholdings in other companies at book value, thereby avoiding reporting unrealized capital losses. Second, they were allowed to re-evaluate their land holdings at market prices which, despite the decade's decline, were still usually much higher than original cost. At the same time, introduction of prompt corrective action, planned for April 1998, was delayed a year for banks that do not have international operations, which meant for most banks.

A New Approach

The Financial Crisis Management Committee (Kin'yu Kiki Kanri Iinkai) was set up to evaluate the applications by banks for public funds. Banks initially were reluctant to apply for public funds, fearing such an action might reveal the size of their problems. In the end, however, all the major banks decided to apply for an identical amount, and all the applications were accepted. ¥1.8 trillion was distributed to 18 major banks and 3 regional banks by the end of March 1998. The convoy system was still marching along.

The capital injection did not end the banking crisis. Soon after, the Long-term Credit Bank, a major recipient, was reported to be in serious trouble. In June its share prices tumbled and those of other banks that were considered weak also fell substantially.

By June 1998 the Liberal Democratic Party (LDP), the largest party in the coalition government, started discussing more systematic ways to resolve the banking crisis and to limit the cost to the real economy as much as possible. This led to a "bridge bank" plan, designed to secure credit lines for healthy borrowers of failed banks while the banks were reorganized under receivership.

Before the bridge bank plan was enacted into law, the LDP suffered a massive loss in the July Upper House election, and Prime Minister Hashimoto resigned. The election sent a clear message of voter dissatisfaction with the government's management of the economy and the financial system mess. It was clear that the government had to come up with a decisive scheme to end the banking crisis and to bring about economic recovery. The new Prime Minister, Keizo Obuchi, moved ahead on both fronts, proposing major banking system reforms and massive fiscal stimulus.

The Democratic Party, which became the principal opposition party as the result of election, came up with a "nationalization" plan to counter the LDP's bridge bank plan. Under it, a failed bank would be nationalized immediately and reorganized for later re-privatization. In early October, a compromise was reached and the Diet passed the Financial Reconstruction Act. According to this Act, a newly created Financial Reconstruction Commission (FRC) decides whether a failed bank should be nationalized and reorganized (the Democratic Party plan) or put under receivership and reorganized as a bridge bank (the LDP plan). In addition, a weak bank can apply for nationalization before it fails. This was what Long-Term Credit Bank did immediately after passage of the law. Another troubled long-term credit bank, Nippon Credit Bank, was nationalized, despite its objections, in December.

The government also passed a bill to inject capital into under-capitalized (but presumably healthy) banks. The Rapid Recapitalization Act allows a healthy bank to apply for public funds. To implement the Rapid Recapitalization Act and Financial Reconstruction Act, the government raised its commitment from

¥30 trillion to ¥60 trillion: ¥17 trillion for depositor protection (already committed), ¥18 trillion for the nationalization of failed banks, and ¥25 trillion for capital injection (an increase from ¥13 trillion).

The Financial Reconstruction Act and the Rapid Recapitalization Act constitute the framework for the Japanese government to deal systematically with the banking crisis, and with any subsequent difficulties. The Financial Reconstruction Commission (FRC) and Financial Supervisory Agency (FSA) have been very active in implementing the framework.

After the Long-Term Credit Bank and Nippon Credit Bank were nationalized, the remaining major banks were encouraged to apply for an injection of capital. This time, most applied. Bank of Tokyo-Mitsubishi refused any public funds, instead successfully recapitalizing itself through a stock subscription taken up by Mitsubishi group-member firms. Some banks were too weak to apply. Yasuda Trust decided to be reorganized under Fuji Bank; Mitsui Trust and Chuo Trust were allowed to apply only on the condition that they merge.

In total, some ¥7.5 trillion were injected into 15 major banks, with varying terms. Details on the amount and terms of the government capital infusion and on the raising of private funds from existing allied shareholders are provided in Nakaso (1999). In the fall of 1999, FRC started accepting applications for capital injections from regional banks. As of September 1999, four regional banks have been approved to receive a total of ¥260 billion.

The FSA, established in June 1998, started by examining all the major banks. Then it moved on to the regional banks and regional banks II. By the summer of 1999, FSA had completed examination of all of them. This led to closure of four regional banks II (as of August 1999).

The Bad Loan Problem in 1999

The nonperforming loans problem is still serious, but the government and the financial industry finally seem ready to resolve it. Active implementation of the Financial Reconstruction Act and Rapid Recapitalization Act by FSA and FRC has been especially encouraging. Table 1.4 shows the estimates of bad loans for banks as of March 1998 and March 1999.

There are three definitions of "bad loans" in Japan (see Section 4 of Hoshi and Kashyap (1999) for more details). The first is the measure of "risk management loans," which is published by each bank in its financial statements. Risk management loans include loans to failed enterprises, loans on which payments are suspended for more than three months, and restructured loans. As of March 1999, the sum of bad loans according to this definition was to close to ¥30 trillion, or 6% of GDP.

TABLE 1.4. Bad Loans as of March 1998 and 1999 (in billion yen and percents)

	Fiscal 1997	Fiscal 1998
Risk management loans		
Total, as % GDP	*5.9*	*6.0*
Total	29,758	29,627
Loans to failed enterprises	6,843	4,424
Past-due loans	10,771	15,504
3-months-past-due loans	3,246	1,633
Restructured loans	8,899	8,063
Classified Loans		
Total, as % GDP	*14.2*	*13.0*
Total of categories II–IV	71,836	64,258
Category IV	0	74
Category III	6,073	3,160
Category II	65,763	61,024
Classified Loans, FRA[1]		
Total, as % GDP	—	*6.9*
Total	—	33,943
Unrecoverable	—	10,321
Risk	—	17,415
Special attention	—	6,207
Allowance for loan losses	17,815	14,797
Cumulative direct write-offs from 1 Apr 1992[2]	19,911	24,620

Fiscal years end on 31 March of the following calendar year.

Hokkaido Takushoku, Tokuyo City, Kyoto Kyoei, Naniwa, Fukutoku, and Midori Bank, which failed or merged with other banks during fiscal 1997 are excluded. Long-term Credit Bank of Japan, Nippon Credit Bank, Kokumin, Koufuku and Tokyo Sowa Bank, which were closed during fiscal 1998 or early fiscal 1999 are excluded from the fiscal 1998 numbers.

1. Loans classified using Financial Reconstruction Act definitions.
2. Direct write-offs include write-offs of loans, loss on sales of loans, loss on supports to other financial institutions. However, the data before fiscal 1994 includes only write-offs of loans and losses on sales to the Cooperative Credit Purchase Corporation (CCPC).

Sources:

Financial Supervisory Agency (FSA), "The Status of Risk Managment Loans Held by All Banks . . . " (for 1999) and "The Current Status of Risk Management Loans Held by Deposit-Taking Financial Institutions . . . " (for 1998).

Financial Reconstruction Commission (FRC), "Self-Assessment Result of Asset Quality . . . " (for 1999 FRC-classified loans).

The data are available in English at www.fsa.go.jp and www.frc.go.jp.

The second definition is based on the classification of loans that FSA uses in bank examinations. The banks are asked to classify their loans according to their collectability. The loans that have no chance of being recovered are classified as Category IV, those with doubtful collectability are Category III, and those that may become uncollectible without special attention are Category II. The remaining, "normal," loans constitute Category I. It is customary to consider the sum of categories II, III, and IV as a definition of bad loans. According to this definition, the amount of bad loans as of March 1999 is ¥64 trillion or 13% of GDP. This is substantially more than the amount of the risk management loans, but one should note that a majority of Category II loans are considered recoverable.

Finally, starting in March 1999, each bank is required to publish yet another set of bad loans numbers, as mandated by the Financial Reconstruction Act. This definition is slightly broader than that for risk management loans but substantially narrower than the supervisory definition. As of March 1999, Japanese banks collectively have about ¥34 trillion (close to 7% of GDP) of bad loans according to this definition.

The table also shows the cumulative amount of loans that were written off by banks since fiscal 1992 and the current outstanding amount of Specific Allowance for Loan Losses. The numbers imply that the banking sector still has a massive bad loan problem, even after substantial write-offs (close to ¥25 trillion). The current level of loan loss allowance (less than ¥15 trillion) is still far less than the amount of bad loans. This suggests banks will continue to have to devote earnings to provision against bad loans; how much depends on the rate and degree of economic recovery (which reduces the amount of bad loans as companies do better) and on stock market rises (which generate unrealized capital gains on securities held).

Late 1998 and early 1999 was a significant turning point. The "crisis" in the banking system is finally over, though most banks still have substantial restructuring problems. Japan is now in the process of building a new financial system.

AN OVERVIEW OF THE BOOK

The chapters that follow build upon the well-known descriptions of Japanese financial institutions, government policies, and financial and economic trends we have summarized above, to provide further analyses and greater detail of specific topics and issues. Each author has a perspective and approach that enriches the book.

Since Japan has a bank-based financial system, inevitably much of the focus is on commercial banks and government policies to deal with their huge and worsening bad- and problem-loan difficulties. But the approach is substantially more comprehensive than the banking system alone. The entire financial system is rapidly changing as Japan moves toward market-based finance. The securities industry in particular is being dramatically transformed. So too, though much more slowly, are the life and casualty insurance industries. Financial institution behavior and reform have macroeconomic as well as microeconomic effects and implications.

The book is divided into three parts. Part I considers the origins of Japan's banking crisis. The crisis has engendered wide-ranging responses in policies, institutions, and financial structures, and interacted with the macroeconomic performance of the real economy. Part II focuses on five particularly important areas of major actual and potential changes. Part III addresses the Big Bang and its effects and potential systemic externalities.

In Chapter 2 Cargill examines what led to the crisis in Japanese banking in 1997–98. He identifies five factors that were responsible. First, the highly regulated financial system, which worked well during the rapid economic growth period, failed in the new environment that began to emerge in the 1970s. The Ministry of Finance was especially slow to evolve its regulatory and supervisory framework. Second, the Bank of Japan created too much liquidity in the late 1980s, with low interest rates, and followed it by too abrupt a tightening of monetary policy. These policy failures led to wild fluctuations in asset prices. Third, the government was extremely slow in responding to the problems in the financial system even after their existence was clear. Fourth, Japanese taxpayers provided little support for the government to use public funds to rescue the banking system until late in the game. Finally, lack of disclosure and transparency by banks, other financial institutions, and regulators alike contributed to the delay in responding to what became ever-deepening difficulties.

Kazuo Ueda, in Chapter 3, also addresses the causes of the banking crisis from a different perspective, and comes up with a similar set of factors with different emphases. He considers the heart of the problem to have been the speculative real estate-related lending of the 1980s, which turned bad when urban land prices plummeted in the 1990s. He attributes both the rise and fall in real estate prices to the volatile movements in monetary policy since the mid-1980s. Regulatory forbearance and non-transparency aggravated the difficulties. Using cross-section regression analysis for 147 commercial banks, he shows that banks located in areas where land prices increased rapidly, and where their proportion of loans collateralized by real estate were higher, tended to have a higher proportion of real estate loans in their portfolios, and higher ratios of bad loans, by the end of fiscal 1995 (31 March 1996). The variance in bad loan ratios is very wide. With the exception of trust banks, all of the banks with a then-reported bad loan ratio of 8% or higher have subsequently been liquidated, merged with another bank, or nationalized.

As both Cargill and Ueda stress, the initial reaction of the government to the bad loans problem was forbearance, which is clearly observed in the *jûsen* case described above and by Ito in Chapter 4. When it was clear that the problems of the Japanese financial system would not just go away, the government tried several measures to contain them, as discussed in these and several other chapters, notably Packer (Chapter 6).

Part II's analysis of important areas of major actual and potential changes begins with Takatoshi Ito's examination, in considerable detail, of the combination of deepening bank nonperforming loan problems and mistakes in macroeconomic and regulatory policies as well as mistakes by banks themselves. The consequences were poor macroeconomic performance in the 1990s, culminating in Japan's recession from the fourth quarter of 1997 until early 1999, and the financial crisis of late 1997 to early 1998. Ito identifies the causes of the recession as, first, the major fiscal policy error of increasing taxes so much in April 1997, followed by the Asian crisis beginning that summer (which reduced Japanese exports), and then the domestic financial crisis of late 1997. Addressing still-controversial policy issues, he argues that, with a monetary policy of a zero (overnight interbank) interest rate and of preventing further yen depreciation, in 1998 Japan was in a liquidity trap that limited the benefits of further monetary stimulus. Initially reluctant, the government finally came to use strong fiscal stimulus. Ito proposes continued stimulus, with more aggressive use of tax cuts relative to government expenditure increases, and special incentives for housing investment.

One of the most surprising and fascinating events of the tumultuous 1990s has been the sharp decrease in the power and position of the hitherto seemingly omnipotent Ministry of Finance, the most powerful and elite central government bureaucracy in a country where bureaucrats ruled and politicians (for long, the Liberal Democratic Party) simply reigned. At the same time, the various categories of private financial institutions have considerable political powers; the handling of the *jûsen* crisis is one important example. MOF supervisory and regulatory responsibilities and powers over the banks and other financial institutions have been taken away, transferred to the newly established Financial Supervisory Agency and the Financial Reconstruction Commission, as is noted in a number of chapters. This is political economy at the highest political level.

In Chapter 5 Nobuhiro Hiwatari discusses the process by which political leaders were forced to deal with the inability of MOF to resolve the bank bad loan problem effectively and to bring about financial system reform. In the 1990s the LDP lost control of the government and coalition politics took over. Eventually the LDP regained power as it skillfully created coalitions and alliances with a series of opposition political parties. No politicians wanted to be blamed for costing voters (as taxpayers) heavily to clean up the financial mess; Hiwatari explains how restructuring the financial regulatory bureaucracy was a strategy of blame avoidance, by non-LDP parties in particular.

From the perspective of both banks and regulatory authorities, the big problem has been how to cope with their immense and ever-worsening bad and problem loans. In Chapter 6 Frank Packer provides a careful and fascinating case study of the main effort from the early and mid 1990s, namely, establishment by banks of the Cooperative Credit Purchasing Company (CCPC). CCPC has bought, at a discount, bad loans collateralized by real estate, enabling selling banks to obtain hitherto-difficult tax benefits. CCPC was then supposed to dispose of those assets, with further losses reverting to the original bank. CCPC was initially quite useful in a limited way but ultimately, as Packer well argues, was not a success story. Indeed it has represented a microcosm of failures of Japanese policy toward the bank bad loan problem. The CCPC has been superseded in scale, scope, and effectiveness by the Resolution and Collection Corporation, which began operations in April 1999.

In Chapter 7 Kazuo Ogawa and Shin-ichi Kitasaka provide a careful, detailed, empirical analysis of the determinants of bank lending and its macroeconomic implications, notably the relationship between bank lending and business fixed investment. First, they estimate loan supply and demand functions in a dynamic framework, utilizing bank balance sheet annual panel data for 1976–95, disaggregated for major banks and regional banks, large and small enterprise borrowers, and manufacturing and non-manufacturing firms, testing the effects of interest rates, deposit growth, use of real estate as collateral, and changes in real estate prices. They find significant differences in bank lending behavior. Small firms and non-manufacturing firms have been more sensitive to bank loan supply, and major banks in particular dealt with asymmetric information problems in lending to small firms by requiring real estate collateral—to note only a few of the author's findings. In the second step of the analysis, Ogawa and Kitasaka address the extent to which business investment has depended on the fundamental profitability of investment, measured by Tobin's marginal q, and on the availability of bank loans. They estimate the coefficients of these determinants on the fixed investment of small, medium, and large firms; and they show that small firms in particular, and especially in non-manufacturing industries, are sensitive to the availability of bank loans. The authors do an informative simulation analysis of the effects on business investment of two events: bank loan supply contraction under the monetary tightening of the early 1990s, and the credit crunch of late 1997 to early 1998. They show that both events substantially reduced business investment, particularly by non-manufacturing small firms, which fed recessionary pressures during both periods.

The Japanese government itself is a major financial intermediary. It collects funds from the postal savings and postal life insurance systems and lends to a range of central government financial institutions, among other activities. Thomas Cargill and Naoyuki Yoshino in Chapter 8 provide an institutional, quantitative, and policy analysis of the postal savings system and of the Fiscal Investment and Loan Program (FILP), administered by the Ministry of Finance's Trust Fund Bureau, which allocates available funds. The authors address the various incompatibilities between the goal of a modern, competitive, market-based financial system and the realities of the government as financial intermediary. FILP lacks transparency and it appears that many of its loans to various government special accounts and agencies cannot be repaid. The authors propose an evolutionary process of reform since the system is so large, and adjustments will have substantial impacts on financial markets and private financial institutions.

Part III addresses the Big Bang and its effects and potential systemic externalities. The first two chapters treat the Big Bang itself, and the next two address broader implications for the legal system and for the corporate governance of both financial institutions and large industrial corporations.

The gradual process of financial deregulation was dramatically accelerated when Prime Minister Hashimoto in November 1996 announced a comprehensive deregulation and reform policy, popularly termed the Big Bang, an allusion to the London financial market reforms of October 1986. However, it is Japanese rather than British in approach and style. The Japanese government's plan is far more comprehensive, in part because it starts farther from their common final objectives than did the London reforms.

First, its goals are to establish free, globally competitive financial markets; to have markets fair, based on transparent and reliable rules; and to ground them in an institutional framework embodying international legal, accounting, and supervisory standards. Second, following a year of policy planning, the program being implemented over a three-year period beginning in April 1998 and scheduled to be completed by 31 March 2001 (the end of fiscal 2000). Third, it has thus far left unaddressed or unresolved some important matters such as postal savings and the government financial system, and the nature and timing of liberalization of the life insurance industry.

Akiyoshi Horiuchi in Chapter 9 provides a comprehensive overview of the Big Bang. He stresses that the Big Bang reflects and symbolizes the regime changes from a MOF-dominated, highly regulated financial system to a competitive, market-based one. Like other chapter authors, he notes the earlier process of gradual and slow deregulation that sought to protect inefficiently managed financial institutions. MOF had no exit strategy for weak financial institutions; they were not supposed to fail and, accordingly, MOF provided a comprehensive, opaque safety net that encouraged morally hazardous behavior. However, due to its policy mistakes and inability to move away from its traditional regulatory behavior, MOF power waned dramatically. The Big Bang has focused mainly on the development of efficient capital markets, including reduction of financial sector compartmentalization and making cross-entry easier. It has major implications for asset management and corporate finance. Horiuchi stresses the importance of making the financial services industry more contestable. He cogently identifies some important issues remaining even after the Big Bang is fully implemented.

Shoichi Royama, who has been a core member of the Securities and Exchange Council, in Chapter 10 argues that capital market reforms and the creation of an effective and efficient securities market system as outlined by their report is at the heart of Big Bang financial deregulation. As corporate borrowers move away from bank financing and individual investors shift away from bank deposits, the role of securities markets becomes more important. Royama explains how the proposal by Securities and Exchange Council, when implemented, will improve the workings of the Japanese securities markets. Many proposed reforms have already be implemented by the time of this writing (October 1999), but some major ones have not. Royama suggests it is too early to tell whether the Big Bang reforms in the securities markets will be successful or not.

In Chapter 11 Hideki Kanda, recognizing the importance of Big Bang legislation to the extensive overhaul of the regulatory and institutional structure of the financial system, stresses the implications for Japan's legal system and for corporate governance. Making capital markets rules-based and more important requires changes in legal rules and in their implementation; the judicial system will become larger, the style of bureaucratic governance will change, and legal provisions will become more specific. Corporate governance, like all systems, is viewed as consisting of sub-systems which can be substitutes or complements, and which vary and interact with each other depending on a country's specific institutional and behavioral arrangements. Kanda considers these subsystems for potential changes in Japanese corporate governance. He notes the importance of the costs of enforcement, which differ according to each country's specific sub-system complementarities and substitutibilities. The nature and degree of convergence across countries will depend on the respective costs of enforcement of different systems of rules. Kanda judges that a general convergence of Japanese corporate law rules with those of other industrial countries in general, and the United States in particular, is unlikely to occur. There will, however, be convergence for some categories of rules, for which he provides illustrative examples. He concludes that it remains to be seen whether the Big Bang will affect Japan's legal and corporate governance systems as a whole.

Michael Gibson in Chapter 12 stresses that improving the performance of the Japanese economy depends on increasing significantly the very low return now earned on Japanese wealth, and that reform of the corporate governance system is substantially more important than the Big Bang and related measures for financial deregulation, though both are necessary. However, reforms in general and the Big Bang in particular have not aimed at corporate governance. He argues the low returns to shareholders are due to a corporate governance system for all large companies, industrial as well as financial, that gives primacy to inside stakeholders; to the weakness of institutional investors; and the lack of a market for corporate control. While the Big Bang will remove regulatory and legal obstacles, the impediments to changes in the corporate governance system are mainly organizational. He considers six ways to change the corporate governance system so as to focus corporate managers on shareholder returns.

PROSPECTS AND REMAINING PROBLEMS

Neither the presumably successful completion of the Big Bang program by 31 March 2001 nor the 1998–99 banking system reforms will complete the process of financial deregulation, or establish a fully competitive, effective, and efficient financial system. All chapter authors allude, often explicitly and in some detail, to remaining problems and issues. Here we consider five sets of difficulties.

The Future of Japanese Commercial Banking

The first set has to do with the future of Japanese commercial banking. While the crisis for the Japanese banking system is over, almost all banks have severe problems: there are still large amounts of nonperforming and problem loans and bloated costs, which means very low profitability. There is also inadequate technological infrastructure to provide existing and new financial products quickly and cheaply. The banks need to restructure and reallocate resources to profitable financial services while stripping away unprofitable activities. Virtually no Japanese bank has capital adequacy commensurate with US and European banks, but the banking system as a whole ironically probably employs too much capital, especially given future prospects.

This implies the need to reduce the number of banks by merger or liquidation. In fact this is happening among both smaller and major banks, and the competitive pressures engendered by recent legislation and implementing policies of the FSA and the FRC assume this will persist. As few as five years ago, the disappearance of a major bank seemed unthinkable. Yet in 10 months of 1999, Mitsui Trust Bank and Chuo Trust Bank agreed to merge (February), Fuji Bank, Daiichi Kangyo Bank, and the Industrial Bank of Japan in August announced a mega-merger to create the largest bank in the world, and in October Sakura Bank (part of the Mitsui *keiretsu*) and Sumitomo Bank announced an alliance. If this leads to a merger, it would be the second largest bank in the world. It also appears Tokai Bank and Asahi Bank will merge. We should note, however, that mergers alone do not lead to efficient reorganization of the Japanese banking sector.

Lack of substantial restructuring in past mergers of Japanese banks (such as those between Mitsui and Taiyo Kobe to create Sakura in 1990, Kyowa and

Saitama to form Asahi in 1991, and Mitsubishi and Tokyo to create Tokyo-Mitsubishi in 1996) casts serious doubt on the role of mergers. However, legislation now makes possible the establishment of financial holding companies that own banks, securities companies, asset management companies, and insurance companies, and this provides a potentially powerful framework for even more dramatic restructuring. The way the government disposes of the two nationalized long-term credit banks (Long-Term Credit Bank of Japan and Nippon Credit Bank) also will affect the reorganization of the financial industry. The decision to sell Long-Term Credit Bank of Japan to Ripplewood, a US private equity group, suggests that foreign investors and financial institutions may play an important role in such a process. GE Capital, one of the largest financial institutions in the world, has been an active buyer in Japan for several years.

The banking system must deal in due course with two longer-run problems. One is disintermediation—the loss both of loan demand and supply of deposits over time. The other is achieving a capital base adequate to support strong banks able to undertake the degree of risk inherent in the banking business in a competitive financial system where the government will not guarantee against failure. Financial deregulation has encouraged many large Japanese firms to switch from bank financing to capital market financing. The Big Bang only intensifies the change, as relatively small firms gain access to capital market financing. Moreover, banks will feel serious competition on the liability side as Japanese households finally are attracted to capital market alternatives to bank deposits. The shift two decades ago of American savers from bank deposits to safe, higher-yielding money market funds, and then to stock and bond mutual funds (termed investment trusts in Japan) is suggestive, though it may take some time to wean Japanese households away from traditional financing instruments. According to Hoshi and Kashyap (1999), such a change could reduce the size of the traditional banking business (taking deposits and making loans) by 20% to 40%. The banks could adjust to this trend by trying to generate more income through non-traditional business (such as capital-market related business, derivatives, and fee-based services), but how successful Japanese banks will be in moving into these lines remains to be seen.

While the risk-adjusted capital adequacy rates of 8% for banks engaged in international banking was agreed upon through the Bank of International Settlements, most globally oriented banks now maintain somewhat higher ratios, including those few Japanese banks still internationally active. In the long run Japanese banks, like all banks, will have to obtain high credit ratings in order to compete by keeping the cost of funds borrowed in global markets at a minimum. Any persistence of a Japan premium spells doom for international competitiveness.

Probably even more important for Japan is a redevelopment of a strong domestic banking system. The present 4% capital-adequacy ratio for banks engaged solely in domestic business should be considered a temporary expedient. International experience suggests banks will have to maintain a substantially higher ratio to compete effectively.

Safety Net

The safety net for bank depositors is a second set of problems. Until 1995 deposits were insured by the Deposit Insurance Corporation for up to ¥10 million for each depositor in any single commercial bank. In an attempt to reassure depositors after the failure of banks in the summer of 1995, MOF announced that all deposits and financial debentures would be fully protected in the event of bank failures until April 2001. Debentures and deposit accounts that exceed ¥10 million will be uninsured again after that. As 2001 approaches, there is now an active discussion on whether the government should continue full protection. Many admit the danger this poses in encouraging moral hazard, but as Horiuchi (Chapter 9) notes, the current uncertainty about the process of paying off insured deposits in failed banks may generate depositor concern about what will happen after 2001. Weaker banks, especially those with substantial deposits from small and medium company clients, fear that deposits will be shifted to banks that are deemed stronger.

It is important to resolve such uncertainty by clearly setting up the details of the future safety net. How much the limit of insured deposits will be, whether the limit is per account or per depositor (people often hold multiple accounts in a bank under assumed names), how long it would take for depositors to get bank-insured deposits when a bank fails, and so on, need to be clarified. Having a clear picture about the future safety net system is also important in establishing a credible bank closure policy. Otherwise closure of failed banks may be delayed in the name of depositor protection. Establishing a credible rule on depositor protection and loss allocation of failed banks will be the final step from the historical discretionary approach to bank insolvency administered by MOF to a more rule-based approach based on Prompt Corrective Action administered by the FSA and the Finance Agency to be established by 2001. (For an incisive analysis of these issues, see Milhaupt (1999)).

Non-Bank Financial Institutions

The financial system more broadly, in particular certain other of its components where potential insolvency difficulties may develop into a crisis, pose a third set of issues. The sector that faces the largest problem appears to be the life insurance industry.

In addition to bad loan problems similar to those in the banking sector, the life insurance industry faces a problem on the liability side of its balance sheet. The companies set an interest rate when they sell policies that return cash to the buyer at maturity. Although they can change the set rate for a group insurance policy during its life, the set rate for an individual policy must be honored for its duration. During the bubble period, many insurance companies competed by offering high set rates (hence lower premium payments). Since the bubbles burst and interest rates have came down to historic lows in the 1990s, these guaranteed rates have become much higher than the rates of return the companies can earn, so there has been a negative spread. As a result, life insurers' liabilities have been expanding faster than their assets.

Some companies already have become insolvent and reorganized. Nissan Life failed in April 1997 and, although the MOF tried to convince its group members—Hitachi and Nissan Auto—to rescue it, they refused and policy holders ended up suffering losses. Toho Life was sold to GE Capital in 1998 and has been going through a restructuring. Daihyaku Life is being acquired by ManuLife. To prepare for likely further failures, the Life Insurance Policy Holders Protection Corporation (a life insurance equivalent of deposit insurance) was introduced in December 1998; however its funds, contributed by the companies themselves, appear to be woefully inadequate. Prompt Corrective Action was introduced for life insurers starting with April 1999. The Financial Supervisory Agency has begun on-site examination of the companies. Preventing a crisis in the industry will be an important test for the new system of financial regulation.

The agricultural credit cooperatives, and their prefectural and national organizations, also appear to have substantial bad loan problems. The general outline of those difficulties became known in the 1995–96 *jûsen* crisis and in the sources of funds for the Long-Term Credit Bank. However, this is a particularly opaque topic about which there has been little disclosure. As of March 1998, the agricultural credit cooperatives and their prefectural and national organizations reported they held just ¥1.3 trillion of bad loans against their total loans of ¥46 trillion (Domon 1998, p 37). The general expectation is that the agricultural credit cooperative system is so politically powerful, and its lending so intertwined with the interests of many politicians, that a crisis will not be allowed to happen. How potential insolvencies will be resolved and financed is unclear.

The absence of arm's-length urban commercial real estate markets has made the resolution of bad loans much more difficult for banks, and indeed all financial institutions having real estate as collateral for loans, as suggested by a number of the authors, particularly Packer (Chapter 6). While banks have provisioned against loan losses, the disposal of real estate collateral claimed against those losses has proceeded slowly. Gradually banks have been selling off their bad loan portfolios, but securitization remains difficult. A number of legal and other institutional changes are underway, but the development of an efficient and effective urban commercial real estate market will be difficult to achieve.

The combination of extraordinarily low interest rates, restrictive regulation, a weak stock market, and mediocre asset management has created serious problems of under-funded corporate pension programs and inadequate returns on government pension programs. These issues are particularly salient given the aging of Japanese society. The government is drafting legislation to create both corporate and individual defined-contribution pension programs analogous to 401(k) plans in the United States. One major stumbling block is MOF resistance to allowing tax incentives. This will be a politically as well as financially important issue. With pension funds likely to increase substantially, development of transparency and competition among a wide range of asset management institutions will become increasingly important.

Japanese financial institutions face increasing competition in domestic markets not only from each other but from foreign financial institutions. The penetration of foreign financial institutions has become surprisingly vigorous, and offers both opportunities and challenges to domestic providers and purchasers of financial services. In some sectors, foreign firms have technological and global market superiority over their Japanese competitors, while (thus far) Japanese institutions have superior access to customers, especially at the retail and small-business level. The growth of foreign financial institutions is likely to be in the areas of their competitive strength: investment banking, international merger and acquisitions, asset management, creation of mutual fund products, and life insurance. Foreign banks have a minuscule share of Japanese deposits and loans, and that probably will persist.

In manufacturing, foreign firms were allowed to invest directly in Japan only after Japanese competitor-firms were strongly established. In contrast, the easing of rules for foreign financial institution entry into Japanese markets is accelerating at a time Japanese financial institutions are particularly weak.

As Japanese finance transforms from a bank-centered and relationship-based system to a market-based and competitive system, we need to recall that the old system had its benefits and mitigated important problems in financial transactions. The costs now probably outweigh those benefits, and certain benefits are irrelevant for some firms. For example, many large Japanese firms are internationally well known. For them, the historic role of banks in reducing information problems and costs is probably irrelevant. However, information problems in financial markets do continue to exist for many firms, especially smaller ones. Similarly, the experience of the 1990s recession reminds us that even large firms are not immune to distress.

As the bank-centered financial system declines, there will be an increasing demand for alternative institutions that mitigate the information problems of financial transactions. These include rating agencies that provide information to capital markets, improved court-based resolution of financial distress, emergence of a market for corporate control, a safety net for labor outside rather than inside of firms (or a group of firms), and others. How these institutions develop in the near future and how existing financial institutions adjust to these changes will determine the future of the Japanese financial system.

Government Financial Institutions

As a number of chapter authors stress, particularly Cargill and Yoshino (Chapter 8) and Ito (Chapter 4), the postal savings system, postal life insurance, the Ministry of Finance Trust Fund Bureau's FILP, the activities of government financial institutions, and the seeming insolvency of some government special accounts, all constitute a potentially huge and politically very difficult set of problems, especially because the amount of funds collected from individuals participating in the postal savings and life insurance programs are so immense. This is the most important financial issue the Big Bang deregulation program failed to address.

One key question is whether the postal savings system and postal life insurance system will persist as relatively aggressive competitors of counterpart private financial institutions in their pricing and creation of new instruments, or will become relatively more passive suppliers of a relatively limited number of financial products as a locational convenience for individuals. The system has considerable political support, so it will not be easy to change policy.

A related issue is how these funds should be allocated. The scheduled termination of automatic transfer of most of the collected funds to the Trust Fund Bureau implies that government financial institutions will be borrowing directly from the postal savings system, which will raise issue of creditworthiness and government guarantees; and indeed the appropriate future role, if any, of the government financial institutions.

The Role of the Financial System

While the specific channels of the flows of funds will alter in importance, with capital markets and asset management institutions becoming more important, both domestic and international financial intermediation will continue to be very important. A rules-based, competitive-market financial system will be a key ingredient in the transformation of Japan as a whole into a more rules-based, competitive-market-based economic system. As Kanda (Chapter 11) and Gibson (Chapter 12) have stressed, this involves far more than deregulation of the financial system. It involves changes in the legal system and the enforcement of its rules, and changes in the Japanese system of corporate governance.

Economic recovery in the near term—and sustained, stable economic growth in the longer run—will make this process of change and transformation easier and less costly. It may also reduce the perceived urgency of change somewhat. After all, look how long it took Japanese regulators and banks to tackle the bad loan problem fully and effectively, and then perhaps only because a crisis was imminent. Nonetheless, we are convinced that the deregulatory forces cannot be halted, and that the competitive pressures on all Japanese financial institutions cannot be contained. Change and transformation will take place; it has to. In that sense we are both optimistic.

REFERENCES

Aoki, Masahiko and Hugh Patrick, editors. 1994. *The Japanese Main Bank System: Its Relevance for Developing and Transforming Economies.* Oxford University Press.

Aoki, Masahiko, Hugh Patrick, and Paul Sheard. 1994. "The Japanese Main Bank System: An Introductory Overview." In Masahiko Aoki and Hugh Patrick, editors, *The Japanese Main Bank System: Its Relevance for Developing and Transforming Economies.* Oxford University Press.

Campbell, John, and Yasushi Hamao. 1994. "Changing Patterns of Corporate Financing and the Main Bank System in Japan." In Masahiko Aoki and Hugh Patrick, editors, *The Japanese Main Bank System: Its Relevance for Developing and Transforming Economies.* Oxford University Press.

Cargill, Thomas F and Shoichi Royama. 1998. *The Transition of Finance in Japan and the United States: A Comparative Perspective.* Hoover Institution Press.

Domon, Takeshi. 1998. "Chogin Mondai wo Yugameta Nokyo Kin'yu no Jidai Sakugo (Anachronism of Nokyo-Finance Distorts the LTCB Problem)." *Kin'yu Business* 162: 34–37 (Nov).

Hoshi, Takeo, Anil Kashyap, and David Scharfstein. 1990. "The Role of Banks in Reducing the Costs of Financial Distress in Japan." *Journal of Financial Economics* 27: 67–88.

Hoshi, Takeo, Anil Kashyap, and David Scharfstein. 1991. "Corporate Structure, Liquidity, and Investment: Evidence from Japanese Industrial Groups." *Quarterly Journal of Economics* 106: 33–60.

Milhaupt, Curtis J. 1999. "Japan's Experience with Deposit Insurance and Failing Banks: Implications for Financial Regulatory Design?" Bank of Japan, *Monetary and Economic Studies* 17, 2: 21–46.

Milhaupt, Curtis and Geoffrey Miller. 1997. "Cooperation, Conflict, and Convergence in Japanese Finance: Evidence from the 'Jusen' Problem." *Law and Policy in International Business* 29: 1–78.

Nakaso, Hiroshi. 1999. "Recent Banking Sector Reforms in Japan." Federal Reserve Bank of New York *Economic Policy Review*, July.

Patrick, Hugh. 1971. "The Economic Muddle of the 1920s." In James W Morley, editor, *Dilemmas of Growth in Prewar Japan.* Princeton University Press.

Peek, Joe and Eric Rosengren. 1999. "Determinants of the Japan Premium: Actions Speak Louder Than Words." Paper presented at the Japan Economic Seminar, Columbia University, 20 Feb.

Sheard, Paul. 1989. "The Main Bank System and Corporate Monitoring and Control in Japan." *Journal of Economic Behavior and Organization* 11: 399–422.

Sheard, Paul. 1994a. "Delegated Monitoring Among Delegated Monitors: Principal-Agent Aspects of the Japanese Main Bank System." *Journal of the Japanese and International Economies* 8: 1–21.

Sheard, Paul. 1994b. "Main Banks and the Governance of Financial Distress." In Masahiko Aoki and Hugh Patrick, editors, *The Japanese Main Bank System: Its Relevance for Developing and Transforming Economies.* Oxford University Press.

Suzuki, Yoshio. 1986. *Money, Finance and Macroeconomic Performance in Japan.* Yale University Press.

Suzuki, Yoshio, editor. 1987. *The Japanese Financial System.* Oxford University Press.

Ueda, Kazuo. 1994. "Institutional and Regulatory Frameworks for the Main Bank System." In Masahiko Aoki and Hugh Patrick, editors, *The Japanese Main Bank System: Its Relevance for Developing and Transforming Economies.* Oxford University Press.

PART I

The Origins of Japan's Banking Crisis

Chapter 2

WHAT CAUSED JAPAN'S BANKING CRISIS?

Thomas F Cargill
University of Nevada at Reno

The banking and financial crisis that started with the collapse of asset prices in 1990 and 1991 and dominated the 1990s stands in stark contrast to Japan's previous postwar record of economic growth, financial stability, and progress toward financial liberalization.[1]

Identification of the causes, both qualitatively and quantitatively, would thus appear straightforward. The task, however, is not so easy. Many of the "causes" —such as moral hazard and agency conflicts—are difficult, if not impossible to quantify. Those that are susceptible to measurement are subject to the "sample of one" problem in that the banking crisis is clearly an outlier in the postwar economic history of Japan. Most important, the very concept of the phrase "cause" implies a one-way process of discrete event-to-outcome not likely to apply to Japan's banking crisis in the 1990s. This point requires an illustration.

Bank of Japan policy after 1986 contributed to asset inflation, and the subsequent collapse of asset prices generated recession and nonperforming loan problems; thus, Bank of Japan policy can be regarded as a "cause" of the banking crisis. At the same time, had the government responded aggressively to the nonperforming loan problem in 1992 or 1993, the banking and financial problems would be a part of economic history rather than the focal point of international discussion and concern in the second half of the 1990s. Agency problems and the mind-set of Japanese regulatory authorities are thus the "cause" of the banking crisis.

The objective of this chapter is to discuss the various "causes" of Japan's banking and financial problems in the 1990s without attributing unidirectional causal meaning to any one factor and without focusing on any one factor as the unique causative agent. Many factors were involved, each with important feedback relationships with other factors. (Patrick (1999) provides an account of the causes of the banking crisis that reflects some of the points raised in this chapter.)

Five Factors

There are five aspects of the Japanese financial situation that together constitute the cause of the banking problems.

First, Japan relied on a rigid financial regime. This "Japanese financial regime" provided a more than satisfactory financial infrastructure for rapid and fairly stable economic growth from 1950 to the mid-1970s. However, it became increasingly incompatible with economic, political, and technical forces that emerged in the 1970s. Despite liberalization, the old regulatory and supervisory framework remained in place and generated a predictable response of delay, forgiveness, and forbearance when financial distress emerged in the wake of the collapse of asset prices in 1990–91. Throughout the 1990s the regulatory authorities have been slow to abandon the old regime.

Second, policy failures on the part of the Bank of Japan in the second half of the 1980s generated asset inflation and provided liquidity to a fundamentally weak financial and regulatory structure. Monetary policy further contributed to the banking problems by a delayed "cold turkey" shift to restrictive policy in May 1989, after asset prices had accelerated to levels unjustified by fundamentals.

Third, government response to the emerging banking and financial problems in the first half of the 1990s was slow, indecisive, and, in most cases, counterproductive. In many instances the government response was rooted to principles of the old financial regime that emphasized mutual support, nontransparency, and a policy attitude that market forces could be managed. As a result, the private-sector response was slow as private institutions anticipated government bailouts and other policies based on preventing failures of financial institutions or markets.

Fourth, the government found little support from the taxpaying public to deal with troubled institutions with public funds. The public perceived it had not been a beneficiary of the old financial regime and, starting in 1997, public support was further weakened by a series of scandals at the Ministry of Finance and the Bank of Japan regarding regulatory oversight. The government also had little support from the public to make fundamental reforms in one of the most complicated and significant elements of the financial system - postal savings. The public regarded postal savings as the one element of the system that was devoted to serving the public. The lack of public support delayed a solution to the nonperforming loan problem and delayed important reforms.

Fifth, institutions that limited open criticism, combined with the undeveloped state of financial disclosure and inadequate public dissemination of available information, contributed to government delay and lack of transparency.

The remainder of this chapter discusses each of these under separate headings. The chapter ends with a summary of the causes of the banking crisis that attempts to tie the factors together.

THE JAPANESE FINANCIAL REGIME

The Japanese financial regime is considered from three perspectives: characteristics of the regime as it existed prior to the liberalization that began in the second half of the 1970s; conflicts between the regime and a variety of economic, technological, and political forces that first emerged in the 1970s; and continued reliance in the 1990s on key elements of the regime that contributed to the banking crisis.

Evolution and Characteristics

The postwar financial regime that supported Japan's impressive growth and financial stability through the mid-1980s first emerged at the time of the Meiji Restoration in 1868, was modified in response to the banking problems of 1927, was further modified in response to war mobilization and war in the 1930s and '40s, and reached maturity during the High Growth Period from 1950 to 1970. Postwar finance was thus a continuation of prewar trends and reflected the influence of the Allied Occupation only at the margin. The regime as it existed in the postwar period and prior to the start of financial liberalization in the second half of the 1970s is characterized in Table 2.1.

These characteristics are a summation of many previous discussions of the Japanese financial system. For example, see Aoki and Patrick (1994) and Cargill (1998).

The financial system was an instrument of industrial policy maintained and protected by mutual support, restraints on competition, and insularity between the domestic financial sector, the Ministry of Finance, the Bank of Japan, and politicians.

This regime assumed a specific set of objectives: support reindustrialization, support domestic investment and export-led economic growth, ensure international isolation, and ensure that household saving was directed to the business sector rather than used to support consumer or housing expenditures.

These objectives were achieved by a rigidly regulated and administratively controlled financial system. Market forces were not absent, but regulatory and administrative directions were more important than market forces in the flow of funds. The financial system was highly segmented, interest rate movements were subject to administrative control and guidance (with the exception of two short-term interest rates - *gensaki* bond repurchase and interbank loans), money and capital markets played a minor role in the flow of funds, and capital inflows and outflows were restricted. (Aoki and Patrick (1994), Cargill and Royama (1988), Horiuchi and Hamada (1987), Patrick (1994), and Suzuki (1980 and 1987) provide detailed discussion of many of these points.)

TABLE 2.1. Characteristics of the Old Financial Regime

1	The financial system was viewed as an instrument of industrial policy.
2	It was designed to transfer the majority of funds from surplus to deficit units through intermediation markets, especially banking channels.
3	It was designed to encourage household saving, but at the same time to limit household access to consumer and mortgage credit.
4	Highly leveraged nonfinancial businesses, dominated by large business groups, were thc primary recipients of large-bank finance. Smaller firms obtained credit from small banks and other types of institutions. That is, intermediation finance was highly segmented.
5	Foreign financial institutions were prohibited or restricted to limited participation in the financial system and external debt was avoided.
6	Inflows and outflows of capital were restricted and exchange rates were either fixed or managed.
7	Government credit allocation policies - including extensive interest rate controls designed to maintain a low cost of capital - played a major role in allocating funds through intermediation markets.
8	Public financial institutions via the Fiscal Loan and Investment Program (FILP) System provided a major channel of finance from the household sector in the form of postal deposits, life insurance, and pension funds to ultimate borrowers through a system of government financial institutions. Only a small percentage of these funds returned to the household sector. The majority of funds financed infrastructure, business, and agriculture.
9	Financial regulation and supervision were designed with opaqueness and nontransparency in mind, to provide an environment for political favors and concessions between politicians, government bureaucrats, and the business sector.
10	The Bank of Japan lacked independence and served as an agent of the government via the Ministry of Finance to ensure a steady flow of credit to the business sector and to provide funds to support weak financial institutions.
11	A system of pervasive deposit guarantees was maintained through regulation, "convoy" approaches to dealing with troubled institutions or markets, and the discount window of the Bank of Japan.
12	An explicit policy of "no failures of financial institutions or markets" was supported by opaque financial regulation, supervision, and central bank policy.
13	There was reliance on long-term multi-dimensional relationships between banks, individual borrowers, and business groups to assess and monitor risk. This is generally referred to as the main bank system.

This type of financial regime differs from financial regimes in western economies (Cole 1993). Western financial systems are a service industry available to all borrowers. They are focused on short-term two-dimensional (price and quantity) transactions and involve money and capital markets, financial disclosure, limited government credit allocation influences, and relatively independent regulatory and central banking institutions. In addition, western economies such as the United States limit concentrations of nonfinancial business and thereby limit the opportunity to extract rents from the financial system.

Japan's banking crisis in the 1990s should not detract from two important aspects of its financial regime. First, despite its problems, with few exceptions the regime met all of its objectives and played an important role in Japan's emergence from World War II to be the second largest economy in the world by the late 1970s. The regime was widely imitated by other Asian economies, though frequently with differences in structure and efficiency. (Cargill (1998) discusses the similarities and differences between the Korean and Japanese financial regimes. Also, see Huh and Kim (1994) for a Korea-Japan comparison.)

Second, the regime was not a manifestation of "Asian culture," nor did it lack an economic rationale. In the context of a national consensus to reindustrialize and resume prewar economic growth, the regime represented a rational solution to the provision of liquidity, distribution of credit and risk, and monitoring of risk in an environment of capital shortage and a financial system with limited financial disclosure and direct markets.

Conflicts Since the 1970s

Krugman's (1994) provocative paper on the Asian growth miracle emphasized the narrow and unsustainable foundation of economic growth in Asia during the 1970s and '80s. Likewise, the success of the Japanese financial regime relied on a narrow and unsustainable set of conditions: restrained market forces, limited number of financial channels between surplus and deficit units, international economic and financial isolation, export oriented growth, and rapid real GDP growth that made it politically possible to achieve consensus among different sectors and avoided any serious test of the stability of the financial infrastructure.

These circumstances could not be maintained in the new economic, financial, political, and technological environment that emerged in the 1970s. The old regime was fundamentally incompatible with market forces and the internationalization of finance because of its pervasive moral hazard, lack of transparency, and mutual support between financial institutions, regulatory authorities, and politicians.

The first manifestation of conflict came in the late 1960s and early '70s in the form of government-directed pressure brought on the Bank of Japan to use expansionary monetary policy to continue high growth rates into the 1970s and, later, to limit yen appreciation during the collapse of the Bretton Woods fixed-exchange-rate system. Instead of high growth and exchange rate stability, however, the expansionary policy generated inflation that reached 30% in 1974. This was corrected and, in fact, the success of the Bank of Japan's price stability policy led to enhanced political independence for the Bank (Cargill 1989; Cargill, Hutchison, and Ito 1997), thus weakening an important component of the old regime.

The second conflict was more fundamental and continues to the present. In response to the oil price shock and downward shift in the natural growth path of real GDP, Japan's flow of funds pattern changed and brought pressure on the financial regime to become more flexible (Feldman 1986; Cargill and Royama 1988). Banks, corporations, and securities companies saw liberalization as a means to reestablish or enhance market share, and the Ministry of Finance was willing to relax constraints on the financial system as a cost of marketing the large amounts of government debt needed to finance the central-government deficits that began in 1973. The shift to a flexible exchange rate regime and political pressure, especially from the United States, created additional pressure on Japan to liberalize.

Liberalization and Perseverance of the Old Regime

Japanese liberalization commenced in 1976 with official recognition of the *gensaki* market and continued in a slow and discrete series of small steps through the early 1990s. While Japan was frequently criticized for the slow pace of financial reform, considerable progress was achieved, as indicated in Table 2.2.

TABLE 2.2. Liberalization Since the Late 1970s

- Interest rate controls have been mostly eliminated
- Short- and long-term capital flows are essentially unrestricted
- Foreign financial institutions and market participants play a significant, but still small, role in the financial system
- Households have increased access to the system
- Some reduction in market segmentation has occurred, such as increased competition between banks and securities companies
- Some effort has been made to close insolvent financial institutions and adopt a more aggressive "prompt and early correction" policy
- Some effort has been made to make the system more transparent
- Bank of Japan operations are more independent
- Regulatory powers of the Ministry of Finance have been weakened by establishment of the Financial Supervisory Agency, which has shown more independence than many expected

TABLE 2.3. Elements of the Old Regime in Government Policy in the 1990s

- Nontransparency
- Mutual support or convoy system
- Government deposit guarantees
- Inefficiency in the delivery of financial services
- Close relationships between business, financial institutions, and regulatory authorities
- Government intermediation finance

These changes, however, pale in comparison to the reluctance of government policy, at least through the early 1990s, to depart from some of the most important elements of the old regime, listed in Table 2.3 and discussed in the remainder of this section.

Thus, even as liberalization weakened the old regime, the authorities continued to pursue a policy of forbearance and forgiveness. A financial supervisory and regulatory framework that delayed an appropriate response to the growing financial distress and increased the ultimate economic and political resolution cost remained largely in place.

Lack of Transparency

A lack of detailed financial disclosure is a major characteristic of the old regime and has limited the ability of market participants to monitor the condition of nonfinancial businesses, financial-institution balance sheets, and nonperforming loans. In the early 1990s the Ministry of Finance did not report individual estimates of nonperforming loans for the largest 21 banks. When official estimates finally were made available for each bank, there was a general consensus that they were grossly understated because they relied too heavily on bank self-reporting and loose definitions of nonperforming loans.

Nontransparency extended to nonbank financial institutions. The Ministry of Finance, for example, knew the magnitude of the housing loan corporation (*jûsen*) problem as early as 1993, yet no action was taken until June 1996 when the problem could no longer be denied. There is every indication the nonresponse policy was based on the hope land and equity prices would soon recover. Other examples of lack of transparency are cited in Cargill, Hutchison, and Ito (1997).

Hokkaido Takushoku, smallest of the 12 city banks, reported ¥300 billion in equity and paid dividends in March 1997; when it failed November 1997, actual equity was a negative ¥1.1 trillion. Likewise, the failure of Yamaichi Securities in late 1997 revealed losses of ¥270 billion that had until then been hidden. (Figures for both Hokkaido Takushoku and Yamaichi are from Fukao (1998).) Until early 1998 estimates of bank nonperforming loans relied far too heavily on the banks' assessment rather than independent auditing. Even in mid-1998 when financial disclosure was a high priority, the government continued to be less than transparent in reporting nonperforming loans. There was little information, for example, about the likely large amounts of nonperforming loans held by government financial institutions.

Reluctance to Depart from the Convoy System

The government has been reluctant to abandon the convoy system in which weaker institutions are supported by stronger institutions or, in other terms, when a political rather than an economic solution to insolvent institutions is adopted. The Ministry of Finance brought considerable pressure on larger financial institutions to absorb the 11 small institutions, mainly credit cooperatives, closed over the 1991–95 period. In the closing of these institutions, no large depositor with uninsured deposits took a loss. Shareholders did take a loss, but in some cases were able to maintain some value in the merger and acquisition process.

The solution to the *jûsen* problem was clearly the outcome of a political process in which the burden sharing had only moderate relationship to those who had funded the housing loan companies. The government did take a more aggressive approach to the failure of Hokkaido Takushoku Bank in November 1997, announcing that it would be treated differently since it was allowed to fail after the Ministry of Finance was unable to secure help from any other bank.

This positive policy was offset, however, by the allocation of the first tranche of the ¥30 trillion committed by the government in early 1998 to protect depositors (¥17 trillion) and provide capital to major banks (¥13 trillion). The government provided an across-the-board capital injection of ¥1.8 trillion to 21 banks irrespective of their individual condition, showing that regulatory authorities had not yet reached a point where they were willing to abandon the convoy system.

Deposit Guarantees

The Japanese banking system has a pervasive system of deposit guarantees, but is more importantly dependent on the willingness of the Bank of Japan to provide funds at the discount window and the willingness of the Ministry of Finance to arrange mergers and acquisitions.

Japan established a deposit insurance system in 1971, but it was never intended to provide a foundation for the system of guarantees. The Deposit Insurance Corporation was understaffed, had no independent power, and was underfunded. The deposit amount insured was increased gradually to ¥10 million, the limit prior to 1995 (a much smaller deposit insurance agency for small financial institutions was also established. See Cargill, Hutchison, and Ito (1996) for more detail on deposit insurance in Japan).

Prior to 1991 official policy was "no failures of financial institutions"; however, after 1991 this policy was abandoned and over the 1991–95 period, 11 small banking institutions were declared insolvent. A close examination of how each of these institutions was handled reveals an unwillingness to impose any penalty on large depositors and in some cases a reluctance to impose penalties even on shareholders.

Pervasive if implicit deposit guarantees by the Ministry of Finance have been a hallmark of the old financial regime and not until 1998 did Japan initiate a serious discussion of deposit insurance, moral hazard, and how far the government should go in bailing out insolvent banks. The postal savings system plays a critical role in these discussions because of its complete government guarantee of the maximum postal deposit of ¥10 million. The 1990s exhibited periods of flight to postal savings from bank deposits in response to increasing bank failures and increased awareness of nonperforming loans. As a stopgap measure, in 1995 the government announced a complete deposit guarantee through March 2001. However, as noted above, this guarantee was not adequately funded until early 1998.

Inefficient Private Financial Institutions

Despite their size and growth, Japanese financial institutions have not been as efficient as their counterparts in more open and competitive economies, as judged by various measures of profitability. There are many reasons to explain this lack of concern with profits: banks have been the beneficiaries of government protection in all forms and thus have less incentive to price their services according to economic principles; the *keiretsu* system and the practice of *amakudari* diverts bank attention away from rational pricing of services; the large holdings of equities in bank portfolios further reduces incentives to price services rationally to borrowers; and the lack of human capital in finance further contributes to an emphasis on goals other than profitability; and the permanent employment system gives greater priority to employee stakeholders than to stockholders. The problem is not confined to the financial industry but extends to the real sector, where corporate governance also faces incentives to remain inefficient. While Big Bang reforms promise a more efficient financial system, incentives for inefficiency are so embedded in the structure of the Japanese economy that change will come slowly.

System of Mutual Support

Strong mutual support persists between business, financial institutions, regulatory authorities, and politicians. Close relationships based on practices such as *amakudari* and the interdependence of elements makes it difficult to initiate change in any direction. That is, the mutual support system, combined with a general lack of transparency, makes it relatively easy to adhere to the old regime and adopt a policy of forbearance and forgiveness as a substitute for meaningful reform.

Government Financial Intermediation

The view that the old financial regime continues in Japan is clearly manifested in the growth of the Ministry of Finance's Fiscal Investment and Loan Program (FILP) and the postal savings system on which it is largely dependent. The postal savings system continues to expand, as has the role of government financial intermediation.[2]

The entire FILP System is in need of reform, but was generally regarded as off limits for serious discussion until 1998. It was ignored in the November 1996 Big Bang announcement of Prime Minister Hashimoto and was little discussed during the flurry of legislative action during 1997. Only in June 1998 was the issue brought to the public's attention, via a report of the Financial Reform Committee of the Trust Fund Bureau, Ministry of Finance. Shortly after the report was released, the law was changed to separate the postal savings system from the FILP. Effective March 2001, the FILP will no longer have access to postal deposits, postal life insurance, or pension funds (Cargill and Yoshino 1998). The final reform of the postal savings system and the FILP has yet to be decided, but this is a significant development in terms of dismantling the old financial regime. (See Cargill and Yoshino, Chapter 8 in this volume.)

BANK OF JAPAN POLICY

Monetary policy played an important role in the banking and financial crisis of the 1990s. In hindsight the asset inflation in Japan from 1987 to 1989 is a classic speculative bubble in which prices depart from economic fundamentals and price increases are predicated only on the expectation that prices will increase further in the future. Cargill, Hutchison, and Ito (1997) provide a detailed review of the second half of the 1980s, showing how the initial rise in asset prices was justified by economic fundamentals, but that sometime in 1987–88, asset prices lost touch with fundamentals.

It is also clear that monetary policy was easy in terms of the growth of high-powered money, growth of the money supply, and the frequency and magnitude of reductions in the discount rate. Bank of Japan policy thus supported the asset inflation and, likewise, the May 1989 shift to a tight monetary policy, with an increase in the discount rate, is responsible for the start of the asset deflation process. Asset deflation in turn deteriorated bank and other financial institution balance sheets and generated Japan's most serious recession since 1950.

There are four issues that need to be addressed regarding the role of Bank of Japan policy in the banking crisis. Why did the Bank adopt an easy policy during the critical 1986–89 period? Why did it delay a shift to a tight policy too long? Do the policy errors suggest a pattern in the context of postwar monetary policy? Will the changes in the Bank of Japan Law effective in 1998 prevent similar policy errors in the future?

Easy policy in the second half of the 1980s can be explained. The Bank, as an outcome of the Plaza Agreement and Louvre Accord, increasingly directed policy toward limiting the appreciation of the yen and, because official price indexes showed little or no inflation, it concluded that the excessive liquidity would have no adverse effects on the economy. This is now considered a mistake, but as Cargill, Hutchison, and Ito (1997, p 113) have noted, "critics of the Bank of Japan's monetary policy stance at the time . . . have more credibility after the fact."

Despite this concession to forgiveness, the Bank can be faulted for focusing too much attention on external considerations. Lowering the discount rate in the presence of rapid real growth in the fall of 1986 and early 1987 seemed even at the time an inappropriate central bank policy despite low inflation.

The Bank of Japan became concerned about the inflation rate in mid-1989 and raised the discount rate. The discount rate was raised four times in the rest of 1989 and 1990. That the Bank delayed the shift to tight monetary policy so long and, as a result, was forced to adopt a more aggressively restrictive policy, ruled out any type of "soft landing".

Bank of Japan policy in the second half of the 1980s represents the second failure of monetary policy in postwar Japan. The first was excessive monetary growth in the early 1970s, attributed partly to political pressure from the Tanaka government, but also to concern about limiting the appreciation of the yen. In fact, a close qualitative and quantitative review of postwar monetary policy suggests that exchange rate considerations have been an important consideration in Bank policy and contributed to the two most serious policy failures of the Bank in the postwar period.

In June 1997 the 1942 Bank of Japan Law was revised to provide the Bank with enhanced "open" and "formal" independence. (Cargill, Hutchison, and Ito (forthcoming) provide a detailed review of the old and new Bank of Japan. Also see Mikitani and Kuwayama (1998).)

The new law went into effect April 1, 1998. Ueda (Chapter 3) has argued this is a desirable development because it will help prevent the type of policy errors made in monetary policy during the second half of the 1980s. According to Ueda, Bank of Japan policy was overly influenced by the Ministry of Finance and, hence, formal independence will help prevent the same type of error in the future.

It is premature to make such a prediction for several reasons. First, it is unclear how independent the Bank of Japan will be under the new legal structure, though Bank policy in 1998 and 1999 suggests the Bank intends to use its new formal independence. Second, the Bank had already achieved a considerable degree of political independence during the 1980s, despite formal dependence on the Ministry of Finance. Third, exchange rate considerations will likely continue to play an important role in policy, irrespective of the formal relationship of the Bank to the government. Fourth, the independence issue in 1997 was a politically motivated effort by the Ministry of Finance to divert attention from its poor performance in handling the nonperforming loan problem. Preventing future policy errors resulting from a focus on external considerations was not a high priority of either the Ministry or the Bank.

GOVERNMENT RESPONSE

The government response to emerging financial distress in the early 1990s was inadequate by any measure. While various institutional reforms occurred in 1995 and 1996, Japan continued to rely on a policy of delay, forgiveness, and forbearance. That is, the policy response was rooted in the old financial regime and based on hope that asset prices and economic growth would recover and eliminate the financial distress. This did not occur.

Conditions improved in 1996 and, in fact, made it possible for the Hashimoto government to make the November 1996 Big Bang announcement. However a fiscal policy change from expansionary to sharply contractionary aborted the recovery and contributed substantially to the creation of the recession that has persisted since. This involved a swing of almost 2 percentage points of GDP from an increase in the consumption tax, the ending of a temporary income tax reduction, and introduction of various user fees.

Economic and financial distress intensified in late 1997 and reached crisis proportions. The failure of Hokkaido Takushoku and Yamaichi on the heels of the Asian crisis initiated an economic reversal of major proportions. The situation in 1998–99 was the worst at any time since the collapse of asset prices.

The lack of a meaningful government response to the problem has already been discussed in the context of the Japanese financial regime. This section summarizes the main elements of the government response and argues that it prolonged the crisis. While the initiatives taken from late 1997 through early 1999 reflect a more realistic assessment of the situation, their impact has been more difficult to predict because of the delay in dealing with the financial distress.

The first response in the early 1990s was to deny that any problems existed and to argue that moral hazard was not a problem in Japan. When outright denial was no longer credible, the Ministry of Finance and other regulatory authorities consistently minimized the problems and permitted accounting and reporting changes that allowed private banks to cover up nonperforming loans. Nonetheless, each announcement of an estimate of the magnitude of the problem was higher than the previous one - a pattern reminiscent of the US regulatory experience during the 1980s and early '90s with regard to the savings and loan (S&L) and banking industries. Some changes were made to bring more transparency in 1996 and 1997, but the fundamental approach of nontransparency, inadequate recognition of the moral hazard problem by relying on forbearance and forgiveness, and market manipulation remained. These aspects of the policy approach have more to do with policy attitudes than with actual policy.

The emphasis on nontransparency was evidenced by the lack of meaningful information on potential nonperforming loans among government financial institutions, changing accounting rules to permit banks to meet the BIS capital requirements, and permitting banks to report the values of equity holdings at historical cost, thus placing a floor under the value of bank equity positions.

Delay continued to be an element of policy in dealing with nonperforming loans and troubled institutions throughout most of the 1990s, until late fall 1998. The government showed little enthusiasm for preemptive closing of financial institutions and aggressive selling off of nonperforming loans.

Reform of the Deposit Insurance Corporation in 1996 was designed to permit a "prompt corrective action" system based loosely on the "trip wire" system of the 1991 Federal Deposit Insurance Corporation Improvement Act legislation in the United States. This was intended to go into effect April 1, 1998 but was postponed for one year to provide banks an opportunity to improve their balance sheets.

The ¥30 trillion government commitment in early 1998 was partly intended for capital injection to major banks through purchases of preferred stock, subordinate bonds, and loans in return for cost cutting, reducing nonperforming loans, and improving management practices. The committee overseeing distribution of the funds held the criteria were not binding and encouraged all major banks to apply (Craig 1998, p 17).

The government has sponsored or financed three nonperforming loan warehouses since 1992: the Cooperative Credit Purchasing Credit Company, the Resolution and Collection Bank, and the Housing Loan Administration Corporation. In October 1998 the latter two were combined into the Resolution and Collection Corporation modeled after the Resolution Trust Corporation in the United States established to dispose of S&L assets. There has been little effort by these institutions as of 1999 to sell off nonperforming assets (See Packer, Chapter 6). As a result, they are part of further delay in the recovery process. The bridge bank proposal of 1998 has the potential to end up as yet another forbearance institution.

In 1992 postal life insurance funds were used to support the Tokyo stock market. This was discontinued but then revived a few years later. In March 1998 about ¥900 billion of postal life and savings funds were transferred to trust banks for purchases of equities of domestic companies. There have been calls from the Liberal Democratic Party to use the large amount of funds collected in the postal life and savings system to support the stock market and banks. This illustrates a policy attitude that market forces can be manipulated, and that this is a substitute for structural reform.

The government's delayed response to the problem has slowed the private sector's response throughout much of the 1990s. Although banks did increase loan loss reserves and sold assets, in light of the government's response, they had incentives to conduct business as if no change in the environment had taken place. Banks continued to pay dividends, continued to support financially weak companies, and continued to operate with high staff levels. The one major change in bank behavior was from 1995 to set aside increasingly large loan reserves, which nonetheless were insufficient. The government policy of forbearance and forgiveness combined with the convoy philosophy provided little incentive for either weak or strong institutions to improve their own balance sheets.

This describes the situation as of mid-1998. The situation has begun to change subsequently. The Liberal Democratic Party's defeat in the July 1998 elections for the Upper House signaled widespread public rejection of the government's approach to economic and financial distress and led to the resignation of Prime Minister Hashimoto. This was a significant turning point. The new prime minister, Keizo Obuchi, initiated a more aggressive approach to dealing with the distress.

In late 1998 the amount of funding to deal with troubled institutions was increased to ¥60 billion, two large banks were nationalized (Long Term Credit Bank and Nippon Credit Bank), and the Bank of Japan and Financial Supervision Agency displayed a more aggressive independence than many had expected. New institutions, such as the Financial Reconstruction Committee and the Resolution and Collection Corporation, were established and serious discussion commenced on what to do with the postal savings system and the entire deposit guarantee system. While it might be premature to conclude a new financial supervision and regulation approach has taken hold in Japan, the evidence does suggest a transition is now firmly in place.

LACK OF PUBLIC SUPPORT

The government until early 1998 was reluctant to use public funds to deal with the banking and financial problems. In 1996, ¥685 billion of public funds were used to address the *jûsen* loan problem. Many observers and government officials were surprised at the level of public opposition to such a small sum relative to the magnitude of the problem—¥6.4 trillion in nonrecoverable loans. As is discussed elsewhere in this volume, this issue was politically mishandled.

As a result, the government was understandably reluctant to make public funding part of a bank bailout package, thus delaying further the resolution of the nonperforming loan problem. The situation changed in late 1997 with the spread of financial distress to other Asian economies and the failures of Hokkaido Takushoku and Yamaichi Securities Company. In the wake of these events and an emerging sense of incipient crisis, public attitudes regarding using taxpayer funds changed. As already noted, in early 1998 the government committed ¥30 trillion of bonds, with the funds pledged to protect depositors and inject capital into the banking system. The distribution of the first ¥1.8 trillion, however, showed that the government was neither aggressive in forcing concessions from receiving banks nor willing to decide which banks were deserving and which were not.

In October 1998 the committed public funding to dealing with the financial distress was increased to ¥60 trillion, maintaining the part allocated to protect depositors and the rest allocated to recapitalize weak but fundamentally healthy banks and to absorb losses of failed banks. Other changes, such as nationalization of two banks and new institutions to deal with nonperforming loans, also helped build public support. How funds will actually be used and whether regulatory authorities will impose real penalties in dealing with troubled institutions remain a concern, however. Thus, public support, while substantial as of mid-1999, is tenuous and could readily evaporate.

Japanese public opposition stands in contrast to public reaction to the US government's efforts to deal with the S&L crisis in the 1980s. In the S&L case, one would have expected much public criticism of the use of taxpayer funds to dispose of assets of failed S&Ls after 1989; however, there was little public comment. The difference is partly explained by the respective roles provided to the public in each financial regime.

The US system is open and designed to serve all demands for funding and, as a result, the public or, more technically, the household sector has had extensive access to the financial system. In particular, the S&L industry provided mortgage credit at favorable terms that imposed no interest rate risk on the borrower in that mortgages had fixed rates and borrowers had the option to refinance if rates declined. The favorable mortgage market supported widespread home ownership, which in turn increased household wealth in the 1970s and '80s as real estate prices rose faster than the general inflation rate and capital gains on housing outpaced the stock and bond markets. Thus, the household sector was a net beneficiary of financial regulation even in the context of the S&L bailout.

This has not been the case in Japan, where the financial regime was designed to support high savings and provide funds to the business sector to support industrialization while limiting household access. In the past, high rates of economic growth and wage increases compensated the household sector for limited access, but since the 1970s lower and unstable economic growth provided little offset. In addition, there is widespread consensus among the public that the financial system has been designed and regulated primarily to serve the interests of the government, financial institutions, and the business sector in ways that many regard as corrupt. Thus, efforts to deal with the financial distress in the 1990s have been viewed merely as efforts to protect banks and bankers who many regard as part of the problem.

The reluctance to seek public funding in the early years of the nonperforming loan problem contributed to delay in resolving it. With significant public funding committed in late 1998, there remain concerns among the public as to whether the funds will be used to support the old convoy system. Scandals in the Ministry of Finance in 1997 and 1998 and in the Banking Bureau of the Bank of Japan in 1998 (which led to the resignation of the Bank's Governor) have eroded public support of government efforts to solve the problem.

NONTRANSPARENCY AND A LACK OF CRITICAL OBSERVERS

In the face of substantial financial problems in the 1980s and early '90s, US regulatory authorities adopted many of the same practices for which Japanese regulatory authorities are now being criticized. Yet the differences in policy outcome are striking. The United States eventually acknowledged, at least to a limited degree, the magnitude of the problem and in 1989 began to take decisive action to close large numbers of insolvent institutions and dispose of their assets through the Resolution Trust Corporation. Banking problems had become apparent after 1988 when the Federal Deposit Insurance Corporation reported its first earnings loss since being established in 1934. The 1991 Federal Deposit Insurance Corporation Improvement Act achieved meaningful reform. It may be premature to conclude that the US financial system is now on a firm foundation, but there is no disagreement that the solvency problems and nonperforming loan problems of the 1980s have been reasonably resolved.

There are many reasons why the United States was able to deal with its financial problems adequately while Japan, even with the US experience as a guide, has had considerable difficulty. Differences in public support of the government's efforts have been discussed already. Another relates to differences between Japan and the United States in the context of minimizing agency-incentive conflict problems.

There now exists a large body of literature highlighting agency problems in financial regulation. Regulatory authorities face incentives to pursue policies adverse to the general public but consistent with their own utility or the utility of the regulated constituency. That is, as long as the authorities possess discretion, there is a tendency to adopt concealment and delay policies in the hope troubled institutions can work their way out of the problem.

In the United States these incentives were more constrained than in Japan for two reasons. First, the United States possesses an extensive financial disclosure system that is accessible and available to the public at nominal cost. Second, institutions exist that permit large numbers of academics and other observers to take strong public stands against government efforts to delay and conceal.

The lack of detailed financial information in Japan is so well known it needs no further comment here. One hopes the government is serious about the goal of transparency, a stated objective of the recently established Financial Supervisory Agency and the Financial Reconstruction Commission.

The institutional situation is more subtle and complex. Japan is a consensus society and, while there is often intense debate over policy issues, there is a high cost to criticizing the status quo. In contrast to the United States, Japanese institutions make it difficult to openly criticize government policy. The press club system in Japan, for example, creates incentives for the press to be less critical because access to government information is controlled. The system of research councils and Ministry institutes, in which academics consult with government agencies, probably limits the supply of those willing to criticize policy publicly.

More important, the Japanese policy-making process is controlled by bureaucrats with little reliance on economists or other specialized policy-making individuals (see Hiwatari, Chapter 5 in this volume). The bureaucracy in general has been closed to economists and has hired staff primarily with law degrees. (It should be noted that this is an undergraduate major in Japan, as it once was in the United States.) As such, economics, finance, and policy are self-taught in many bureaucracies in Japan. There are many able economists and policy analysts in Japan, but they generally are left out of policy making. In contrast, economists and academics play important roles in the US process and the US bureaucracy includes many graduate school-trained economists.

Japanese institutions have not encouraged an active and credible system for public discussion of policy mistakes and misuses of regulatory power, especially one capable of influencing policy. The absence of active and vocal non-government observers willing and able to challenge government efforts to cover-up and delay financial problems needs to be considered a cause of the financial crisis.

A SUMMING UP

The Japanese financial regime reached maturity at the start of the High Growth Period in 1950. During the next two decades, the regime satisfied all of its objectives and importantly contributed to Japan's emergence by the late 1970s as the second largest economy in the world. The regime's success, however, depended on an environment that, after the early 1970s, was vanishing and Japan's rigid financial system came into conflict with new forces, calling for a shift to a more open and competitive financial system.

Internationalization of finance, domestic liberalization in many countries, and advances in computer and telecommunications technology made it difficult to enforce, and easier to circumvent, the constraints on portfolio choice, and political forces increasingly stressed the benefits of markets over regulation. Since the 1970s Japan has achieved partial liberalization with many significant achievements, but many elements of the old regime remained in place. These remaining sources of rigidity include nontransparency, mutual support (convoy) system, pervasive deposit guarantees, inefficient financial institutions, and close relationship among banks, regulatory authorities, and politicians. The combination of liberalization with continued adherence to important elements of the old regime generated conflicts.

Market participants gained more portfolio flexibility than earlier in the postwar period, and took on new risks in new markets in an effort to reestablish or enhance market share. However, this occurred in the absence of an adequate system for monitoring risk. Administrative guidance is incapable of such monitoring and liberalization weakened the main bank system. The absence of good governance (basic accountability) in the corporate sector compounded the problem.

During the 1980s, special conditions in Japan with regard to real estate, such as a price-inelastic supply of land and extensive regulation of building activity, combined with rapid real GDP growth and an influx of foreign financial institutions, provided the basis for a speculative real estate bubble. Banks could no longer rely on a captive corporate market and were forced to seek new markets. They became overly dependent on real estate lending. The role of equities in bank capital ensured a feedback relationship would exit between bank lending, real estate price inflation, and increased equity prices. Smaller institutions also became active participants in the real estate sector. Like S&Ls in the United States during the 1980s, small Japanese credit-union-type depositories aggressively pursued lending in speculative ventures, and, like their US counterparts, did so without oversight. Credit cooperatives were not under the supervision of either the Bank of Japan or the Ministry of Finance but rather were under the supervision of local prefectures.

The main bank system had served as an effective system to evaluate and monitor risk, but it began to unravel in response to financial liberalization and no widely available financial-disclosure framework was available to replace it. The expansion of credit was not accomplished by increased disclosure.

"Administrative guidance" could not keep pace with the fast changing financial environment and the regulatory monitoring system lagged market developments. Complete deposit guarantees, lack of transparency, and adherence to a system of mutual support provided incentives to assume imprudent levels of risk. In addition, the human resources available to monitor the newly emerging financial system were small relative to the task at hand.

In this context, the Bank of Japan's easy monetary policy after 1986 provided the liquidity, and financial liberalization provided the asset-diversification powers, that together supported asset inflation in the late 1980s. Loans for real estate expanded, increasing land prices, which expanded collateral for lending, and rising equity prices increased bank capital.

The collapse of asset prices revealed fundamental weaknesses in Japan's financial and regulatory structure. The mutual support system made it difficult for banks and other depositories to price loans efficiently and to penalize low-quality debtors. The government's belief in managed finance and nontransparency made forbearance and forgiveness the preferred policy.

The failure to resolve the nonperforming loan problem generated a credit crunch that has contributed to stagnant or declining real GDP growth for almost a decade and has interfered with efforts by the Bank of Japan to stimulate the economy.

The regulatory authorities' denial of a problem was followed by understatement when denial was no longer credible. The authorities adopted a policy of delay, forgiveness, and forbearance based on the hope economic growth and asset prices would recover and solve the problem. Lack of critical outside groups made it easier to adopt such a policy. There was no public support for a bailout.

A significant turning point was reached when Japan came close to a financial and economic abyss in late 1997 and early 1998. The failure of several major financial institutions shifted public sentiment, so taxpayer funds were made available. A clear public rejection of the government's past approach came in the July 1998 Upper House elections. However, public support remains tenuous due to past policy failures and scandals at the Ministry of Finance and the Bank of Japan. Moreover, adherence to a mutual support system in the funds first distribution showed the authorities had yet to break fully with the past.

The near collapse of the economic and financial system clearly shows that the old regime is finished and that significant reform is needed to return Japan to sustained economic growth and financial stability. The public is now more focused on how the government handles the problem and has demonstrated a willingness to reject a government that it sees as failing to resolve the problems.

The 1990s are Japan's lost decade in terms of economic and financial development, but new policies and institutions in 1998 and 1999 suggest a transition from the old rigid regulatory and supervisory framework to a new framework consistent with open and competitive financial institutions and markets.

CONCLUSION

The discussion has highlighted five factors that together constitute the cause of the banking and financial crisis that defined Japan's performance in the 1990s. Each plays a role and each is important, so that specific problems generally can be attributed to various combinations of factors.

In many respects, the Japanese financial regime prior to the crisis was an "accident waiting to happen." The continued reliance on a regulatory and supervisory framework embedded in the old rigid system would have generated a response of delay, forgiveness, and forbearance to any shock, internal or external. While Bank of Japan policy is a cause because it provided an internal shock to a speculative asset bubble which then collapsed, the inherent nature of the financial regulatory and supervisory framework insured that a banking crisis would result.

The sheer number and interrelatedness of the "causes" of Japan's banking and financial problems mean recovery and reform will be a difficult task and will represent a major departure from past practices. Japan has faced more difficult transitions and, while the issue was in doubt as recently as 1998, there are meaningful signs the country's political leaders and regulatory authorities have made the decision to move to the type of financial system outlined in Big Bang.

Japan is now in the process of developing a new financial regulatory and supervisory framework divorced from the old financial regime. The new framework has the potential to return Japan to sustained economic and financial development.

NOTES

1 Postwar economic and financial development, with emphasis on the period since 1970, is discussed in Cargill, Hutchison, and Ito (1997); financial liberalization through the mid-1980s is discussed in Cargill and Royama (1988).

2 Japan's postal savings system is the largest financial institution in the world with ¥2.4 trillion in deposits in 1998. Cargill and Yoshino (1998), Cargill and Yoshino (Chapter 8 in this volume), and Kuwayama (1997) provide detailed discussion of this complex and important part of Japan's financial structure. Kuwayama compares the Japan's system with the US postal savings system in existence from 1910 to 1966.

REFERENCES

Aoki, Masahiko and Hugh Patrick, eds. 1994. *The Japanese Main Banking System*. Oxford: Oxford University Press.

Cargill, Thomas F. 1988. "Korea and Japan: The End of the Japanese Financial Regime." In George Kaufman, ed, *Bank Crisis: Causes, Analysis and Prevention*. London: JAI Press, Inc.

Cargill, Thomas F. 1989. *Central Bank Independence and Regulatory Responsibilities: The Bank of Japan and the Federal Reserve*. Salomon Brothers Center for the Study of Financial Institutions, New York University.

Cargill, Thomas F, Michael M Hutchison, and Takatoshi Ito. 1996. "Deposit guarantees in Japan: Aftermath of the bubble and burst of the bubble economy." *Contemporary Economic Policy*, 1996 July: 41–52.

Cargill, Thomas F, Michael M Hutchison, and Takatoshi Ito. 1997. *The Political Economy of Japanese Monetary Policy*. Cambridge MA: The MIT Press.

Cargill, Thomas F, Michael M Hutchison, and Takatoshi Ito. Forthcoming. *Financial Policy and Central Banking in Japan*. Cambridge MA: The MIT Press.

Cargill, Thomas F and Shoichi Royama. 1988. *The Transition of Finance in Japan and the United States*. Stanford CA: Hoover Institution Press.

Cargill, Thomas F and Naoyuki Yoshino. 1998. "Too big for its boots." *The Financial Regulator*, 3 (1998 Dec): 39–43.

Cargill, Thomas F and Naoyuki Yoshino. "Postal Savings and Policy Based Finance." Chapter 6 in this volume.

Cole, David C. 1993. "The Political Economy of Korean-U.S. Financial Relations." *Korean-U.S. Financial Issues*. Washington DC: Korea Economic Institute of America.

Craig, Valentine V. 1998. "Japanese Banking: A Time of Crisis." *FDIC Banking Review*, 11 (2): 9–17.

Feldman, Robert Alan. 1986. *Japanese Financial Markets: Deficits, Dilemmas, and Deregulation*. Cambridge MA: The MIT Press.

Fukao, Mitsuhiro. 1998. "Japan's Role in the International Trading System: Prospects for Market Liberalization and Economic Reform." Testimony before the Committee on Finance, United States Senate, 1998 July 14.

Hamada, Koichi and Akiyoshi Horiuchi. 1987. "The Political Economy of the Financial Market." In Kozo Yamamura and Yasukichi Yasuba, eds, *The Political Economy of Japan*, v I. Stanford: Stanford University Press.

Huh, Chan Guk and Sun Bae Kim. 1994. "Financial Regulation and Banking Sector Performance: A Comparison of Bad Loan Problems in Japan and Korea." *Economic Review, Federal Reserve Bank of San Francisco*, 1994 (2).

Krugman, Paul. 1994. "The Myth of Asia's Miracle." *Foreign Affairs*, 1994 Nov–Dec: 62–78.

Kuwayama, Patricia Hagan. 1997 Oct. "Postal Banking in the United States and Japan: A Comparative Analysis." Center on Japanese Economy and Business, Columbia Business School, Working Paper 139. To be published in Monetary and Economic Studies, the Bank of Japan.

Mikitani, Ryoichi and Patricia Hagan Kuwayama. 1998 Aug. "Japan's New Central Banking Law: A Critical View." Center on Japanese Economy and Business, Columbia Business School, Working Paper 145.

Patrick, Hugh. 1994. "The Relevance of Japanese Finance and its Main Bank System." In Masahiko Aoki and Hugh Patrick, eds, *The Japanese Main Banking System*. Oxford: Oxford University Press.

Patrick, Hugh. 1999. "The Causes of Japan's Financial Crisis." Pacific Economic Papers #288, Australia-Japan Research Centre, the Australian National University.

Suzuki, Yoshio. *Money and Banking in Contemporary Japan*. Yale University Press, 1980.

Suzuki, Yoshio, ed. 1987. *The Japanese Financial System*. Oxford: Claredon Press.

Ueda, Kazuo. 1999. "Causes of the Japanese Banking Instability in the 1990s." Chapter 3 in this volume.

Chapter 3

CAUSES OF JAPAN'S BANKING PROBLEMS IN THE 1990s

Kazuo Ueda
Bank of Japan

This chapter discusses the causes of the instability of the Japanese financial system in the 1990s. Bad loans have been the immediate cause of many of the problems facing the Japanese financial system in the 1990s, and real estate lending during the boom period of the late 1980s is generally considered a principal source of the bad loans. This chapter seeks to explain why the real estate lending took place, and to measure the actual impact it has had since the bubble burst. Real estate lending is, however, only one source of Japan's banking problems, so data on bad loans at individual banks are used to estimate the importance of several other variables as contributing factors. The volatility of monetary policy that led to wide swings in asset prices, the impact of liberalization on bank behavior, and the role bank regulation has played in aggravating the situation are considered.

Given its focus on causes, the concern here is mainly with the period up to the failure of three large financial institutions in November 1997. It is useful to divide the last 20 or so years leading to those failures into several periods; this is done in the next section. This is followed by a review of the state of the bad-loan problem as of March 1998 and the statistical analysis of possible causes. I then turn to Bank of Japan monetary policy, especially during the mid to late 1980s, as the root cause of the swings in asset prices. The role played by public policy towards banks in aggravating the bad-loan problem is also examined.

The definition of bad loans has changed over time, has become more severe, and has been a source of confusion. The definition was revised again in March 1999. Table 3.1 shows how the definition has evolved.

Bank classification has also changed during the 1990s. Where before generally one spoke of the city banks (of which there were 13 until 1990), long-term banks (3), and trust banks (7) separately, they are now commonly grouped as the "top-tier" or major bank category, sometimes further modified by the number of banks in the group. This number has declined to 17. During the period covered by this paper, there were 20. Between 1989–92, 67 *sogo* (mutual)

TABLE 3.1. The Evolving Definition of Bad Loans Reported on Bank Financial Statements

What is included in bad loans, and the terms used to describe them, have changed through time. The situation is further complicated by the fact there are three sets of numbers (as well as estimates made by analysts in the private sector). This table gives the definition of bad loans used by banks in the financial statements issued for the report dates shown. (For convenience, which fiscal-year reports are covered by a definition are listed in parentheses.) This series is used in Table 3.2 and the regression analysis. These loans are now referred to by the banks as *"risk management loans (non-performing loans)."*

March is the end of Japanese banks' fiscal years and interim reports are issued in September. (For example, fiscal 1992 ended on 31 March 1993 and the interim report is as of 30 September 1992.)

1993 Mar – 1995 Sep (Fiscal 1992–95)

Loans to borrowers in legal bankruptcy.
Past-due loans (reported by top-tier banks only), defined as no payment of interest or principal for 6 months or more.

1996 Mar – 1996 Sep (Fiscal 1995–96)

Loans to borrowers in legal bankruptcy.
Past-due loans, (now reported by all banks) defined as no payment of interest or principal for 6 months or more. Also called *loans in arrears.*
Interest-waived loans, defined as loans with interest rates lowered to less than the BOJ discount rate at the time the rate is lowered. Sometimes also called *restructured* (narrowly defined).

1997 Mar – 1997 Sep (Fiscal 1996–97)

Loans to borrowers in legal bankruptcy.
Past-due loans, defined as no payment of interest or principal for 6 months or more.
Interest-waived loans, defined as loans with interest rates lowered to less than the BOJ discount rate at the time the rate is lowered.
Loans to borrowers in informal workouts.

1998 Mar – (Fiscal 1997–)

Loans to borrowers in legal bankruptcy.
Past-due loans, defined as past-due loans on which there has been no payment of interest or principal for 6 months or more.
3 months Past-due loans, defined as past-due loans on which there has been no payment of interest or principal for 3 to 6 months. Also called *non-accrual* loans.
Restructured loans, defined as loans on which the original interest rate or maturity terms have been eased. This makes the definition of restructured used in Japan comparable to the corresponding concept in the United States. This category includes loans listed as *interest-waived* in earlier years. Note that a literal translation of the Japanese term is "loans with relaxed conditions."

TABLE 3.1. Continued

1999 Mar – **(Fiscal 1998–)**

Beginning with March 1999 reports, banks have tightened the definitions of bad loans so that the new definitions are compatible with those of self-assessment. (See below.) As a result, all the Category III and IV problem loans in self-assessment are now included. Specifically, the sum of Category III and IV loans in self-assessment is equal to loans to borrowers in legal bankruptcy and Past-due loans, except that self-assessment includes non-loan exposures such as customer liability for acceptance & guarantees, securities lending etc. Three month Past-due loans and restructured loans are now a subset of Category II loans in self-assessment. The remainder of Category II loans are those to debtors subject to specific management risk but are still making interest payments.

Problem Loans Based on Banks Self-Assessment

1998 Mar **(Fiscal 1997–)**

With the introduction of Prompt Corrective Action banks have started to carry out the self-assessment of their balance sheets. The format of the assessment roughly matches that of inspection by regulators. Under PCA problem loans are classified in order of seriousness Category IV, Category III and Category II loans. Banks are not required to disclose to the public the results of self-assessment. The aggregate figures are, however, reported by the FSA, which are used in Table 3.2. Some individual banks themselves have opted to disclose the results. Note that the criteria used for classifying loans into the above categories were tightened in fiscal 1998 under the guidance of FSA. Hence, March 1998 and March 1999 figures are not strictly comparable.

For a full discussion of definitions of bad loans, see Hoshi and Kashyap (1999, Section 4).

banks and one *shinkin* were successively reclassified as regional II (second-tier) banks, in addition to the 64 existing regional banks, which were classified as Regional I (first-tier) banks.

CHRONOLOGY

It is useful to divide the last 20 or so years into several periods. First is the period from the late 1970s to the mid 1980s, which can be characterized as the start of financial deregulation in Japan. Second, the mid to late 1980s was a period of substantially rising asset prices supported by massive bank lending. Third, the 1990s have seen dramatically falling asset prices, the resulting problems in the banking sector, and the government's slow attempts to address them.

The 1990s may be further divided into three. Until 1994 banks and regulators only slowly came to recognize the seriousness of the bad-loan problem. Starting in late 1994, regulators embarked on serious resolution attempts. They thought the problems were most serious among the credit cooperatives and housing finance companies (*jusen*). Attempts to mobilize public money faced serious objections from taxpayers and, in the end, the use of public funds was confined to closing credit cooperatives, and *jusen*. The problems unfortunately did not disappear with these actions.

Since late 1997, when three large banks and securities companies went under, leading to a serious credit crunch, more extensive action has been taken. The government finally decided to put aside a large sum of public money, ¥60 trillion, to protect creditors of insolvent banks and to inject equity into solvent but undercapitalized banks. In addition, the introduction of prompt corrective action (PCA) in April 1998 was designed as a way to make the regulatory approach more transparent and rule based.[1]

At the time of summer 1999, serious strains on the financial system have subsided. It remains to be seen how quickly the system will recover health and begin to intermediate funds smoothly.

THE EXTENT OF THE BAD-LOAN PROBLEM

The situation of the banking system just before serious attempts to address the problems of unhealthy banks were taken is summarized in Table 3.2.

For the top-tier and 128 regional banks as of March 1998, problem loans based on self-assessment, as shown in the table, totaled ¥71.8 trillion yen. In comparison, bad loans based on the official definition stood at ¥19.5 trillion. Apart from technical details, the major reason for the discrepancy is that self-assessment includes a large amount for Category II loans, which are the relatively healthiest of problem loans. Category II loans amounted to ¥68.0 trillion in March 1998. Past experience suggests only a relatively small fraction of these are unrecoverable.

The ratio of problem loans to total loans is highest for credit cooperatives (*shinso*). This accords with the fact that many of the restructuring efforts so far have involved credit cooperatives.

Loss provisions can be made out of own capital, operating profits, and realization of latent gains on securities. Own capital alone exceeds the required loss provision for all segments of the industry except credit cooperatives, and for them, including another year of operating profits provides full cover. Thus, it has been perceived that banks have had enough capital to make loss provisions. However, credit cooperatives would have almost no capital left once required provisions are made.

For top-tier banks, the BIS ratio after loss provisions falls short of the required 8% even with the inclusion of another year of operating profits and of subordinate loans and debentures (which are equal to about 3.5% of risk as-

TABLE 3.2. The Bad Loan Problem as of March 1998
(Trillion yen, except the number of banks and percents)

Top 20	Regional	Shinkin	Shinso[1]	
20	128	401	351	Number of banks
11.1	11.0	13.6	16.6	Problem as % all loans
50.5	21.6	10.1	2.5	Problem loans[2]
11.2	4.3	1.9	0.6	Required loss provision[3]
13.6	9.4	5.1	0.5	Capital
3.6	1.9	0.8	0.2	Operating profits (fiscal'97)
2.7	2.6	0.6	0.0	Unrealized gains[4]
747	265	111	23	Total assets

1. *Shinso* are called credit cooperatives in English.
2. Category II and III loans, as determined by self-assessment of each bank (see Table 3.1 for definition).
3. Based on data from past inspections, BOJ (1997) reports that the probabilities of problem loans becoming non-recoverable within three years are 16.7% for Category II and 75.3% for Category III. I have use these probabilities to arrive at an estimate of the required loss provision.
4. On securities. (Unrealized gains on real estate, primarily the banks' buildings, are not included.) Historically, assets have been carried on corporate books at cost. These unrealized gains are thus sometimes called "hidden reserves."

Source: Financial Supervisory Agency, "The Status of Risk Management Loans." July 1998.

sets). Only after inclusion of unrealized capital gains in real estate holdings and tax allocation effects, does the BIS ratio come close to 8%.[2]

The amount of bad loans written off in the last few years is striking. As of March 1993, official bad loans outstanding were ¥12.8 trillion for the 20 banks then in the top tier. In the subsequent five years, the banks wrote off ¥37.6 trillion and as of March 1998 still had bad loans of ¥14.5 trillion yen on their books, using the same definition as in 1993, higher than in 1993![3]

The slow progress in reducing the level of bad loans relates primarily to three factors: underestimates of bad loans, regulatory forbearance, and genuine increases in them resulting from the stagnation in the economy. That is, in addition to the progressive tightening of reporting standards of bad loans by banks as reported in Table 3.2, regulators have increasingly encouraged banks to recognize and write off large amounts of bad loans. BOJ (1999) identifies four points at which regulatory recognition of bad loans expanded significantly. Since 1993 MOF has made it easier for banks to write off bad loans using after tax profits. In 1995 bad loans to *jusen* were written off. Since 1997 write offs and loss provisions based on self-assessment have started. Since 1998, following guidance from the Financial Supervisory Agency (FSA), the criteria for bad loan classification under self-assessment has been tightened, and loan provisioning increased accordingly.

REAL ESTATE-RELATED LENDING

The role real estate-related loans played in causing the bad-loan problem has been widely discussed. At the aggregate level, Table 3.3 shows real estate loans as a percentage of total loans for each of six segments of the banking industry. (All data for the analyses in this section, unless otherwise noted, can be found in the Nikkei Needs Data Bank.)

Among the segments, trust banks and long-term banks generally have had the greatest share of their loans in real estate—with the long-term banks greatest before 1981 and during 1987–90 and trust banks greatest in 1982-86 and 1991–95. Looking at changes in relative exposure, except for trust banks, the pattern is the same across the industry during the 1980s: the ratios started going up at the beginning of the decade and reached a peak in 1989. Trust banks actually reduced their relative exposure to real estate after a 1986 peak, but still ended the decade with a greater absolute exposure than 10 years earlier. Both trust banks and long-term credit banks substantially increased exposure during the first half of the 1990s, while exposure at the other types of banks was more or less flat or down slightly.

Figure 3.1 shows year-over-year growth rates of the price index for land for commercial use in six large cities.

TABLE 3.3. Share of Real Estate Industry Lending in Total Loans by Bank Type

	City	Regional 1	Regional 2	Trust	Longterm	*Shinkin*
1975	5.0	6.2	6.7	7.3	10.4	5.5
	4.8	5.6	6.2	7.5	10.1	5.2
	4.7	5.3	6.4	9.7	10.4	5.4
	5.1	5.4	7.0	10.4	10.5	5.8
	4.9	5.1	7.1	9.9	10.0	6.5
1980	4.8	5.0	7.4	9.1	9.8	6.8
	5.0	5.2	7.9	9.8	9.6	7.1
	5.5	5.5	8.3	10.6	9.5	7.3
	5.9	5.7	8.7	11.1	10.3	7.3
	6.3	5.9	9.2	11.3	10.5	7.6
1985	7.7	6.5	10.3	14.3	11.4	8.2
	10.4	7.3	10.7	15.8	13.5	9.2
	10.5	8.1	11.6	13.0	13.6	10.6
	11.2	8.9	12.5	11.8	14.0	10.9
	11.9	9.5	13.3	11.4	14.1	11.6
1990	11.5	9.3	12.4	11.5	13.7	10.5
	12.0	9.7	12.0	14.1	13.8	9.7
	12.9	10.0	12.0	15.9	14.2	9.7
	11.8	9.0	11.4	16.0	14.7	9.9
	12.1	9.3	11.9	16.9	15.5	9.7
1995	12.2	9.2	11.8	17.5	16.4	

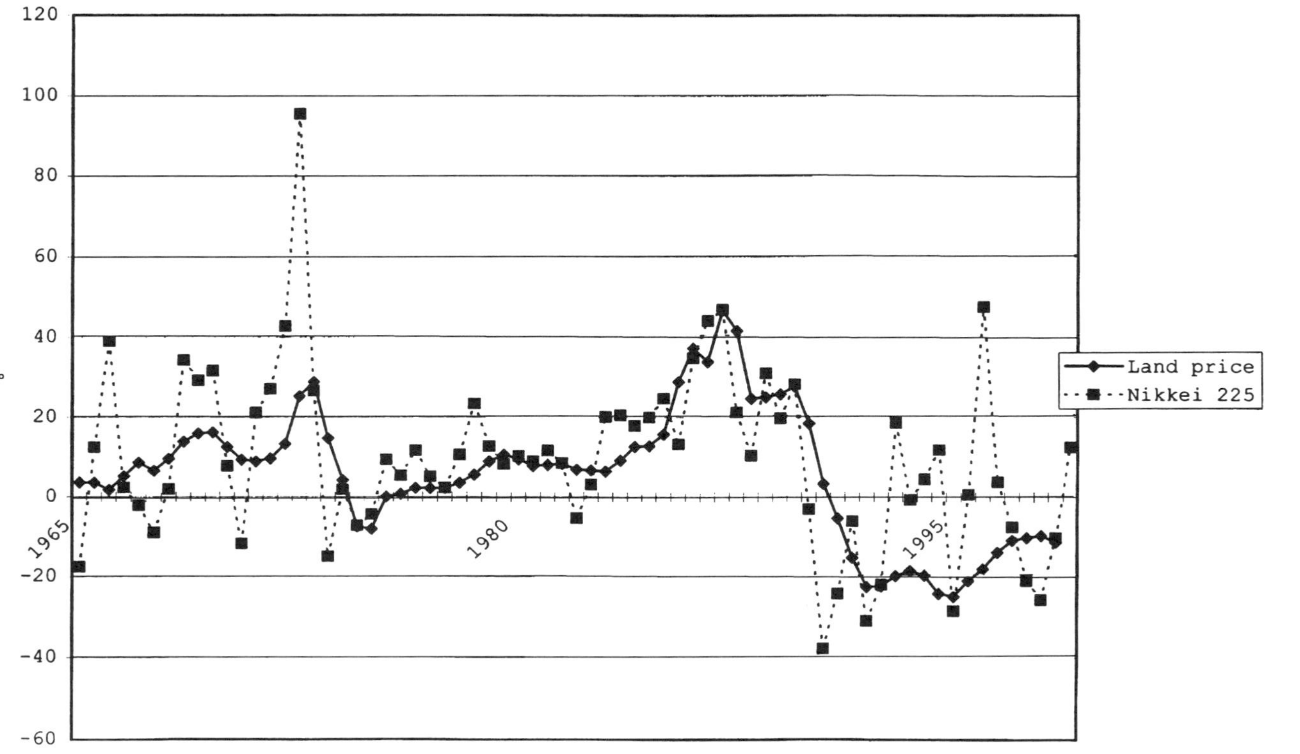

Note: This figure plots annualized changes in the price index for real estate for commercial use in six large cities and in the Nikkei 225 index, semi-annually.

FIGURE 3.1. Annualized rates of change in stock and Japanese urban land prices (1965–98).

The increases in real estate loans in the late 1980s occurred in the context of accelerating increases in urban land prices. In contrast, land prices consistently declined in the 1990s, quite sharply so in 1995. Such an observation is consistent with the view that the collapse in land prices has been a major cause of the bad-loan problem. Because land is a common form of collateral, declining urban land prices affected more than just loans made directly for real estate-related purposes.

The decline in land prices in the 1990s was largely an unexpected shock. With the exception of a brief period around oil-shocked 1975, postwar Japan had never previously experienced a decline in land prices. Some years saw greater increases than others, but always there were increases, and usually they exceeded general price increases for goods and services. Thus, no time series analysis of Japanese land price data through the late 1980s would have given a high probability to the possibility of a sharp fall in land prices in the 1990s. This means adoption of value-at-risk analysis would not of itself have prevented Japanese banks from lending massively to real estate-related sectors. Of course, history abounds with banking crises generated by boom and bust cycles in real estate prices, so one can argue that Japanese banks could have learned from the experience of other economies.

OTHER CONTRIBUTING FACTORS

In addition to real estate loans, a number of hypotheses have been advanced concerning causes of the bad-loan problem. These include the effects of liberalization, the nature of bank regulation, and poor judgment by bank managers.

Financial liberalization, which has been steadily taking place since the late 1970s, is sometimes claimed as a cause of the financial problems. (For a longer discussion along similar lines, see Ueda (1994) and Hoshi and Kashyap (1999).)

Liberalization benefited the securities markets first. Large nonfinancial firms that once were good customers of major banks started to use the bond and stock markets. However, financial products for retail customers backed by bonds and stocks did not grow rapidly so funds continued to flow into banks. The introduction of CDs in 1979 and the liberalization of time deposit interest rates, which began in 1985, increased the cost of funds for banks. Such a chain of events forced banks to look for lending opportunities with low screening costs. An easy place to go was real estate-related loans, where credit analysis was just a matter of estimating the future path of real estate prices. Given the historical record of land price increases, the perceived risk of such loans may have been low. Large banks also began to seek customers among smaller firms, which were pleased to have the prestige of being clients. This meant a loss of customers for smaller banks, so some of them also increased real estate loans.

Inefficient or lax bank management is sometimes regarded as a cause of bad loans. This is considered to be important in the analysis of US banking crises historically. (For example, Wheelock and Wilson (1995) find that the probability of bankruptcy was higher for inefficient banks in the banking crisis in Kansas during 1910–25.) However, its significance for Japan in the 1990s is yet to be established, if only because it is a bit stretched as a cause of an economy-wide bad-loan problem. One must argue that many banks became suddenly inefficient. Still, there could be important differences among banks in the degree of exposure to real estate-related loans. Such information can be utilized to test the effects of management efficiency on bad loans.

Some safety nets have been blamed for contributing to banking problems by creating moral hazard. This view is especially strong in the literature on the US banking crisis in the 1980s. That is, troubled banks chose to get into high-risk investments, only to aggravate the situation (see, for example, Brumbaugh & Carron (1987)). The strategy was supported by regulatory forbearance. To my knowledge, a similar analysis on Japanese banks has not been carried out yet. Examples of such behavior in Japan, however, abound. Many of the banks that went under were collecting deposits at above-average interest rates and using the funds for insecure investments. Presumably, this factor intensifies the effects of other factors such as land price movements and any bank management inefficiency. Consequently, finding its effect independently of others would not be easy unless one resorts to international comparison or historical analysis.

HYPOTHESIS TESTING

In the following, I use information contained in cross-sectional variations in the degree of seriousness of the bad loan problem at individual banks to test some of these hypotheses. Unfortunately, balance sheet data on small banks such as the *shinkin* and *shinso* (credit cooperatives) are not available on an individual-bank basis. Hence, the analysis is of the top-tier and regional banks. Specifically, I use balance sheet data for 147 banks in order of their type and in order that they appear in Figure 3.2 below: long-term (3), city (10), regional I(59), regional II (67), and trust (8).

The analysis examines causes of bad loans as of March 1996. The choice of the end of fiscal 1995 is a compromise between two considerations. The more recent the bad-loan data become, the more accurate they probably are. On the other hand, more recent data include many loans that became bad because of the stagnant behavior of the economy in the 1990s, not just those generated by sharp declines in assets prices in the early 1990s. Further, using data from 1997 or 1998 excludes the banks closed during these years which had very high bad-loan ratios.

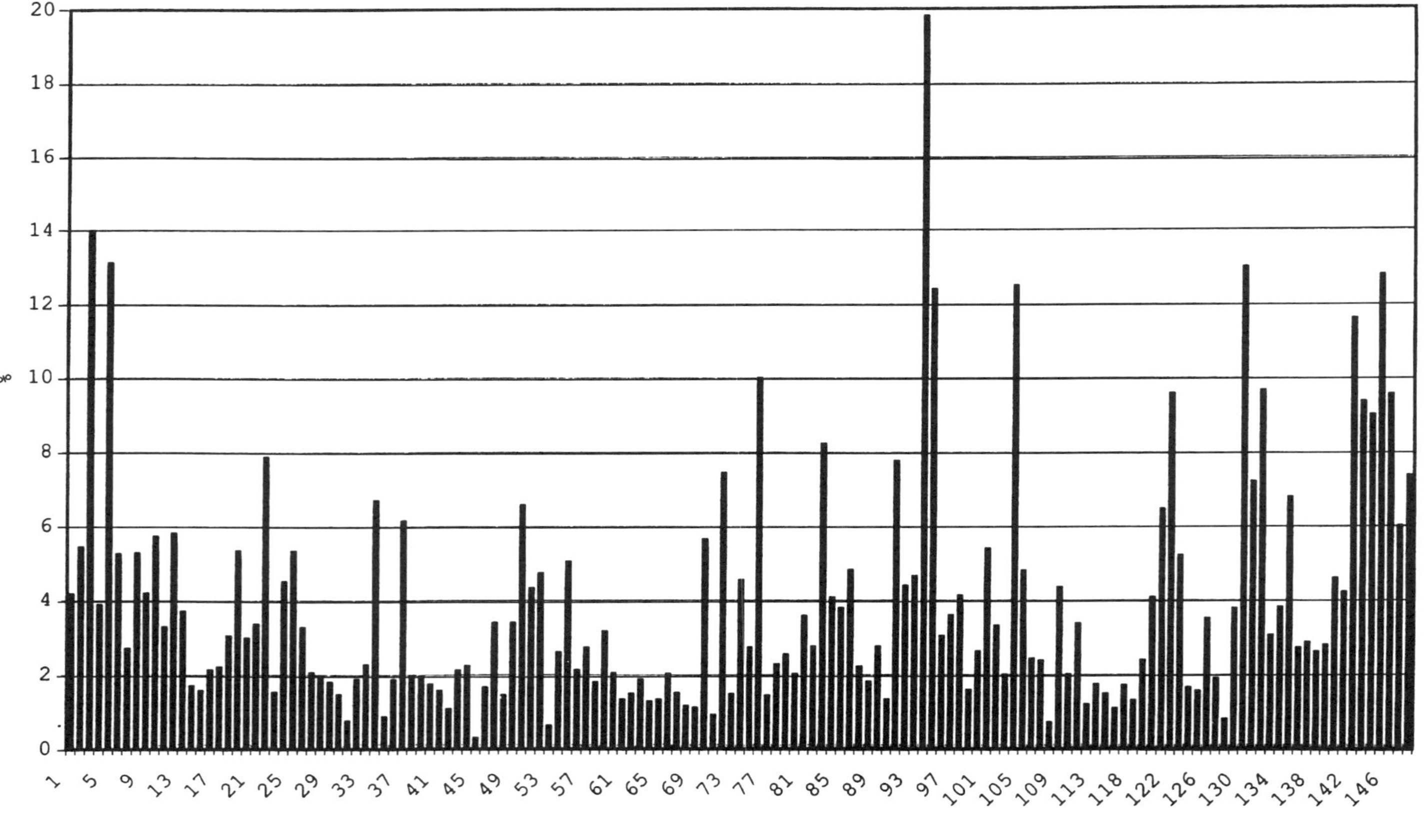

FIGURE 3.2. The bad-loan ratio of 147 sample banks (March end, 1996).

Despite criticisms to the contrary, the official bad loan data reported by banks contain important information about their soundness. Figure 3.2 shows the bad loan ration of the sample banks. The ratios go as high as 20%, but only eight go over 10% and there are quite a few below 2%.

The bad-loan ratio tends to be higher for long-term credit and trust banks which sharply increased real estate loans in the late 1980s. There are also several regional banks with very high ratios.

With the exception of trust banks, the banks with a bad-loan ratio equal to or greater than 8% in March 1996—there were 10 of these in the sample plus one not in the sample—have all subsequently been liquidated, merged with another bank, or nationalized. On the other hand, less than 5 banks with a bad loan ratio less than 8% in 1996 are no longer independent.

Figure 3.3 presents the correlation between the bad-loan ratio in 1996 and the share of loans in 1990 to real estate-related industries (the real estate, construction, and non-bank financial sectors). A clear positive correlation is found, again highlighting the role played by real estate-related loans. The non-bank financial sector consisted primarily of *jûsen* and other non-bank financial institutions, predominantly bank-related, which borrowed from banks, credit associations, and agriculture credit cooperatives, and lent for real estate projects.

Explaining the Bad-Loan Ratio

Let us now seek to explain the bad-loan ratio using three sets of variables. First, data on land price movements (LP) are used, as they directly affect the viability of real estate-related loans. The LP variable is the sum of the rate of land price inflation between 1986 and 1990 and the rate of land price deflation between 1990 and 1996. Thus, it represents the tremendous swing in land prices in the time frame between the mid-1980s and the mid-1990s. The land price data have been taken from *Chika-Kouji* (*Kokudo-Cho*), and correspond to the highest-price data in the capital city in which the main office of a sample bank is located. For most city, trust, and long-term banks that is either Tokyo or Osaka; for the regional banks it is a prefectural capital.

The second set of variables is designed to capture bank management efficiency. I include the rate of return on capital (Profit 86), and the current cost to current profit ratio (Current 86). The latter was used extensively by regulators as the most important proxy for bank efficiency, especially during the first half of the postwar period (see Ueda (1994) for details). A rise in the ratio indicates that the bank requires more resources, that is it has to incur more costs, to earn the same amount of revenue.

Third, a variable that shows how well banks are capitalized, either explicitly or implicitly, is included to address the hypothesis that well-capitalized banks

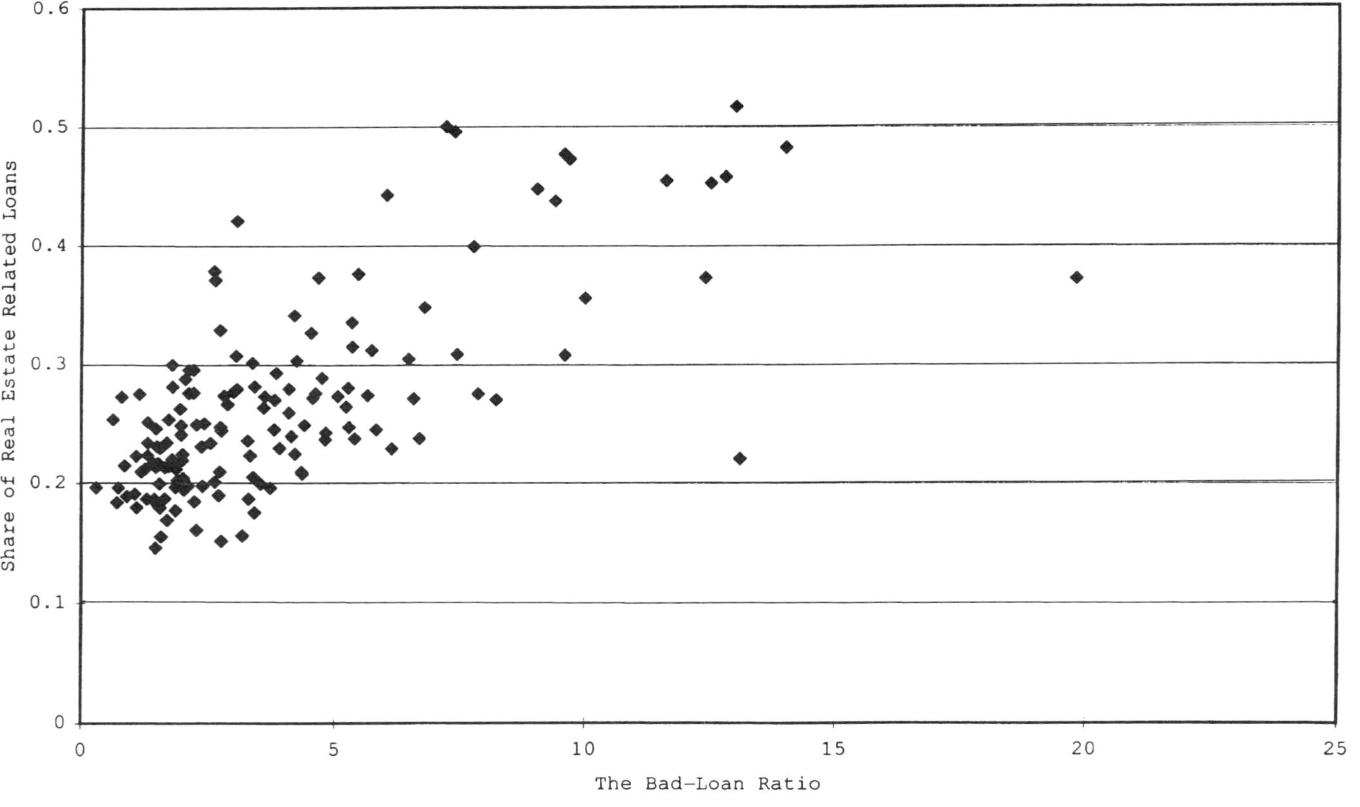

FIGURE 3.3. Real estate related lendings and the bad-loan ratio.

are less prone to carry out go-for-broke investments. (Horiuchi and Shimizu (1996) have analyzed a similar hypothesis.) For want of a better measure of the capital ratio, I simply use the sum of own capital, loss provisions, and unrealized capital gains, divided by total assets (Cap 86).

A variable is included to capture the effect of financial liberalization on bank franchise value. Specifically, total loans divided by the number of branches (Branch) is assumed to represent the resources banks hold in terms of branch offices and loan officers that can be used to increase retail loans. The number of branches is as of March 1980, which roughly corresponds to the start of financial liberalization. Given the stability of the number of branches, however, the choice of year made no difference. The variable captures the effect on bank franchise value of the unevenness of deregulation in the following sense. Starting in the late 1970s deregulation in securities markets, and in restrictions on banks opening branches and regulations prohibiting banks from entering nontraditional banking services, led to a significant decrease in traditional sources of income for banks without many branch offices. These banks lost large borrowers, while being placed at a disadvantage in making loans to small borrowers. Put differently, other things equal, banks with a higher value for the variable Branch may have had a tendency to make large real estate loans for which credit analysis was deemed relatively easy.

Finally, I add the share of loans using land as collateral as of 1986 (Colla 86). The effect of this variable may be regarded as coming from any one of the three mechanisms discussed above. For example, it may be thought of as another mechanism by which land price movements affect the performance of loans, or as representing a lack of credit analysis capability at banks either as a result of inherent bank inefficiency or of regulation.

Table 3.4 presents the results. I regressed both the bad-loan ratio and the share of real estate-related loans on the variables discussed above. In Equation 1, the swing in land prices, the importance of land as collateral, the capital ratio, and the amount of loans per branch all have the expected signs and are statistically significant. The bad-loan ratio in 1996 is higher for banks in regions with greater swings in land prices, with more use of land as collateral, with smaller amounts of capital, and more limited size of branch networks,and the variables related to capital ratios have the expected signs and are statistically significant. (The Colla 86 variable may simply be playing the role of a proxy for a bank's inclination to increase real estate-related loans. Hence, I also estimated the equations without the variable, with no substantive changes in the results.) Although the R-squared of the equation is not very high, of the 30 banks with the highest actual bad-loan ratios, 18 (60%) are in the top 30 of the fitted values of the regression.

The regression fnr the exposure to real estate related industries, Equation 2, shows that the four variables affect real estate-related loans in the expected direction, although the capital ratio is insignificant.

TABLE 3.4. Regression Results for the Bad-Loan Ratio & the Share of Real Estate Related Loans

	Dependent Variable	LP	Colla 86	Profit 86	Cap 86	Branch	Current 86	R-squared
Equation 1	The Bad-Loan Ratio	0.865	4.59	0.102	–1.66	0.154	–0.314	0.332
		3.18	*2.55*	*2.48*	*–4.33*	*2.39*	*–2.49*	
Equation 2	Share of Real Estate	0.0285	0.0836	0.000696	–0.0135	0.00677	–0.00553	0.276
	Related Loans	*3.96*	*1.76*	*0.643*	*–1.34*	*3.98*	*–1.67*	

Notes: 1. Data definitions are:

LP: The rate of increase in the land price of the capital city of the prefecture where the main office of a sample bank is located between 1986 and 1990+The rate of decrease in the same land price between 1990 & 1996.

Colla 86: The share of loans backed by land collateral in 1986.

Profit 86: The rate of return on capital in 1986.

Cap 86: <own capital+loan loss provisions> divided by total assets in 1986.

Branch: Total loans divided by the number of branches in March 1980.

Current 86: Current costs divided by current profits in 1986.

2. The numbers in italics are t-statistics.

3. The equations include a constant, not shown for simplicity.

Somewhat surprisingly, the bad-loan ratio is higher for more-efficient banks. This result may reflect problems with the measures of bank efficiency. (It would be better to estimate a measure of, for example, bank X-efficiency, and use this as an explanatory variable in the bad loans equation. This approach, though attempted, so far has not been successful with the Japanese data.) Alternatively, it may indicate that seemingly more efficient banks simply were earning high returns because of their exposure to potentially riskier loans. On this interpretation, the risks manifested themselves in the 1990s. Equation 2 shows, however, that such risk taking was not particularly confined to real estate-related loans.

More quantitatively, the sample standard deviation of the bad-loan ratio is 3.22. Against this, the contribution of land price (LP) is 0.79 (that is, the standard deviation of LP times the estimated coefficient was 0.79). The contribution of Branch is 0.58, and that of the share of loans using land as collateral (Colla 86) is 0.60. Of course, given the correlation between the variables, one cannot simply regard the size of the standard deviations as showing the importance of the variables.

The Results

The estimation result indicates that in the absence of any swing in land prices, the bad-loan ratio would have been 2.70% on average against an actual 3.96%.

To summarize, statistical analysis indicates that the tremendous rise and then fall in land prices between the mid 1980s and the mid 1990s was a significant cause of the bad-loan problem. In addition, regulations limiting banks' ability to diversify in the face of liberalization of transactions in the securities markets seems to have been a factor in prompting some banks to increase real estate-related loans. Low capital ratios may have played a role as well. The role differences in bank management played in the bad-loan problem are difficult to identify.

MACROECONOMIC BACKGROUND

We now turn to a brief discussion of macroeconomic factors behind the tremendous swings in assets prices. I focus mostly on monetary policy. (This section is based on Ueda (1997).)

Since 1971, when the United States exhorted other countries to appreciate their currencies against the dollar, movements of Japanese macroeconomic variables have shown a definite pattern. In periods of, or slightly after, a large current account surplus, asset prices such as real estate and stock prices have risen sharply, followed by strong growth of real GDP. This in turn has led to a decline in the current account surplus and to a temporary depreciation of the yen.

The key to this correlation was BOJ monetary policy. That is, the most important feature of BOJ policy in the 1970s and '80s was its close relationship with the current account and the exchange rate.

Let us look at the this more closely. Figure 3.4 shows on the left axis the ratio of the current account to GDP (NX/GDP), and the share of investment in GDP (with a minus sign, as investment share actually moves inversely to the others); and on the right axis the rate of change in the yen against the dollar since 1970, and the rate of change in the Nikkei 225. Though land prices are not shown in the figure, they have moved in line with stock prices (see Figure 3.1). It also shows the timing of shifts in monetary policy. An "L" stands for the first lowering of the discount rate after a period of tight monetary policy. A "T" stands for the first increase in the discount rate after a period of looseness. An exception is early 1986, when an L appears after an earlier L, because there was no tightening in the sense of a discount rate increase in between.

The figure reveals clearly that all these variables are closely related. Thus, a current account surplus causes an appreciation of the yen. It also worsens trade conflicts with foreign economies. The presumption has been that an appreciation of the yen exerts a strong deflationary impact on the economy. The public calls for measures to increase aggregate demand and reverse the trend of the exchange rate. Foreign governments also ask Japan to pursue an expansionary macro-policy. For these reasons, interest rates are lowered, leading to increases in asset prices and, with a lag, to a rise in investment and a worsening of the current account.

There is, of course, the question as to why BOJ wanted to expand if one of the policy targets was to create a worsening of the current account. It could be that a monetary expansion led to a worsening of the current account through expansion of domestic demand, which outweighed the effect of exchange rate depreciation.

The figure shows that this pattern has repeated four times in the last 25 years, exactly following the cycle in the current account. The late 1980s were no exception. BOJ decreased the discount rate five times starting in early 1986 and created a sharp inflation of asset prices.

The period of loose monetary policy in the late 1980s went on too long, but for at least three reasons. First, goods and service prices were not increasing. Second, in late 1987, there was a sharp worldwide fall in stock prices, which made BOJ somewhat reluctant to raise interest rates. Third, MOF reportedly put pressure on BOJ not to tighten for the sake of international policy coordination (see, for example, Funabashi (1988) and Ueda (1993)).

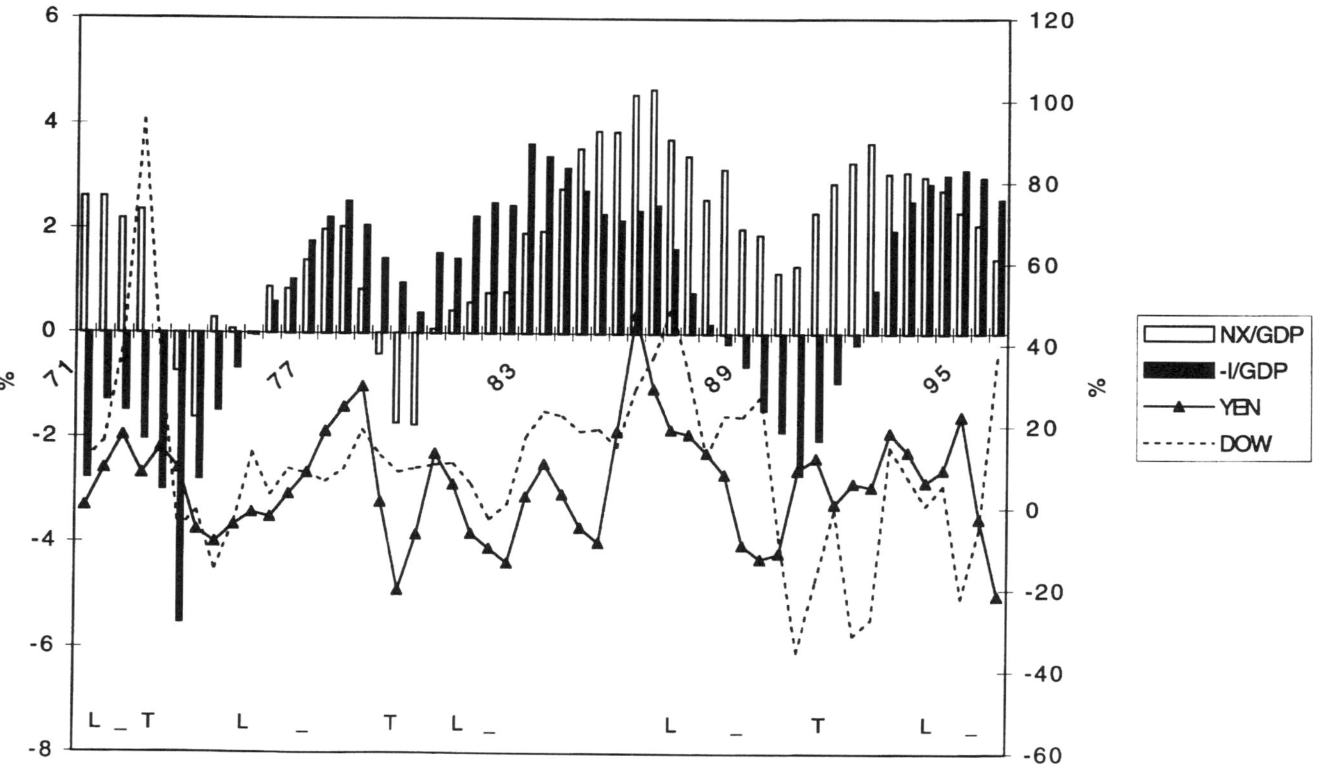

Note: The mean ratio of investment to GDP has been adjusted to make it comparable in the figure to other series. The annual rates of change in NX/GDP & –I/GDP are shown on the left axis, while those of the yen and the Nikkei 225 stock index are on the right axis.

FIGURE 3.4. Japanese macro-economic fluctuations & monetary policy.

MOF also had the memory of the large budget deficits of the late 1970s and early 1980s and was reluctant to carry out strong fiscal expansion, which further contributed to pressure on BOJ to carry out an easy monetary policy.

Monetary tightening started only in 1989. The delay permitted asset prices to continue rising in 1988 and 1989 and made the declines in the 1990s sharper. Interestingly, there was a temporary drop in the rate of increase in land prices in 1988 and a resurgence in 1989, before peaking in 1991.

It is hard to determine whether BOJ would have behaved differently in the absence of pressure from MOF and others. Nonetheless, the swings in monetary policy seems to have been a major cause of swings in asset price movements and, in turn, of the bad-loan problem.

PUBLIC POLICY

To what extent are bank regulators to blame for the bad-loan problem? To answer this, I divide the discussion into the period up to the late 1980s and the years since.

Financial deregulation started in the late 1970s for a variety of reasons, including the large issuance of government bonds and pressure from the United States to open Japan's financial markets. The salient features were gradualism and maintenance of segmentation. An example of gradualism is interest rate control on time deposits: deregulation started in 1985 but was only completed nine years later in 1994. Segmentation has meant that different types of financial services have been provided by different types of financial institutions, with fairly strict barriers between them. Banking and securities businesses have been strictly separated and trust banking services have been provided almost exclusively by trust banks. But it has gone further in Japan: long-term and short-term banking have been separated and clients were distributed in part by size—for example, smaller banks have been encouraged to lend to small businesses.

This policy of segmentation, when coupled with liberalization in other fields such as development of the securities markets, has limited the scope for diversification and created serious difficulties for banks. For example, long-term credit and trust banks were created to specialize in term loans to large firms. Under deregulation, these banks increasingly lost large borrowers to the bond and equity markets. In rethinking their purpose, segmentation meant they were precluded from moving aggressively into investment banking. Expanding real estate-related loans was one of the few avenues open to them. Statistical evidence consistent with such a view has been presented above.

Similarly, smaller banks and *jûsen* increased commercial real estate loans because the city banks—which were losing their traditional, large borrowers—

aggressively sought customers among the smaller firms and individuals than had been the smaller banks' customary clientele.

The 1980s was a period when non-Japanese financial institutions started to develop innovative financial techniques. Many of these techniques—for example, securitization of bank loans—fell on the boundary between traditional banking and securities business. Ambiguity regarding entry regulations prevented Japanese financial institutions from developing through competition the skills its international competitors were acquiring.

With a lag of about a decade, Japan decided to carry out a more full-fledged financial deregulation under the name of the Big Bang. With hindsight, however, it would have been much less painful in terms of the costs of deregulation, and much more effective in terms of mitigating the speculative real estate boom, had it been possible to carry out the Big Bang in the 1980s.

Another problem with policy concerns bank risk management. Traditionally, tight control of bank behavior by regulators was a substitute for risk management by the banks themselves, and for monitoring by shareholders and depositors. But the controls were progressively relaxed during the 1970s and '80s even though banks were not simultaneously introducing more comprehensive risk management techniques. Depositors still had faith in the ability of regulators to protect them. Thus, a vacuum emerged in risk management. This may have been a factor behind the massive lending to real estate activities.

Regulatory Forbearance

Without doubt, regulators in the 1990s long underestimated the size and negative effects on the economy of the bad-loan problem. As a result, their approach was forbearance. (Early warning against forbearance was issued by a number of people, including, for example, Kane (1993).)

Since the early 1990s, both banks and regulators have been trying to achieve at least two objectives: reducing bad loans and meeting the BIS capital standard, sometimes with only few instruments at hand.

Large Japanese banks had capital ratios barely above 8% at the start of the 1990s, with about half of the 8% accounted for by unrealized gains on their equity positions. (The inclusion of such gains had been a concession to Japanese banks when the capital ratios were negotiated.) Banks have been realizing these gains to off-set write-offs of bad loans. BOJ (1999) estimates that between fiscal 1991 and fiscal 1998 Japanese banks wrote off ¥56.6 trillion in bad loans. This was financed by ¥37 trillion in operating profits, ¥3.2 trillion of realized gains on bonds, ¥12.4 trillion realized on equities, ¥1.7 trillion yen on real estate, and a reduction in capital base of ¥17.4 trillion. This meant that when equity prices were dropping, banks faced the possibility of not being able to meet the BIS standard or having to slow the pace of acknowledging and writing off bad loans.

As of March 1998, unrealized gains on securities holdings stood at ¥2.2 trillion for the top-tier banks, only 12% of what they had been in 1993 and a negligible portion of their capital base. What filled the gap has been a sharp increase in other tier-2 capital, mostly subordinated debentures and loans. As noted above, banks have been allowed since March 1998 to use the book-value accounting method for their holdings of securities when calculating the BIS ratio. Hence, for some banks the official capital ratio does not reflect unrealized losses in their security holdings.

For domestic banks, the BIS standard was not applied and hence was not a constraint. Aggressive bad loan write offs, however, were sometimes not possible because they would have rendered some banks insolvent.

Difficulties

The difficulties banks and regulators faced reflected several constraints on their behavior. First, public money for protecting depositors in the event of a bank failure was very difficult to obtain. It required the financial panic of November 1997 to persuade the public and politicians of the necessity of using significant amounts of public funds for the resolution of the bad-loan problem. Second, asset markets were not cooperative. It has been very difficult to issue new shares in the equity market. Some suspect that the so-called price keeping operations (of government-controlled pension and other fund purchases of equities) resulted in the malfunctioning of the market. Ironically, the operations were a reflection of the recognition that further large price declines in the stock market would add to the instability of the financial system.

Consequently, provisions for bad loans have been made only gradually. Insufficient loss provisions have been accompanied by limited disclosure. Forbearance in the early stage of the problem forced regulators to continue forbearance as the problems became more serious. As a result, the amount of taxpayer money necessary for resolution must have increased relative to resolution at an earlier stage.

I fully realize that the international financial community would not have accepted a Japanese decision to introduce a radically different capital standard, but requirements such as the BIS regulation and its domestic equivalent, prompt corrective action (PCA), have had the unfortunate feature of intensifying the effects of negative exogenous shocks on the economy. Introduction of the regulations into a weak banking sector may have aggravated the financial instability. Additionally, the inclusion of unrealized gains in the definition of the capital base has increased the destabilizing nature of the regulations.

To avoid misunderstandings, let me stress that the right remedy was not to have avoided the introduction of the capital requirements, but to have addressed the bad-loan problem seriously at a much earlier stage. An important lesson one can draw from this experience is the difficulty of designing appropriate regulations and introducing them at the right time.

CONCLUSION

At the heart of the bad-loan problem in Japan in the 1990s is the speculative real estate lending of the 1980s, which turned bad as urban land prices plummeted in the 1990s. The increase in real estate-related lending was mainly caused by the sharp rise in urban land prices in the late 1980s and the perception that land price movements would be sustainable. Both the rise and fall of land prices were to a significant degree due to major swings in monetary policy since the mid 1980s. In addition, financial liberalization in the securities markets and the maintenance of segmentation between banking and securities services proved an unfortunate combination that added to the extent of bank lending for real estate.

After the collapse in land prices, regulatory forbearance has aggravated the problems. Forbearance was initially caused by underestimation of the seriousness of the impact of asset price declines on the economy. Declines in asset prices had two direct effects on the capital base of banks: they made bad a significant portion of real estate-related loans, and the unrealized gains on securities held by banks, a major component of tier-2 capital, decreased sharply. The erosion of the capital base, coupled with the difficulty of obtaining public funds to clean up the system, led regulators to adopt a non-transparent approach to the problem.

Lessons from the Japanese experience abound. Stable monetary policy is a prerequisite for a stable financial system. Regulations limiting the ability of financial institutions to diversify can become a cause of financial instability. Prudential policy should pay more attention to assessing the vulnerability of banks and the financial system to shocks that do not occur very frequently and hence are not fully taken into account by usual risk management techniques. Capital ratio regulations should be modified to lessen pro-cyclical features.

ACKNOWLEDGEMENTS

The views expressed are those of the author and do not represent those of the Bank of Japan. The author would like to thank Charles Calomiris, Takeo Hoshi,

Edward Kane, and Hugh Patrick for extensive comments on earlier drafts, and Larry Meissner for editing the final draft.

NOTES

1 Under an amendment to the banking law (passed on 18 June 1996) which became effective on 1 April 1998, bank regulators can issue corrective orders as a bank's total risk-based capital adequacy ratio falls below each of three thresholds: 8%, 4%, and 0%. In category I (below 8%), a bank is required to create and implement a business improvement plan. For category 2 (below 4%), the bank must formulate a plan to increase capital, restrain gross asset growth, or cease expanding into new businesses, as deemed warranted. Banks falling in category 3 (below 0%) in principle must suspend business. The Financial Supervisory Agency enforces PCA.

2 Reported BIS ratios are different from those based on the estimates of bad loans in Table 3.2, since less bad loans are provisioned for. Since March 1998, banks have been allowed to use the book value accounting method for their security holdings if they so choose, which means banks with unrealized losses can report a higher level of capital assuming they report securities at cost rather than market.

3 During the 1970s and '80s banks wrote off (removed from their balance sheets as worthless) only some 0.01% of outstanding loans each year (0.02% for city banks). The exception was 1977, when restructuring related to the first oil shock led to city-bank write-offs of 0.06%. One reason for these low levels is that the tax authority did not allow banks to freely write off bad loans from after tax profits.

REFERENCES

Bank of Japan. 1997. "On the Use of Self-Assessment for Improving Credit Risk Management." *Bank of Japan Monthly Review* (Oct). In Japanese.

Bank of Japan. 1999. "Financial Statements of All Banks in Fiscal Year 1998." In Japanese. *Bank of Japan Monthly Review* (Aug). In Japanese.

Brumbaugh, Jr, R Dan, and Andrew S Carron. 1987. "Thrift Industry Crisis: Causes and Solutions." *Brookings Papers on Economic Activity* 2.

Financial Supervisory Agency. 1998. "The Status of Risk Management Loans," July 17.

Funabashi, Youichi. 1988. *Tsuuka Retsuretsu*. Asahi Shinbunsha. In Japanese.

Horiuchi, Akiyoshi and Katsutoshi Shimizu. 1996. "The Deterioration of Banks' Balance Sheets in Japan: Risk-Taking and Recapitalization." Discussion Paper 96F13, University of Tokyo.

Hoshi, Takeo and Anil Kashyap. 1999. "The Japanese Banking Crisis: Where Did It Come From and How Will It End?" *NBER Macroeconomic Annual*.

Kane, Edward J. 1993. "What Lessons Should Japan Learn from the US Deposit Insurance Mess?" *Journal of the Japanese and International Economies* 7 (Dec).

Kokudo-cho. *Chika-Koji*. Various issues.

Nakaso, Hiroshi. 1999. "Recent Banking Sector Reforms in Japan." *Federal Reserve Bank of New York Economic Policy Review* 5(2).

Ueda, Kazuo. 1993. *Kokusai-shushi-Hukinkou kano Kinyu-seisaku* (The Current Account Surplus and Monetary Policy). Toyo Keizai. In Japanese.

Ueda, Kazuo. 1994. "Institutional and Regulatory Frameworks for the Main Bank System." In Masahiko Aoki and Hugh Patrick, editors, *The Japanese Main Bank System*. Clarendon Press, Oxford.

Ueda, Kazuo. 1997. "Japanese Monetary Policy, Rules or Discretion: A Reconsideration". In Iwao Kuroda, editor, *Towards More Effective Monetary Policy*. MacMillan Press Ltd.

Wheelock, David and Paul W Wilson. 1995. "Explaining Bank Failures: Deposit Insurance, Regulation, and Efficiency." *Review of Economics and Statistics* 77: 689-700.

Zenginkyo (Federation of Bankers Associations of Japan). 1998. "Japanese Banks, 1998." The Federation's annual report.

PART II

Responding to Crisis

Chapter 4

THE STAGNANT JAPANESE ECONOMY IN THE 1990s: THE NEED FOR FINANCIAL SUPERVISION TO RESTORE SUSTAINED GROWTH

Takatoshi Ito
Ministry of Finance

In the 1990s the dream economy that had impressed the world and brought Japan to the forefront of the advanced economies has become more like a nightmare. What went wrong? What will lift the Japanese economy from stagnation? These are questions addressed in this chapter. In answering them, I also consider the inter-relationship between Japan and the Asian economies, and the parallels between them.

After outlining Japan's macroeconomic situation, I analyze the developments leading to the 1997 financial crisis. In many ways 1997 can be considered a turning point in Japanese financial development, as the cumulative effects of policy mistakes, including how the nonperforming loans problem was being dealt with, combined with ongoing reforms of Japan's financial system and exogenous events to shake Japan's financial structure.

The second section examines several aspects of the banking system as they relate to the structural weaknesses that have contributed to—and been exacerbated by—Japan's stagnation. These include capital adequacy, moral hazard, deposit insurance reform, and the postal savings system. I also take up the question of how to use public money effectively in resolving the problems.

The usual counter-cyclical macroeconomic policies have not worked in Japan in the second half of the 1990s, or at least not well enough. In the third section, I consider why and offer some alternatives to move Japan out of its stagnation. This is followed by an explanation of the reasons for the Asian financial crisis. Parallels to Japan are discussed.

An Overview of the Economy

Japan's real GDP grew more than 4% each year from 1985 to 1990, except for 2.9% in 1986. During these years, the Nikkei stock index and typical urban land prices tripled. Stocks peaked in late 1989 and declined 40% in 1990. By 1992 business activity had definitely slackened, with growth at just 1.0%. The Nikkei in August 1992 was back to its level of April 1986, 60% below its peak.

Japan grew less than 1.5% a year in 6 of the 7 years 1992–98, a performance much worse than most other market economies. The last quarter of 1997 and all of 1998 saw declines in GDP. This made it the most severe recession in Japan's postwar history. The first half of 1999 witnessed some recovery, and in the second half growth forecasts were being increased, but problems remain.

In 1996 the growth rate climbed to 5.1%, reflecting a boom in housing construction and consumer durables in the latter half of the year. This was, however, spending in anticipation of a consumption tax rate increase set for April 1997. As scheduled, the consumption tax rate was raised from 3% to 5%, a temporary income tax cut was repealed, and social security insurance premiums were raised. Together these took ¥9 trillion out of the economy annually. Aggregate consumption acted predictably negative, what was not expected was the duration of the negative reaction. Consumption and investment were still weak six months after the tax increases.

Then two other major shocks hit. First, the Asian currency crises dampened Asian demands for Japanese exports. As Asian economies went into a severe recession, their domestic demand plummeted. As excess supply and excess capacity became evident in Asia, Japanese exports of parts, machinery, tools, and other semi-finished goods, declined.

Second, major financial crises shook Japan in November 1997. Sanyo Securities, the Hokkaido Takushoku Bank, and Yamaichi Securities failed one after another. In the face of all this, Japanese consumer confidence was lost.

The crises of the Japanese and Asian economies in 1997–98 are also reflections of regional interdependence. The yen's depreciation against the US dollar from its April 1995 peak of 80 yen to about 140 yen in June 1997 was a factor in Thailand's devaluation of the baht on 2 July 1997. The yen was depreciating partly as a correction of excess appreciation and partly as a reflection of weak Japanese fundamentals. Because Asian currencies were pegged to the dollar, yen depreciation reduced their export competitiveness and exports plummeted. Post-devaluation weakness in the region was reinforced by the weakness of Japan as a market. It is also evident that weak Japanese exports to Asia have pulled down Japan's growth rate.

In addition to macroeconomic mismanagement, Japan and the Asian economies share structural weaknesses in their banking systems. Japanese banks are beset by nonperforming loans due to a sharp decline in land prices, and many Asian banks are burdened by excessive borrowing from abroad or nonperforming loans attributable to sharp currency depreciations. Japan and Asian countries did not have a legal framework to close insolvent banks before the crises, and this has contributed to protracting resolution of the problem.

Recovery has been hindered by the extreme fragility of the financial sector. Japan's weakened banking system cannot provide financing for viable industries. Asian exporters suffer from a credit crunch. Restoring a robust financial sector is a high priority for Japan and many Asian economies.

THE DEVELOPING JAPANESE CRISIS, 1992–97

Bank analysts at brokerage firms began to comment on a potential nonperforming loans problem in 1992–93, but regulators were reluctant to force banks to determine and disclose specific amounts. The emerging problems simply were not addressed early or decisively. (Some institutional and theoretical analysis in this chapter draw on Cargill, Hutchison, and Ito (1997).)

The problems arose because real estate and construction companies could not pay interest on their loans or sell assets to pay off the loans. Even if banks repossess the collateral, its market value has often became much lower than the loan balance. So banks continued to lend to these companies, hoping that the market would recover.

Policy was reactive and sought to ameliorate consequences rather than address causes. As a result, a series of mini crises from 1994 to 1997 gradually gave the public an ever-grimmer picture of Japan's financial institutions. The problems of the *jûsen* were the first to receive notice, in 1992, and a rehabilitation plan, which later turned out to be too optimistic, was hammered out.

Banks generally continued to generate operating profits, but as land and stock prices fell sharply, supervisory agencies began to find shaky balance sheets. Specifics were not revealed to the public and the reticence regarding the true magnitude of nonperforming loans only multiplied suspicion among investors. Uncertainties about the future of banks and other financial institutions depressed stock prices, which in turn put further pressure on the banks' balance sheets (which had been relying on unrealized capital gains as a source of capital). Because banks were under pressure to increase their risk-adjusted capital ratio, they were forced to curtail lending, which further worsened macroeconomic conditions.

Avoiding the Problems

Bank regulators long were reluctant to force banks to disclose the extent of problem loans. Indeed, at times it actively allowed the banks to conceal the problem. Thus, on 18 August 1992, the government announced a temporary rule change that allowed corporations to defer reporting stock-portfolio losses until the end of the fiscal year (March 1993), rather than with their September

1992 interim reports. This delayed revelation of the impact stock and land price declines had on balance sheets. In specçal cases where a loan default would have adverse social effects, banks were allowed not to report interest concessions as taxable income, unlike the standard procedure.

By 1994 banks were publishing numbers that were called "full disclosure." However the definition of nonperforming was softer than in the United States. The Japanese definition for overdue loans was nonpayment of interest for six months, compared to three months in the United States. In Japan, a rescheduled loan was one with an interest rate lowered to below the official discount rate at the time of rescheduling. In the United States, it is any loan on which the interest rate or other payment terms have been eased.

Further, many argued that Japanese banks have simply lent additional money so that the borrower could meet interest payments (called *oigashi*, it is a practice not unique to Japan). *Oigashi* is suggested by the increases in lending to real estate and construction after 1994, even as lending to other sectors was decreasing.

Regulators felt justified in providing less-than-candid estimates of the magnitude of the nonperforming loan problem. Initially, the delay in disclosure and the softer standards were a reflection of regulators' wishful thinking that land prices and stock prices would soon rise. Then, when the problems became more serious (say by 1994), the reluctance became more a fear that a sysòemic crisis might result from full disclosure.

The public nonetheless became acutely aware of the nonperforming loan problem in December 1994 when two credit cooperatives failed and it was necessary to set up a special bank, Tokyo Kyodo Bank, to take over their remaining assets. Because of allegations of fraud by the bank managers, these cases were widely publicized. It was also pointed out that credit cooperatives unions, which were under the supervision of the prefectures rather than of the Ministry of Finance (MOF) or the Bank of Japan, were not adequately supervised.

The Tokyo Metropolitan government was asked to contribute to fill the gap, but the Governor of Tokyo and the Tokyo Metropolitan Assembly refused. It became clear that there was no clear rule or framework to close financial institutions and assign losses while protecting depositors.

Another series of financial problems and scandals took place in 1995. Although small financial institutions had been merged with help of the Deposit Insurance Corporation (DIC) beginning in 1991, it was not until August 1995 when Hyogo Bank became insolvent that a bank listed on the first section of the Tokyo Stock Exchange was closed.

By the end of 1995 the *jûsen* problem, the problem of nonperforming bank loans, and the risk of exposure of large numbers of small financial institutions were seen as major and indeed unprecedented policy issues.

The *Jûsen* Problem

Jûsen were created in the mid 1970s as subsidiaries of banks, securities firms, and life insurance companies, initially to provide housing mortgage credit to households. Much like consumer finance companies in the United States, they were not permitted to accept deposits and so obtained funds by borrowing from other institutions. As the corporate sector reduced its dependence on bank credit after 1975, banks began to turn to consumer finance and, in the 1980s, became aggressive lenders to individuals. In response, the *jûsen* turned to real estate lending in the second half of the 1980s.

In April 1990 MOF introduced guidelines to banks to limit total lending to the real estate sector; however, lending by *jûsen* was exempted. During 1990 and 1991, *jûsen* lending increased rapidly as a result of funds provided by agricultural cooperatives and their prefecture federations. By now they had evolved into housing-loan companies.

Concerns over the quality of assets held by *jûsen* were raised as early as 1992, and a 10-year rehabilitation plan was arranged for seven of the eight *jûsen* in the spring of 1993. Lending to them was restructured so that parent banks (which were major shareholders) were required to reduce the interest rate on outstanding loans to 1.5% and agricultural cooperatives (and their prefectural federations) were to receive 4.5%. At the time, the interbank rate was about 3.2%, so effectively insolvent *jûsen* were borrowing at rates less than the country's leading banks.

The problems of the *jûsen* became the focus of an intense political debate in 1995 and even overshadowed the issue of bank nonperforming loans. In August 1995 MOF conducted a special examination to determine the extent of the problem. Of ¥13 trillion in *jûsen* assets, nonperforming loans were estimated at ¥9.6 trillion (74%), of which ¥6.4 trillion was considered unrecoverable and ¥1.2 trillion was considered a possible loss. This is more than one-fourth of all losses incurred by financial institutions by then.

The majority of *jûsen* funding came from the 21 major banks and from agricultural credit cooperatives, each providing about the same levels of funding (¥5 trillion from the 21 banks, ¥5.5 trillion from the cooperatives). Other funding sources were regional banks (¥1.1 trillion), life insurance companies (¥0.8 trillion), and others (¥0.6 trillion).

That agricultural cooperatives were the largest supplier of funds posed a major policy issue. If the potential loss of ¥7.6 trillion was divided proportionally among funders, cooperatives would have had to write off more than ¥3 trillion. This was not possible, however, as they operated with small capital bases.

In December 1995 the government proposed a resolution plan for the seven insolvent *jûsen*. The burden was not shared equitably. Rather, its distribution reflected the political strength of the agricultural sector. The Director General of MOF's Banking Bureau secretly signed a memorandum of understanding with his counterpart at the Ministry of Agriculture during the debate over cost sharing. Banks that had founded *jûsen* were asked to absorb losses in excess of their equity stakes and lending. This heavier burden reflected the public perception that the founder banks were providing personnel to manage operations and were referring potential borrowers (who turned out to be high-risk customers) to *jûsen*.

The precedent for disproportionate sharing had been established when banks had been required to absorb a larger share of losses in schemes for dealing with the failures of Cosmo Credit Cooperative, the Kizu Credit Cooperative, and the Hyogo Bank in July and August 1995. Banks not related to these institutions were asked to contribute to the loss-sharing scheme by contributing capital or by making below-market loans to banks that assumed the assets of the insolvent institutions. The argument made to justify requesting accepting responsibility beyond the legal framework was based on the public-good character of the financial system and the need to maintain stability. Requiring unrelated bank to contribute directly to bail-outs was referred to as the "all-Japan" rescue scheme, an important element of the so-called convoy system.

MOF and the suppliers of funds to the seven *jûsen* agreed to dissolve them and in July 1996 the Jûsen Resolution Corporation, now known as the Housing Loan Administration Corporation, assumed the ¥6.4 trillion of unrecoverable loans. Because the problem had not been not dealt with earlier, total losses far exceeded the equity of the *jûsen*.

Political opposition to using tax funds was strong. Initially ¥1.1 trillion was proposed, but in the end just ¥685 billion was made available.

Other smaller institutions, such as credit cooperatives, have problems as well. They have diversified significantly away from their traditional specialization on loans to farmers for agricultural operations—indeed, most hold significant amounts of real-estate-related loans. However, they are not regulated or supervised by MOF or the Bank of Japan, and local regulation and supervision are uneven in extent and sophistication. Some credit cooperatives have strong ties to the local community and to local politicians. Significant risk resides in these small institutions because of the substantial uncertainty as to where they stand in Japan's deposit-guarantee system.

Bank Credit Ratings

In the wake of the *jûsen* insolvencies, a "Japan premium" emerged in the Eurodollar market: Japan's banks, once regarded as among the most financially secure in the world, were required to pay a premium over LIBOR (the London interbank interest rate). The premium increased in September 1995 when Daiwa

Bank was discovered to have covered up at least $1 billion derivative losses caused by a "rogue" trader in New York.

Japanese banks have been continually downgraded by credit rating agencies in the 1990s. In August 1995 Moody's Investor Service released a new rating system for the major Japanese banks. It is designed to rate banks on a "stand alone" basis, without government support, and is a "measure of the likelihood that a bank will require assistance from third parties such as its owners, its industry group, or official institutions." No Japanese bank received a rating of A (exceptional intrinsic financial strength) or B (intrinsic financial strength), and the top 50 Japanese banks received an average rating of D (adequate financial strength limited by a variety of factors).

Still Avoiding the Problems

Japan's banks have been setting aside funds in special accounts to eventually write off losses. Special provisioning by the top 21 banks increased from ¥1.9 trillion in March 1993 to ¥3.0 trillion in March 1994, and to ¥4.3 trillion in March 1995. Sumitomo Bank took a more drastic step, reporting an overall loss for fiscal 1994 as a result of charging off ¥826 billion for bad loans. However, even as they reserved for nonperforming loans, the banks continued to pay dividends, so that the dividend pay-out increased as a percentage of earnings.

At the end of September 1995, the volume of nonperforming loans was officially estimated at ¥27 trillion, equal to 10% of Japan's GDP and 6% of all the loans held by Japan's depository institutions. This estimate might have been too low, however: published estimates from private sources typically ranged from ¥50 trillion to ¥60 trillion. These higher estimates often included loans overdue between 60 and 180 days (not included in MOF data at the time); loans restructured above the official discount rate (the official definition counted only those granted rates below the ODR); and sometimes estimated an amount for loans made to allow paying interest payments (termed *oigashi*).

When the economy grew in 1996, there was a hope that the economic downturn was over. However, as the economy turned to a recession again in 1997, bad debts continued to increase. In March 1998, 19 major banks reported bad debts of ¥15.8 trillion (old standard) and ¥22 trillion according to a newly implemented broader standard. (See Ueda's Table 3.1 in Chapter 3 for the evolving definition of problem loans.)

The banks could have pursued more aggressive remedies. These include organizational restructuring, such as selling assets and subsidiaries (branches or foreign operations) and cutting personnel costs, in order to reduce operating costs. But these things were not done.

There has been a widespread perception among Japanese that bankers have been highly paid, only to make mistakes. Thus, initially the public was quite unwilling to see tax money used to bail-out the banks.

However, the reality pointed to the opposite conclusion if depositors were to be protected. When a bank is insolvent, someone has to pay. Depositors are protected in order to prevent a run and systemic risk. The maximum that shareholders can be asked to pay is their equity, although this principle was violated in the *jûsen* resolution. The most lenders can do is to forgive the debt. Then, if the remaining asset value is less than the deposits, there is a problem. This simple arithmetic was not appreciated in the discussion.

The Cooperative Credit Purchasing Company (CCPC), established in December 1992, was the first visible effort to deal with the problem of nonperforming loans. It is discussed by Packer in Chapter 6. The CCPC now appears to have been set up primarily to provide accelerated tax benefits to large banks without requiring the banks to directly write off loses and acknowledge the losses in their public reports. Banks were required to lend the CCPC an amount equal to the face value of the assets transferred to it, so if the assets are finally sold by the CCPC at a loss, the banks are effectively still responsible. This was revised in July 1998 so that the CCPC can buy loans and the like without recourse against the banks. It is unclear how the CCPC is managing these risks of further price decline after purchasing imperiled assets from banks.

Policy Mistakes and Regulator Credibility

In 1995 a trader in the New York branch of Daiwa Bank was found to have hidden a huge loss. The delay in reporting this to US regulators cost the bank its operating license in the United States. Because Japanese authorities knew of the loss and tacitly accepted its concealment, the credibility of bank supervision by MOF was further damaged.

With ample signs of financial distress in 1995, policy responses were less than adequate. First, regulators believed that, by solving the *jûsen* problem by burdening the banks, a major part of the nonperforming loan problem had been solved. The monetary authorities proclaimed that none of the 21 largest banks would be allowed to fail. However, it soon became obvious that the authorities would not be able to maintain the too-big-to-fail policy. Moreover, moral hazard among bank executives became prevalent after the too-big-to-fail policy was announced.

Second, by denying the seriousness of the situation, the authorities could not prepare a scheme that would inject fiscal funds to solve the problems, or even to inject enough funds into the Deposit Insurance Corporation. This made it impossible to act decisively to close insolvent or near-insolvent banks and incur losses when selling the assets. Third, the monetary authorities failed to enforce accurate accounting rules. They even changed rules to help hide nonperforming loans. These mistakes prolonged the nonperforming loan problem until it finally erupted into a full-blown crisis in November 1997.

The November 1997 Financial Crisis

In November, Sanyo Securities, the seventh largest securities firm, filed for creditor protection under the Corporate Rehabilitation Law, which froze its assets and led to the first postwar default in the interbank market. That sent a shock wave, and changed the behavior of foreign financial institutions. The interbank market generally is very liquid, but it became less so, which proved too much for financial institutions that had been relying on it to meet emergency shortfalls in liquidity.

Hokkaido Takushoku Bank (Takugin), one of Japan's top 20 banks, failed on November 17 and Yamaichi Securities, one of the Big Four securities firms, closed on November 24, three days after its debt was downgraded to junk bond status by Moody's. Although both were rumored to have had problems, many believed something would be worked out to rescue them. For example, it had been announced on 1 April 1997 that Takugin would merge with Hokkaido Bank (Dogin, for short). However, talks broke down over the summer. Takugin was the largest bank failure in postwar Japan. Yamaichi's main bank, Fuji, had been expected to join with the government in keeping it open.

When an internationally active bank fails, there is risk of spillovers to other countries through the payments system and money markets. International risk was minimal in the failures of Takugin and Sanyo Securities as neither had much international business. However, Yamaichi had an extensive banking business abroad through subsidiaries, and there was a fear that it might trigger a crisis. One reason Yamaichi chose to "decertify" itself rather than enter "bankruptcy rehabilitation with protection from creditors" was to avoid the types of problems in the interbank market that had followed Sanyo's failure.

The way Takugin and Yamaichi failed was widely regarded as evidence of past mistakes in government policy. First, in 1995 the government had extended a blanket guarantee of deposits because the deposit insurance system was running out of funds. Second, how other weak financial institutions would be dealt with was unclear. There was now a sense that no institution was too big to fail.

The market interpreted the failures as a sign that the government had lost its grip. The stock prices of other financial institutions perceived as weak plummeted in Tokyo and the "Japan premium" charged Japanese banks for short-term funds from international markets soared to 50 basis points from less than 10 basis points. It was feared that further collapses of financial institutions in Tokyo would seriously disrupt the function of world financial markets.

Strong pressure came from abroad to do something to avoid a melt-down of the Japanese financial system. The government announced plans to make ¥30 trillion yen available to help banks recapitalize and consolidate. The government screened the banks and purchased preferred stock and subordinated debt in the 18 largest banks and 3 regional banks in March 1998, just in time to help their capital ratios for the fiscal year ending 31 March.

STRUCTURALLY WEAK BANKING SYSTEM

This section looks at several aspects of the banking system as they relate to the structural weaknesses that have contributed to—and been exacerbated by—Japan's stagnation in the 1990s. These include capital adequacy, moral hazard, deposit insurance reform, and the postal savings system. I also take up the question of how to use public money effectively in resolving the problems.

Capital-Adequacy Requirements

One issue that complicates resolution of Japan's banking problems concerns stock price fluctuations and the application of capital-adequacy requirements. Japanese banks traditionally have large holdings of securities as a part of their relationship with firms. Accounting rule dictated (until March 1998) that bank balance sheets show the lower of book or market value. The difference was unrealized capital gains (*fukumi*, sometimes translated as latent gains). The amount of *fukumi* was large in the second half of the 1980s, because the shares held had been bought in the 1940s and '50s. These gains had been a huge buffer in the capital positions of Japanese banks, which otherwise would have been relatively undercapitalized.

In 1988, at the time of the adoption of the Basle capital-adequacy requirements for banks doing international business, Japanese monetary authorities negotiated successfully for 45% of unrealized capital gains to be counted as part of near-capital (Tier 2). This was expected to make it easier for Japanese banks to meet the requirements and looked reasonable in 1988 and early 1989, before the bubble burst. However, as stock prices plummeted, banks suddenly faced a shortage of capital because their unrealized gains diminished significantly.

Whenever stock prices declined sharply, banks became squeezed. Such stock-market induced credit crunches happened in 1992, 1995, and 1997. Although the decline in prices in 1992 was largely offset by issuing subordinated debt (*retsugo sai*), which also is counted toward Tier 2, there has been a limit to this in subsequent years. Increasingly, banks that were particularly damaged by stock price declines limited lending, but the reluctance to lend extended even to stronger banks. (See Ito and Sasaki (1998).)

Some gains were realized to offset bad debt losses and build up reserves between 1992 to 1998. Some of the sold shares subsequently were replaced, which meant the book values of securities increased. With the increased book value and decreasing market value (because of sharp stock price declines in the second half of 1997 and the first quarter of 1998), banks had lost most of their *fukumi* by 1998. Faced with an erosion of the banks' capital bases, regulators changed the rules for fiscal 1997 reports, allowing banks to use either book value or the existing rule of the lower of book or market. Many banks chose the former to avoid showing a loss of capital.

Moral Hazard

Moral hazard—incentives to assume more risk because deposit guarantees remove the discipline of depositor flight as a constraint on risk-taking—is a serious problem despite a general unwillingness by Japanese regulatory authorities to recognize it.

The two credit cooperatives that failed so spectacularly in 1995 suffered from classic moral hazard in their last two years. Deposits at the two institutions increased from ¥139 billion in March 1992 to ¥244 billion in November 1994 (an annual rate of 32%). This rapid increases was made possible by offering above-market deposit rates. Meanwhile, lending increased from ¥137 billion to ¥225 billion (an annual rate of 22%). The majority of the new loans ultimately were classified as nonperforming. Total nonperforming loans increased from ¥250 billion (of a total ¥1,371 billion) in March 1992 to ¥1,769 billion (out of ¥1,990 billion) in March 1994. Moreover, unrecoverable losses increased from ¥65 billion in March 1992 to ¥1,118 billion in March 1994.

Another moral hazard was apparent after 1995. Efforts by large banks to write off nonperforming loan were not enough. Dividends were still paid out, and management stayed. No major consolidation or restructuring took place until after the crisis of November 1997.

Deposit Insurance Corporation Reforms

Before the start of liberalization in the mid 1970s, Japan's deposit guarantees were supported by an extensive set of constraints on portfolio decisions. From the 1950 to the early 1970s, Japan's financial system was one of the most regulated and administratively controlled in the world. These controls limited the ability of financial institutions to assume and manage risk; at the same time, they left the deposit-guarantee system untested.

The Deposit Insurance Corporation (DIC) was established in 1971. DIC covers deposits in deposit taking institutions—commercial banks, long-term credit banks, trust banks, regional banks, *shinkin* banks, and credit cooperatives. There is a separate deposit insurance mechanism for agriculture and fishery cooperatives.

In the first 20 years there were no bank failures, and thus no DIC payouts. Premiums just accumulated in the fund. The manner in which the DIC can assist has evolved over time. Even before the first payout, organizational changes were made. Before 1986, liquidating the bank and paying off depositors up to the deposit insurance amount was the only option for DIC, and the insurance ceiling was ¥10 million per customer. After 1986, DIC was allowed to make a "gift" to a white-knight institution that would merge with an insolvent institution, up to a "payoff equivalent." This was approximately equal to what would have been paid in a liquidation.

In 1991, regulators, for the first time in the postwar period, officially assisted the mergers of insolvent depository institutions with stronger institutions, using resources from DIC.

In 1995, after the assisted merger of Kizu Credit Union, which consumed more than ¥1 trillion, DIC's reserves were almost exhausted. A lack of funds was not the only problem. It was becoming difficult to find white-knights: franchise value was decreasing because the limitation on branch opening was being deregulated. The authorities had to create a white-knight institution, the Tokyo Kyodo Bank, to deal with two failed credit cooperatives in Tokyo in 1995. And MOF announced that all bank deposits would be guaranteed until March 31, 2001, though without directly providing DIC resources.

The ceiling on financial assistance sometimes was not enough, so that contributions from "related" institutions were sought. (See Cargill, Hutchison, and Ito (1997, Chapter 6, especially Table 6.4) for cases of assistance.) Resolution took time because each individual case had to be handled differently.

The Deposit Insurance Corporation law was revised in 1996, expanding DIC's role. The revised law allows DIC to pay off depositors and represent depositor interests in the bankruptcy proceeding. DIC also was allowed to purchase bank assets, so the payoff ceiling constraint was effectively removed. Both changes allowed DIC to move quickly. The premium was raised from 0.012% to 0.084% of total deposits. The Tokyo Kyodo Bank became the Reorganization and Collection Bank (RCB), designated as a public white knight for credit associations.

In February 1998, in an effort to contain the turmoil after the November 1997 crisis, further changes to DIC were made. In response to criticism that

DIC had insufficient funds after the Hokkaido Takushoku Bank failure, the government announced it would back DIC with ¥17 trillion to absorb losses of bankrupt institutions, and an additional ¥13 trillion as a capital injection into viable financial institutions. Of the ¥17 trillion, ¥7 trillion was in the form of government bonds given to DIC, which it can cash as necessary, and ¥10 trillion was a government guarantee. Of the ¥13 trillion, ¥3 trillion was bonds and ¥10 trillion was a guarantee.

Changes also were made so that assisted mergers no longer had to involve at least one insolvent institution. The RCB became a general bad-bank which assumes the assets of failed institutions that are not merged with other private institutions.

As of May 1998, the total amount DIC had expended directly reached ¥2,560 billion, and purchased assets came to ¥403 billion. In addition, there are subsidized loans of ¥8 billion yen (the first case), and debt assumption of ¥4 billion yen (from the liquidation of Hanwa Bank).

The steps described above are a series of strengthening measures for DIC. The remaining issues are as follows. First, coordination with supervisory agencies is crucial. The supervision of financial institutions is now done by the Financial Supervision Agency (FSA) and bank examination is by the Bank of Japan. Second, there is a blanket guarantee by the government until March 31, 2001 that all deposits are safe (overriding the DIC law protecting only ¥10 million yen). This prevents bank runs. However, it may increase moral hazard. Again, early detection of problem institutions is crucial.

The Role of Postal Savings

The Postal Savings System has been a focal point of discussion during the past two decades. See the discussion by Cargill and Yoshino in Chapter 8.

Two issues seem particularly important in the context of the deterioration of the financial system in the 1990s. First, a significant part of the flow of funds is likely to be allocated on the basis of political connections rather than on the basis of economic criteria. Postal savings have been easily accessible to MOF to bail out troubled financial institutions. This was done with the *jûsen*, and in 1992 MOF even directed the Ministry of Posts and Telecommunications to use postal life insurance funds to support equity prices on the Tokyo stock exchange.

Second, at some point Japan needs to deal explicitly with postal savings because of its size and its potentially destabilizing role in the deposit-guarantee system. Privatization, apparently the most efficient long-term solution, is bound to run into stiff political opposition.

The immediate crises have made it complicated to carry out a reform. A flight to safety has made postal savings more popular. Small savers responded to the crises of November 1997 and summer of 1998 by shifting deposits to postal saving. Subsequently, one-third of incremental household saving in financial form has gone into postal savings. It is good that the government guarantee means individuals' savings will be there, otherwise money might have fled overseas, causing a crash of the yen, but in the long run, this is not sustainable.

A major part of postal savings is recycled back into the economy through loans from government financial institutions. The financial crisis, with its resulting credit crunch among private-sector banks, has made the role of government financial institutions more important.

These positive arguments have to be balanced against the long-term needs to reform the postal saving system.

How To Use Public Money Effectively

A plan to appropriate ¥30 trillion was first floated in December 1997 in a response to the panic that followed the failures of Hokkaido Takushoku Bank and Yamaichi Securities. Of this, ¥13 trillion was to be used to inject capital into solvent, but thinly capitalized, banks, while ¥17 trillion was to be used to protect depositors in insolvent, failing institutions.

In March 1998, a first wave of capital injection, less than ¥2 trillion, was made to 21 banks (the top 18 banks plus 3 regional banks). The size of the injections, in the form of subordinated loans and preferred shares, were very similar across major banks that accepted funds and, overall, were not enough to raise the capital-adequacy ratio significantly. Moreover, due diligence, which was supposed to be a precondition, was less than adequate. This became apparent when the Long Term Credit Bank (LTCB), which had received an injection of ¥177 billion, saw its stock battered in the stock market after a credible report was published in May that its nonperforming loans were far more than had been believed.

LTCB was forced to seek a rescue merger, and initially it was arranged for Sumitomo Trust Bank and LTCB to merge, after due diligence. In resolving the LTCB crisis, whether some part of the ¥13 trillion could be used became an issue. The Liberal Democratic Party proposed tapping this pot to strengthen LTCB's capital base but opposition parties complained that LTCB would not qualify for getting help from the government because it was essentially bankrupt.

In the Diet session that started in September 1998, two different plans to restore confidence in the financial sector were submitted, one from the LDP and another from a coalition of opposing parties. Following extensive informal discussions, a group of economists had formed the Shadow Financial Regulatory Committee (Japan) in September 1998. Its second recommendation regarding bank supervision was issued in September as part of this debate. The group pointed out that there are important principles, such as shareholder responsibility and management responsibility, that should be pressed when government intervention is attempted. The difference between the LDP's proposal and the opposition parties' proposals actually was fairly small. The shadow group urged politicians on both sides to compromise on how to deal with large banks that are near insolvent, with the case of LTCB in mind. (Their recommendations and other information can be found at their website). (Their recommendations and other information can be found at their web site http://news.fbc.keio.ac.jp/~fukaozem/sfrc.)

After a month-long negotiation, the LDP and opposition parties compromised: LTCB would be nationalized instead of receiving a capital injection and being merged. That left it unclear whether the parties could agree on the conditions under which the ¥13 trillion would be used. When LTCB was nationalized, it was revealed that LTCB and Nippon Credit Bank had been window-dressing their accounts to hide bad debts.

It also was agreed in October 1998 to make ¥60 trillion of public money available to strengthen the financial system and recapitalize the banks, to replace the February ¥30 trillion commitment. Recapitalization was done in March 1999, and this time in return for public money, provisioning for nonperforming loans was done in a more rigorous way. The recapitalization was successful and the Japan premium disappeared in April 1999.

POLICY OPTIONS

The usual counter-cyclical macroeconomic policies have not worked in Japan in the second half of the 1990s, or at least not well enough. As the interest rate approaches zero, the effectiveness of monetary policy is limited. Moreover, further expansion of liquidity would weaken the yen, and yen depreciation further depresses Asian economies.

Yen depreciation combined with an export drive is not a solution because it would create political conflict with the United States and would not help the Asian economies recover, something that is important for a Japanese economic recovery.

Despite large devaluations, Asian export booms are yet to come. First, Japan, which absorbs about one-third of Asian exports, is struggling to restore growth. In fact, Asian exports to Japan declined from 1997 to 1998. Second, Asian banking systems were damaged so that export financing became difficult. Their exporters are suffering from a credit crunch.

Liquidity Trap

The official discount rate (ODR) has been used as a principal tool of countercyclical monetary policy. During the bubble years of the late 1980s, the ODR was maintained at 2.5%. In May 1989 it was raised 75 basis points to 3.25%. More increases followed: in October and December 1989 and March and August 1990. These brought the ODR to 6.0%.

Frequent, sharp increases in the interest rate, along with imposition of land tax and restraints on lending to the real estate sector, made land prices turn down. As stock and land prices started to decline, the real economy started to slow down in 1990–92. However, the growth rate in 1991 was still high at 3.8%.

As the bubble started to deflate and the real economy started to cool, the ODR was lowered. By September 1993, after seven cuts, the ODR was 1.75%. By then the economy was clearly in a recession. It was hoped that this record low interest rate, in conjunction with fiscal stimulus, would revive the economy in 1994. But yen appreciation in 1993 (from 125 to 100) and again in 1995 (from 100 to 80) canceled out the domestic stimulus. The ODR was lowered further, to 1.0% in April 1995 and to 0.5% in September 1995. This record low rate has been maintained since, waiting for a sign of recovery. After Hokkaido Takushoku Bank and Yamaichi Securities failed in November 1997, the financial markets became unstable. Credit lines were cut. Pessimistic expectations made consumers save rather than spend, and poor sales made producers not invest.

As the financial crisis deepened in 1998, the Bank of Japan came under considerable pressure to ease monetary policy. But there was not much room to ease. Considerable debate took place in the spring and summer of 1998 over what set of monetary and fiscal policies was an appropriate response to the declining economy and fragile financial sector. There were those who did not see the effectiveness of monetary policy under the low interest rate environment and those who insisted that monetary policy would still be effective.

Those who noted the ineffectiveness of monetary policy (including myself) emphasized that the economy was basically in a "liquidity trap," in that any increase in the monetary base would not lower the interest rate (since it already was essentially zero). An increase in the monetary base would be used as excess reserves by banks, hoarded by households, or converted for investment abroad to receive higher returns. A yen depreciation would take place. Since the current-account surplus already was at around 3% of GDP and the yen had fallen from 130 in January 1998 to 145 in August, any depreciation from an expansionary monetary policy would not be desirable from the standpoint of international policy coordination, and would be irresponsible for the second largest economy in the world.

It certainly was not tolerable for the US Congress and the steel lobby. Steel was starting a case that has become a series of anti-dumping charges against several nations including Japan over several steel products. Yen depreciation would increase the probability of "dumping" charges by other US industries.

In the framework of IS-LM analysis, the situation can be depicted as a flat LM curve (the interest rate being unresponsive to money supply) and a vertical IS curve (investment being insensitive to the interest rate).

Those who have advocated the effectiveness of monetary policy (for example, Paul Krugman and Alan Meltzer in various forums) emphasize that expanding the monetary base would cause inflation and that would lower the *real* interest rate, and thereby increase investment. The assertion is based on the belief that printing enough money will cause inflation. They think yen depreciation is good because that would cause inflation. The threat of international conflicts has not been a concern of advocates of monetary expansion.

The yield curve had become flat by September 1998, with long-term governments yielding less than 1%. Such low rates are unprecedented in the modern history of any industrial nation. By the end of 1998 there had been no recovery in fixed investment or consumer durables, which would be expected to have responded to the low interest rates in normal circumstances. An expansion in the monetary base (it is increasing at around 9%) has not resulted in much increase in M2 (it is increasing at around 3%). A situation like this is termed a liquidity trap in Keynesian economics. Investment seems to be insensitive to the interest rate. In September, the Bank of Japan lowered the target operational interest rate (uncollateralized, overnight call rate) to 0.25%, while the ODR was maintained at 0.50%. But investment did not respond.

In November, the Bank of Japan broadened the instruments for open market operations. Corporate commercial paper (CP) and corporate bonds (CB) were added to the list of eligible instruments for open market operations, with flexible terms and conditions. These measures were aimed mostly at easing liquidity condition for weaker financial institutions, and have been effective for that purpose. Consumption and investment did not respond in any significant way to these actions.

Fiscal Policy

Fiscal expansion under a liquidity trap will not increase the interest rate, and thus will not crowd out private investment. It seems completely straight-forward to advocate fiscal policy in an environment like Japan's in 1998. Even if reducing fiscal deficits is desirable as a medium-term objective in a society with an aging population, the desirability of a discretionary counter-cyclical policy is not diminished. The credibility of the Japanese government in reducing deficits when the economy booms, as was done in the 1980s, would not be lost if the government exercised discretionary policy in a recession. So far, a straight Keynesian prescription applies.

A fiscal-stimulus package of ¥16.6 trillion was announced on 24 April 1998. The economy was still going down during the summer. Another package, this one for ¥23.9 trillion, was announced in November. This helped stimulate the economy, and the first quarter of 1999 saw positive growth.

Why was the government so reluctant to in use fiscal policy in the first half of 1998? There are three possible explanations, contradictory among themselves.

First, there was a political constraint. The Hashimoto government had passed fiscal consolidation legislation in November 1997. It would have hurt the credibility of the government if it had changed course only a year later. This reason was removed by the fall of the Hashimoto government after the House of Councilors election in July 1998. The Hashimoto government should have reflected more on the consequences of explaining the need for temporarily shelving a medium-term fiscal consolidation plan compared to a slow decline in political support caused by a contracting economy.

Second, some economists believe that the textbook Keynesian formulation, on which the above reasoning is based, is wrong. In other words, a Keynesian fiscal stimulus is ineffective. As evidence there is the record of Japanese fiscal stimulus in the six years through mid 1998. In that time the government adopted five stimulus packages cumulating to ¥60 trillion yen. Although it is debatable how much of each package was genuine increment and how much was repackaging of previous packages, a sizable fiscal stimulus appears to have had little impact. Average annual growth was only around 1%.

This objection clearly overlooks the issue of a benchmark. Without any fiscal stimulus, the economy undoubtedly would have contracted. The underlying economy was so weak that fiscal stimulus did not bring the economy all the way to its potential growth rate but it arguably kept things from becoming worse. The question remains as to what prevented the economy from getting back on a self-sustained growth path. Was it the series of bad shocks? Or has the dynamic spill-over effect of fiscal packages become smaller in the 1990s? Or was the amount of actual stimulus smaller than generally recognized?

Third, public opinion believes fiscal spending in Japan is wasteful. The share of public works spending in the budget has been more or less fixed for years. Agriculture-related investment—including irrigation, rural roads and forestry roads, fishing-port improvements and the like—receive a disproportionate share of the budget. The costs of tunnels and bridges relative to the benefits have been questioned. Therefore, critics argue, fiscal spending is a waste of taxpayer money.

This objection has some merit. If government investment is poured into projects that do not improve productivity or living conditions significantly, is it still worthwhile? A hard-core Keynesians would say, "Yes." Wasteful investment is not as desirable as productive investment, but any spending that increases aggregate demand serves the purpose. Keynes used building a pyramid as an example.

Those who oppose public spending on the basis of waste should look to another avenue for stimulus, namely a tax cut. A hard-core Keynesian would argue that the multiplier from fiscal spending is much higher than for a tax cut. Because some of a tax cut is saved, a ¥1 billion tax cut may not raise GDP by even ¥1 billion, but ¥1 billion of public spending should raise GDP by ¥1–2 billion.

Income-Tax Cut

So what is a real option? Here, I deviate from an old-fashioned Keynesian approach by promoting a tax cut. I have three reasons: fiscal spending has been wasteful from the supply-side point of view; in the medium term, current spending will increase future deficits by committing funds to maintain the wasteful structures being built by current spending; and a tax cut will boost consumer confidence. In the medium term, the dynamic multiplier from a well-designed tax cut will be no less than that of increased fiscal spending.

The tax cut should take the form of a permanent income tax reduction and a temporary consumption tax reduction in specified housing-related expenditures. A temporary income tax cut will not stimulate the economy because it will not affect lifetime (permanent) income on which consumption decisions are based. A temporary consumption tax (VAT) reduction will give the economy a kick, but it will cause a reactionary recession when it is terminated. However, a specific sector, namely housing, can be targeted to stimulate the economy with desirable supply-side effects.

In fact, it was announced in the spring of 1998 that individual and corporate tax cuts would be introduced. However, Prime Minister Hashimoto waffled between a permanent and a temporary income tax cut. This probably cost his party support in the July House of Councilors election.

A Housing-Related Tax Cut and Deregulation

Japanese have invested a lot in housing—the ratio of housing investment to GDP has been high compared to other G7 countries—but the quality has not improved because costs are so high. Indeed, housing is probably the least-satisfactory aspect of the Japanese living standard, both absolutely and compared to the United States and even to Europe

In this context, tax breaks for homebuilding are good social policy. However, the notion of burdening "luxury" homes with taxes has prevailed for several decades. The problem is that the definition of "luxury" has not changed much, while incomes have grown dramatically. Many programs designed to encourage owner-occupied housing, such as reduced rates of property and registration taxes and subsidies such as government Housing Finance Agency loans, do not apply if a house is larger than 240 square meters. Public housing, including government-employee housing, also has been rather Spartan, with floor space and amenities strictly regulated.

Currently available breaks for owner-occupied housing include an income tax credit for new homeowners. This is limited to moderate earners (up to ¥15 million in taxable income) with moderately sized houses (up to 150 square meters) and loan balances of up to ¥30 million. Calculating the credit is quite complex, and the ceiling is ¥300,000 a year for 6 years.

Larger houses will encourage purchases of consumption durables. In many Japanese households limited floor space is holding back purchases of larger refrigerators, TVs, personal computers, and other household goods. Japanese "salary-men" stay late at work or wine and dine with colleagues, rarely seeing their children while awake, partly because there is no space for them at home.

Another reason for low-quality housing is excessively strong tenant protection. Tenancy cannot be terminated at the expiration of a lease unless the tenant agrees or the landlord has a "righteous" cause. Righteousness is very narrowly defined, such as the landlord having no choice but to reclaim the property for personal use. Even when there is no lease, evicting a tenant is extremely difficult. Thus, potential landlords do not want to put up high-quality rental housing.

In sum, the following incentives are recommended: eliminate the 5% consumption tax on housing structures; eliminate size restrictions on reductions of property and registration taxes; replace restrictive and limited income tax credits for homeowners with a US-type deduction from taxable income of housing loan interest payments, without limitation as to house size, taxable income level, or length of time one can claim the deduction.

Public Works Reform

If there is a way to insure that public works spending is for productive projects, that should be done both for counter-cyclical and long-run supply-side reasons. It is just too wasteful right now to continue the current bureaucratic and political system to decide which projects are funded.

One way to force evaluation is to fund public works with project-specific bonds rather than with direct government spending. The market will evaluate the viability of the project and price the bonds accordingly. Some critics say that most projects have social purposes and are not viable on commercial terms.

In such cases of public goods and externalities, there can be interest subsidies or government guarantees on the principal. But it is important that investors evaluate each project on its own merits. If some projects command a high interest rate, reflecting a risk premium, this broadens the market for high-risk high-return financial products. This currently involves primarily samurai bonds, which are issued in yen by emerging-market government entities. Would projects in Japan, say the Hokkaido bullet train project or the Chubu New International Airport near Nagoya be as risky as those sovereign bond issues? If Japanese invest in project bonds for structures built in Japan, that would stimulate the domestic economy, which desperately needs a push.

Project-bond schemes should be applied to most public works: agricultural irrigation, fishing ports, agricultural roads, forestry roads, intercity highways, metropolitan highways, airports, bullet trains, dams, and so on. The market mechanism will make it harder for wasteful projects to be adopted. As wasteful projects are not realized, fiscal deficits will be contained (both as current expenditures and future maintenance).

Non-project-based government spending should be concentrated on other kinds of social infrastructure. Urban sewer systems (not even all of Tokyo's households are hooked to sewers) and improved sidewalks in cities, for example, can be achieved by increased general spending.

ASIAN COUNTRIES: SOME PARALLELS?

It has been shown that a currency crisis and a banking crisis occur simultaneously in a mutually reinforcing manner (Goldstein (1997); Kaminsky and Reinhart (1999)). A country with a banking crisis often develops a currency crisis, either by capital flight or by being attacked by speculators. Currency devaluation often puts banks with foreign-currency denominated liabilities into serious trouble. East Asian countries were no exceptions.

Thailand had problems with its financial institutions before its July 1997 currency floatation. The finance company industry (a form of nonbanks) were just like the *jûsen* in Japan in terms of their funding, investment, and how they got into trouble. (For the structure of banking systems in Asia before the crisis, see Institute of Global Financial Studies (1998).) Asset prices in Thailand increased sharply in 1993–94 and then, as the prospect for growth waned, plummeted in 1996. By the end of 1996, one commercial bank (Bangkok Bank of Commerce) and several finance companies had developed serious nonperforming loan problems. Bangkok Bank of Commerce failed in 1996. The Bank of Thailand supported the finance companies with emergency loans through the deposit insurance fund (FDIF). However, 16 finance companies were suspended in late June (just before the devaluation of July 2), and 42 more were suspended in early August (just before the IMF support package). (See Ito (1998) for details.) Those who lent to finance companies were affected by their failures.

Indonesia has had a history of weak state banks. A policy of encouraging private-sector banks also failed because supervision was not strengthened, and political influences over banks remained.

Korean banks were extending loans to *chaebol* (business groups). As the chaebol expanded into industries in which they had no experience, banks were forced by the government to lend money to them. When the "diversification strategy" failed, banks were left with nonperforming loans. Other problems in Korea came from merchant banks (nonbanks), which escaped banking regulation and lent to real estate sectors.

In summary, the banking problem in Asia is either a trigger or a complicating factor of the currency crisis. It is easy to say that the over-presence of the banking sector increased vulnerability, and that the equity and bond markets were underdeveloped. However, for developing countries, human capital in the financial sector is limited, and it is a difficult to determine whether the banking or securities industries should develop first. The Asian experience poses this question.

CONCLUSION

In this chapter I have described the challenges that Japan and Asia face. Despite the large devaluation, Asian export booms are yet to come. Japan, a large absorber of Asian exports, is struggling to restore its growth. The weakened banking system cannot provide financing for viable industries. Asian exporters suffer from a credit crunch. Japan has few monetary or fiscal options to lift the economy because of the weak banking system.

The situation in Japan is more inexcusable than for the Asian economies. As its economy was integrated into a global system, a better policy should have been devised earlier.

Regulation was too much. Segmentation of markets among banks, long-term credit banks, trust banks, smaller financial institutions, securities firms, life-insurance companies, and non life-insurance companies should have been ended earlier. "Gradualism" allowed rent-seeking financial institutions to make crucial mistakes during the bubble years. With hindsight, the Big Bang should have taken place a decade earlier.

At the same time, regulation was too little. Financial deregulation should have been accompanied by strengthened supervision and a restructured legal framework. For example, Japan should have had a procedure to deal with failed banks. Without hindsight, the Big Bang should have taken place half a decade ago.

The current deterioration of the financial system may force the Bank of Japan to give increasing consideration to prudential objectives in formulating policy—and those objectives may conflict with domestic price stability. The Financial Supervision Agency created in 1998 has a difficult task in implementing stringent standards and forcing banks to take action. Concerns with prudential policy are always present. However, the willingness to subsidize the banking sector directly on the basis of vague arguments of systemic risk has imposed serious costs on the economy at large. With the failures of Hokkaido Takushoku Bank and Yamaichi Securities, no bank or securities firm feels safe from market pressure. Combined with a new regime of financial supervision, the Japanese financial system is undergoing significant changes. Without a strengthened supervision regime, the Big Bang will result in a Big Failure.

ACKNOWLEDGEMENTS

The author gratefully acknowledges comments from Alan Meltzer.

REFERENCES

Cargill, Thomas, Michael Hutchison, and Takatoshi Ito, 1997. *The Political Economy of Japanese Monetary Policy*. MIT Press.

Goldstein, Morris. 1997. *The Case for an International Banking Standard*. Institute of International Economics.

Institute of Global Financial Studies, Foundation for Advanced Information and Research. 1998 July. *Banking Systems in Asia*. The Committee of Financial Technical Assistance in Asia.

Ito, Takatoshi. 1998. "The Development of Thailand Currency Crisis: A Chronological Review." *Journal of Research Institute for International Investment and Development*. 24 (9): 66–93.

Ito, Takatoshi and Yuri Nagataki Sasaki. 1998 Sep. "Impacts of the Basle Capital Standard on Japanese Banks' Behavior." National Bureau of Economic Research, working paper.

Kaminsky, Graciela and Carmen Reinhart. 1999. "The Twin Crises: The Causes of Banking and Balance of Payments Problems." *American Economic Review* 89 (3) (Jun).

Chapter 5

THE REORGANIZATION OF JAPAN'S FINANCIAL BUREAUCRACY: THE POLITICS OF BUREAUCRATIC STRUCTURE AND BLAME AVOIDANCE

Nobuhiro Hiwatari
The University of Tokyo

In September 1998 the Obuchi Cabinet decided to create the Financial Reconstruction Commission (FRC, *Kinyû Saisei I'inkai*), a new administrative body headed by a cabinet minister, to cope with Japan's ailing banks. The council has under its jurisdiction the Financial Supervisory Agency (FSA, *Kinyû-Kantoku-chô*), which is in charge of financial supervision, inspection, and policy-making. Once the FRC completes its mandate, it is expected to become the Finance Agency (*Kinyû-Chô*). The decision to create the FRC concluded a three-year debate over the breakup of the Ministry of Finance (MOF), and the exact authority of the Finance Agency was finally decided in April 1999. MOF's financial arm, which underwent internal reorganization in the mid 1990s, is expected to become the Finance Agency. The agency will have what once were MOF's financial responsibilities, except those pertaining to financial crises and the collapse of financial institutions, which will be co-managed with the 'new' MOF.

Conventional explanations by journalists and researchers for what caused MOF's initial reorganization and eventual breakup, and the creation of a new agency, are not persuasive. The press focused only on the breakup and described it as a struggle over "the divorce of its fiscal and financial arms (*zasei-kinyû bunri*)", in which the ministry was defeated in "the battle between the political will and the administrative won't."[1]

The titles of the books on MOF's breakup testify to the common wisdom. They can be translated as, Why Was MOF Entrapped? (*Ôkurasho wa naze oitumeraretaka*, by Masaru Mabuchi), The 850-day Run Loss of MOF Bureaucrats (*Kyodai na rakujitu: Ôkura kanryo haisô no 850-nichi*, by Sô'ichiro Tahara), and Testimony: the Collapse of MOF (*Kensho: Okurasho hôkai*, by Nobuto Kishi). Indeed, the leading authority on MOF politics, Masaru Mabuchi (1997, p 338), claims that the Liberal Democratic Party (LDP) struck down the ministry in reaction to having been maltreated by it when the LDP was out of power in 1993–94. Kishi argues (1996, p 161–77) that there was support within MOF for the separation of its fiscal and financial arms.

MOF in fact willingly reorganized itself internally in order to prepare for financial liberalization—what has come to be known as the Big Bang. Furthermore, in the five major battles over MOF between 1996 and 1999, the LDP remained MOF's guardian. The splitting of MOF came only as a concession to the LDP's coalition partners—the Socialist Party and the *Sakigake* in 1996, and the opposition parties in 1998—that cooperated in passing legislation to inject public funds into troubled banks.

If we accept that bureaucratic restructuring was enacted as a concession to non-LDP parties, but not necessarily to the opposition parties, and that this took place mostly during the process of financial policy reform, then we have on our hands puzzles that are overlooked, and cannot be explained, by fixation on a tug-of-war between the LDP and MOF. To explain MOF's internal reorganization, as well as the splitting off of its financial arm and creation of a new agency, it is necessary to set up a framework that both draws on the insights of the existing literature on bureaucratic restructuring and incorporates the specific Japanese institutional context into the analysis. This is done in the next section.

The remainder of the chapter is then divided into three parts. In the first part, I argue that the banking crisis and the stock market slump, exacerbated by financial globalization, crippled the existing regulatory regime, making it a liability for financial institutions, and thus forcing MOF to create a new policy regime for troubled banks and to liberalize the Tokyo stock exchange. In the two specific cases examined—liquidation of the housing loan corporations and the creation of policies for troubled banks—I will show that it was the severity of the banking crisis that forced politicians to enact cost-imposing reforms and to demand the breakup of MOF. In the second part I examine five rounds in the battle over MOF's breakup between 1996–99 and show that the LDP conceded to the non-LDP parties only when it involved blame avoidance.

Alternative explanations are then briefly examined. This is followed by an examination of the implications of this study for an understanding of the characteristics and functioning of Japanese institutions, especially after the 1980s when the government has been increasingly compelled to enact unpopular policies that imposed costs on the electorate.

THE FRAMEWORK: BLAME AVOIDANCE IN BUREAUCRATIC RESTRUCTURING

One still-to-be explained puzzle has to do with interest group mobilization of bureaucracies. Existing theory seems to expect bureaucratic restructuring to be brought about by the mobilization of politicians by interest groups. An obvious place to start thinking about bureaucratic restructuring is the work of Terry Moe (1989, 1990, and 1995). Moe argues that by mobilizing politicians, interest groups create and shape new agencies in order to set up new policy regimes. Thus, he has difficulty explaining why, in the absence of interest group mobilization, politicians are at times eager to restructure bureaucracies.

The insights contained in E.E. Schattschneider's (1966) study of political participation enables us to include an examination of certain *processes* in an analysis of institutions. According to Schattschneider, the expansion of groups affected by a particular policy can widen the conflict arena and change institutionally vested interests. This conception of the broadening of the conflict arena fits well with the case of the troubled banks in Japan, because financial globalization has created a situation in which the problem of troubled banks can easily become a banking sector and macroeconomic crisis that threatens to destabilize international financial markets.

However, both authors would predict that a restructuring of the bureaucracy would be motivated by the mobilization of politicians by interest groups. Although this may explain the internal reorganization of MOF in preparation for the Big Bang, the fact is that during the banking crisis, interest groups were indifferent to the restructuring of the financial bureaucracy. The same can hardly be said of political parties.

One can understand why politicians might be eager to restructure the bureaucracy without first being mobilized by interest groups if we loosen the assumption, underlying both Moe's and Schattschneider's theories, that politicians seek to claim credit for representing interest groups.

The idea that politicians do not always try to seek credit, they also try to avoid blame, is developed in the works of R. Kent Weaver (1986). According to Weaver, sometimes there is little credit to be claimed. When there are significant costs compared to the minor or diffused benefits that accrue from the decision, politicians try to avoid being blamed for the decision. Only when the benefits outweigh the costs will politicians claim credit for their policy choices. Where both the benefits and costs are insignificant, politicians can act statesman-like. Thus, the behavior of politicians in the same institutional setting will differ according to the issue at stake. What is important to keep in mind is that they are not always the mere agents of interest groups.

The idea of blame avoidance has become increasingly important in the 1990s as governments in advanced industrial democracies are being compelled to make unpopular decisions that impose significant costs on the electorate. Financial globalization has made it increasingly difficult for governments to pursue unilateral economic reflation during economic downturns or otherwise accumulate large government deficits, and this can negatively affect interest groups.

Other conspicuous cases are moves to retrench costly public welfare schemes and to privatize state-owned firms.

Japan's banking crisis is a good example of a situation in which politicians were motivated to try to avoid being blamed. Although the reforms they supported were critical to the revitalization of the economy and the stabilization of international markets, they also imposed significant costs on taxpayers. Thus, the theory of blame avoidance better explains why politicians would insist on the breakup of MOF during cost-imposing reforms than does the existing theory on bureaucratic restructuring. However, simply applying blame avoidance to a case of bureaucratic restructuring is not sufficient to understand the particular situation under examination; it would lead to the prediction that the LDP would be the most intent to avoid blame—and therefore the most compelled to sacrifice MOF—since it was responsible for enacting the unpopular policy of fiscal reform. It remains a puzzle why it was the non-LDP parties that insisted on MOF's breakup and on the creation of a new agency.

Both the theory of bureaucratic restructuring and that of blame avoidance actually tell us where to look to understand the second part of the puzzle: why parties other than the ruling LDP demanded bureaucratic restructuring and insisted on MOF's breakup. Both Moe and Weaver state that the outcome of bureaucratic restructuring and blame avoidance depends on the institutional context of the system under investigation. Moe claims that US bureaucracies are ineffectively structured as a result both of the three-way contest among the president and congressional friends and foes, and the shifting coalitions to which this contest gives rise. The interest groups that create an agency not only fear that it might be weakened or dismantled once their opponents gain strength in Congress, they also have to compromise with such opponents. Both groups fear efforts by the president to put the agency under hierarchical control. Compromise among the contestants creates procedures and devices that make the agency both difficult to control and to dismantle.

By contrast, in cases in which the possibilities for a change in administration are small, as in Japan, interest groups have the power to shape their relations with an agency without having to mobilize politicians or create a new bureaucracy.

Furthermore, as Weaver points out, blame avoidance strategies will play out differently in non-US institutional contexts of cabinet systems and organized parties. Thus, it is necessary to take the Japanese institutional context into account in order to explain why MOF's breakup was not the result of specific interests mobilizing politicians to change the regulatory regime but rather was insisted upon by parties other than the LDP.

THE EVIDENCE

The two cases examined in this section—the liquidation of the housing loan corporations and the creation of policies for troubled banks—show that the repercussions of the bank issue led MOF and the banks to abandon the old regime and compelled politicians to address the problem. In the 1990s the increasing burden of bad loans and the reaction of international investors made it more and more difficult for MOF's financial arm to force healthy banks to subsidize failing ones. The impact of financial globalization transformed the problem of troubled banks into a banking-sector and economic-policy crisis. International investors reacted to rumors of troubled Japanese banks by selling stocks and yen and by increasing the Japan premium. (Interest rates in international capital markets are often benchmarked against LIBOR, the base inter-bank lending rate in London. Japanese banks at various times in the 1990s paid a premium to LIBOR.) The Japan premium indicated a lack of confidence in the credibility of Japanese banks and MOF as regards the extent of bad loans. This further depleted the lending power of healthy banks and damaged their overseas activities.

Consequently, the banking sector and the financial arm of MOF concluded that the existing regime no longer served their interests. Moreover, the deflationary spiral caused by the banking sector's accumulation of bad loans pushed the economy into a deep recession, which threatened to destabilize international markets. Thus, financial policy reform became an issue to be dealt with by government leaders and by the fiscal arm of MOF, which is in charge of macroeconomic and currency management. There was no political mobilization by interest groups; rather it was the severity of the issue that compelled government leaders to make unpopular decisions. Because the solution imposed costs on the electorate, the political parties that had to cooperate with the LDP in passing such measures insisted on the breakup of MOF.

The Jûsen Crisis and the Collapse of the Old Regime

The well-documented crisis of the housing loan corporations (*jûsen*) shows how the old regulatory regime lost the support of its participants because it could not internalize the enormous losses. The case has four major features.

First, MOF's financial arm always favored methods that contained the costs of solving problems within financial circles. MOF was forced to reconsider this approach only when international concern over Japan's bad loans problem had detrimental effects on the banks and on the economy. Second, financial institutions rejected MOF's attempts to distribute the costs among them; this effectively destroyed the old regime. Third, neither MOF's financial arm nor the banks tried to mobilize politicians to solve the housing loan mess. Rather, it was the agricultural credit cooperatives, as lenders to the *jûsen*, that mobilized politicians to protect their interests.

Finally, the non-LDP parties, which had to cooperate with the LDP's policy of imposing costs, were able to raise the issue of MOF's breakup. The outcry over the use of taxpayer money to liquidate the *jûsen* and help the agricultural credit cooperatives led political parties to push for MOF's breakup in order to avoid blame. It might be claimed that this was a special case because it involved both the liquidation of non-bank financial institutions and the mobilization of politicians by agricultural co-ops. This claim is addressed in the following discussion of the creation of a policy regime in order to deal with the problem of troubled banks.

The *jûsen*, of which there were eight, were created in the 1970s as subsidiaries of groups of banks to help finance home purchases using funds borrowed from the inter-bank money market. They expanded rapidly during the asset boom of the mid-1980s in a way that ensured that their collapse after the bubble burst would inflict severe damage on their creditor banks. Because the major banks had a number of non-bank subsidiaries similar to *jûsen* that catered to the real estate industry, the way the *jûsen* damaged the major banks during their downfall provides insight into the way in which the collapse of the asset bubble caused the banking crisis. In the 1980s *jûsen* assets ballooned as they lent heavily to the real estate and land development industries. The parent banks provided credit, introduced prospective borrowers, and sent managerial staff.

In early 1990 MOF and the Bank of Japan (BOJ) began to address the problems of the asset bubble. MOF ordered banks to reduce the growth of real estate-related loans and to report all loans made to the three problematic industries, namely real estate, construction, and non-bank finance. Exempt from this rule, the *jûsen* continued to finance the real estate industry by borrowing from the agricultural co-ops, which were supervised by the Ministry of Agriculture (MOA) and also exempt from MOF regulations. As a result, loans by the co-ops to *jûsen* doubled from ¥2.9 trillion in 1990 to ¥5.9 trillion in 1993.

When, in 1992, MOF faced the imminent collapse of the largest *jûsen*, Nihon Jûtaku Kinyû (NJK), it resorted to its traditional policy of bailing out failing institutions by cross-subsidization. MOF assembled a rescue plan with Sanwa Bank, NJK's largest shareholder. Both MOF and Sanwa agreed to reduce NJK's interest payments to creditors rather than liquidate the company. In early 1993 MOF distributed the reduction of interest payments among three groups of NJK creditors: the nine parent (shareholder) banks, other creditor banks, and agricultural credit cooperatives. The first group was to forgive all interest payments;

the second group's interest rate was reduced to 2.5%, and the third group's was reduced to 4.5%.

The seven smaller parent banks had argued that the two main banks should bear more responsibility; and the agricultural credit cooperatives refused to shoulder any losses, claiming that they provided credit to the *jûsen* because, as subsidiaries of major banks and supervised by MOF, the *jûsen* were considered safe bets. Thus, MOF's compromise plan bridged the conflict between, on the one hand, the two main parent banks (Sanwa Bank and Sakaura Bank) and the other parent banks, and, on the other, between the parent banks and the co-ops. To ease acceptance of this plan, MOF further promised the MOA that the co-ops would be given priority in loan repayment and that the parent banks would rehabilitate NJK by infusing new capital into it.

However, after 1994 as the *jûsen*'s bad loans ballooned as a consequence of the general fall in land prices, it became clear that the whole *jûsen* industry had to be liquidated and the old regime could no longer cope with the crisis. In mid-1995, after the failure of a number of small credit institutions and the Daiwa Bank Incident, new concerns over the viability of the banks caused the Japan premium rate to jump—especially for the main creditors of the industry, which were the long-term credit and trust banks.[2]

In addition, the Nikkei index of stock prices dipped below the critical 15,000 threshold in August 1995. Prodded to act by the market, MOF tried to distribute the costs of *jûsen* liquidation but it failed due to strong opposition from financial institutions. By the time of *jûsen* liquidation in 1996, about half of their ¥13 trillion in outstanding loans were judged non-retrievable. The final settlement forced *jûsen* creditor banks to forgive ¥6.3 trillion. The government contributed ¥685 billion.

Initially, however, MOF had proposed that creditors write off the ¥6.3 trillion of non-retrievable loans (class IV) and the ¥1.2 trillion yen of near-non-retrievable loans (class III) without injecting public money. Parent banks were to forgive all of their claims and the remaining losses would be distributed proportionately to the amount lent. Under this formula, the parent banks were to lose ¥3.5 trillion, creditor banks ¥1.7 trillion, and co-ops ¥2.3 trillion.

Anticipating strong resistance from the agricultural credit cooperatives, MOF instead decided to require forgiveness of creditor claims equal only to the total class IV loans (¥6.3 trillion). However, this would be done without reducing the ¥5.2 trillion in losses assigned to the parent and creditor banks when class III loans were included. This effectively more than halved the burden on the co-ops, from ¥2.3 trillion to ¥1.1 trillion. However, the parent banks vehemently opposed this solution because they would have losses exceeding their entire loans to the *jûsen* when the ¥1.2 trillion in class III loans went bad.

The non-viability of the old regime became apparent when the agricultural credit cooperatives mobilized politicians to inject pubic funds. The co-ops earlier had opposed the injection of public funds, insisting instead that parent banks reconstruct the *jûsen*. However, when the collapse of the *jûsen* became inevitable, the co-ops mobilized LDP politicians to make the government pay ¥685 billion to reduce their burden to ¥530 billion. These were ballpark figures meant to prevent individual regional co-ops from recording losses. (Agricultural credit cooperatives are organized in a three-tier hierarchical system with a single central co-op—Nôrinchûkin—at the top, regional federations, and then the local credit cooperatives. The regionals invested most heavily in *jûsen*.)

Journalistic accounts of this process attest to the critical importance of co-op pressure on Diet members in the resolution of the problem. Within MOF, the Budget Bureau favored spending taxpayer money, against the objections of the Banking Bureau, because it feared a delay in the budget bill if the liquidation plan fell through. Neither the Banking Bureau nor the banks were resolute in mobilizing politicians.

In addition to its injection of public funds, the government and the banks created a new loan-retrieval company (the Jûsen Management Fund) to take over the remaining ¥6.8 trillion of *jûsen* loans. Half of whatever losses this fund had recorded at the end of its mandate were to be covered by the government. (Kishi 1996, p 142; Yutani and Tsujihiro 1996, p 1–66 and 98–257; Satô 1998, p 295-322; Takao 1998, ch 5.)

During the *jûsen* debates in the Diet, the parent banks and the co-ops attacked both each other and MOF's compromise plan, while a public outcry erupted against the injection of public money. It was only after this unexpected backlash against the *jûsen* settlement that the LDP's coalition partners, which had to cooperate with the LDP in passing the necessary legislation, started to advocate breaking up MOF.

The *jûsen* case shows that international investors no longer allowed MOF to ignore the bad-loan problem, and the enormity of the debts vitiated MOF's efforts to continue its traditional methods, including cross-subsidization. The *jûsen* case also reveals another important point: the large banks that eventually collapsed suffered from the fact that they could not retrieve the loans their non-bank subsidiaries had made to real estate firms after the general fall in land prices. Thus, the *jûsen* case shows how the collapse of the land market spread into a banking crisis through non-bank financial subsidiaries.

Creating the New Framework for Troubled Banks

By October 1998 a comprehensive policy framework for troubled banks was more or less complete. The new framework created the Financial Reconstruction Commission (FRC), a temporary minister-led committee to supervise the Financial Supervisory Agency (FSA). The FSA was now either to put failed banks under receivership or temporarily to nationalize them, and then separate their performing from their non-performing loans, selling the latter to the Resolution and Collection Corporation (RCC), and the former to other banks. Unless there is an immediate acquirer, the Deposit Insurance Corporation (DIC) can send receivers to operate the bank as a "bridge bank" for up to three years and continue to write off bad loans until a purchaser is found.

A total of ¥17 trillion is earmarked to protect the depositors of failed banks, and there is ¥18 trillion to nationalize failed banks, set up bridge banks, and purchase bad loans. In addition, ¥25 trillion has been allocated by the government to increase the capital of healthy banks by purchasing their equity and bonds.

This reflected a radical shift in the policy toward troubled banks away from bailing them out, either by cross-subsidization or by the injection of public money, to helping only the healthy ones and facilitating the liquidation of the rest. The FRC was created specifically to supervise this regime and has been given vast powers to inspect the operation of banks, infuse capital into the healthy ones, and terminate the operation of the ailing banks. Part of the FRC's power had belonged to MOF. Thus, the creation, via the FRC, of a policy regime for troubled banks also marked the final step in MOF's breakup.

The new policy framework created to deal with troubled banks was first applied to credit cooperatives in 1996. It was expanded to include ordinary banks in 1997 after the collapse of a major bank, and became comprehensive in 1998 amidst a political and economic crisis.

The process of creating the new policy framework unfolded in a way that resonates with the four observations made in the *jûsen* case (see p 113–14). First, MOF's financial arm always favored methods that contained the costs of solving problems within financial circles. When a bank fell into trouble, MOF would invariably try to save it by arranging acquisitions or mergers. This was its approach in 1995 in the cases of the failed credit cooperatives and of the local banks and then in 1997 during the crisis of Hokkaido Takushoku Bank and Nippon Credit Bank. Second, such attempts failed because partner banks would not bail out the failing banks.

Third, neither MOF's financial arm nor the banks mobilized politicians to help them out. Instead, it was the macroeconomic and international financial impact of the banking crisis that put the issue into the hands of politicians. By the time of the collapse of the Hokkaido Takushoku Bank in November 1997 and the imminent failure of the Long Term Credit Bank in June 1998, Japan's banking crisis had become an international concern that forced political leaders to take action. In other words, unlike in the *jûsen* case, which was driven by the mobilization of politicians by agricultural credit cooperatives, it was the serious consequences of inaction that put the issue of the banking crisis on the agenda for government leaders.

Finally, as in the *jûsen* case, it was when the LDP had to win the cooperation of the opposition parties in order to pass the legislation that would create the new policy regime that the issue of dividing MOF came up. This meant the LDP had to concede to demands to deprive MOF of more of its power over financial institutions than the party had intended, and to strengthen the future FSA (provisionally headed by the Financial Reconstruction Commission).

Beginning with the failure of two credit co-ops in Tokyo in late 1994, which was followed by a series of similar failures in 1995, including the collapse of a second-tier regional bank, the Hyôgo Bank, in April, MOF was faced with the refusal of healthier banks to participate in bail outs. MOF thus abandoned its method of dealing with each case individually and started to set up a generalized liquidation scheme.

At first, it asked creditor banks to forgive their loans. MOF also wrote off bad loans, and transferred the remaining operations to the newly established Tokyo Cooperative Bank with money provided by the Credit Cooperative Association, local governments (which supervised the credit co-ops), the Bank of Japan, and the Deposit Insurance Corporation. In all of these cases, however, bitter disputes erupted among the various participants over the distribution of the burdens of liquidation. Thus, for the remainder of 1995—amid criticism by credit rating companies, the IMF (August 1995), and participants at the G7 Meeting in October 1995 regarding Japan's tardiness in addressing the bad loan problem—a government advisory committee discussed how to set up a scheme of credit co-op liquidation. As a result, MOF decided temporarily to increase annual bank contributions to the deposit insurance fund by seven-fold, turned the Tokyo Cooperative Bank into a resolution trust for credit co-ops, renamed Resolution and Collection Bank (RCB), and set a deadline for the introduction of limits on deposit guarantees.

Although it committed the government to paying for the loans the RCB could not recover, MOF restricted the liquidation scheme to credit co-ops. It sought to strengthen healthier banks by compelling them to increase their capital and declared it would rigorously apply BIS capital requirements (albeit with a lower ratio for domestically operating banks). Legislation to implement these measures was presented in 1996 at the same time as the *jûsen* bills. Because of the public outcry over the *jûsen* settlement, the government left the issue of compensating the losses of the Jûsen Management Fund and the Resolution and Collection Corporation (RCC) deliberately vague and to be dealt with at the end of their mandate. (Nihon Keizai Shinbun-sha 1996, Part I; Satô 1998, p 262–95; Takao 1998, p 113–37.)

By 1997, as the banking crisis spread, MOF was forced to figure out what to do in the event of a failure of a major bank. Again, MOF first tried to merge troubled banks with healthier ones. Such was the proposed joining of the Hokkaidô Takushoku Bank (Takushoku) with Hokkaidô Bank, and the alliance between the Nippon Credit Bank (NCB, a long-term credit bank) and New York-based Bankers Trust. MOF also compelled major banks and the Bank of Japan to provide loans to the troubled NCB in exchange for promises of extensive cost-cutting and rationalization. However, the Takushoku merger fell through when Hokkaidô Bank realized it could not absorb the bad loans.

When Takushoku failed in November 1997, MOF decided to create a regime for troubled banks by expanding the deposit insurance fund, this time relying on public money instead of contributions from the financial sector. Still, MOF was reluctant to resort to public funds until it was driven to do so by another surge in the Japan premium and by politicians and business leaders responding to concerns voiced by US Treasury officials. In order to quell possible opposition, MOF decided to fund the expansion of the deposit insurance fund by using Bank of Japan loans and paid-upon-call government bonds rather than by earmarked government spending.

The expansion of the deposit insurance fund had two purposes. One was to enable the RCC to acquire non-performing loans from failed banks in general, not just from credit co-ops, in order to make it easier for healthy banks to take over the normal operations of failed banks. This measure was a response to the Takushoku case, where liquidation had been stalled because Hokuyo Bank, which was to take over most of the failed bank's operations, refused to accept the questionable loans.

The other purpose was to inject capital into healthy banks by purchasing their equity and bonds. Thus, instead of prodding banks to meet the BIS capital requirements by administrative guidance, MOF decided to increase their capital directly. A total of ¥17 trillion was prepared to ensure full safety of deposits (until 2001) and to cover losses incurred by bad loans, and another ¥13 trillion was prepared to help the healthier banks.

MOF tried to assure policy-makers that it would not create a moral hazard by using public funds to help ailing banks. Among the earliest recipients of capital infusions were the two long-term credit banks, which shortly were shown to be in trouble. The opposition condemned this measure for wasting taxpayer money on healthy banks; economists criticized it for spoiling ailing ones. (Nihon Keizai Shinbun-sha 1998, p 123–32 and 202–45; Takao 1998, Ch 7; Asahi Shinbun 1999, Chs 5–7.)

A radical shift in political and economic circumstances in mid-1998 forced MOF to address this dilemma and to increase the amount of funds drastically. This led to the final phase in the creation of a policy regime for troubled banks.

Facing the imminent failure of the Long Term Credit Bank (LTCB), MOF initially tried to merge it with Sumitomo Trust and Banking Corporation. However, talks stalled because Sumitomo Trust refused to absorb LTCB's non-performing loans. Meanwhile, international concern over the bad-loans problem caused the yen and Japanese stock prices to tumble in June 1998, dragging down Asian and European stock markets and causing alarm among US and

Asian leaders. China issued strongly worded warnings, and international financial leaders held emergency meetings. It reached the point that top government leaders and MOF's fiscal arm had to make a pledge to the international community that they would fix the banking problem.

Thus, MOF, prodded by the LDP, hastily decided to create a system of "bridge banks" that would take over failed banks, selling their performing loans to other banks and their non-performing loans to the Deposit Insurance Corporation. This would make it easier for other banks to acquire the healthy operations of failed banks. The bridge-bank solution, which emerged as the July 1998 Upper House election approached, was to let the Financial Supervisory Agency appoint a receiver to take over a failed bank's management and sell off its bad loans to the RCC. If the receiver could not find an acquirer of the performing loans within two years, the bank was to be nationalized and rid itself of its questionable loans to make it more attractive to potential buyers. However, the question remained whether the government was willing to help only healthy banks and to let large banks, such as LTCB, fail.

Even before the bridge-bank solution was passed into law in October 1998, the banking issue had grown into a political and economic crisis to which top government leaders were forced to react. Discontented voters punished the LDP with a defeat in the Upper House election on 12 July, thereby forcing Ryutaro Hashimoto to step down as prime minister. He was replaced by Keizo Obuchi, whose mandate was undermined by the political uncertainty generated by the LDP's lack of a majority in the Upper House.

Meanwhile, domestic and international leaders urged the government to solve the banking problem and revive the economy. Thus, the matter was no longer in the hands of the financial bureaucrats, but in the hands of top government leaders and MOF's fiscal arm, which was in charge of macroeconomic management. Opposition parties demanded that the government abolish measures to help healthy banks, nationalize all failed banks, integrate the existing liquidation funds into the Resolution and Collection Bank, and create a new Financial Reconstruction Commission (FRC) which was to be responsible for reviving failed banks. The opposition also demanded that MOF's power over financial crisis management be transferred to the FRC.

The LDP was under more and more pressure to reach a compromise ahead of the Clinton-Obuchi summit meeting in New York on 22 September. It also wanted to save the LTCB. In the end, the LDP-led government agreed to adopt a modified version of the opposition bill and discard its own proposed legislation. As a result of negotiations between the LDP and the Democratic Party, it was agreed to create the FRC, allow the FRC either to nationalize or appoint receivers for failed banks, nationalize the LTCB, and abolish measures to help healthy banks.

This basic agreement was announced on 18 September. It was greeted with skepticism, reflected by the fact that on 21 September, the first full day of trading after the announcement, the Nikkei index fell to its lowest level since early 1986, touching 13,597. After reaching basic agreement, the two sides spent an excruciating 10 days debating two minor points: the extent of MOF's breakup and whether the government could help healthy banks in the interim until a new measure was agreed upon.

At their summit meeting, Obuchi was urged by Clinton to inject public money into healthy banks to save the economy. The same demand was echoed at the 7 October G7 meeting of finance ministers and central bank directors. With this shift of events, the opposition parties no longer had to fear being blamed for using public money in order to help healthy banks. Instead, they risked being blamed for holding the economy hostage and for causing an international credit crunch if they refused to compromise with the government. Thus, Komeito and the Liberal Party became eager to work with the government, thereby effectively isolating the Democratic Party.

Because the issue did not give politicians an opportunity to claim credit but rather compelled them to avoid blame, the parties competed to increase the money available for the banks. They increased the funds for healthy banks from ¥13 trillion to ¥25 trillion and doubled the amount available for troubled banks from ¥17 trillion to ¥35 trillion. (See Satô 1998, p 397–403; Suda 1998, chs 1–3 and 6; Asahi Shinbun 1999, Ch 10.)

By late October 1998, the existing regime had been drastically revised and a new bureaucratic structure had been set up to facilitate the liquidation of ailing banks and inject an unprecedented amount of money into healthy ones to avoid a credit crunch. The new FRC was given the power to inspect the assets of both failed and healthy banks, to liquidate ailing banks and dismiss their management, and to order managerial changes to healthy banks in exchange for capital infusion.

It is important to note that the agency has had to get the cooperation of the major banks in making rules for how it exercises its supervision, and it has had to persuade the reluctant healthiest banks to apply for public money. Thus, although the FRC exercises more transparent, codified, and rule-based regulatory power than did MOF, it still is dependent on the major banks for implementation of policies (Asahi Shinbun 1999, chs 1 and 11).

The liquidation of the *jûsen* and the setting up of policies for troubled banks show that the collapse of the old regime ignited a crisis that compelled politicians to confront the issue of imposing costs on the public. It was in these two cases, in which the LDP had to enact such cost-imposing policies, that the party made concessions to the demands of its cooperative partners that MOF be split. Before examining the process of MOF's breakup, it is necessary to see how a transformation of policy regimes could have been accommodated by an internal reorganization of MOF.

Financial Market Reforms

MOF's old regulatory regime was based on a segregated financial service industry—divided not just between banks and securities but also between several kinds of banks—and MOF's informal negotiation of conflicts, and its distribution of the costs of bank failures, within the industry. This regime was created under the US Occupation, and MOF continued to coordinate the interests of the segregated financial regime throughout the high growth period, thereby avoiding the intervention of political parties, into the 1980s (Hiwatari 1991, ch 2). Frances Rosenbluth (1993) sees this pattern extending to the period of financial liberalization and deregulation after the 1980s. Steven Vogel (1996) claims that MOF's ability to coordinate such interests allowed the state to play an autonomous role in directing the orderly desegmentation of the financial service industry.

The preference of financial institutions for negotiating the rearrangement of policy regimes within the traditional regulatory system rather than mobilizing politicians or creating a new agency is apparent if we examine the reforms aimed at making the Tokyo financial market more accessible and attractive—Japan's Big Bang. MOF developed a policy of desegmentation as part of the reform effort to meet challenges from international markets, with the goal of making the Tokyo market more accessible and attractive. In general, the Big Bang catered to the general shift in global finance from credit-based to market-based financial services ("securitization") and from collusive to rule-based regulation. There were, as yet, no demands for a new agency. (See Moran 1991, Chs 1 and 5; Moran 1994; Lawrence 1996; Underhill 1997.)

Faced with the separation of the banking and securities industries and the new regulatory push, in October 1996 MOF proposed to integrate its Bank and Securities Bureaus into the Financial Planning Bureau. However, at the height of MOF's negotiated introduction of competition by the accommodation of opposing interests—what Steven Vogel calls "strategic re-regulation"—MOF was confronted by the problem of failing banks. As a result, the old regulatory regime was replaced by one that is more rule-based.

A brief examination of the process that led to the Big Bang will show that MOF and the financial institutions ultimately were willing cooperatively to rearrange the old regime and to inaugurate new rules that would accommodate financial globalization without having to mobilize politicians or create a new agency. Thus, this case supports the claim that the bureaucratic restructuring of MOF took place only because of the involvement of politicians in necessary but unpopular reforms as a result of the non-viability of the previous regime.

After the 20 October 1996 general election, then Prime Minister Hashimoto described the Japanese Big Bang as one of his top policy priorities. In the 1990s a depressed stock market forced securities firms to realize that they could not hope to survive, much less expand, if they protected their markets. From its peak at the end of 1989, the Nikkei average had lost almost two-thirds of its value by mid 1992 and has spent the remainder of the 1990s fluctuating between 14,000 and 21,000. Annual trading volume on the Tokyo exchange quickly dropped by over two-thirds from its 1989 level and has stagnated since. Meanwhile, trading in New York and London has continued to grow (Takao 1994, Ch 1).

The banking crisis rendered the banks desperate for new business opportunities. This was especially the case for the special purpose banks — the long term credit and trust banks; the fact their opportunities were limited was the reason they made massive loans to speculative real estate development companies. In the end, despite significant costs, the banks and securities firms reluctantly agreed to further weaken market segmentation and enhance market competition by carrying out the Big Bang.

MOF had already started to loosen the boundaries among financial institutions with the 1992 Financial System Reform Law by allowing banks to move into other areas by way of subsidiaries, and by allowing banks to engage in some areas of securities trading. As discussed by Vogel (1996, ch 8) and Suginohara (1997), MOF pursued this policy and negotiated the attendant conflicts between the long-term credit banks and other banks over the proper methods of boundary-crossing, and between banks and securities firms over the scope of desegmentation.

For instance, one proposed way to cross boundaries, the multifunctional subsidiary formula, in which a subsidiary could operate in several segmented markets, was opposed by all except the long-term credit banks, which could become investment banks without creating subsidiaries. MOF rejected two other approaches—licensing of universal banks and multi-market holding companies—because both benefited the large banks over the securities firms. Instead, MOF adopted the compromise solution of requiring that separate bank subsidiaries be created for each market segment. MOF also controlled the extent to which the banks could enter the securities business by engineering a compromise between the banks and the securities houses. As a result, MOF retained control over market boundaries that had been critical to its power over the industry. (See Rosenbluth 1993, p 115–19; Vogel 1996, Ch 9.)

However, the banking crisis rapidly eroded the benefits of protecting such boundaries. By the time of the *jûsen* crisis, it was evident that the long-term credit banks and trust banks, which were the largest creditors to the *jûsen*, could no longer survive within the confines of their designated businesses.

Thus, in early 1997, MOF withdrew its earlier objection and allowed financial institutions to diversify through the creation not only of subsidiaries but also of holding companies, thereby making it easier for large banks to expand across boundaries by acquiring existing banks or securities firms. Also in 1997, MOF liberalized the licensing of foreign exchange operations and started to relax the principle of separate subsidiaries for each market segment. In the following year it abolished the long-term credit bank law.

With passage of the Big Bang laws in June 1998, the government expressed its commitment to liberalization of entry into the securities industry, abolition of the remaining restrictions on bank subsidiaries, and liberalization of the insurance market.

The securities industry became structurally depressed and its troubles were exacerbated by a series of scandals (related to compensation of insiders) and the collapse of Sanyo Securities and Yamaichi Securities in November 1997 (Nihon Keizai Shinbun-sha 1998, p 134–74). In order to survive, securities firms have had little alternative but to accept the reforms and merge or align with domestic and international investment or commercial banks. These developments continued to undermine the foundations of MOF's traditional regulatory regime (Takao 1998, Ch 1; Asahi Shinbun 1999, Ch 9).

In the 1980s, securities firms, fearing competition from banks, were opposed to the creation of new markets for security-type services, such as warrant bonds, CDs (certificates of deposit), and CP (commercial paper), or to the opening of the stock exchange to foreign firms. However, the stagnation of the industry in the 1990s changed their preferences. (Sobel 1994, p 29–34 and 97–110; Laurence 1996, p 330–34.)

The blurring of the boundary between banks and securities firms and the shift to rule-based regulation were reflected in the integration of MOF's Banking and Securities Bureau into the Financial Planning Bureau, agreed upon in October 1996. In the old regime, MOF regulated financial institutions and sectors separately. Instead of this agent-based regulation, which implies close, negotiated relations between each financial institution and the bureaucracy, the bureaucracy must now codify laws to govern markets. MOF could not appease demands for its partition with the offer of this reorganization, but it nonetheless carried it out.

Anticipating that it would have to supervise *markets*, in which firms enter, exit and cross boundaries, rather than *sectors* which characterized by stable participants, MOF's Financial Planning Bureau was reorganized in a way that no longer reflects sector-based divisions. Thus, the foundation of MOF's old regime, segmented financial markets, was eroded and the basis of relations between the state and financial institutions shifted from consensus to codified rules in the areas both of helping troubled banks and supervising financial markets.

The preparation for the Big Bang was efficiently accommodated by MOF and financial institutions without the involvement of politicians. However, the injection of public funds into troubled banks led political parties to demand the breakup of MOF. In fact, it was the reaction of politicians to a specific kind of policy that led to the decision to break up MOF.

BLAME AVOIDANCE, POLICY COOPERATION AND THE SPLIT-UP OF MOF

MOF's modus operandi of containing the 1990s banking crisis within financial circles failed, and thereby exacerbated the problem until it reached such proportions that it threatened the health of the banking sector, the economy, and international markets, and required a large amount of public spending. The old regime was structured in a way that tended to exclude politicians. However, the severity of the issues compelled politicians to address the banking crisis.

In this section, I argue that the breakup of MOF can be explained as an instance of political blame avoidance. Two features stand out in the five major rounds of debate over MOF's partition between 1996 and 1999.

One feature is that the political parties which insisted on the breakup of MOF were those that cooperated with the LDP to pass legislation which imposed costs on the public. Thus, the position of a party changed on this issue depending on its relations with the LDP at the time. The other feature is that the LDP made concessions to such demands when it feared an electoral backlash or needed the cooperation of the non-LDP parties to implement unpopular measures. Conversely, the LDP declined concessions to its coalition partners when such elements were missing. This was mainly because the LDP needed MOF's expertise in dealing with the financial crisis and accepted MOF's plea that reorganizing the ministry amid a crisis would only distract officials and weaken the government's ability to cope with the pending problems.

These features were apparent in the first round of debate after the *jûsen* bill deliberations in 1996 when the LDP-led government agreed to create the Financial Supervisory Agency (FSA) and in the fourth round in 1998 when the government agreed to create the Financial Reconstruction Commission (FRC). I have already described the broader context of these two rounds of debate. The other rounds were the debates over the independent status of the FSA in late 1996 (round 2), the transfer of financial policy-making functions to the new agency in late 1997 (round 3), and a final settlement in April 1999 (round 5) on the power of the FSA after the Financial Reconstruction Commission ends its temporary mandate in April 2000.

In the two interim rounds, and in the last round, when both the LDP and non-LDP parties had a chance to claim credit for the breaking up of MOF, the LDP made only minimal or cosmetic concessions to its coalition partners' demands to further strip MOF of its powers. The parties that cooperated with the LDP, but could not monopolize credit for enacting necessary reforms, had a stronger incentive to insist on a popular issue like MOF's breakup. The LDP, by contrast, had to make concessions to its coalition partners in order to avoid being the sole target of a voter backlash by being able to share blame with the non-LDP parties.

Round 1 (early to mid-1996): The Decision to Split-up MOF

The first and critical stage of MOF's partition began with the legislative debate on *jûsen* liquidation in early 1996 and continued until the three coalition parties agreed, on the eve of the 20 October 1996 general election, to transfer MOF's financial supervisory and investigatory functions to a separate agency. Within the coalition, the Sakigake and the Socialist Party insisted on MOF's breakup because they had to share the blame for enacting an extremely unpopular policy without being able to claim the credit for protecting the agricultural credit cooperatives, as the LDP could do.

As the election approached, however, the leaders of the Sakigake and the Socialists re-ignited the issue. They were particularity vulnerable, and urgently needed an issue to boost their standing not just because of their cooperation with the LDP but also because most of their Diet members were about to launch a new party. The coalition parties had, to their advantage, a Socialist finance minister who yielded to the demands of his party instead of protecting the ministry, and some support from members of the LDP leadership who were willing to sacrifice MOF to appeal to voters and thereby tighten the three-party alliance. As a concession, MOF's leaders proposed to integrate its Banking and Securities Bureaus and to elevate its Financial Investigation Department to being a bureau. Such concessions, however, could not prevent the coalition parties from agreeing, on the eve of the election, to break up MOF and to create the Financial Supervisory Agency (FSA).

Round 2 (late 1996): Deciding the Powers of the FSA

The extent to which the Financial Supervisory Agency (FSA) was to be independent of MOF was discussed after the election as the second round of debates over MOF's breakup began. This round proved sensitive to the shift in power within the coalition and party system. The LDP had fared better than expected in the election, whereas the Sakigake, which had been reduced to a fraction of its former size due to a mass exodus just before the election, and the Socialists were defeated and needed to justify their continued alignment with the LDP. Thus, the two parties demanded that the FSA be completely independent of MOF and the cabinet. The LDP refused to claim credit for the decision to break up MOF and showed no eagerness to make concessions. Instead, the LDP returned to its usual position of protecting MOF and its powers.

Emerging anti-mainstream groups in the LDP criticized the leadership for continuing to cater to the two small parties instead of aligning with the opposition parties that had emerged as winners in the election, the New Frontier Party and the Democratic Party. Once the talks began, the LDP proposed that the FSA be placed under MOF like the Tax Agency, while the Socialists and the Sakigake demanded that it be independent like the Fair Trade Commission. The LDP leadership, eager to maintain the three-party coalition and fend off attacks by anti-mainstream groups, proposed a compromise, on Christmas Eve 1996, to make the FSA an independent agency in the Prime Minister's Office, and to allow MOF to retain its authority in financial policy-making. (See Nihon Keizai Shinbun 1997, p 35–45; Mabuchi 1997, p 134–255; Tahara 1998, p 15–96.)

Round 3 (late 1997 to early 1998): Administrative Reorganization Deliberations

The third round of debate lasted from late 1997 to early 1998. It concerned the relationship between MOF and the FSA in the context of Prime Minister Hashimoto's plan to overhaul the central government by consolidating the existing 22 departments into 13 by 2001. The outcome was asymmetrical because the government decided to transfer some part of MOF's financial policy-making functions to the FSA in the future, while the LDP refused to make any concessions despite strong threats from the Sakigake that it would break up the coalition unless the LDP agreed to transfer more of MOF's power to the FSA. The FSA will be transformed into the Finance Agency (*Kinyû-chô*) as part of the administrative reorganization.

This outcome can be explained by the fact that the government had become absorbed in the management of the banking crisis and needed MOF's expertise, while the changing political situation made the LDP less dependent on its coalition partners for the passage of legislation. Indeed, MOF accepted the decision by Prime Minister Hashimoto that it keep its powers concerning the schematic management of financial crises and bank failures while it shared its other powers with, or transferred them to, the FSA.

In response to a media campaign urging further severing of MOF's fiscal and financial arms, Prime Minister Hashimoto reworded the interim report of the Administrative Reform Council (*Gyôkaku Kaigi*); it proposed to keep matters pertaining to the stability of the financial system under MOF. The Prime Minister was eager to get credit for this change, while the Council itself was critical of redrawing the boundaries between MOF and the future Finance Agency. Some council members argued that further separation would undermine the already agreed justification for separating the FSA from MOF, while others argued it would create another agency and that this went against the announced administrative reform, which was aimed at reducing the number of departments. The Prime Minister's ruling was opaque; it deliberately left vague what constituted crisis management of the financial system and the distinction between that and the stability of the financial system. Therefore, it remained unclear what would change in the year 2001. (Gyôsei Kaikaku 1998, p 273, 389–92, 445, 449–51, 582, 648–49, 895–97, 996, and 1077; Tahara 1998, p 99–123.)

In contrast to the quiet acceptance of this decision by MOF bureaucrats, the shifting political situation in late 1997 transformed the MOF issue into a coalition crisis. The Sakigake, supported by the Socialists, insisted that MOF retain no financial-policy powers, including those related to international finance and currency, and kept threatening to break up the coalition. The demand to relieve MOF of its international financial functions, however, was quietly dropped, as it was obvious that foreign exchange management had become a critical part of fiscal and monetary policy-making. The LDP stood firm in its opposition to any further restructuring of MOF.

Meanwhile, the largest opposition party, the New Frontier Party (NFP), was disintegrating due to internal feuds. The Sakigake was obstinate regarding MOF's breakup; it had to spearhead a popular issue in order to reassemble the fragmented opposition groups, and it reasoned that LDP leaders could not afford to break up the coalition when they faced challenges from internal anti-mainstream groups. However, once it became clear that former NFP members were going to the Liberal Party, the Democratic Party, or Komeito—but not the Sakigake or the Socialists—the two parties realized that they needed the LDP to remain in power. As a result, the Socialists struck a face-saving compromise with the LDP which stated that MOF could retain its powers "for the time being." (According to an LDP official widely quoted in the media, "'The time being' can mean forever.") The Sakigake had no choice but to go along.

Round 4: The Fall 1998 Crisis

The MOF issue remained the final point of contention in negotiations between the government and opposition in the fall of 1998 over the establishment of a new policy regime to deal with failed banks. The LDP agreed to adopt the opposition's proposed legislation. Although this included creation of the FRC and the transfer of MOF's power over financial crisis management to the FRC ahead of the scheduled reorganization of the central bureaucracy, it also forced the opposition to share blame with the LDP for using public money to help troubled banks.

In the initial debate on the future of MOF, both sides agreed to separate its financial powers by the end of the 1999 Diet session. The conflict over the interpretation of this compromise forced the parties to renegotiate the agreement, thereby causing a delay in implementation of the new policy framework. The LDP interpreted this as a confirmation of the deadline by which the proposed Administrative Reform legislation was to be passed, while the opposition claimed it meant an earlier and complete transfer of MOF's power to the FRC.

The reworded compromise made crisis management of the financial system and bank failures the co-jurisdiction of MOF and the FRC "for the time being," thereby shelving the issue until mid 1999 when the parties were to finalize the Administrative Reorganization bills. However, the opposition's earlier insistence on reducing MOF's power has had the effect of equipping the new FRC with more power.

Round 5 (early 1999): The Final Settlement

The fifth round was completed in April 1999 and confirms this chapter's hypothesis. In early 1999, the parties finally clarified the 1998 agreement to finalize the deliberation of the Administrative Reorganization bills. This had been the thorniest issue. During talks between the LDP, the Democratic Party (the largest opposition party), and Komeito, the Democratic Party demanded MOF's "crisis management" functions be transferred to the Finance Agency by the beginning of 2000. The LDP consistently refused to make such concessions. The talks broke down when Komeito decided to support the LDP bill, after proposing several compromises to reach a three-party consensus in vain. Thus, it was decided that MOF will co-manage crisis management functions with the Finance Agency when the agency is inaugurated in July 2000.

CONCLUSION

This chapter has argued that MOF's partition can be understood as an instance of bureaucratic restructuring, used as a partisan blame-avoidance device, in the context of broader efforts to set up a new regime for troubled banks. Structural arguments that examine the institutionalized relations between interest groups, political parties, and the bureaucracy are inadequate to explain why the split up of MOF proceeded at certain times and not at others. In order to incorporate temporal variations into the explanation, I have adopted the theories of conflict expansion and blame avoidance. The theory of conflict expansion explains why the interests of financial institutions and MOF converged to abandon the old regime and why the politicians were compelled to address the banking crisis. The theory of blame avoidance explains why MOF's restructuring was associated with the setting up of a cost-imposing policy framework to help troubled banks. Politicians had to justify the unpopular policy of injecting public money into the banks, even though it was necessary to revive the domestic economy and stabilize international markets. The Japanese institutional context of one-party dominance explains why the dilemma was acute for those cooperating with the LDP, compelling them to seek popular approbation by advocating the break up of MOF, and why the LDP had to make concessions to these parties.

Alternative Arguments

Alternative arguments based either on institutional characteristics or contingent aspects cannot fully account for the puzzles addressed in this paper. For instance, the argument that opposition parties took up popular issues like MOF's breakup to differentiate themselves from the LDP cannot explain why it was the coalition partners, and not the opposition, that insisted on the issue or why the LDP made concessions only in conjunction with the passing of unpopular financial reform legislation. Similarly, the composition of the government—LDP majority government, LDP coalition government, and LDP Upper House minority government—cannot explain the variations in outcomes because MOF's breakup both progressed and was stalled under LDP majority governments, while its breakup progressed during LDP coalition and LDP Upper House minority governments.

Explanations which stress contingent factors have obvious limitations in their ability to explain MOF's breakup and the creation of a new agency. The argument that a string of scandals by MOF officials made the ministry vulnerable to attacks by politicians cannot be sustained because the government was protective of MOF during the scandals. In the scandals of 1995 and 1998, the government opposed the resignation of all the MOF officials involved except those who received favors, and it accepted the early retirement or resignation of MOF's vice-minister and minister only after being pressured to do so (see Asahi Shinbun 1999, Ch 8). Furthermore, in the 1998 scandal the government refused demands by the media and non-LDP parties to reopen the issue of the breakup of MOF.

The argument that MOF's incompetence led to its breakup is simplistic; it cannot explain the mechanism and causal relations that produced such a result.

The Role of Institutional Setting

I have stressed that it was the Japanese institutional setting that made parties other than the ruling LDP demand bureaucratic restructuring as part of a policy regime shift. The same pursuit of blame avoidance entails different outcomes when pursued in different institutional settings. For instance, Weaver lists examples of blame avoidance behavior by lawmakers in the US setting of a decentralized Congress and loose party discipline, and finds a broad agreement to surrender discretion as one of the important policy effects of blame avoidance. However, this chapter argues that in the Japanese case of one-party dominance, it might be in the ruling party's interest to wait until the problem becomes critical, and broad agreement in favor of policy reform surfaces. In such cases it can monopolize the credit for implementing necessary policies, although it also has to shoulder the blame for them. Furthermore, in such cases the opposition parties face a dilemma between opposing the necessary but unpopular reforms, thereby being criticized as populist or obstructionist, and acting "responsibly" and supporting the policies, which puts them in the position of having to share the blame.

In a one-party dominant system, where the chances of the opposition replacing the government in a single election are bleak, policy participation is the only way a non-LDP party can show it is fit to govern. However, policy participation forces such non-LDP parties to support the government's necessary but unpopular policies, which puts them in the position of having to share the blame without being able to claim much credit. This case shows that parties formally aligned with the LDP tried to ease their dilemma by pursuing other measures beyond the policy in question, such as MOF's breakup, in order to garner some public approbation.

This chapter also offers one potential explanation for why new agencies are rarely created in Japan and have never been created as a result of political mobilization by specific interest groups, a fact which is in marked contrast to the situation of the United States as it is described by Moe (1989, 1995). As we saw with the case of the Japanese Big Bang, MOF and the financial institutions were able to restructure the regulatory regime by themselves without creating a new agency. In stable one-party regimes, the bureaucracy can anticipate the ruling party's need to attract a broad coalition of diverse interests and therefore accommodate new policy demands made by interest groups or coordinate conflicts among them. This has been the case, for example, in the areas of financial desegmentation and service liberalization.

The role of bureaucrats reduces the need for interest groups to mobilize politicians in order to institutionalize their policies. Thus, it is only in a crisis, when the existing policy regime fails dramatically, that the restructuring of existing agencies is contemplated. In such rare cases, it is not the ruling party but other parties that attack the government and demand a new agency. This was seen in the only other case of agency partition in postwar Japan: the 1971 creation of the Environment Agency, which resulted from of the breakup of the Ministry of Health and Welfare (MHW).

In the Environment Agency case it was the non-viability of MHW's anti-pollution control policy that led to the passage of a dozen anti-pollution bills and the creation of the new agency as the major concession to the opposition. The major difference is that the opposition attacked the government in order to claim credit for addressing the pollution issue, while the government enacted the measures to avoid being blamed for being soft on the industry and on MITI. (See McKean 1977; Kôseishô 1988, p 982–1165.)

Both this case and the banking case show that it was the non-LDP parties that demanded the splitting of an existing agency, without pressure from specific interest groups; it also shows that it was the non-LDP parties that forced the LDP to create an agency that was stronger than what the government had desired. The irony of Japanese bureaucratic restructuring is that it creates agencies that are not expected to serve their most devoted creators, the non-LDP parties.

Implications

This case study also has some broader implications about what is changing in Japanese politics. For instance, if bureaucratic restructuring was part of a policy regime shift, then most of the expected changes would be in the relations between the agency and the interest groups, despite MOF's restructuring, and not between the ruling party and the agency, or among the political parties. The evidence presented here refutes Mabuchi's claim (1997) that the changing relationship between the LDP and MOF caused the latter's breakup. On the contrary, the LDP protected MOF and resisted changes in the existing party-agency relations.

In addition, it is doubtful whether the relationship between the LDP and other parties changed after LDP's brief removal from power or its experience with coalition governments. The dilemma of the non-LDP parties supporting the LDP's unpopular but necessary policies appears in my analysis of neo-liberal reforms in the 1980s (Hiwatari 1998). I argue there that the parties that cooperated with the LDP in tightening welfare schemes and increasing taxes to ease the budget deficit could not broaden their electoral appeal; they could only win minor policy concessions for their constituents.

What I did not address there is the dilemma of the non-cooperative populist opposition that might be rewarded in the following election for opposing an unpopular policy but is forced, after its victory, to prove it is fit to replace the ruling party and carry out necessary policies. Such was the case of the Socialists who scored a victory in the 1989 Upper House election by opposing the new sales tax. If such parties aim to establish themselves as viable contestants for power, they face the same dilemma as the parties that cooperated with the ruling party. The dilemma was evident after the 1998 Upper House elections when the LDP adopted the opposition's proposed legislation for troubled banks. Thus, this case shows that inter-party relations have not changed significantly from the early 1980s despite the LDP's experience of being out of power and of forming coalition governments.

This case also shows that, unlike the relations between the LDP and the bureaucracy or the LDP and other parties, some changes are in process in the relation between the bureaucracy and the financial sector since the destruction of the old regulatory regime. Although the change is not expected to transform the "meso-corporatist" nature of financial regulation (see Moran 1991) which is confined to experts in the agency and the industry, it is expected to change the way the two interact.

A new policy regime for troubled banks has replaced the old system in which MOF would rescue troubled banks by informally coordinating mergers and cross-subsidizing losses within the financial community. Now, the FRC must liquidate failed banks (those with a capital ratio below 2%) and order major banks below the 8% BIS requirement to reduce (or freeze) dividends and executive pay, cut the number of branches and personnel, and retire executive officials, according to a scale based on the bank's capitalization ratio.

The rules have become more transparent and codified and their implementation is expected to be more quasi-juridical. An identical development is seen in the new rules of the Japanese Big Bang pertaining to transparency, accounting, insider trading, investor protection, and capital adequacy. As a result, the basis of what Vogel (1996) has called "strategic re-regulation"—MOF's negotiated introduction of competition by the accommodation of opposing interests—is rapidly dissolving. Instead of coordinating interests among fixed participants, the financial bureaucracy must now supervise measures that encourage actors to move in and out of the market.

Although the FRC is still dependent on the banks in assessing their health and supervising the market with diverse new services, the future Finance Agency can no longer use its newly acquired power in an informal and concerted way as MOF once did. The irony of Japanese bureaucratic restructuring is that the non-LDP parties are likely to present the LDP with an agency more powerful and highly insulated than any of the players would have wanted.

NOTES

1 Words uttered by Dorothy, an advisor to Prime Minster Jim Hacker, fictional characters in the BBC TV series "Yes, Prime Minister" written by Jonathan Lynn and Antony Jay (BBC Videos).
2 Daiwa Bank's US subsidiary had accumulated huge losses which the bank and MOF failed to report to US authorities. The incident damaged the credibility of Japanese banks and MOF by fueling widespread suspicion that they colluded to conceal bank losses, especially bad loans. See Kishi (1996, p 160); Takao (1998, Ch 6).

REFERENCES

Newspapers and Periodicals

Nihon Keizai Shinbun (*www.nikkei.ac.jp*) (Daily)

Asahi Shinbun (*www.asahi.com*) (Daily)

Yomiuri Shinbun (*www.yomiuri.ac.jp*) (Daily)

Kinyû Zaisei Ji'jyo (Weekly)

Official Reports by the Ministry of Finance

(*www.mof.go.jp*)

Ôkurashô. 1996a. "Sôgô Bukai Ronten Seiri." Shôken Torihiki Shingi-kai.

———. 1996b. "Kiyû Kinou Kasseika I'inkai no Koremade no Giron no Sieiri to Kongo Kento-subeki Jikô ni tsuite." Kinyû Seido Chôsa-kai.

———. 1997a. "'Gaikoku Kawase oyobi Bôeki Kanri Hô' no Kaisei ni tsuite." Gaikoku Kawase-tou Shingikai.

———. 1997b. "'Kinyû System Kaikaku' no Genjyo Seiri." Ôkurashô.

———. 1997c. Yûka Shôken Kanren no Tento Derivative Torihiki ni tsuite." Shôken Torihiki Shingi-kai, Derivative Tokubetsu Bukai.

———. 1997d. "Shôken Torihiki Shingi-kai, Sôgô Bukai, Working Party Shusa Hokoku" Parts 1–3. Shôken Torihiki Shingi-kai.

———. 1997e. "Shôken Shijyô no Sôgô-teki Kaikaku." Shôken Torihiki Shingi-kai.

———. 1997f. "Waga Kuni no Kinyû System no Kaikaku ni tsuite." Kinyû Seido Chôsa-kai.

———. 1998. "Kinyû System Kaikaku Hôan ni tsuite." Ôkurashô.

Books and Articles

Asahi Shinbun Keizai-bu, editor. 1999. *Kinyû Dôran*. Tokyo: Asahi Shinbun- sha.

Cerny, Philip G. 1993. "The Deregulation and Re-regulation of Financial Markets in a More Open World." In Philip G Cerny, editor, *Finance and World Politics: Markets, Regimes and States in the Post-hegemonic Era*. Hants: Edward Elger, 51–85.

Gyôsei Kaikaku Kaigi Jimukyoku OB-kai, editor. 1998. *21-Seiki no Nihon no Gyôsei: Gyôsei Kaikaku Kaigi Ktsudo Kiroku.* Tokyo: Gyôsei Kanri Kenkyu Senta.

Hiwatari, Nobuhiro. 1991. *Sengo Nihon no Shijyô to Seiji.* Tokyo: Tokyo Daigaku Shuppan-kai.

———. 1998. "Adjustment to Stagflation and Neoliberal Reforms in Japan, the United Kingdom, and the United States." *Comparative Political Studies* 31 (5): 602–32.

Kishi, Nobuhito. 1996. *Kensho, Ôkurashô Hôkai.* Tokyo: Tôyô Keizai Shinpo-sha.

Kôseishô, editor. 1988. *Kôsei-sho Go-jyu-nen-shi (Kijyutu-hen).* Chuô Hoki Shuppan.

Laurence, Henry. 1996. "Regulatory Competition of Financial Market Reform in Britain and Japan." *Governance* 9 (3): 311–41.

Lincoln, Edward and Robert E Litan. 1998. "The 'Big Bang'?: An Ambivalent Japan Deregulates its Financial Markets." *Brookings Review* 16 (1): 37–40.

Mabuchi, Masaru. 1996. "Ôkurashô no Moral Hazard." *Asteion* 40: 138–48.

———. 1997. *Ôkurashô wa Naze Oitusme-raretanoka?.* Tokyo: Chuo Koron-sha.

McKean, Margaret A. 1977. "Pollution and Policymaking." In T.J. Pempel, editor, *Policymaking in Contemporary Japan.* Ithaca: Cornell University Press, 201–38.

Moe, Terry M. 1989. "The Politics of Bureaucratic Structure." In John E Chubb and Paul Peterson, editors, *Can the Government Govern?* Washington DC: The Brookings Institution, 267–329.

———. 1990. "Political Institutions: The Neglected Side of the Story." *Journal of Law, Economics, and Organization* 6: 213–53.

———. 1995. "The Politics of Structural Choice: Towards a Theory of Public Bureaucracy." In Oliver E Williamson, editor, *Organization Theory. Expanded Edition*). Oxford: Oxford University Press), 116–153.

Moran, Michael. 1991. *The Politics of Financial Services Revolution: The USA, UK and Japan.* London: Macmillan.

———. 1994. "The State and the Financial Revolution." *West European Politics* 17 (3): 158–77.

Nihon Keizai Shinbun-sha, editor. 1996. *Dare ga Ginkô wo Tsubushitaka?: Documento, Kansai Kinyû no Hatan.* Tokyo: Nihon Keizai Shinbun-sha.

———. 1997. *Dônaru Kinyû Big-Bang.* Tokyo: Nihon Keizai Shinbun-sha.

———. 1998. *Nihon ga Furueta Hi: Documento, 97-aki Kinyû Kiki.* Tokyo: Nihon Keizai Shinbun-sha.

Pierson, Paul. 1994. *Dismantling the Welfare State?* Cambridge: Cambridge University Press.

———. 1996. "The New Politics of the Welfare State." *World Politics* 48 (2): 143–79.

Rosenbluth, Frances McCall. 1993. "Financial Deregulation and Interest Intermediation." In Gary D Allinson and Yasûnori Sone, editors, *Political Dynamics in Contemporary Japan.* Ithaca: Cornell University Press, 107–29.

Satô, Akira. 1998. *Documento: Kinyû Hatan.* Tokyo: Iwanama Shoten.

Schattschneider, E. E. 1960. *The Semisovereign People: a Realist's View of Democracy in America.* New York: Holt, Rinehart and Winston.

Suda, Shin'ichiro. 1998. *Chôgin Hatan.* Tokyo: Kôdan-sha.

Suginohara, Masako. 1997. *Kinyû Jiyû-ka no Seiji Katei.* University of Tokyo, Master's thesis.

Sobel, Andrew C. 1994. *Domestic Choices, International Markets: Dismantling National Barriers and Liberalizing Securities Markets.* Ann Arbor: University of Michigan Press.

Tahara, Sô'ichiro. 1998. *Kyodai na Rakujitu: Ôkura Kanyo Haisô no 850-nichi.* Tokyo: Bungei Shunjyu-sha.

Takao, Yoshikazu. 1994. *Heisei Kinyû Fukyo.* Tokyo: Chuo Koron-sha.

———. 1998. *Kinyû Defure.* Tokyo: Tôyô Keizai Shinpô-sha.

Underhill, Geoffrey RD. 1997. "Private Markets and Public Responsibility in a Global System: Conflict and Co-operation in Transnational Banking and Securities Regulation." In Geoffrey RD Underhill, editor, *The New World Order in International Finance.* London: Macmillan Press.

Vogel, Steven K. 1996. *Freer Markets, More Rules: Regulatory Reform in Advanced Industrial Counties.* Cornell University Press.

R Kent Weaver. 1986. "The Politics of Blame Avoidance." *Journal of Public Policy* 6 (4): 371–98.

Yutani, Shyôyô and Fumiaki Tsujihiro. 1996. *Documento: Jûsen Hôkai.* Tokyo: Diamond-sha.

Chapter 6

THE DISPOSAL OF BAD LOANS IN JAPAN: THE CASE OF THE CCPC

Frank Packer
Federal Reserve Bank of New York

A theme of Japan's banking problems in the 1990s was the consistently inadequate disclosure of the scale of bad loans outstanding. The major banks began publishing outstanding loans to bankrupt and 60-day-overdue borrowers in 1993. By March 1995, this amount stood at ¥12.5 trillion, or 3.3% of all loans (Figure 6.1).

When additional categories of problem loans, including those restructured at rates less than prime and those made to companies requiring financial assistance, were added to the disclosed bad-loan total starting with fiscal 1995, the figures were nearly double those based on the prior definition. For instance, virtually all the outstanding loans of the major banks to the seven housing loan finance companies (*jûsen*)—around ¥8 trillion—had been restructured to allow the borrowers to waive interest payments, or the banks had provided new money to pay the interest. Another large chunk of previously undisclosed bad loans—those past due for more than 3 months and restructured at any below-market interest rate—were unveiled starting with fiscal 1997. The inadequacy of bad loan accounting was underscored by the fact that for all three major banks that failed or were nationalized in 1997–8, bad loans subsequently were found to be a much greater percentage of assets than had been disclosed prior to failure, even by later, more inclusive, standards. (The evolving requirements of what banks must disclose regarding problem loans are summarized in Ueda, Chapter 3, Table 3.1.)

One result of inadequate disclosure was a lack of sufficient pressure on banks to more actively dispose of nonperfoming loans. Although it was true that the major banks started to record provisions for bad loans in the mid-1990s, it was too rarely accompanied by the sale of the underlying collateral (real estate) that would have established a cap on losses. By the summer of 1998, as economists and policy makers debated plans to restructure the banking sector with government assistance, a commonly shared goal was to accelerate the disposal of bad debts.

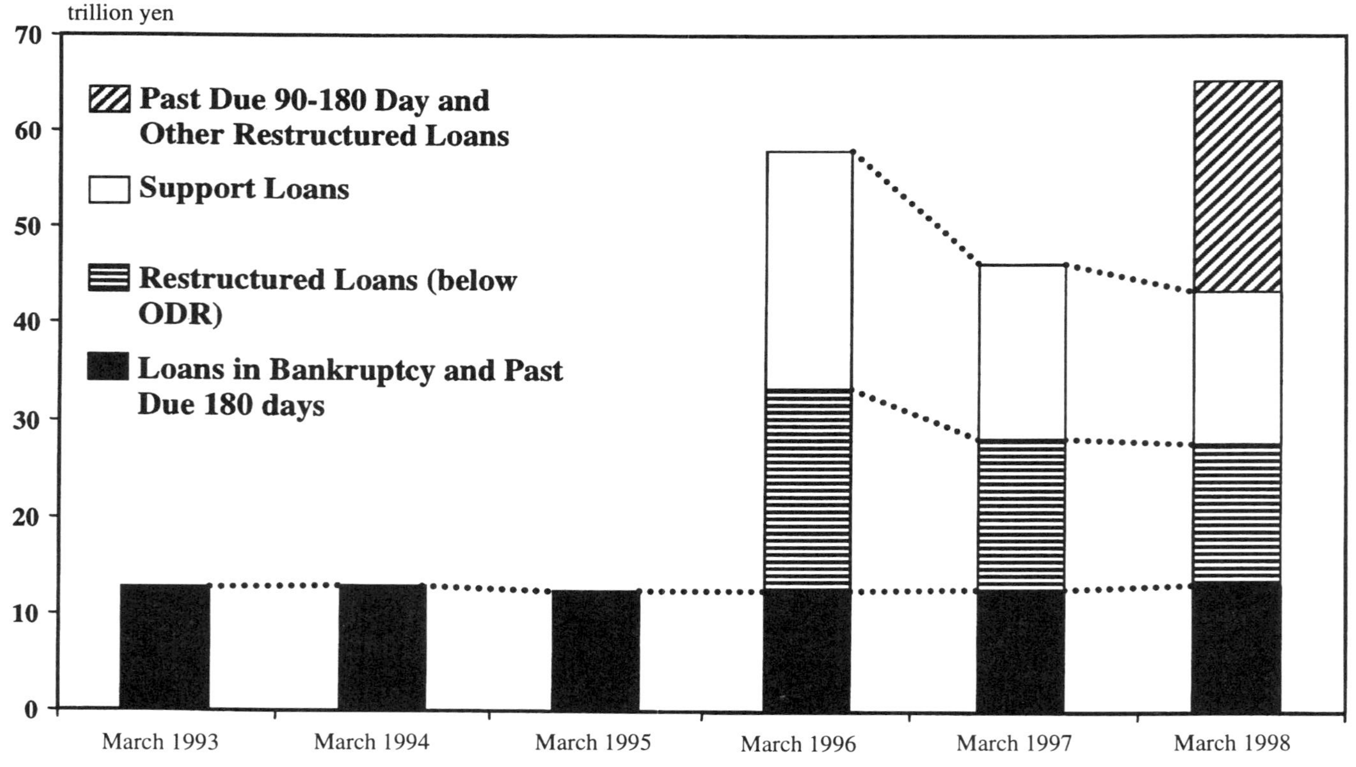

FIGURE 6.1. Balance of disclosed nonperforming loans major bank totals.

This same goal had been on top of the policy agenda much earlier. In the summer of 1992, the government under then Prime Minister Miyazawa issued statements outlining a disposal plan for the nonperforming assets of banks. Shortly thereafter, the banks formed the Cooperative Credit Purchasing Company (CCPC) to specialize in the purchase and sale of bad loans with real estate as collateral. By removing problem loans from bank balance sheets, its activities were to "strengthen the public credibility of financial institutions and improve their ability to meet loan demand." But six years later, most Japanese and foreign observers agreed that Japanese banks generally, and the CCPC in particular, had made inadequate progress toward the disposition of bad loans.

In this chapter, I review the origins, structure, and operations of the CCPC through April 1999. In many respects, the CCPC represents a microcosm of the failures of Japanese policy regarding the bad loan problem in the 1990s. In terms of the relatively modest goal of facilitating the deduction from income of bad-loan losses, it was successful. But in terms of increasing transparency about bank asset quality, reducing exposure to real estate on the part of banks, and increasing liquidity in the real estate market, the CCPC was not successful. Moreover, to the extent it allowed Japanese banks to put off a more active disposal of bad loans, it increased the eventual costs of bank recapitalization borne by Japanese taxpayers.

THE CREDIT COOPERATIVE PURCHASING COMPANY (CCPC)

In August 1992, when it was clear that Japanese banks had a huge amount of nonperforming loans in the construction and real-estate sectors that needed to be disposed of, the Japanese government proposed the formation of a company to buy real estate held by banks as collateral on bad loans. Explicitly stated in subsequent policy statements was the intention to channel some ¥1.5 trillion of a larger emergency fiscal package into purchases of land held by the new company. However, protests ensued from non-financial industries that this would represent a taxpayer bailout of the banking sector. Banks were unpopular because of the higher-than-average salaries they paid, as well as their financing of the bubble economy. In addition, the projected increase in demand for real estate contradicted other promises by the government to bring land prices down to more affordable levels. As a result, plans for a public capital infusion were dropped.

Banks went ahead with meetings on the initiative and announced the formation of a new company to buy bad debts, the Credit Cooperative Purchasing Company (CCPC) in December 1992. The operations of CCPC as planned by its founders and revealed in its "Notice of Establishment" are reviewed in Figure 6.2.

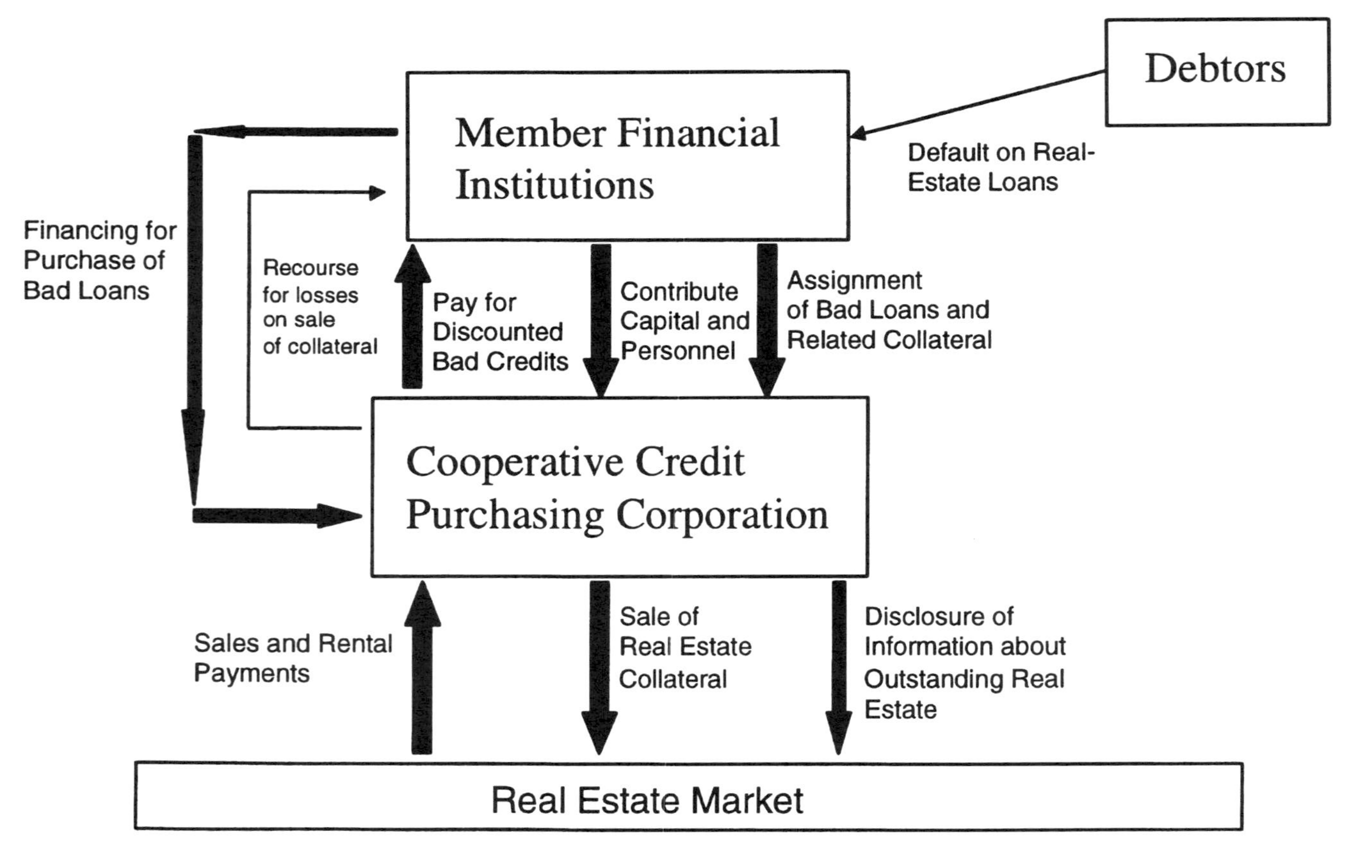

FIGURE 6.2. The structure of the CCPC (founded December 1992).

Initially it was capitalized at ¥7.9 billion from 162 financial institutions. (As of April 1998, it was 165 financial institutions that had contributed capital.) Contributing institutions also were to second employees, who numbered 35 as of April 1998.

Banks brought bad credits to the CCPC for sale. The credit had to be secured by domestic real estate, and neither the credit nor collateral could be subject to any dispute or legal proceeding that would be difficult to handle. The selling bank also had to have fulfilled any legal requirements necessary for third-party assignment of the credit and accompanying collateral. Few of the loans transferred are likely to have been in legal bankruptcy or liquidation, as the disposition of such debts would have been subject to the jurisdiction of bankruptcy court if there had been a filing and the ability to charge losses against income was already allowed in principle for debts owed by companies in bankruptcy.

If applications were not rejected due to insufficient documentation, the price of each transaction was determined by an independent appraisal committee made up of experts in the fields of law, accounting, taxation, and real estate appraisal. The relevant loan purchasing transaction was then funded by the bank that brought the original loan to the CCPC. That is, the selling bank loaned the CCPC the funds necessary to buy the loan.

According to the Notice, there were informal limitations on the amount any one institution could bring to the CCPC. Amounts to be accepted from each financial institution were to be decided flexibly in consideration of administrative capacity, and "equitable treatment for financial institutions wishing to sell credits."

Sales to the CCPC left the selling bank with a contingent liability. The Business Division of the CCPC is responsible for collecting revenue from the debtor or underlying real estate, including any ultimate disposal. However, if there proved to be a "significant" difference between ultimate collections and the initial purchase price, the CCPC has recourse to the seller of a loan. Though not stated in the Notice, it was later reported that the recourse amounted to as much as 95% of the losses incurred on disposal (NKY, 12 Jul 1996).

At the time of its establishment, the CCPC was expected to be in operation for about 10 years, with the purchases of loans backed by real estate scheduled only for the first 6 fiscal years (through March 1998). Any loans or underlying collateral not sold after 10 years presumably was to revert to the originating bank.

Taxes

Notwithstanding occasional exceptions for loans to less developed countries in difficulty and loans to major companies in industries considered of national importance, the write-off of bad debts against taxable income traditionally had not been allowed until a bankruptcy procedure began, or an excess of liabilities over assets had existed for at least two years.[1]

Nor were interest concessions on outstanding loans recognized for tax purposes. Indeed, *imputed* interest revenue was generally taxed even if not actually received. Such rigorous tax treatment of troubled loans may have reflected an attempt to control profit shifting among main banks and borrowers for the purpose of minimizing taxes.

In August 1992, both as part of a (short-lived) bailout of Nippon Housing Finance and to encourage city banks to assist the troubled Nippon Credit Bank in restructuring the debt of three of its affiliated non-bank institutions, the authorities gave banks the right not to report interest concessions as taxable income in special cases in which the borrower's survival and social interests were deemed at risk. That is, only interest actually collected, rather than imputed interest, would be included in taxable income. Another tax policy change was an expansion in September 1992 of the definition of the terms by which loans could be deemed unrecoverable for purposes of establishing special reserves.

The CCPC extended the relaxation of tax policy to the reduction of principal, as all losses on sales made to the CCPC would count as deductible expenses and hence would provide a tax shield. That is, the discount between appraised and face value was in principle accepted as an expense.

The CCPC was a harbinger of further tax policy changes and clarifications making it easier for banks to deduct loan losses for tax purposes. Starting in fiscal 1994, most major banks began to liberally deduct loan losses taken for the purpose of assisting related borrowers, in addition to taking losses on loans transferred to CCPC.

Particularly given the scarcity of public funding to address the bad loan problem in the mid-1990s, the principal carrot that Japanese authorities relied on to encourage the recognition of loan losses was modification of tax policy. The CCPC represented the centerpiece of such modifications.

Purchase Volume

Initially, sales to CCPC significantly reduced reported nonperforming loans of Japan's major banks. From the beginning of its loan-purchase operations through fiscal 1995 (that is, through 31 March 1996), over 8000 loans, with a face value of ¥12.14 trillion were sold to CCPC. Estimates are that ¥8.23 trillion of this was from major banks. (Table 6.1).

Assuming that the loans sold would otherwise have been reported as problem loans (including restructured and support loans), the amount of problem loans reported at the end of March 1996 by the 21 major city, long-term credit,

TABLE 6.1. Loans Sold to the CCPC: March 1993–March 1999 (yen amounts in billion)

Fiscal Year	Number of Loans Sold	Face Value (yen)	Appraised Value (yen)	Claimed Losses (yen)	Claimed Losses As % of Face
1992	229	681.7	452.1	229.6	33.7
1993	1,891	3,838.3	1,777.4	2,060.9	53.7
1994	3,077	4,038.1	1,591.0	2,447.1	60.6
1995	3,154	3,577.4	1,182.2	2,395.2	67.0
1996	1,425	1,444.8	41.2	1,034.6	71.6
1997	1,254	1,336.2	350.4	985.8	73.8
1998	435	348.5	37.7	310.8	89.2
Total	—	—	5801.0	9464.0	62.0

Fiscal years end in March of the following calendar year.
Source: CCPC

and trust banks was about one-fourth less than it otherwise would have been (¥25.7 trillion instead of ¥33.8 trillion).

By the time purchase operations were suspended in April 1998, usage had dropped considerably, however. The face value of loans purchased in fiscal 1996 and 1997 were only around one-third of the fiscal 1994 peak. The drop in usage was particularly apparent among the major banks. While they are estimated to have accounted for more than 70% of the cumulative loans sold to the CCPC as of April 1996, in fiscal 1996 and 1997 they accounted for only an estimated 56%. Over the course of the six fiscal years ending with March 1998 a face value of ¥14.9 trillion in loans and associated collateral was sold to CCPC.

It is likely that the slowdown in operations was because fewer loans were available for this route. Recall that only loans with real estate as collateral were accepted. Moreover, they had to have relatively uncomplicated claims, which meant the CCPC could handle bad loans only where one or a few lenders had claim to the underlying real estate collateral. In addition, loans with recalcitrant borrowers were not appropriate for the CCPC, as debtor approval of the sale of properties was required. Another factor underlying the drop off was probably the increased reliance of Japanese banks on other forms of loan sales, as discussed later.

Banks tended to wait until the very last month of a reporting period before selling loans to the CCPC. In the first half of each fiscal year, more than 70% of the loans bought by the CCPC (measured by face value) were bought in the last month, September; 66% of loans bought in the second half also occurred in the last month, March. Monthly data released by CCPC indicate that this concentration was just as pronounced in 1997 as it had been in 1993. Banks clearly had the ability to choose a quantity of loans to sell to CCPC, and the related loss on the disposition of the assets, after approximate values of other items in their income statements (such as net gain on securities sales) had been determined.

Purchase Prices, Discounted Value, and Second-Stage Reserves

The discount between the face value of the loans sold to the CCPC and the value as determined by the Price Appraisal Committee has steadily increased over time. In the second half of fiscal 1992, the appraised value of loans purchased was reported to be 66% of face, implying a loss of one-third of the face value of loans sold. By 1995, the loss was nearly two-thirds the face value; losses amounted to more than three-fourths of face value for fiscal 1996 (Table 6.1, Figure 6.3).

This increased discount is consistent with a continued decline in the value of underlying real estate during the period. If we assume that CCPC valuations reflected market prices at the time they were sold, and that properties are more likely to sell the more recently CCPC has purchased them, then the estimate of unrecognized losses at the CCPC as of 1 April 1998 is ¥1.8 trillion, or 31% of the book value of CCPC properties. Banks' off-balance sheet liabilities associated with assets sold to the CCPC—the undisclosed current value of the recourse—thus amounted to around ¥1.7 trillion. This is 95% of estimated losses; the remainder of the loss, CCPC's share, was four times CCPC's paid-in capital.

These estimates are relatively conservative. A July 1996 report based on CCPC internal data estimated ¥1.5 trillion of losses (NKY, 12 Jul 1996). This is larger than my estimate for the same period, which is based on data released to the public. In January 1997, a private research institute estimated there were losses of ¥3.1 trillion on loans purchased by CCPC as of September 1996, or 60% of book value (NKY, 14 Jan 1997). In addition to falling land prices, the institute cited excessively optimistic valuations by the Appraisal Committee at the time of transfer to CCPC, a matter discussed below. All these estimates would be greatly increased if extended to 1998 or 1999, given the continued deflation in real estate prices.

Starting in fiscal 1996, most of the major banks began to put aside reserves for expected losses from loans sold to CCPC. The Bank of Tokyo-Mitsubishi, which reports according to US GAAP, had done this on the recommendation of its accountants, and a number of other major banks followed suit (NKY, 13 Feb 1997).

Although the move towards reserving was an overdue recognition of losses at the CCPC, the amounts put aside were inadequate. As of April 1998, according to their financial statements, city banks had put aside ¥0.4 trillion, which is

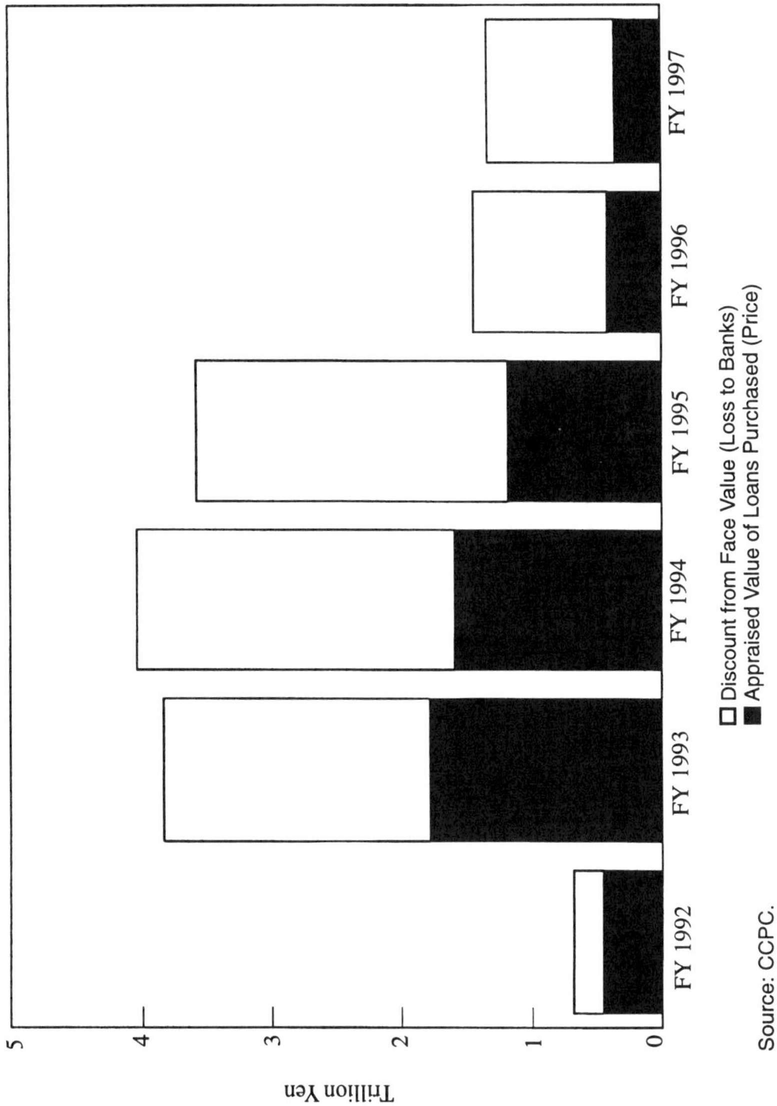

Source: CCPC.

Note: Data are for fiscal years ending March 31 of the following calendar year.

FIGURE 6.3. Loan purchases by CCPC: face and appraised values.

just 12.4% of their estimated loans to the CCPC. The long-term credit banks' reserves were even less, at 9.3%, while the trust banks (as of October 1997) had set aside 12.6%. These numbers are well below the 30% to 60% loss estimates cited above.

Sales and Income

In the first years of its existence, CCPC was virtually dormant on the sales side of its operation. Through the end of March 1994, it had sold 88 properties for ¥27.2 billion, and obtained rental fees and interest payments from the secured loans of ¥3.8 billion. Total revenue at that point was around 1.4% of the appraised value of the properties it owned.

Part of the reason sales were such a small fraction of assets in the early years was that the Ministry of Finance (MOF) and the major banks had agreed that valuations of the land would be generously high both for the purpose of providing a floor for real estate prices and to limit the tax write-off (Kasahara 1994, p 12). As early as October 1993, a former high-level Ministry of Construction official was quoted as saying that the prices of most of CCPC's land holdings would have to go to 10% of face value to attract buyers, instead of the 50% at which they were being transferred to CCPC at the time (NKS, 10 Oct 1993). The head of CCPC noted in early April 1994 that financial institutions were selling CCPC loans that were "difficult to liquidate" and that the recession had further delayed liquidation (Nikkei Weekly, 11 Apr 1994, p 12).

Table 6.2 shows that liquidation of properties picked up dramatically in later years. By the end of March 1998, cumulative revenue had increased more than thirty-fold to ¥1.2 trillion. A total of 6,847 properties had been sold for ¥1.1 trillion, representing over one-third of the 19,391 properties owned by the CCPC, but only around 19% of the appraised value of all properties purchased. More than four-fifths of the appraised value of properties remained unaccounted for. These figures improved even more dramatically in fiscal 1998, as is discussed below.

Rental income has been sparse and also indicates substantial overvaluation of properties. Subtracting proceeds from real estate sales from the CCPC's total revenue each fiscal year, and dividing this difference by the book value of the properties at the beginning of the year net of prior-period asset sales, consistently gives an upper bound for an annualized return on CCPC assets through fiscal 1997 of between 0.4% and 0.5%. This is an upper bound because net assets (the denominator) expanded every year through fiscal 1997.

As a result, even considering the historically low interest rates during much of its existence, CCPC did not have the income to pay interest at market rates to its funding banks. At the higher rates of interest of the early years of CCPC, the comparisons are even more stark. At the long-term prime rate of 4.9% in March

TABLE 6.2. Income and Collateral Disposed of by the CCPC: March 1993–March 1999 (yen amounts in billion)

Fiscal Year	Rental, Interest Income, and Other Income (yen)	Real Estate Sales		Cumulative Returns (yen)[1]	% of Cumulative Loans to CCPC[2]
		Number of Properties	Amount Received (yen)		
1992	0	0	0.0	0.0	0.0
1993	3.8	88	27.2	31.0	1.4
1994	9.4	591	131.3	171.7	4.5
1995	18.3	1,305	241.7	431.7	8.6
1996	22.7	2,294	360.0	814.4	15.0
1997	27.4	2,569	343.1	1,184.9	20.6
1998	172.0[3]	3,620	401.0	1,757.9	30.3
Total	—	10,467	1,504.3	1,757.9	30.3

Fiscal years end in March of the following calendar year.
1. Cumulative returns include rental and interest income and amounts received from sale of properties.
2. Cumulative returns as a percentage of cumulative loans made to the CCPC to finance its activities.
3. The large rise in rental interest and other categories in fiscal year 1998 is due to bulk loans sales in March 1999 by the CCPC to outside investors (NKS, 16 April 1999).

1993, total interest paid or accrued by April 1994 on the ¥452.1 billion of CCPC borrowing as of March 1993 would have amounted to around ¥22 billion, well in excess of the sum not just of rental and interest income but also of paid-in capital (¥9.3 billion).

Tax Savings

A vital advantage of utilizing the CCPC was that deducting the discount between appraised and face value from taxable income was approved by the tax authorities. This discount amounted to about ¥9.15 trillion for fiscal 1992–7, thus reducing the taxes of Japanese banks and other financial institutions by around ¥4.6 trillion. This compares to ¥2.0 trillion in taxes actually paid by the major banks during the period.

Table 6.3 shows that the major banks have dominated use of the CCPC, particularly in its early years. In 1992 and 1993, they accounted for between 74% and 95% of losses on loans sold to the CCPC. Although the percentages declined slightly in later years, in fiscal 1997, the share of the major banks were two-thirds of the total. City banks accounted for 53% of the losses on loans sold; trust banks, 6%; and long-term credit banks, 6%.

TABLE 6.3. Losses on Loans Sold to the CCPC: March 1993–March 1998 (in billion yen and percents)

Fiscal Year	Loans Sold by Major Banks A	All Loans B	Losses on A as % of B
1992	217.6	229.6	94.8
1993	1,510.8	2,059.4	73.4
1994	1,527.8	2,447.0	62.4
1995	1,010.9	2,395.1	42.2
1996	510.6	1,035.3	49.3
1997	661.4	985.8	67.1
Total	5,439.1	9,152.2	59.4

Fiscal years end in March of the following calendar year.

Major banks include 11 city banks (10 from 1995), 10 trust, and 3 long-term credit banks.

Source: CCPC, Major Bank financial statements.

OTHER LOSSES REALIZED ON BAD LOANS

Despite the initial rapid expansion in the use of the CCPC to claim losses on real-estate loans in default, there remained a large chunk of other loans seriously burdening Japanese banks. Many loans to non-banks had been "restructured" so as to charge low (often zero) interest rates, yet were not officially disclosed as problem loans until 1996. A good portion of these consisted of loans to housing finance companies (*jûsen*). These amounted to ¥4.9 trillion among the 21 major banks at the end of March 1994, compared to officially recognized bad debt of ¥13.5 trillion.

Early on, some non-bank loans ended up in the CCPC; as of October 1993, 12.4% of the loans transferred were loans originated by non-banks and sold to the CCPC through the non-banks' sponsor institutions. However, relative to their holdings of bad real estate loans, non-banks were very inactive in their use of the CCPC. This is in large part because their main banks had been required to sponsor any sales to CCPC, and to take on the full contingent liability implicit in the sale of bad loans to CCPC. Given the large number of creditors for major non-banks such as the *jûsen*, major banks often found this burden unacceptable. (This subsequently played a role in the *jûsen* crisis. For details, see Cargill, Hutchinson, and Ito 1997; Milhaupt and Miller 1997.)

In early 1994, MOF announced the framework for a new approach to deal with these loans. The new guidelines permitted creation of "Special Purpose Companies" (SPCs) that accept restructured loans in return for a specified number of shares in the new entity (Ministry of Finance 1994).

Again, a tax break was involved: the difference between the face value of the loans and the appraised market value of the shares could be deducted from income for tax purposes. The appraised value at the time of transfer was to be determined by discounting the contracted cash flow from the loans at a market interest rate. The figure was to be updated every year, and changes in the figure reported as bank income, as well as interest payments that passed through the SPC (Figure 6.4).

As with the CCPC, the SPC framework allowed Japanese banks to realize tax benefits from troubled loans more quickly than before, while at the same time giving them the ability to time the realization of these benefits according to the strength of operating earnings and gains on sales of stock-holdings.

The proposed scheme and related tax deductions took effect in fiscal 1994. There were numerous advantages to the banks in using the new scheme as opposed to a tax-equivalent write-down of principal. Clearly, they did not have to recognize the restructured loans as nonperforming. Further, since the SPC did not transform the claim on the ultimate obligor, banks could maintain the pressure on the non-banks to restructure their operations, as well as gain any upside benefits from a prospective recovery. Finally, discounting of a loan by any individual bank did not affect the priority of its claim vis-a-vis other creditors in case the non-bank failed.

Although this measure had the potential to have beneficial effects on bank tax bills of the same order of magnitude as the CCPC if it been applied to the *jûsen* problem, usage of the mechanism turned out to be quite limited. If the ¥4.9 trillion of loans to the *jûsen* had been transferred to the SPCs at 60% of face value, ¥2 trillion of losses would have been claimed for those loans alone. (MOF suggested the 60% figure in the 14 February 1994 and 28 February 1994 issues of its weekly publication, *Kinyu Zaisei Jijo*.) At a tax rate of about 50%, the 21 major banks would have saved ¥1 trillion, more than the ¥0.8 billion they paid in taxes in fiscal 1992, and more than twice the ¥0.35 trillion they paid in fiscal 1993. (Negative taxable income can be carried forward up to five years.) However, in 1994 only five major banks—including two long-term credit banks and two trust banks—used the SPC structure, reporting losses of ¥61 billion, less than 4% of the losses reported that year on sales to the CCPC. There was subsequently no reporting of loan losses on sales to SPCs.

Because long-term credit banks and trust banks were relatively more exposed in terms of restructured loans to non-banks than were city banks, the projected benefits of the measure, had it been used more widely, were asymmetrically distributed across classes of banks. Although only one-third of official nonperforming loans among major banks as of March 1994 were on the accounts of trust and long-term credit banks, 70% of the (explicit) major bank exposure to the *jûsen* was at the long-term credit and trust banks. According to an article in the Nikkei Kinyu Shimbun, the Industrial Bank of Japan was responsible for proposing the SPC guidelines, but many city banks were not as enthusiastic.

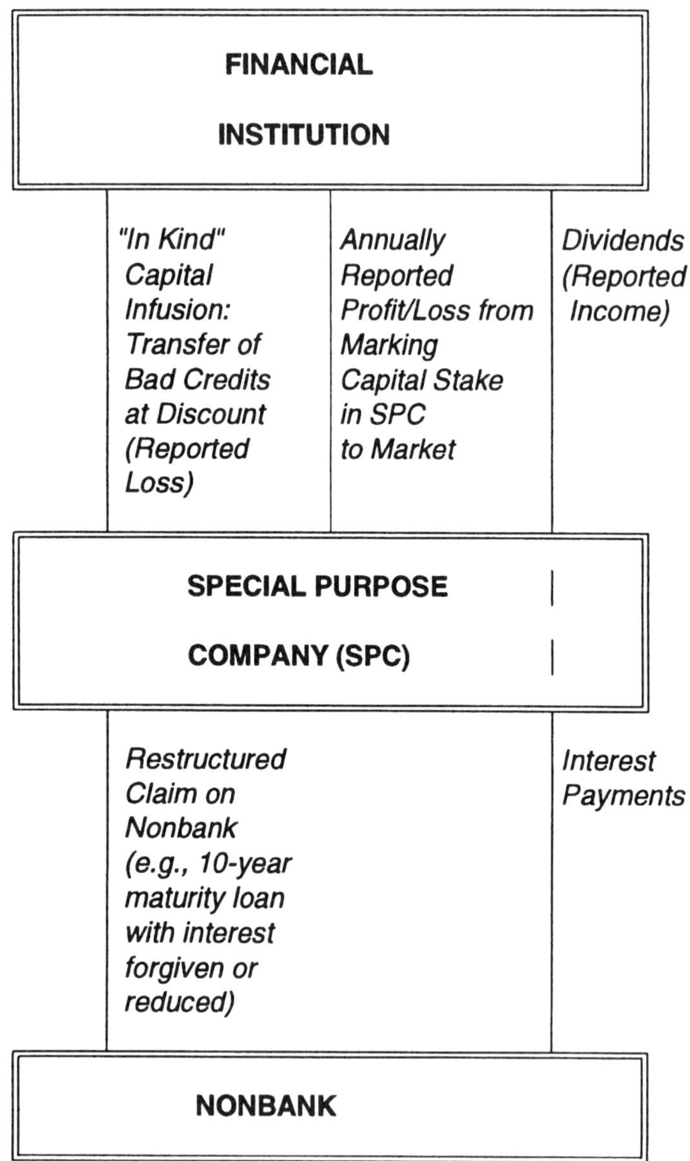

Source: Kinyu Zaisei Jijo, Feb. 14, 1994.

FIGURE 6.4. Proposed structure for transferring bad loans to SPCs.

Many banks feared that the scheme—which at least in theory allowed sales of bad loans without the consent of other creditors—would legitimize a pro-rata solution to the distribution of losses for loans to non-banks. In fact, many parties believed that the parent banks should be responsible for bearing a disproportionate, if not the entire, share of the losses in the event of default of an affiliated non-bank (Milhaupt and Miller 1997). In part for this reason, the *jûsen* problem was ultimately resolved via a separate institutional structure after negotiations and a prolonged public debate in 1995–6, as is discussed in Ito (Chapter 4) and Hiwatari (Chapter 5).The reason SPCs were not used for loans to other non-bank borrowers was probably because it became easier to claim losses for tax purposes by other means, as discussed below.

Starting in 1994, a clarified and liberalized tax policy on the part of MOF resulted in more reporting of loan losses outside the CCPC structure. The category frequently reported in financial statement footnotes was losses on loans assisting related companies. Starting in fiscal 1996, these began to greatly exceed the loan-loss expenses on sales to CCPC. Over fiscal 1992–4, stated losses on loans sold CCPC were more than four-fifths of the ¥4.4 trillion written off by the major banks for loans to domestic companies; over the next three fiscal years, 1995–7, they were less than one-third of the ¥7 trillion written off. Clearly, the status of the CCPC as the leading vehicle for obtaining a tax-free write off has diminished over time.

Increasingly, actual loan sales to third parties (without recourse) are being reported by the major banks. Often sold to foreign investors and in bulk form, loan sales such as these, which permanently remove the bad loans from a bank's balance sheets, have long been recommended by economists and bank analysts (Corrigan 1994; Atkinson 1998). Through March 1998, ¥240 billion of losses through actual loan sales had been reported on the financial statements of the major banks, more than 90% of it in the two preceding fiscal years. This still comprised less than 4% of all the other domestic loan write-offs taken during the two year period.

However, loan sales, most noticeably to foreign banks, appeared to increase greatly in 1998. In March 1999, it was announced that Sumitomo Bank, IBJ, and Sanwa Bank expected to report about ¥1.25 trillion of bad loans sold to third-party investors in fiscal 1998. Fuji Bank, Bank of Tokyo-Mitsubishi, and DKB were reported to have sold an additional ¥350 billion to foreign investors. These reported sales significantly exceeded the amounts sold to CCPC in fiscal 1998.

PROPOSALS FOR REFORM OF THE CCPC AND THE RENEWAL OF PURCHASE OPERATIONS

While continued asset deflation has made banks more reluctant to recognize the full degree of losses on transferred loans, other structural factors have also hampered the sales side of CCPC operations. First, the continued recourse CCPC has against the bank that first brought the collateral diminishes the incentive of the selling bank to approve a sale by CCPC at a loss. Second, one principle followed by the CCPC is that the debtor must agree to the sale of the property; however, banks have often had great difficulty in gaining such approval (NKY, 31 Mar 1998).

Third, the limited capacity of the bankruptcy court system has proved to be a bottleneck. In 1996 CCPC established a new rule whereby if the underlying real estate could not be sold within three years, it would automatically go to the courts for disposition at competitive auction. While CCPC had sent 300 properties to the court as of April 1998, there were only a few cases where returns had been realized, as it takes 2 to 3 years for an auction to be completed, given current court overcrowding (NKY, 31 Mar 1998).

In June 1998 in coordination with the LDP's announcement of a tentative "Total Plan for Financial Revitalization," the CCPC itself issued a detailed statement in which its plans for self-reinvention were described. Plans for the revision of purchase operations included: (1) expansion of the loans eligible for purchase, including loans without the approval of the debtor and bank-guaranteed subsidiary debt; (2) use of different procedures for evaluation of real estate, specifically taking into account a property's cash flow; and (3) raising funds from parties other than the selling bank, and without recourse for any losses incurred on liquidation of the real estate. Plans for the revision of selling operations included an active pursuit of securitization and bulk sales with related financial institutions and use of a special committee to resolve inter-creditor differences of opinion over the disposal of collateral.

Although the plans for reform were laudable, they were extremely ambitious given the resources of the CCPC. The goal of establishing bulk sale and securitization capabilities would have required many more employees than the 35 planned for by the CCPC. The elimination of recourse also would have necessitated careful analysis of the value and marketability of the properties before purchase. And collecting on loans from uncooperative borrowers would have required legal skills and investigative powers.

The role of the CCPC was part of the debate in mid-1998 regarding the future of the Long Term Credit Bank. Proponents of a "soft landing" suggested that CCPC be used to buy LTCB's bad assets after the prospective merger partner, Sumitomo Trust, said it would not absorb them (NKS, 7 Jul 1998). This raised the specter of CCPC being used to support the use of the convoy system and the merger of weak banks with strong ones.

In retrospect, the key event for decisions about banking reform in general, and the future of the CCPC in particular, was the defeat of the LDP in the upper-house elections in July 1998. The vote sent the message that the public wanted the government to clean up the banking mess, and forced the LDP to compromise with the opposition to strengthen the proposed banking reforms (Patrick 1999).

Plans to bail out LTCB, which included the use of CCPC as a government-funded mechanism to buy up the bad debts, were dropped, and the bank was nationalized instead. Plans for a special Real Estate Lien Adjustment Committee—perceived by some as a vehicle for further politicizing the process of debt workout and delaying necessary restructuring—also were dropped. In laws passed by the Diet in October 1998, a cabinet-level Financial Reconstruction Commission was formed to use the leverage it got from providing public funds to recapitalize banks to aggressively promote restructuring. A new state-authorized organization, the Resolution and Collection Corporation, was formed to purchase bad loans from banks and dispose of them.

After the LDP's election loss, the CCPC moved ahead independently of legislation and announced, in a notice on 7 August 1998, that it planned to start loan purchase operations again in September in response to public demands for a fundamental and quick solution to the bad loan problem. Its staff would use new procedures for evaluating land prices, and would continue the loan purchase operations for three years (CCPC 1998).

Three trends are apparent since the CCPC resumed loan purchase operations. First, the low level of loan purchases evident before purchases had been suspended in April 1998 has continued. The total face value of loans purchased in the six months ending with March 1999 (that is, the second half of fiscal 1998) was ¥348 billion, about one-fourth the amount purchased in fiscal 1997. (For the three months April-June 1999, purchases total only ¥2.3 billion). The loans brought to the CCPC are smaller than before, ¥800 million on average. There did appear to be more realistic pricing of loans than before—the estimated discounts from face value of new loans purchased averaged nearly 90%.

Recovery operations by the CCPC—which had never been suspended—did pick up considerably in fiscal 1998, rising to ¥573 billion on the sale of 3673 properties. The number of properties sold that year was nearly half the total for the previous six years. On a percentage basis, the ratio of recoveries to the value of property originally brought to CCPC rose from 20% to 30%. Thus, even though CCPC was not taking on a new life, efforts to mop up existing assets had renewed vigor.

Fiscal 1998 had also been the first year of operations under the new Financial Supervisory Agency, which was much more skeptical of banks' self-evaluations of problem loans, and thus maintained pressure on the banks to improve asset quality and dispose of problem loans (Choy 1999; Hoshi and Kashyap 1999). Perhaps for this reason, the remaining major banks increased their provisions for second-stage losses on loans to the CCPC by ¥433 billion. (These are losses incurred when the CCPC takes recourse against the selling bank.)

This nearly doubled their previous year-end provision totals, even though relatively few new loans had been taken to the CCPC.

THE RESOLUTION AND COLLECTION CORP (RCC)

The CCPC probably became a less popular place for the disposal of bad loans in part because of anticipation of the establishment of a new and powerful institution, the Resolution and Collection Corporation (RCC), to collect bad loans. Authorized in October 1998, the RCC began operations in April 1999. It was the product of the merger of the Housing Loan Administration Corporation (HLAC), which had been handling the disposition of failed *jûsen* loans, and the Reconstruction and Collection Bank (RCB), which had been handling the disposition of bad loans of failed banks and credit cooperatives. Unlike its predecessor institutions, it was given authority to buy bad loans from solvent financial institutions, as well as from failed ones.

The resources of the RCC dwarf those of the CCPC. The RCC started operations with about 2600 employees, mostly from failed financial institutions, as well as lawyers, bankers, and government officials from MOF and the National Tax Agency. To the extent there are economies of scale in loan collection, the RCC could realize them. It took over loan claims of about ¥4.5 trillion from the HLAC and RCB, and was scheduled to take over about ¥8 trillion in bad loans from the temporarily nationalized Long Term Credit Bank and Nippon Credit Bank by the end of September 1999.

RCC's predecessors had already had a fair degree of success in collection and recoveries. In 1998 HLAC collected ¥634 billion, well above the recoveries of the CCPC. RCC announced an intention to collect ¥710 billion in 1999 (NW, 31 May 1999).

As there was no recourse to financial institutions bringing the loans, to assure that loan pricing reflected fair value the RCC established a four-stage process for pricing the nonperforming loans it was to purchase. First, a real estate appraiser would submit a valuation of the property; then, in sequence, the RCC, a pricing committee at the Deposit Insurance Corporation, and the Financial Reconstruction Commission would review and approve the valuation. Officials expected that banks were likely to choose loans for sale to the RCC that were not considered attractive in the loan sale market (NKS, 18 Jun 1999).

The RCC was expected to be much more aggressive in extracting returns from bad loans than CCPC had been. RCC's first president, Kohei Nakabo, had formerly directed the Housing Loan Administration Corporation, and become very popular among the Japanese public for aggressively pursuing returns from the nonperforming loans of the *jûsen*. At the time the RCC was established, he stated that its priority was to prevent secondary losses to taxpayers. Nakabo's plan for the RCC at the outset was to buy the very worst of the bad loans, and to concentrate on buying loans that were either deliberately hidden or involved the criminal underworld (NKS, 1 Apr 1999).

The RCC is much better equipped for the collection of loans from uncooperative borrowers than is CCPC. By virtue of a mandate from the Deposit Insurance Corporation, it has special powers of investigation and the authority to impose penalties. To build further expertise, the RCC established a special task force, staffed by police officers, to handle the illegal disruption of loan collection, as well as former prosecutors to file criminal complaints (Yomiuri, 31 Mar 1999).

The major banks choose to take advantage of the RCC's willingness to buy problem loans beyond the traditional scope of the CCPC. By 1 August 1999, the RCC had received offers to sell nonperforming loans with a face value of ¥223 billion from 39 financial institutions, including ¥150 billion from the major banks. The bulk of the loans were believed to be especially hard to recover, with a variety of problems including underlying real-estate collateral with illegal occupants (Nikkei Weekly, 19 Jul 1999).

CONCLUSION

At the time of its formation, the CCPC greatly facilitated the realization of losses for tax purposes. In the first few years of its existence, losses on transfers to CCPC comprised the vast majority of loan losses claimed for tax purposes, and Japanese banks saved very substantial sums in taxes. To this extent, the CCPC is representative of the Japanese authorities' preference during the mid-1990s to rely on tax breaks to assist banks rather than using the more politically controversial method of direct funding.

Unfortunately, the CCPC also is representative of the authorities' failed policy of forbearance during the period (Cargill, Hutchinson, and Ito, 1997). By the end of the formal term of loan purchases, more than five years after its foundation, loan sales to the CCPC had been accompanied by relatively little of the sort of asset disposal—such as market sales of land or bulk sales to third-party investors—that would have reduced bank exposure to real estate. As a result, the CCPC did not gain for banks any of the following:

1 Liquidity.
2 More certainty about future asset valuations.
3 Less diversion of management effort. (Time was spent monitoring the management of the assets sold with recourse, and reserves have been taken by the healthier of the major banks for loans sold to the CCPC.)

4 Greater availability of risk capital. (In the United States the disposal of bad loans often was combined with measures to recapitalize once investor confidence has been restored. The recapitalization of Japanese banks was, if anything, only hindered by the establishment of the CCPC, which leading bank analysts quickly identified as a warehouse for bad loans at inadequate discounts (see, for example, Ogawa 1994).)

Many of the flaws of the CCPC were structural, and were recognized in the proposals to reform it in the summer of 1998. Recourse to the selling bank and over-optimistic valuations warehoused second-stage loan losses. Limitations on the loans it bought to those with undisputed claims, and limitations on its recoveries to those with debtor approval, greatly constrained its activities. At the same time, the staff did not consist of the lawyers and investigators necessary to go after the worst of the bad loans.

But perhaps the ultimate structural limitation was that it was the banks that owned, staffed, and managed the CCPC. Given the governments' explicit and implicit guarantee on all bank deposits, the principal-agent problems in asset salvage were even greater than those documented for US savings and loans (Kane 1991). It was in the interest of the taxpayer, but not the banks, to achieve a rapid disposal of underlying collateral at market valuations.

ACKNOWLEDGEMENTS

Many thanks to the editors of this volume, the participants and attendees of the conference, and Jeffrey Young (the discussant) for comments on the preliminary draft. Sabina Goldina provided invaluable assistance on the figures. The opinions expressed represent those of the author and not those of the Federal Reserve Bank of New York or the Federal Reserve System.

NOTE

1 For instance, when Japan Line, a terminally distressed company in the shipping industry, needed to obtain a reduction in debt outstanding prior to a merger in 1989, its main bank (the Industrial Bank of Japan) was allowed to claim deductions from income for reductions in principal after negotiations with the Ministry of Finance (Packer 1994).

REFERENCES

Atkinson, David. 1998 May 19. "Resolving Japan's Bad Debt Crisis: Implications of the Government's Total Plan." Goldman Sachs.

Cargill, Thomas, Michael Hutchinson, and Takatoshi Ito. 1997. *The Political Economy of Japanese Monetary Policy*. MIT Press.

Cargill, Thomas, Michael Hutchinson, and Takatoshi Ito. 1997. "Preventing Future Banking Crisis in Japan." Paper presented at the conference, Preventing Banking Crises and Lessons from Recent Global Bank Failures, Federal Reserve Bank of Chicago, 11–13 June.

Choy, Jon. 1999. "Japan's Banking Industry: The "Convoy" Disperses in Stormy Seas." *Japan Economic Institute Report*, 12 Mar.

Corrigan, E Gerald. 1994. "The Importance of the Creation of Liquidity in the United States." Speech published in "Bad Debt Securitization II," Goldman Sachs, Japan Research, 22 Feb.

Cooperative Credit Purchasing Company. 1992 22 Dec. "Notice of Establishment."

___. 1998 Jun 23. "The Reopening of Loan Purchase Operations Along with the Expansion of the Functions of the CCPC."

___. 1998 Aug 7. "The Reopening of Loan Purchase Operations."

Fukao, Mitsuhiro. 1998 Mar. "Japanese Financial Instability and Weaknesses in the Corporate Governance Structure." Conference paper.

Horiuchi, Akiyoshi. 1998 Jun. "Financial Fragility in Japan: A Governance Issue." University of Tokyo, discussion paper.

Hoshi, Takeo and Anil Kashyap. 1999. "The Japanese Banking Crisis: Where Did It Come From and How Will It End?" In *NBER Macroeconomics Annual 1999.*

Kane, Edward. 1990. "Principal-Agent Problems in S&L Salvage." *Journal of Finance* 45: 755–64 (July).

Kasahara, Shigehisa. 1994 Jan. "A Rescue Plan for the Post-Bubble Japanese Economy: The Establishment of the Cooperative Credit Purchasing Company." United Nations Conference on Trade and Development, discussion paper.

Mieno, Yasushi. 1993. "Economic and Financial Conditions in Japan and the Necessity of Strengthening the Financial System." Speech on 24 Mar 1993, published in *Bank of Japan Monthly*, Apr 1994 p 1–12. (In Japanese.)

Milhaupt, Curtis, and Geoffrey Miller. 1997. "Cooperation, Conflict, and Convergence in Japanese Finance: Evidence from the *Jusen* Problem." *Law and Policy in International Business*, Fall.

Ministry of Finance. 1994. "Policy Guidelines on the Problem of Non-Performing Loans Held by Financial Institutions." 8 Feb translation.

NKS = Nihon Keizai Shimbun.

NKY = Nikkei Kinyu Shimbun.

Ogawa, Alicia. 1994. "Bad Debt Write-Offs: What's Going On Here?" Salomon Brothers, Japanese Equity Research, 13 Apr.

Packer, Frank. 1995. "The Role of Long-Term Credit Banks within the Main Bank System." In Masahiko Aoki and Hugh Patrick, editors, *The Japanese Main Bank System.* Oxford University Press.

Patrick, Hugh. 1999 Feb 8. "Japan's Banking Mess: Is the Worst Over?" Processed.

Ueda, Kazuo. 1998. "Japan's Total Plan Can Work." Asian Wall Street Journal, 20 July 20.

Chapter 7

BANK LENDING IN JAPAN: ITS DETERMINANTS AND MACROECONOMIC IMPLICATIONS

Kazuo Ogawa
Osaka University

and

Shin-Ichi Kitasaka
Kobe University

November 1997 saw unprecedented failures of Japanese financial institutions as Hokkaido Takushoku Bank and Yamaichi Securities went into bankruptcy. This prompted risk-averse households to shift deposits from banks perceived to be in trouble to safer banks. The increase in the level of deposits during December, compared to the previous year, was 6.2% for postal savings, 4.7% for city banks and only 1.6% for first-tier regional banks. Second-tier regional banks had a decline in deposits of 2.1%. Many argue that quick shifts of deposits, together with a fall in share prices, make banks very cautious in making loans or, even worse, lead them to withdraw loans to maintain capital requirements. It is further asserted that a contraction of bank credit in turn chokes off the real activity of bank-dependent firms and thus aggravates the current stagnancy of the Japanese economy.

Such an assertion presumes that bank credit plays an important role in supporting real activity in the Japanese economy. It should be noted, however, that this assertion hinges crucially on the substitutability of items on the balance sheets both of banking firms and of borrowers. Suppose a negative shock hits the deposit level of one bank. When the substitutability of deposits and other items on the balance sheet of the bank is perfect, the bank can offset the deposit shock completely and its lending behavior will not be affected at all. When the substitutability between bank loans and other ways of financing is perfect for the borrowers, they can offset the reduction in bank loans by raising funds from sources. Thus, it is only when the degree of substitutability is imperfect for both banks and borrowers that shocks to a bank's balance sheet are propagated into the real economy by way of bank loans. This propagation channel is the well-known lending channel and bank credit does play a vital role in transmitting a change in monetary policy.[1]

The purpose of this chapter is to examine the role of banks in the Japanese economy. We proceed in two steps. First, we analyze the lending behavior of Japanese banks based on a set of panel data for commercial banks in the period 1976–95. Then we analyze borrowers. We focus on the effect of bank loans on fixed investment by non-financial firms, which constitutes a key component of business fluctuations.

There are four features in our study. Three are associated with the analysis of banking firms and the fourth with that of non-financial firms. First, we estimate the Euler equation of bank loans derived from the inter-temporal model of banks. There are very few studies examining the lending behavior of Japanese banks from the viewpoint of the inter-temporal maximization principle.[2]

Second, because our data set contains four different types of banks (city banks, long-term credit banks, trust banks, and regional banks), the analysis is conducted by categorizing the sample banks broadly into two types: regional banks and major banks (city banks, long-term credit banks, and trust banks). (Members of the Second Association of Regional Banks are included in regional banks.) There are noticeable differences between the two types of banks in terms of size, position in the inter-bank market, composition of liabilities, and so forth. It is interesting to see how lending behavior differs between the two types.

Third, the sample period 1976–95. These two decades include numerous important events. There was significant financial liberalization and internationalization, and large firms became less dependent on bank loans. In the midst of the bubble period from the late 1980s to early 1990s, banks enormously increased credit tied to real estate. Soaring asset prices was followed by a sharp fall, which plunged a number of banks into financial trouble. The Basle Accord, reached in June 1988, constrained banks engaging in international business by requiring that the ratio of bank capital to bank assets must be above 8%.

The virtue of our dynamic modeling is its ability to empirically examine the effects of such episodes on bank lending behavior. We focus on three episodes and examine how each affected lending behavior.

One is the role of real estate as collateral in loan contracts during the bubble period. We examine for which type of banks and borrowers real estate is important as collateral.[3] The second episode is the introduction of regulation of bank capital (the Basle Accord), which took full effect in 1993. The third episode is the extent to which the shift of deposits from one bank to another, which occurred soon after the collapse of large financial corporations in November 1997, affected bank lending behavior. This involves investigating the substitutability of deposits and the other items of balance sheet of banks.

We estimate the investment function of non-financial firms by industry and firm size. Large firms have many more ways to finance activities than do small firms. Therefore it is expected that bank loans are more important for small firms. Estimation of an investment function by firm size enables us to examine this conjecture. Further, based on the estimates of an investment function, we simulate the extent to which a change in loan supply affects investment activities by firm size to obtain the impact on the aggregate investment.

Let us preview our main findings. Real estate played a vital role as collateral for loans made by major banks to small and non-manufacturing firms. Financial liberalization enabled large non-financial corporations, especially in manufacturing, to raise funds directly from the capital market, leading banks to lend to small and non-manufacturing firms with which they had not previously had close ties. The problem of asymmetric information is severe in this situation, and it is real estate collateral that mitigated the problem by decreasing the default risk. Note that real estate had been correctly judged to be the safest form of collateral for the entire postwar period until 1990, as prices had never declined significantly, or for long, and loans were in principle only for a certain proportion (60–80%) of the appraised market value.

Second, loans by regional banks are quite sensitive to deposits, and this is especially so for loans to small and non-manufacturing firms. Third, the introduction of BIS requirements had a significant effect on the lending behavior of major banks. Fourth, expenditure on fixed investment by small firms is much more sensitive to bank loans than that of large firms. Our simulation results indicate that the contraction of loan supply in the early 1990s, as well as the collapse of large financial institutions in fall of 1997, had tremendous negative effects on the fixed investment of small and non-manufacturing firms.

Taken together, our evidence implies that shocks in the asset markets are propagated into the real activity of bank-dependent firms via bank loans, and thus the lending channel is especially important in the Japanese economy.

The next section describes the major characteristics of lending behavior of the Japanese banks from the late 1970s to the middle of the 1990s, followed by the major characteristics of investment activities of Japanese non-financial firms in the study period. We then develop a dynamic model of banking firms and derive an Euler equation of loans. The data set employed for estimation is then described. This is followed by a discussion of the econometric issues in estimating the Euler equation and testing hypotheses on bank lending behavior. We then present and interpret our results.

We present estimates of the investment function by firm size, with special focus on the role of bank loans and evaluation of the effects of changes in loan supply on investment quantitatively using a simulation technique.

LENDING BEHAVIOR FROM THE LATE 1970s TO THE 1990s

The task in this section to describe the characteristics of bank lending on the basis of our panel data set, which is collected from the Nikkei NEEDS Data

Base. The data cover fiscal 1976 to fiscal 1995 (Japanese fiscal years begin on 1 April, so we cover 1 April 1976 to 31 March 1996). The sample contains 139 banks: 7 city banks, 3 long-term credit banks, 7 trust banks and 122 regional banks. We exclude the 11 banks in the NEEDS data that engaged in mergers during the sample period.[4]

Let us first examine the growth rate of bank loans for each of the four types of banks, for the sample period. Table 7.1 summarizes the average growth rate for the whole period and the three subperiods.

The pattern is quite similar across the four types of banks. There are spikes in the growth rate in 1982, 1985, and 1990. Except for trust banks, the rates also share a common increasing trend from 1986 to 1990—the bubble period. Growth fell sharply in 1991, with a declining trend prevalent for the rest of our sample period. In particular, the rate plunged into negative territory in 1993 for long-term credit banks and in 1994 for city banks and trust banks. Contrasted with double-digit rates during the bubble period, the average growth of loans was only 1.07% for city banks, –0.02% for long-term credit banks, 0.06% for trust banks, and 3.81% for regional banks during 1991–95. Note that restrictions on loans to the real estate industry took effect in April 1990, which might have had a direct effect on bank lending.

Shift in Lending

Three aspects of bank lending during the study period deserve discussion. First, lending shifted from large firms to small firms, irrespective of the type of banks. Second, there was a shift in lending to non-manufacturing, especially tertiary industries. The third is that the share of real estate lending in total lending displays different patterns for different types of banks.

Lending shifted from large firms to small firms, irrespective of the type of banks. (Small firms are defined as unincorporated enterprises and corporations

TABLE 7.1. Growth Rate of Bank Loans, in Percents

	1977–86	1987–90	1991–95	Whole Sample Period
City banks	10.58	14.07	1.07	8.81
Long-term credit banks	10.67	12.62	–0.02	8.27
Trust banks	10.17	11.31	0.06	7.75
Regional banks	9.65	10.50	3.81	8.29
Total	9.75	10.77	3.40	8.29

Notes: The figures are average values of the sample period shown.
Source: Nikkei NEEDS Company Data Base.

with book capital of less than ¥100 million or with fewer than 300 regular employees; for wholesalers, the limits are less than ¥30 million yen or 100 employees; for retail trade, eating and drinking places and service industries, ¥10 million or 50 regular employees.) Table 7.2 presents the average of the percentage of loans to small firms for the whole period and the three subperiods.

The largest shift is observed for trust banks. The share of small firms was merely 18% in 1977 but jumped to 44% in 1988. The share of small firm loans also increased by more than 20 percentage points for city banks and long-term credit banks. Even the regional banks, the traditional lenders to small firms and whose proportion of total loans to small firms is far larger than that of any other type of banks, increased the percentage of loans going to small firms.

The second characteristic is a tilt of bank loans toward non-manufacturing, especially tertiary industries. What is common to all types of banks is an increasing trend of loans to non-manufacturing until 1990. The trend is especially noticeable for long-term banks and trust banks. The share of loans to non-manufacturing is 56.4% for long-term banks in 1977, rising to 90.5% in 1990. For trust banks the shares are 62.0% and 93.1%.

Table 7.3 gives the average growth rate of loans to major industries for the study period and each subperiod. Growth is highest for financial institutions for 1977–86 and 1987–90, followed by personal loans excluding housing, real estate, and service industries. The growth of lending to financial institutions is 30% annually for 1977–86 and 25% for 1987–90. Since financial institutions include non-deposit money corporations engaged in the provision of finance, credit and investment, so called non-banks, and they loaned out what they borrowed from banks to real estate and construction industries during the late 1980s and early 1990s, the average growth rate of loans to real estate industry in Table 7.3 probably underestimates the actual figures.

TABLE 7.2. Loans to Small Firms as a Percentage of Total Loans

	1977–86	1987–90	1991–95	Whole Sample Period
City banks	38.55	48.33	52.17	44.20
Long-term credit banks	27.97	34.57	38.40	32.11
Trust banks	31.30	43.39	43.74	37.12
Regional banks	77.97	82.26	80.49	79.54
Total	72.55	77.57	76.31	74.60

Notes: The figures are average values of the sample period shown.
Source: Nikkei NEEDS Company Data Base.

TABLE 7.3. Growth Rate of Loans by Industry, in Percents

	1977–86	1987–90	1991–95	Whole Sample Period Excluding 1991
Manufacturing	5.29	1.333	1.147	3.39
Construction	11.01	6.51	7.30	9.09
Wholesale and retail trade	12.36	3.11	0.64	7.46
Financial institutions	30.55	25.03	–0.74	21.96
Real estate	13.27	17.61	5.40	12.45
Service	14.99	13.75	5.22	12.42
Personal and others	12.21	13.43	1.85	10.08
Personal excluding housing loans	17.06	23.61	–1.45	14.28

Notes: The figures are average values of the sample period shown. The loans during 1976–90 exclude overdraft, while those during 1991–95 include overdraft. Since the overdraft figures are not available by industry we exclkude 1991 in computing the growth rate of bank loans.
Source: Nikkei NEEDS Company Data Base.

There is an interesting pattern in loans secured by real estate. Table 7.4 gives the average of loans secured by real estate for the whole period and the three subperiods.

For city banks the percentage rose noticeably from the middle of the 1980s to the early 1990s, reversing a declining trend from 1977 (18.5%) to 1985 (15.1%). The rise started in 1986 and peaked in 1991 (23.0%). Although the proportion exhibits a sharp declining trend for long-term credit banks and trust banks from the late 1970s to the late 1980s, it leveled off in the 1990s. For regional banks the proportion is rather stable in the range of 36.5% (1977) to 39.9% (1993). Casual observation suggests that the sharp run up in land prices during the bubble period might be responsible for a rise in the share of loans secured by real estate for city banks and the greater dependence of loans on real estate for long-term credit banks and trust banks.

Implication

By combining these three characteristics, it is conjectured that real estate was often used as collateral during the bubble period. This was especially so for

TABLE 7.4. Loans Secured by Real Estate as a Percentage of Total Loans

	1977–86	1987–90	1991–95	Whole Sample Period
City banks	17.33	19.79	21.94	19.06
Long-term credit banks	36.68	23.03	27.31	31.34
Trust banks	32.33	24.22	25.53	28.83
Regional banks	37.94	38.97	39.42	38.55
Total	36.59	36.91	37.58	36.92

Notes: The figures are average values of the sample period shown.
Source: Nikkei NEEDS Company Data Base.

new customers, because lenders knew little about them. Real estate was expected to rise in value, or at least not to decline by any serious amount or for any sustained period of time. Major banks pursued small and non-manufacturing firms as new clients. Similarly regional banks also sought new clients (as some of their established clients switched to major banks), in the process taking them away from credit associations and credit cooperatives. We will examine this conjecture empirically, based on an inter-temporal model of banking firms developed later in this chapter.

CHARACTERISTICS OF INVESTMENT BEHAVIOR BY JAPANESE NON-FINANCIAL FIRMS FROM THE LATE 1970s TO THE 1990s

In this section, we describe the characteristics of fixed investment of Japanese non-financial firms from the late 1970s to the 1990s. In particular, we emphasize a comparison of investment behavior across industry and firm size because the effect of bank lending on investment is expected to vary for these characteristics.

We use data in the Ministry of Finance's Quarterly Report of Financial Statements of Incorporated Business (*Hojin Kigyo Tokei Kiho*, abbreviated QRFS). QRFS reports the major items on balance sheets and profit and loss statements by firm size for manufacturing and non-manufacturing industries. The measure of firm size is capital. In original format, there are five size classes, but for the purpose of simplifying the analysis we aggregate these into three. Small firms includes those with less than ¥100 million yen in capital; medium is ¥100 million to ¥1 billion; and large is over ¥1 billion.

There is one problem with using the time series data in QRFS, that of discontinuity. This arises from a complete renewal of the firms in the sample each April, after which they are fixed for a year. It is necessary to adjust the series in a consistent manner. Fortunately the survey contains, for the main items in the balance sheet, the values for the same firms at the beginning and end of each year. This implies that we can compute the time series of flow variables consistently.

As for a series on investment, we use the increment in property, plant, and equipment, plus construction in progress. Loan data include short-term liabilities as well as long-term liabilities. Once the flow series becomes available, a perpetual inventory method can be used to construct the series of capital stock and loans outstanding.

All the data are seasonally adjusted by the Census X-12 ARIMA method. The detailed procedures for constructing the consistent data series are described in Ogawa (1999).

The distribution of gross fixed investment in 1997 nominal private aggregate fixed investment is 3.5% for small firms, 3% for medium, and 13.9% for large in manufacturing industries. For non-manufacturing, the numbers are 11% for small firms, 7.1% for medium, and 24.8% for large. The rest of fixed investment (36.7%) comes from financial institutions and small non-incorporated businesses, with the latter representing most of it.

Characteristics of the gross fixed investment rate from the middle of the 1970s to the late 90s are now in order. The gross fixed investment rate is defined as the ratio of gross fixed investment of the capital stock. Gross investment is constructed as a sum of new increments of construction in progress and physical capital stock excluding land.

We observe three peaks in the investment rate common to all three size groups. They are centered around 1980, 1984–85, and 1989–91. Each corresponds to boom periods in the Japanese economy. However, the peaks are more pronounced for small firms and for the long-lived boom (called *heisei keiki)* which started with the fourth quarter of 1986. We also observe precipitous declines in investment rates from 1991 to 1994 for all firm size groups, this being the severe downturn after the bubble burst (*heisei fukyo*).

For non-manufacturing industries, the peaks of investment rate are less conspicuous except for small firms. For them, the peak reaches as high as 6.6% in the fourth quarter of 1989. Common to all size groups is the sharp fall of the investment rate from 1991 to 1994.

Table 7.5 shows the sample average of the gross fixed investment rate over the whole period as well as the subperiods. The average gross fixed investment rate is highest in the first quarter of 1987 to the first quarter of 1991 (*heisei keiki*), and lowest in the second quarter of 1991 to the first quarter of 1998 (*heisei fukyo*) for both manufacturing and non-manufacturing. This indicates

TABLE 7.5. Fixed Investment Rate by Firm Size, in Percents

1977–86	1987–90	1991–98	1977–98	σ	Firm Size (capital in million yen)
		Manufacturing			
4.10	4.47	2.69	3.74	0.98	10–100
3.72	4.03	2.69	3.47	0.74	100–1000
3.58	3.90	3.00	3.46	0.63	1000–
		Non-manufacturing			
4.19	5.40	3.19	4.11	0.99	10–100
4.24	4.38	3.29	3.98	0.69	100–1000
4.02	4.78	3.77	4.09	0.58	1000–

σ is the standard deviation of the 1977–98 average.

Notes: The gross fixed investment rate is defined as the ratio of gross fixed investment to the capital stock. Gross investment is constructed as a sum of the new increment of construction in progress and physical capital stock excluding land.

Source: Ministry of Finance: Quarterly Report of Financial Statements of Incorporated Business (*Hojin Kigyo Tokei Kiho*), various issues.

that fixed investment was the driving force of the booms in the late 1980s, and it has been stagnant in the 1990s. Note that the volatility of fixed investment in terms of standard deviation is highest for small firms in both manufacturing and non-manufacturing.

INTER-TEMPORAL MODEL OF BANKING FIRMS

We construct an inter-temporal model of banks and derive a Euler equation to be examined empirically. Our model is general enough to test a variety of hypotheses on the lending behavior of banks such as the role of collateral, the effect of regulation on bank capital requirements, and high sensitivity of bank loans. A bank chooses the optimal level of bank loans, call money borrowing, and security holdings given its level of deposits and bank capital so that the value of the firm can be maximized.

Interest rates on time deposits were regulated until 1993. Even after that, the rate paid on deposits does not exhibit a large enough variability across banks to induce a shift of deposits. This justifies our assumption that deposits are exogenous to banks.

Bank stock prices also moved in a narrow range until 1983, which discouraged banks from issuing new equity. This justifies our assumption that bank capital is exogenous to banks.

As for borrowing from the Bank of Japan, the official discount rate is usually set lower than the call rate (inter-bank market rate), so we assume that a bank already borrows as much as possible from BOJ at the current discount rate.

The balance sheet of a bank can be simplified to three assets (reserves, loans, and securities) offset by three liabilities (deposits, call-money borrowing, and capital). In our model, call loans are recorded as a negative figure under liabilities.

The bank is subject to two constraints: a reserve requirement on deposits and a minimum requirement on the ratio of bank capital to bank assets. We assume that the banking firm holds the minimum level of required reserves since reserves bear no interest.

Costs

There are two types of costs associated with making loans. One is the agency cost arising from the asymmetry between lender and borrower, which depends in part on how long a customer has been affiliated with the bank. The other cost is expected default.

The longer the relationship, the less severe the information asymmetry. Especially during our sample period, a large increase in total loans is associated with a large increase in loans to new customers. We thus assume that agency cost is an increasing function of the net change in bank loans. (A gross increase in loans is more closely associated with agency cost than is the net increase, given that all the new loans are for new customers. However, the unavailability of gross loan data forces us to use the flow data.)

It is assumed that default cost is an increasing function of loan stock. However, default cost depends on whether the loan is secured and, if so, on the value of collateral. Land has played a fundamental role as collateral in Japan. We formally examine that role by including the change in land prices as a shift variable in the default-cost function.

Loan-related costs also depend on the size of bank. The same change of loan stock costs less for larger banks because they have the capacity to diversify loan risks. We measure the size of bank by the sum of deposits and bank capital.

To summarize, loan-related costs are an increasing function of the net flow of bank loans and loan stock and a decreasing function of the sum of deposits and bank capital.

Basic Loan Supply Function

Maximization of the value of a banking firm subject to the two constraints and the balance-sheet identity given above yields the first order condition for bank loans. According to the first order condition, the optimal level of bank loans is determined in such a manner that the marginal cost of loans is equal to the discounted marginal revenue of loans in the next period, including the savings of the cost associated with adjusting the loan in the next period and the expected default cost arising from the change in the current loan stock. Note that the marginal cost is higher for banks for which the capital requirement constraint binding.

For the purpose of estimation, we assume the following type of loan-related cost function.

$$(1)\quad C(FL_t, L_{t-1}, D_{t-1} + CAP_{t-1}) = \left[\alpha_0\left(\frac{FL_t}{D_{t-1} + CAP_{t-1}} - \mu\right)\right.$$

$$\left.+\frac{\alpha_1}{2}\left(\frac{FL_t}{D_{t-1} + CAP_{t-1}} - \mu\right)^2\right](D_{t-1} + CAP_{t-1}) + \left[\alpha_2\frac{L_{t-1}}{D_{t-1} + CAP_{t-1}}\right]$$

$$(D_{t-1} + CAP_{t-1})$$

where L_{t-1}: loan stock at the end of period $t-1$
D_{t-1}: deposit stock at the end of period $t-1$
FL_t: net flow of bank loans in period t
CAP_{t-1}: bank capital at the end of period $t-1$
$\alpha_1 > 0$, $\alpha_2 > 0$

Substituting the loan-related cost function above into the first order condition and arranging terms under the assumption that the bank forms expectations rationally, we obtain the following optimal loan supply equation. (See the full version of this paper, Ogawa and Kitasaka (1999) for derivation of optimal loan supply equation.)

$$(2)\quad \frac{FL_t}{D_{t-1} + CAP_{t-1}} - (1 + r_{t+1})^{-1}\left(\frac{FL_t}{D_{t-1} + CAP_{t-1}}\right) = \beta_0 + \beta_1(1 + r_{t+1})^{-1}$$

$$+ \beta_2(1 + r_{t+1})^{-1}(r_{L,t+1} - r_{C,t+1}) - \frac{q}{\alpha_1}\lambda_t + v_{t+1}$$

where $\beta_0 = \mu - \frac{\alpha_0}{\alpha_1}$

$$\beta_1 = \frac{\alpha_0 - \alpha_2}{\alpha_1} - \mu$$

$$\beta_2 = \frac{1}{\alpha_1}$$

r_{t+1}: one-period required rate of return in period t
$r_{L,\,t+1}$: interest rate on bank loans in period $t + 1$
$r_{C,\,t+1}$: call rate in period $t + 1$
λ_t: non-negative Lagrangean multiplier associated with the requirment on bank capital
q: minimum required ratio of bank capital to loans
v_{t+1}: forecast error

Equation 2 is the basic equation to be estimated in the subsequent sections. The ratio of net lending to bank size is a function of interest differentials between the loan interest rate and the call rate, the required rate of return, the non-negative Lagrangean multiplier, and the future lead variables of the ratio of net lending to bank size.

It should be noted that the forecast error v_{t+1} is uncorrelated with any variables contained in the bank's information set in period t under rational expectation assumptions. This property proves to be very useful in conducting a test of some hypotheses on the bank behavior.

PROCEDURES FOR ESTIMATION AND TESTING HYPOTHESES OF BANK LENDING BEHAVIOR

To begin, we modify equation 2 in order to test several hypotheses on bank lending behavior. Then we discuss econometric issues in estimating the Euler equation, followed by a description of the data set.

Formulation of Hypotheses

Let us first state the stripped-down version of the loan supply equation where the regulation of bank capital requirement is not binding. Then the loan supply equation is written without the term of the Lagrangean multiplier in equation 2.

The proportion of loans secured by real estate rose in the bubble period for city banks. For the other types of banks, its declining trend ceased in the same period. These observation suggest that land price might affect the loan supply schedule of the banks. This idea can be incorporated into the model by formulating the rate of change in land prices as a shift variable of the default cost function. Specifically, the parameter α_2 in the loan-related cost function can be expressed as a linear function of the rate of change in land prices[5].

An increase in land prices leads to a rise in collateral value and hence reduces the expected cost of default. In other words the coefficient of the rate of change in land prices is expected to be negative.

Liquidity Constraints

It is a well-known procedure to add extra terms such as cash flow or some kind of proxy for internal funds to an investment function to test the existence of liquidity constraints on non-financial firms. The same procedure is applicable in our case to test whether the bank is constrained in the capital markets.

Suppose a negative shock hits the bank's deposits and a large amount of deposits is withdrawn unexpectedly. When the bank is not constrained, it can offset the shock to deposits completely by borrowing in the call market, or issuing CDs, even if it does not hold securities to cushion the negative shock. Thus its lending behavior will be unaffected by shocks.

When the bank is constrained in the capital market and does not hold enough liquid assets, then its lending volume is sensitive to shocks and the original shock to the balance sheet will be transmitted to the real economy unless the borrowers have perfect substitutes for bank loans.

In the framework of the inter-temporal model developed above, it is easy to test rigorously whether the bank is constrained. Because the forecast error in equation 2 is uncorrelated with any elements in the bank's information set in period t, lending behavior by unconstrained banks is not affected at all by them even if they are added to the explanatory variables. One natural candidate will be the growth rate of deposits.[6]

Augmented Loan Supply Function

When we incorporate the two hypotheses on lending behavior—the collateral role of land in loan contracts and any imperfection of capital markets facing the banks—the basic loan supply (equation 2) is augmented as follows.

$$(3)\quad \frac{FL_t}{D_{t-1}+CAP_{t-1}} - (1+r_{t+1})^{-1}\left(\frac{FL_t}{D_{t-1}+CAP_{t-1}}\right) = \beta_0 + \beta_1(1+r_{t+1})^{-1}$$

$$+\, \beta_2(1+r_{t+1})^{-1}(r_{L,\,t+1} - r_{C,\,t+1}) + \beta_3(1+r_{t+1})^{-1}\frac{p_t^L}{p_{t-1}^L} + \beta_4\frac{\Delta D_t}{D_{t-1}} + v_{t+1}$$

Note that the coefficient of land price change b_3 is positive since land price appreciation reduces the parameter of the default cost function, and hence increases the loan supply.

Identification Problem

Now we briefly discuss the identification problem. We term equation 3 the loan supply equation, but some may argue that land prices are a proxy of future economic activity and appear in the demand equation of loans. Suppose that the loan demand equation is specified as a function of the loan rate, the rate of change in land prices, and an activity level such as GDP or sales. Then it is easy to verify that both the loan supply equation (3) and the loan demand equation are over-identified. One of the key conditions for identification is that access to the call market is limited to financial institutions, which implies that the call rate does not appear in the loan demand equation.

Growth in Deposits

Before proceeding to the formal analysis, let us have a brief look at the growth rate of deposits. Data are in Table 7.6.

When we examine the growth rate of deposits, there are spikes in 1982, 1985 and 1990, which are also found in the growth rate of loans. The growth rate of deposits fell sharply in 1991 and the averaged rate of deposit growth during 1991–95 is negative for all types of banks except regional banks. A similar trend is also observed for the growth rate of loans.

Because the level of deposits is mainly determined by the non-financial sector, and banks take it as given, it seems that the supply of bank loans is sensitive to the supply of deposits. In fact, the simple correlation coefficient between the growth rate of loans and that of deposits over the whole sample period is 0.8336 for city banks, 0.6907 for long-term credit banks, 0.5921 for trust banks, and 0.6836 for regional banks. Further investigation into the relationship between bank loans and deposits is made in the next section.

TABLE 7.6. Growth Rate of Deposits, in Percents

	1977–86	1987–90	1991–95	Whole Sample Period
City banks	11.46	16.22	–3.12	8.62
Long-term credit banks	14.93	16.34	–5.85	9.76
Trust banks	16.32	20.32	–11.18	9.92
Regional banks	9.96	11.13	3.02	8.38
Total	10.46	11.96	1.80	8.50

Notes: The figures are average values of the sample period shown.
Source: Nikkei NEEDS Company Data Base.

Regulation of Bank Capital Levels

The efficacy of regulations on the level of bank capital is formally tested by adding the Lagrangean multiplier in Equation 3. One caveat is that in general the Lagrangean multiplier per se is not observable, so some proxy of the extent to which the regulation is binding should be employed instead. It is quite difficult to choose the relevant measure for this purpose. We decide to use the realized ratio of bank capital to total assets. Whether the regulation is binding or not can be seen simply by testing the hypothesis that the coefficient of the ratio of bank capital to total assets is zero.

Honda (1997) also investigates the implications of the Basle Accord using panel data of banks as well as quarterly aggregate data. Instead of estimating the structural equation, he estimates the reduced-form equation of bank loans. He finds that the introduction of the Basle Accord had significant effects on bank credit. Moreover, it is found that the reaction of banks subject to the international standard is significantly different than those subject to the lower domestic standard.

Ito and Sasaki (1998) also examine how the Basle Accord influenced major Japanese banks' lending behavior between 1990 and 1993. They find that the effect of the risk-based capital (RBC) ratio on lending for city banks is positive and significant, but not different from zero for trust or regional banks. They conclude that the risk-based capital requirement was a serious hurdle only for internationally active banks.

Estimation Method

The loan supply equations are estimated by the generalized method of moments (GMM) technique. We eliminate firm-specific effects by first differencing equations. Under the assumption of rational expectations, candidates for instruments in the first-differenced form are the variables included in the information set in period $t - 1$. Our basic list of instruments includes the constant term, the twice-lagged first-differenced LHS variable, $\Delta(1 + r_{t+1})^{-1}$, $\Delta(1+ r_{t+1})^{-1}(r_{L,t+1} - r_{C,t+1})$, and thrice-lagged $\Delta(1 + r_{t+1})^{-1}(r_{L,t+1} - r_{C,t+1})$. The twice-lagged first-differenced GDP growth rate is also included as an instrument to account for loan demand. The twice- and thrice-lagged variables of p_t^L/p_{t-1}^L are added as instruments to estimate the loan supply equation with land prices as the explanatory variable. On the other hand, the twice- and thrice-lagged variables of $\Delta D_t/D_t$ are added as instruments to estimate the loan supply equation with the growth rate of deposit as the explanatory variable.

Data Set Description

The loan supply equations are estimated on the basis of data from Nikkei NEEDS. As described earlier, there 139 banks, including 17 major banks and 122 regional banks. It should be noted that the regional banks are quite different from major banks in terms of size, loan customers, position in the interbank market and so forth.

Table 7.7 compares balance sheet data for major banks and regional banks. The sample mean of total assets for major banks is ¥16.1 trillion, which is 12.5 times larger than the ¥1.3 trillion for regional banks. The amount of call loans is larger than that of call money borrowing for regional banks, but the opposite is true for major banks. This implies that in general the regional banks supply

TABLE 7.7. Comparison of Balance Sheets of Major and Regional Banks

Regional Banks	Major Banks	
	Balance sheet items in billion yen	
1,285	16,092	Total assets
45.0	366.0	Call loans
20.3	951.9	Call money borrowing
	Balance sheet items as a percentage of total assets	
66.4	81.8	Loans
16.0	17.8	Securities
	Balance sheet items as a percentage of total liabilities	
56.5	30.2	Time Deposits
0.8	2.9	Certificates of Deposit (CDs)

Entries are sample means for the 1976–95 based on our panel data set (see discussion in the text).
Source: Nikkei NEEDS data base.

funds to the call market, while major banks raise funds there. Over 50% of total liabilities are time deposits for regional banks, but only 30% for major banks. However the proportion of certificate of deposits (CD) in total liabilities is higher for major banks (2.88%) than for regional banks (0.83%). To sum up the comparison, it is desirable to conduct the empirical analysis separately for major banks and regional banks.

We disaggregate loans in two ways. First, loans are divided into those to small firms and those to large firms. Banks have increasingly put more weight on making loans to small firms that are relatively new customers. Therefore we conjecture that the degree of asymmetry in information between lenders and borrowers will be more severe for small firms, which might be reflected in the lending behavior of banks.

We also divide loans into those to manufacturing industries and those to non-manufacturing industries. The proportion of loans to non-manufacturing exhibited an increasing trend over the 1980s, especially during the bubble period. The growth pattern of non-manufacturing is quite different from that of manufacturing. Hence the tilt of bank loans toward non-manufacturing might reflect changes in the industrial structure of the Japanese economy. Estimating loan supply equations separately for manufacturing and non-manufacturing controls for these demand-side conditions of loans.

Description of the variables used for estimation is now in order.

The loan and deposits variables are taken from the balance sheets of banks. The deposits variable we employ is core deposits excluding the CDs. CDs are excluded because banks can influence their interest rate and terms and, in testing the imperfection of capital markets facing banks, we need the deposit variable exogenous to banks.

The size of a bank is defined as the sum of its deposits, bank debentures, and bank capital. The flow of loans and deposits are simply calculated as the current end-of-fiscal-year stock minus the previous year. The interest rate on loans is computed as the interest receipts on loans and discounts divided by the end-of-fiscal-year loan stock in the previous year.

The required rate of return is the average over the fiscal year of yields on listed 10-year government bonds. The collateralized overnight call rate is averaged over the year to provide the call rate. All banks are assumed to face the same required rate of return and call rate.

It is assumed that banks face different land prices, depending on the location of their head offices. The land price index of the six largest cities is used when the headquarters is in Tokyo, Kanagawa, Saitama, Chiba, Aichi, Osaka, Kyoto, Hyogo, Nara, or Wakayama prefectures. (These cover the metropolitan areas where land prices soared in the bubble period.) For the other locations, we use the land price index of other cities. The indexes are from Japan Research Institute of Real Estate.

ESTIMATION RESULTS AND INTERPRETATION

Total Loans

The basic loan supply equation, without any consideration for land price, deposit growth, and bank capital regulation, is estimated separately for major banks and regional banks with the ratio of total loans to bank size as a dependent variable. The estimation is conducted for the whole sample period as well as the three subperiods: 1981–86, 1987–90 (the bubble), and 1991–94 (since the bubble burst). By dividing the whole sample period into three, it is expected that we may capture the different responses of bank lending to the changes in economic conditions. (The original sample period covers 1976–95. However, the first five years are used exclusively as instruments for 1981, while the last year is used as a lead variable in the 1994 regression.)

The estimation results of the basic loan supply equation are not satisfactory on the whole. For major banks, as well as regional banks, the coefficients of the interest rate differential are significantly positive for most of the cases, but the J-statistics indicate that over-identifying restrictions are rejected at the standard level for all cases except the 1991–95 regression for major banks. This suggests that the interest rate differential alone cannot adequately explain the growth rate of loans and that the basic model is misspecified.

Tables 7.8 and 7.9 show the estimation results of equation 3.

We first examine the estimation results for major banks, which are shown in Table 7.8. When loan supply is estimated over the whole sample period, the interest rate differential and the growth rate of deposits have positive and significant coefficients. (The estimation results over the whole sample period are not shown here. See Ogawa and Kitasaka (1999), for detailed tables of estima-

TABLE 7.8. Estimation of Equation 3, Total Loan Supply by Major Banks

	Reciprocal of Gross Discount Rate	Interest Differential (bank loan - call rate)	Change in Land Price	Growth Rate of Deposits	J-statistics p-value	Number of Observations
1981–86	−4.3535**	3.6523***	0.9381***	0.3306***	9.8755	102
	(−2.53)	(4.82)	(3.75)	(6.11)	0.130	
1987–90	4.4940	−12.8865**	1.2410***	0.4106***	4.2212	68
	(0.82)	(−2.09)	(3.47)	(2.97)	0.647	
1991–94	−3.7212**	6.8685***	−0.1128	0.2030**	7.7422	68
	(−2.43)	(2.70)	(−1.00)	(2.38)	0.258	

Notes: Significance levels: ***1% **5% *10%
t-values are in parentheses.

TABLE 7.9. Estimation of Equation 3, Total Loan Supply by Regional Banks

	Reciprocal of Gross Discount Rate	Interest Differential (bank loan - call rate)	Change in Land Price	Growth Rate of Deposits	J-statistics p-value	Number of Observations
1981–86	2.5176***	−1.9024***	−1.2432***	1.6914***	2.4046	732
	(3.31)	(−3.73)	(−4.90)	(6.73)	0.879	
1987–90	−7.9713***	3.7159*	0.4192***	0.4169***	1.7880	488
	(−3.05)	(1.77)	(6.67)	(3.70)	0.938	
1991–94	−3.6398***	5.1065***	0.1087**	0.4199***	12.0190	488
	(−6.34)	(5.85)	(2.56)	(5.43)	0.062	

Notes: See the notes in Table 7.8.

tion results.) The over-identifying restrictions are satisfied for the case where both the rate of change in land prices and the growth rate of deposits are included as explanatory variables. Surprisingly, the rate of change in land price has the wrong sign and is significant. However, once the sample period is divided into three, a different story emerges. For 1981–86 all the explanatory variables, including the rate of change in land price, are significant and the over-identifying restrictions are not rejected. For 1987–90 both the rate of change in land prices and the growth rate of deposits have positive effects on loan supply and are significant. For 1991–94 the rate of change in land price loses its significance, but the interest differential, as well as the growth rate of deposits, maintain their significance. The effect of the growth rate of deposits is little affected if bank debentures are added to the deposit variable.

To sum up the results, the rate of change in land prices is a significant variable during the 1980s. Moreover the coefficient of land price change during 1987–90 is 32% larger than in 1981–86 for the case where all the regressors are employed. The coefficient of the growth rate of deposits is positive and significant irrespective of the sample period. It indicates that the major banks faced an imperfect capital market, although the degree of imperfection was somewhat alleviated during 1991–94. The interest rate differential—which is the fundamental variable to measure the profitability of lending activities—is significant except for the bubble period. Given its negative sign, we can infer that the lending behavior of city banks during the bubble was somewhat different than in the other periods.

Results for regional banks are in Table 7.9. When the loan supply equation is estimated over the whole sample period, either the growth rate of deposits or the interest differential is significant, but the over-identifying restrictions are decisively rejected. Turning to the estimation results for the three subperiods, the growth rate of deposits exerts a positive and significant effect on loan supply during 1981–86. Moreover, the over-identifying restrictions are not rejected when all the regressors are taken together. For 1987–90 and 1991–94, all the explanatory variables gain statistical significance and the over-identifying restrictions are not rejected. Note that the growth rate of deposits remains significant irrespective of the sample period chosen. Furthermore, the coefficient estimates of the growth rate of deposits for regional banks are larger than those for major banks for most of the cases. This suggests that regional banks are more vulnerable to shocks to deposits and hence their lending behavior is affected much more by such shocks. In other words, regional banks are constrained in the capital market much more severely than major banks.

The coefficient estimates of the rate of change in land prices is larger for major banks. The shift of bank loans to small and non-manufacturing firms is more noticeable for major banks than for regional banks. This implies that major banks are likely to make loans to relatively new customers about which they know little, so collateral plays a more important role. This can explain why the loans by major banks are more responsive to land prices. We scrutinize this conjecture by estimating the Euler equation separately for loans by firm size and by industries.

Loans by Firm Size

We estimate the loan supply equation (3) for loans to small firms and to large firms jointly.

Table 7.10 shows the estimation results for major banks. Although the rate of change in land prices displays the wrong sign and the over-identifying restrictions are rejected for all cases over the whole sample period, we can detect an interesting pattern of lending behavior once the sample period is split into three. This suggests that the lending behavior of major banks is adaptable and that estimation of the Euler equation without proper consideration for the sample period might lead to misinterpretation.

For 1981–86 the interest differential has significantly positive effects on both small-firm and large-firm loans. Besides the interest differential, the rate of change in land prices and the growth rate of deposits are positive and significant for loans to large firms. Moreover the over-identifying restrictions are not rejected at the 5% level when all the regressors are taken into consideration.

For 1987–90 the growth rate of deposits is positive and significant for both types of loans, but the rate of change in land prices remains significant only for loans to small firms when all the regressors are included.

For 1991–94 both the interest differential and the growth rate of deposits have significantly positive effect on the loans to large firms, but we cannot detect any significant explanatory variables for loans to small firms. Note that in the bubble period the rate of change in land prices has significantly positive

TABLE 7.10. Estimation of Equation 3, Loans by Firm Size, Major Banks

Firm Size	Reciprocal of Gross Discount Rate	Interest Differential (bank loan - call rate)	Change in Land Price	Growth Rate of Deposits	J-statistics p-value	Number of Observations
			1981–86			
Small	−2.1958**	1.0036***	0.2259	−0.0476		
	(−2.11)	(3.29)	(1.49)	(−1.55)	22.5830	
						102
Large	−0.3198	2.2340***	0.5156***	0.3839***	0.067	
	(−0.20)	(3.40)	(2.72)	(8.41)		
			1987–90			
Small	9.2806**	−12.6014***	0.8338***	0.1631*		
	(2.51)	(−3.04)	(3.06)	(1.81)	11.9630	
						68
Large	−4.0512	−0.2732	0.1878	0.2944***	0.609	
	(−0.89)	(−0.05)	(0.66)	(2.82)		
			1991–94			
Small	−0.1527	1.6229	0.0401	0.0393		
	(−0.11)	(0.79)	(0.47)	(0.58)	13.6869	
						68
Large	−5.0037***	6.8697***	−0.1995**	0.1445*	0.473	
	(−3.27)	(3.16)	(−2.00)	(1.73)		

Notes: See the notes in Table 7.8.

effect on loans to small firms, but not to large firms. This supports our conjecture that real estate is more potent as collateral in lowering the cost associated with asymmetric information for loans to borrowers with a shorter customer relationship. Our evidence here is consistent with the findings by Berger and Udell (1995) for the US case. They find that borrowers with longer banking relationships are less likely to pledge collateral.

Table 7.11 shows the estimation results of loan supply equations by firm size for regional banks. Over the whole sample period the growth rate of deposits is the only significant variable in the loan supply equation to small firms and none of the explanatory variables can explain loans to large firms satisfactorily. Moreover, the over-identifying restrictions are decisively rejected. Looking at the subperiods, the growth rate of deposits always has positive and significant effects on loans to small firms but is not significant for large firms. The rate of change in land prices and the interest differential also exert significantly positive effects on loans to small firms during 1987–90.

TABLE 7.11. Estimation of Equation 3, Loans by Firm Size, Regional Banks

Firm Size	Reciprocal of Gross Discount Rate	Interest Differential (bank loan - call rate)	Change in Land Price	Growth Rate of Deposits	J-statistics p-value	Number of Observations
			1981–86			
Small	1.2466	−1.1539	−0.9963***	1.3886***		
	(1.21)	(−1.63)	(−2.81)	(4.03)	20.6269	
						732
Large	0.7843	−0.3775	−0.1559	0.1049	0.112	
	(0.94)	(−0.65)	(−0.53)	(0.37)		
			1987–90			
Small	−19.5984***	13.4277***	0.5107**	0.5838**		
	(−3.04)	(2.57)	(2.56)	(2.05)	15.6614	
						488
Large	11.4605*	−9.4875*	−0.1127	−0.1387	0.609	
	(1.78)	(−1.82)	(−0.59)	(−0.50)		
			1991–94			
Small	−1.1151	2.1147	−0.0996	0.7900***		
	(−0.49)	(0.73)	(−1.20)	(3.52)	22.6460	
						488
Large	−2.5250	2.9520	0.2061***	−0.3738*	0.066	
	(−1.11)	(1.04)	(2.73)	(−1.76)		

Notes: See the notes in Table 7.8.

To sum up, we see that it is the growth rate of deposits that matters for loans to small firms by regional banks. Moreover, in the bubble period land also played a collateral role in lending to small firms and mitigated the problem of asymmetric information between lenders and borrowers.

Loans by Industries

In estimating the loan supply equation by industries, we divide total loans into those to manufacturing and those to non-manufacturing. The virtue of estimating the equation separately for different industries is to control demand-side conditions. It is also expected that we will see how the banks supplied loans in response to changes in industrial structure.

The estimation results of the loan supply Equation 3 are shown in Tables 7.12 and 7.13.

TABLE 7.12. Estimation of Equation 3, Loans by Industry, Major Banks

Industry	Reciprocal of Gross Discount Rate	Interest Differential (bank loan - call rate)	Change in Land Price	Growth Rate of Deposits	J-statistics p-value	Number of Observations
			1981–86			
M	–0.6441	–0.1424	0.0582	0.0025		
	(–1.39)	(–0.80)	(0.76)	(0.15)	28.1423	
						102
NM	–1.6035	2.4055***	0.5887**	0.3716***	0.014	
	(–0.97)	(4.09)	(2.42)	(7.56)		
			1987–90			
M	3.7590***	–3.1744***	–0.0376	–0.0168		
	(4.84)	(–3.85)	(–0.66)	(–0.72)	18.6217	
						68
NM	–2.6388	–8.1926*	1.5411***	0.3152***	0.180	
	(–0.68)	(–1.76)	(4.84)	(2.89)		
			1991–94			
M	0.2115	–0.1965	0.1530***	–0.2599***		
	(0.31)	(–0.22)	(3.48)	(–7.02)	17.6354	
						68
NM	–6.1916***	10.9805***	–0.3182***	0.3942***	0.224	
	(–4.01)	(4.72)	(–3.40)	(4.54)		

Notes: M is manufacturing industries; NM is non-manufacturing industries.
Significance levels: ***1% **5% *10%
t-values are in parentheses.

Table 7.12 shows the results for major banks. When the loan supply equation is estimated over the whole period, some coefficients of the interest differential and the growth rate of deposits are significantly positive, although the over-identifying restrictions are rejected in all cases. This again suggests the need to estimate the loan supply equation by subperiods. For loans to non-manufacturing, the growth rate of deposits always has positive and significant effects on loan supply. Furthermore, the rate of change in land prices gains significance in 1981–86 and 1987–90. Note that the coefficient of land price changes in 1987–90 is 2.6 times larger than in 1981–86 for the case where all the explanatory variables are taken into consideration. The interest differential is also positive and significant for 1981–86 and 1991–94. In contrast, we cannot detect meaningful explanatory variables for loan supply to manufacturing except for land price changes in 1991–94.

TABLE 7.13. Estimation of Equation 3, Loans by Industry, Regional Banks

Industry	Reciprocal of Gross Discount Rate	Interest Differential (bank loan - call rate)	Change in Land Price	Growth Rate of Deposits	J-statistics p-value	Number of Observations
			1981–86			
M	1.4890***	–1.3775***	–0.6701***	0.7407***		
	(4.19)	(–5.49)	(–5.57)	(5.92)	35.5325	
						732
NM	0.7456*	–0.4058	–0.5774***	0.8739***	0.001	
	(1.77)	(–1.44)	(–4.00)	(6.18)		
			1987–90			
M	0.0971	–0.0631	–0.0479***	–0.0246		
	(0.14)	(–0.11)	(–2.65)	(–0.74)	21.6257	
						488
NM	–7.9932***	3.7197**	0.4797***	0.4508***	0.087	
	(–3.46)	(1.99)	(8.07)	(4.71)		
			1991–94			
M	–1.6332***	1.9790***	0.1689***	–0.3727***		
	(–4.49)	(3.58)	(6.42)	(–6.96)	30.0948	
						488
NM	–1.7380***	2.9376***	–0.0426	0.7474***	0.007	
	(–2.94)	(3.28)	(–1.03)	(9.21)		

Notes: See the notes in Table 7.12.

Table 7.13 shows the estimation for regional banks. When estimated over the whole period, some of the coefficients satisfy the sign conditions the theory requires, but the rejection of over-identifying restrictions indicate that the model is misspecified. When we estimate the loan supply equation for the subperiods, we obtain much more reasonable coefficient estimates. For loans to non-manufacturing, we obtain positive and significant coefficients on both the growth rate of deposits and the interest differential irrespective of the sample period. (For 1981–86 the coefficients of both the growth rate of deposits and the interest differential are significantly positive when the land price change variable is dropped from the equation.) In addition, the rate of change in land prices has a positive and significant effect in 1987–90. For loans to manufacturing, the coefficients of the growth rate of deposits are positive and significant for 1981–86, and the interest differential and land price changes have positive and significant effects on loan supply for 1991–94. However, for 1987–90 we cannot obtain the coefficient estimators that are statistically significant or satisfy the sign conditions the theory requires.

What is common to lending to non-manufacturing industries by major banks and regional banks is the sensitivity of loans to deposits irrespective of the subperiod and the positive response of loans to land-price appreciation during the bubble period. Note that the response of loans to land-price changes by major banks is much larger than that by regional banks. This is consistent with our earlier observation that the shift of loans toward non-manufacturing is much more rapid for major banks than for regional banks and hence major banks are more susceptible to the problem of asymmetric information.

Effect of Basle Accord on Lending Behavior

Lastly we examine the introduction of regulation on bank capital that took full effect in March 1993 (The Basle Accord). According to the Accord, banks engaging in international business must maintain a ratio of bank capital to risk-weighted assets above 8%. When this condition is binding, the positive Lagrangean multiplier appears as an additional factor affecting the growth rate of loans.

To test whether the Basle Accord affects the lending behavior of banks, we re-estimate the Euler equation by adding the variable closely correlated with the level of the Lagrangean multiplier since the multiplier per se is not observable. Our candidate for this proxy is the observed ratio of bank capital to bank assets. The ratio, using the BIS standard, is available for the banks that have international operations since 1989, when the requirements became partially effective. Therefore, we re-estimate the loan supply equation with the bank capital ratio as an additional explanatory variable for the period of 1992–94. Now the bank sample is reduced from 139 to 82. (The dropped banks are regional banks not subject to the Accord as well as Hyogo Bank, which is excluded because data are not available.) The estimation of the loan supply equation is conducted not only for total loans but also for loans by firm size and industries. The results are reported in Table 7.14.

The ratio of bank capital to bank assets has positive and significant effects on the lending behavior of major banks, but not that of regional banks. That is, when the ratio of bank capital to bank assets is lowered for some reason, the major banks will decrease lending. Our result that the capital requirement was binding in terms of lending behavior only for major banks with active international business is consistent with the findings of Ito and Sasaki (1998).

When loans by major banks are further broken down into those to small firms and large firms, the capital ratio exerts significantly positive effects on loans to large firms, but not to small firms. We also find that the ratio has larger positive effects on loans to non-manufacturing industries. When the ratio falls,

TABLE 7.14. Effects of the Basle Accord on Bank Lending Activity: 1992–94

	Reciprocal of Gross Discount Rate	Interest Differential (bank loan - call rate)	Change in Land Price	Growth Rate of Deposits	Bank Capital - Bank Assets Ratio	J-statistics p-value	Number of Observations
Total Loans			**Major Banks**				
	−1.3969*	−1.5128	−0.3612***	−0.1440	4.7922***	2.6907	51
	(−1.68)	(−0.53)	(−2.91)	(−0.95)	(3.15)	0.847	
			Regional Banks				
	−2.5401***	3.8531***	0.0329	0.4256*	0.7375	4.2139	194
	(−4.43)	(3.55)	(0.46)	(1.94)	(0.79)	0.648	
Loans by Firm Size			**Major Banks**				
Small	−2.3999**	2.3172	−0.2900	0.0943	2.6576		
	(−2.35)	(1.10)	(−1.54)	(0.58)	(1.46)	14.3690	51
Large	−3.0845**	1.5979	−0.3995***	0.0079	3.2507**	0.348	
	(−2.39)	(0.87)	(−2.59)	(0.06)	(2.43)		
			Regional Banks				
Small	1.2266	1.4290	0.2327	0.1981	−3.8875		
	(0.84)	(0.87)	(0.80)	(0.43)	(−1.09)	14.3690	194
Large	−3.8394***	2.0163	−0.2543	0.2405	5.4244	0.383	
	(−2.59)	(1.11)	(−0.89)	(0.56)	(1.53)		

TABLE 7.14. Effects of the Basle Accord on Bank Lending Activity: 1992–94 (continued)

Loans by Industries			Major Banks				
M	−0.5242**	0.2471	0.0674**	−0.0807***	0.9312***		
	(−2.10)	(0.64)	(2.24)	(−3.20)	(4.28)	12.2131	
							51
NM	−2.2757***	1.0478	−0.3899**	−0.2329	3.3251**	0.510	
	(−2.82)	(0.50)	(−2.50)	(−1.36)	(2.09)		
			Regional Banks				
M	−1.2866***	1.0236***	0.0792***	0.0104	1.6571***		
	(−5.73)	(2.61)	(2.67)	(0.13)	(4.33)	27.9712	
							194
NM	−1.1281**	3.0322***	−0.0091	0.3310*	−1.4824*	0.014	
	(−2.42)	(3.25)	(−0.15)	(1.89)	(−1.86)		

Notes: See notes in Table 7.12.

we also observe a reallocation of loans by regional banks from manufacturing firms to non-manufacturing firms even though total loan volume is unaffected.

BANK LENDING AND ITS MACROECONOMIC CONSEQUENCES: EVIDENCE FROM THE ESTIMATION

Now we evaluate how investment activity is affected by changes in loan supply. Our empirical strategy is to measure the sensitivity of fixed investment to bank loans by industry and by firm size. This can measure the degree of substitutability among alternative financing methods. It is conjectured that investment by smaller firms is more sensitive to bank loans, as they have fewer alternatives when raising funds.

The basic framework of the investment function assumes two types of firms. One is without any constraints in the capital market. For this type, investment is determined solely by the fundamental profitability of the investment, which is measured by Tobin's marginal q (the expected present value of the future marginal product of capital divided by capital stock). The other type of firm faces borrowing constraints. The level of investment for this type is determined by the availability of bank loans, which is measured by the growth rate of loan supply. For these firms, investment will not increase even if the future profitability of investment improves, because they cannot finance the investment project. It is only when the loan supply to these firms increases that they increase investment spending. Note that an increase in loan supply does not affect the investment activities of unconstrained firms as long as the future profitability of investment is unchanged.

Aggregate investment is thus determined by two factors: marginal q and the growth rate of loans. To account for the delayed response of investment to these factors, we introduce distributed lags. We also add the lagged investment rate to cope with the non-stationarity. The investment function to be estimated is presented as equation 4.

$$(4)\quad \frac{I_t}{K_{t-1}} = \gamma_0 + \sum_{i=0}^{N} \gamma_{1,t-i} Mq_{t-i} + \sum_{i=0}^{N} \gamma_{2,t-i} \frac{\Delta L_{t-i-1}}{L_{t-i-2}} + \gamma_3 \frac{I_{t-1}}{K_{t-2}} + u_t$$

where I_t: gross fixed investment in period t

K_{t-1}: capital stock at the end of period $t-1$

Mq_t: marginal q in period t

L_t: loan outstanding at the end of period t

u_t: disturbance term

The coefficients of the growth rate of loans measure the extent to which bank loans can be substituted for another financing method. We exclude the current growth rate of loans from the explanatory variables to avoid the simultaneity problem of loan demand and investment. Therefore, it is expected that the growth rate in equation 4 can measure the effects of loan supply on investment. Because the lagged investment rate is included in the regressors, the significance test of the loan growth rate is equivalent to the Granger causality test from loan supply to investment. In the simulation analysis below, we also show that the supply conditions of loans is very important in determining the observed growth rate of loans.

A series for marginal q is constructed in the following manner. First, the stochastic properties of the two components of marginal q, the profit rate and the discount factor, are examined. The profit rate is taken as the ratio of operating surplus to beginning-of-period capital stock. The discount factor is computed as (1 – the depreciation rate) divided by (1 + the borrowing interest rate) where the depreciation rate is assumed to be constant, at 1.98% per quarter, across industries. (See Ogawa et al 1994, Data Appendix Table A-2.) The unit root test is conducted for these two series and we detect unit roots for all the series in manufacturing and non-manufacturing.

Next we test the cointegration relationship between the profit rate and the discount factor and find no cointegration relationship. Therefore it is assumed that these two series follow the VAR model in first-difference form. Finally, based on the VAR estimates, we construct a marginal q series. (See Abel and Blanchard (1986) for more details on the procedure.)

Figure 1 shows the marginal q of manufacturing industries by firm size. The level is higher for small firms than for medium and large firms for most of the period. We observe two peaks for small firms, in 1979 and 1989, each of which corresponds to peaks in the investment rate. Marginal q falls sharply from 1991 to 1994. The marginal q series of medium and large firms are very much alike and much smoother than that of small firms.

Figure 2 shows marginal q for non-manufacturing industries. Again we observe two peaks in 1979 and 1989 for small firms. The series for medium and large firms move very closely and are much smoother than that of small firms.

The sample average of marginal q is compared over the whole sample period as well as three subperiods. It is highest in the bubble period for small firms in both manufacturing and non-manufacturing. In contrast, the series for medium and large firms during this period are not discernibly different from those earlier. Marginal q is lowest in the third subperiod irrespective of firm size and industry, suggesting the severity of the downturn after the bubble burst. Note that the volatility of marginal q in terms of standard deviation is highest for small firms in both manufacturing and non-manufacturing.

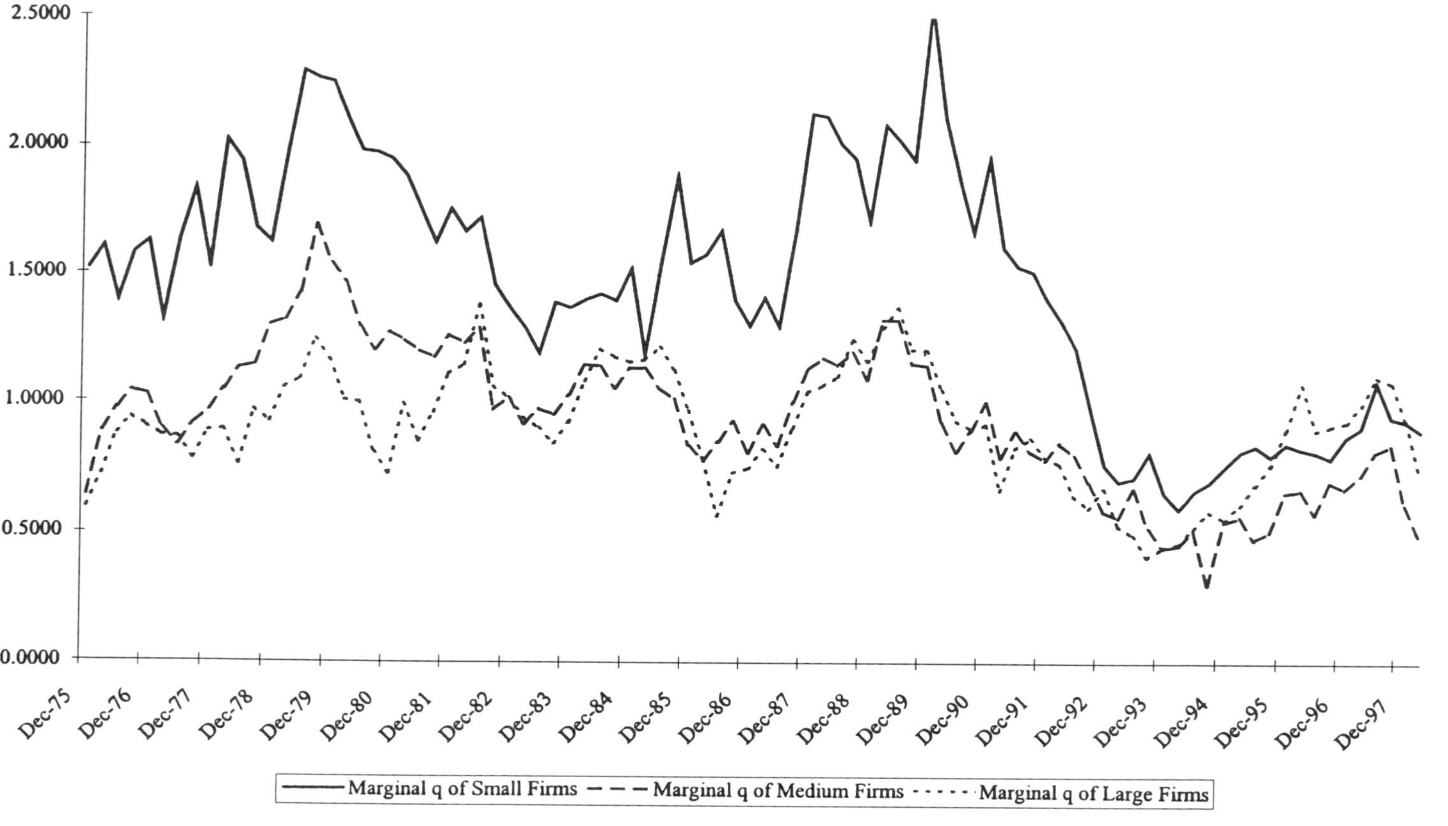

FIGURE 7.1. Marginal q by firm size, manufacturing, 1975–98 from fourth quarter of 1975 to the first quarter of 1998.

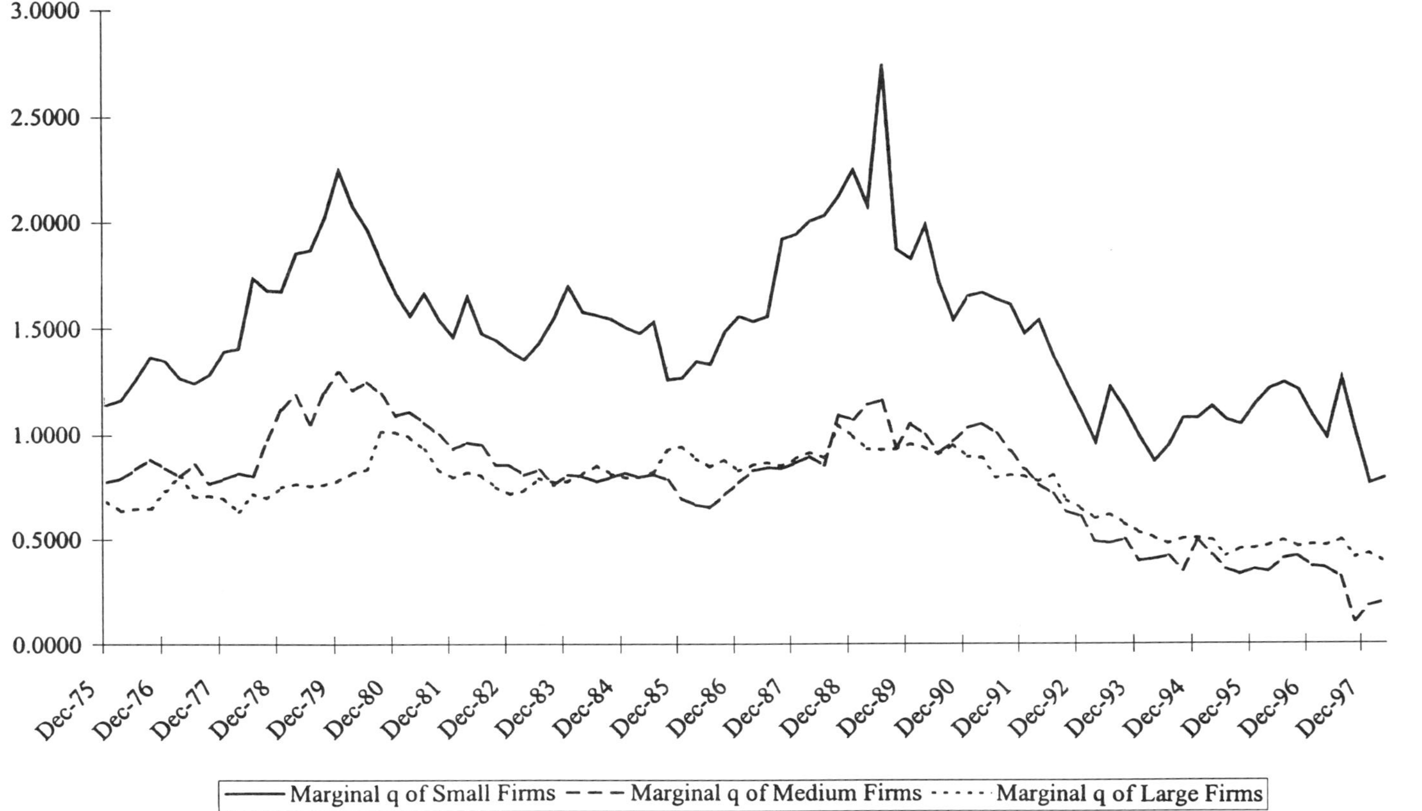

FIGURE 7.2. Marginal q by firm size, non-manufacturing, 1975–98 from fourth quarter of 1975 to the first quarter of 1998.

Equation 4 is estimated separately for each firm size and industry group by applying the Almon lag procedure. The lag length is taken to be 16 quarters. Estimation results are in Table 7.15.

The coefficients of marginal q are positive and significant for all cases except large firms in non-manufacturing. The coefficients of the growth rate of loans are significantly positive for small firms in both manufacturing and non-manufacturing, medium firms in manufacturing, and large firms in non-manufacturing.

It might be argued that measurement error of the operating surplus, a constituent of marginal q, is larger for small firms. If that is the case, then the coefficient estimates of the investment function will be inconsistent. To account for this, we employ the marginal q series of large firms as instruments of the marginal q for the small-firm group. It turns out that for manufacturing the coefficient estimates (t-value in parentheses) are 0.0079 (1.01) for marginal q

TABLE 7.15. Estimation of Investment Function (Equation 6) by Firm Size

Firm Size in Terms of Capital (million yen)	Marginal q of Loans	Growth Rate S.E.	$\bar{R}^2$
Manufacturing Industries			
10–100	0.0092***	0.1675**	0.9215
	(3.51)	(2.44)	0.0029
100–1000	0.0050*	0.2534*	0.9023
	(1.79)	(1.69)	0.0025
1000–	0.0061*	–0.0627	0.9196
	(1.95)	(–0.91)	0.0018
Non-manufacturing Industries			
10–100	0.0016***	0.1640***	0.8546
	(3.60)	(3.27)	0.0040
100–1000	0.0147***	0.0416	0.8011
	(4.27)	(1.33)	0.0033
1000–	0.0002	0.1635*	0.8364
	(0.03)	(1.76)	0.0024

Notes: Significance levels: ***1% **5% *10%
t-values are in parentheses.
$\bar{R}^2$: adjusted coefficient of determination.
S.E.: standard error of the regression.

and 0.1946 (2.34) for bank loan growth. For non-manufacturing they are 0.0292 (3.40) for marginal q and 0.1411 (1.93) for bank loan growth. Although marginal q loses its significance for manufacturing industries, all the other parameters remain significant.

It should be noted that a non-negligible portion of small firms in manufacturing and non-manufacturing are constrained in the capital market and their investment is thus bound by the availability of bank loans. Our results are consistent with Motonishi and Yoshikawa (1998). They find that financial constraints are important for investment decisions of small firms in manufacturing as well as non-manufacturing.

Shocks

To assess the importance to investment behavior of bank loans quantitatively, we use a simulation technique to evaluate the extent to which shocks to bank loan supply affect investment activities.

As context, we first show how two financial events that lead to changes in the lending attitude of banks affected the actual loan amount. One event is the introduction of restrictions on bank lending to the real estate industry, which took effect in April 1990 and lasted until December 1991. The other is the failure of several large financial corporations in November 1997. The empirical strategy is very simple. We compute the average growth rate of loans over the three years prior to the event and then subtract the averaged growth thus computed from the actual growth rate after the event. This estimates the deviation of the growth rate of loans from the recent trend and it shows the effects of the event on actual loan growth.

Table 7.16 shows the effects on actual lending to manufacturing and to non-manufacturing of restrictions on real estate lending. The introduction of regulations had large negative effects on the growth rates of loans to non-manufacturing firms, irrespective of firm size, since real estate firms are a significant component. In 1993, the growth rate of loans decrease on average by 4.5%, 1.8%, and 3.0 % for small firms, medium firms, and large firms respectively. The growth of loans to small firms in manufacturing also was reduced by 1.4% on average in 1992 and 1993. Loan growth increased considerably by 1.2% to 3.2%, for large firms in manufacturing.

Table 7.17 shows the effects of the bank failures in November 1997 on the growth rate of loans. It is seen that the actual growth rate to small firms was hit severely. For small firms in non-manufacturing, the rate decreased by 1.2% in the last quarter of 1997 and by 2.1% in the first quarter of 1998. For small firms in manufacturing, the reduction was 1% in the first quarter of 1998.

TABLE 7.16. Effects on the Growth Rate of Loans of Restriction on Real Estate Lending, 1990–3: Second Quarter of 1990 to the Second Quarter of 1993

Firm Size in Terms of Capital (million yen)	Average Deviation of Loan Growth Rate from the Recent Trend (% per quarter)			
	1990	1991	1992	1993
Manufacturing Industries				
10–100	–0.10	–0.08	–1.40	–1.42
100–1000	0.67	0.42	–0.48	0.14
1000–	2.74	1.18	3.23	2.80
Non-manufacturing Industries				
10–100	0.42	–1.71	–2.82	–4.53
100–1000	0.58	–1.30	–2.05	–1.78
1000–	–0.84	–3.27	–2.87	–3.00

Notes: The figures are averages over each year of the deviation of loan growth rate from the recent trend.
Source: Quarterly Report of Financial Statements of Incorporated Business.

TABLE 7.17. Effects of the November 1997 Bank Failures on Growth Rate of Loans

Firm Size in Terms of Capital (million yen)	Deviation of Loan Growth Rate from the Recent Trend (% per quarter)	
	Fourth Quarter of 1997	First Quarter of 1998
Manufacturing Industries		
10–100	0.57	–1.02
100–1000	–0.38	–0.17
1000–	3.04	2.08
Non-manufacturing Industries		
10–100	–1.18	–2.06
100–1000	0.53	–0.20
1000–	0.64	–0.96

Source: Quarterly Report of Financial Statements of Incorporated Business.

Simulation

Now we simulate the effects of bank lending on investment expenditure. Two simulation exercises are conducted. The first is to measure the effects of loan supply contraction in the early 1990s on investment. The discount rate was raised five times from May 1989 to September 1990. Furthermore, restrictions on loans to real estate took effect in April 1990 and lasted until December 1991. This tight monetary policy reduced loan supply significantly.

The second simulation assesses the effects of the failure of large financial institutions in the autumn of 1997. Banks became very cautious in lending, especially to small firms, after this.

The effects of the reduced loan supply on investment expenditure in these two cases are examined as follows. First, we simulate a model consisting of the investment function and the capital stock identity over the period we are interested in. Then we simulate under the alternative lending scenario. Specifically, we compute the average growth rate of loans over the several quarters prior to the simulation period and use it as the alternative. We can measure the effects of reduced loan supply on investment by subtracting the benchmark solution of investment from the solution under the alternative scenario.

The results of the first exercise are in Table 7.18. It shows, in billion yen and percentage terms, how much investment spending would have been changed if lending behavior had not been changed. To obtain the aggregate change in investment, we assume that investment spending not covered by our sample changes in the same proportion as that of small firms in non-manufacturing. This is justified because the rest of investment comes mainly from small businesses that are not incorporated.

Aggregate investment would have been higher by about ¥3 trillion (15%) per quarter in the first and second quarters in 1993. When disaggregated, we see that the effects are centered on non-manufacturing industries, especially small firms. The investment increase amounts to ¥650 billion to ¥700 billion in the first and the second quarter of 1993 for the small and large firm groups in non-manufacturing. In percentage terms, investment would have increased by 25 to 30% in the same quarters in 1993 for small and medium firms in non-manufacturing.

Our results are in contrast with the findings of Motonishi and Yoshikawa (1998). They report that a significant fall of investment during 1992–94 basically is caused by worsening real factors rather than by financial factors. Their results are based on an investment function using Bank of Japan diffusion indices of 'real profitability' and 'banks' willingness to lend.' To evaluate their assertions in our model, we conduct another simulation where averaged marginal q over the two years prior to the simulation period is used instead of the actual figures. The difference in investment between the alternative and the benchmark is shown in Table 7.19.

TABLE 7.18. The Role of Bank Lending in the 1991–93 Recession Third Quarter of 1991 to the Second Quarter of 1993 (billion yen at 1990 market prices)

	Manufacturing Industries			Non-manufacturing Industries			
	Small Firms	Medium Firms	Large Firms	Small Firms	Medium Firms	Large Firms	Aggregate Investment
91:3	0.0 (0.0)	0.0 (0.0)	0.0 (0.0)	0.0 (0.0)	0.0 (0.0)	0.0 (0.0)	0.0 (0.0)
91:4	15.7 (1.2)	3.8 (0.5)	−9.6 (−0.2)	231.8 (8.4)	48.8 (3.1)	2.7 (0.0)	808.8 (3.7)
92:1	27.3 (2.2)	8.7 (1.1)	−11.2 (−0.3)	406.5 (14.9)	99.7 (6.4)	24.5 (0.5)	1515.5 (7.0)
92:2	46.6 (4.4)	18.5 (2.4)	−31.0 (−0.9)	529.4 (18.8)	159.3 (9.7)	88.9 (1.6)	1909.1 (9.1)
92:3	61.3 (5.4)	30.8 (5.1)	−52.0 (−1.6)	600.3 (21.5)	215.7 (14.4)	192.3 (3.5)	2326.2 (11.2)
92:4	76.7 (7.3)	44.8 (7.5)	−77.8 (−2.4)	695.2 (25.1)	268.4 (17.2)	332.1 (6.6)	2836.2 (14.1)
93:1	85.2 (8.5)	60.0 (9.7)	−70.4 (−2.4)	702.7 (25.9)	321.2 (21.9)	489.5 (9.6)	3149.8 (16.1)
93:2	97.8 (11.2)	73.1 (13.1)	−52.6 (−1.9)	654.0 (21.5)	361.4 (30.3)	654.8 (13.1)	2964.9 (15.7)

Notes: The values in parentheses are percentage change of fixed investment relative to actual figures.

Aggregate investment would have been increased by ¥4.5–5.1 trillion yen (23–27%) in the first and second quarters in 1993. These figures are larger than those in the previous simulation, but not overwhelming so. The figures for 1991 and 1992 are more or less the same as in the bank lending simulation. Furthermore, the effects of bank lending on investment in non-manufacturing are at least as large as the effects of real factors. The difference between the Motonishi-Yoshikawa results and ours appears to be due mainly to the choice of explanatory variables in the investment function. The diffusion indices, and their explanatory variables, give some distributional information across firms on profitability and an evaluation of the lending attitude of financial institutions. However, it is not so clear how they are associated with the traditional explanatory variables such as marginal q, sales, or the interest rate.

TABLE 7.19. Simulation Results: The Role of Real Factors in the 1991–93 Recession (billion yen at market prices in 1990)

	Manufacturing Industries			Non-manufacturing Industries			
	Small Firms	Medium Firms	Large Firms	Small Firms	Medium Firms	Large Firms	Aggregate Investment
91:3	31.8	17.1	19.6	44.5	–2.3	6.5	221.1
	(2.1)	(2.0)	(0.5)	(1.6)	(–0.2)	(0.1)	(1.0)
91:4	85.8	44.2	61.2	129.1	–0.2	22.9	630.2
	(6.8)	(5.4)	(1.5)	(4.7)	(–0.0)	(0.4)	(2.9)
92:1	153.6	65.9	119.1	215.7	12.6	50.5	1126.8
	(12.2)	(8.4)	(3.3)	(7.9)	(0.8)	(1.0)	(5.2)
92:2	232.0	86.9	203.0	336.9	39.6	85.7	1682.5
	(22.1)	(11.3)	(5.7)	(12.0)	(2.4)	(1.6)	(8.0)
92:3	328.6	115.2	308.0	492.6	78.5	131.5	2502.9
	(28.8)	(19.1)	(9.5)	(17.7)	(5.2)	(2.4)	(12.1)
92:4	445.3	154.8	411.8	679.8	130.9	189.1	3475.3
	(42.4)	(25.8)	(12.9)	(24.6)	(8.4)	(3.8)	(17.3)
93:1	567.9	196.9	538.4	900.02	188.4	257.7	4569.2
	(56.4)	(31.7)	(18.5)	(33.2)	(12.9)	(5.1)	(23.3)
93:2	682.1	222.1	673.3	1057.1	254.2	329.8	5120.1
	(78.2)	(39.8)	(24.4)	(34.8)	(21.3)	(6.6)	(27.1)

Notes: The values in parentheses are percentage change of fixed investment relative to actual figures.

Lastly, we examine the effects on investment activity of successive failures of financial institutions in November 1997. The simulation period is from the second quarter of 1996 to the first quarter of 1998. The scenario is based on the premise that the average growth rate of loans over the first quarter of 1995 to the first quarter of 1996 continues over the simulation period. This corresponds to the short-lived recovery of the economy. The differences in investment between the alternative and the benchmark are shown in Table 7.20.

Aggregate investment would have been expanded by ¥1.6 trillion (7.4%) in the last quarter of 1997 and ¥1.9 trillion (9.3%) in the first quarter of 1998. The effects of the credit crunch fall mostly on small firms in non-manufacturing. Their investment would have been increased by around ¥300 billion (15–20%) in that period. The annual growth rate of fixed investment would have been raised by 8.8% if the increment of investment in the first quarter of 1998 had

TABLE 7.20. Simulation Results: The Effects of the 1997–98 Credit Crunch from the Second Quarter of 1996 to the First Quarter of 1998.

	Manufacturing Industries			Non-manufacturing Industries			
	Small Firms	Medium Firms	Large Firms	Small Firms	Medium Firms	Large Firms	Aggregate Investment
96:2	0.0 (0.0)	0.0 (0.0)	0.0 (0.0)	0.0 (0.0)	0.0 (0.0)	0.0 (0.0)	0.0 (0.0)
96:3	–4.1 (–0.6)	–0.1 (–0.0)	–7.6 (–0.3)	153.8 (6.5)	11.1 (0.7)	0.2 (0.0)	665.5 (3.2)
96:4	2.3 (0.3)	–0.3 (–0.1)	–13.1 (–0.5)	264.7 (11.7)	15.4 (1.0)	1.3 (0.0)	1251.2 (5.8)
97:1	6.3 (0.8)	–1.7 (–0.2)	–18.5 (–0.6)	252.2 (9.0)	23.7 (1.5)	4.3 (0.1)	992.3 (4.4)
97:2	13.0 (1.9)	2.8 (0.5)	–16.4 (–0.6)	196.6 (8.1)	26.6 (2.0)	8.1 (0.2)	961.9 (4.4)
97:3	18.6 (2.4)	5.2 (0.8)	–19.7 (–0.7)	209.5 (10.1)	26.0 (1.8)	6.6 (0.1)	1152.8 (5.2)
97:4	23.4 (3.4)	12.0 (1.9)	–17.6 (–0.6)	297.2 (14.5)	29.5 (1.8)	5.1 (0.1)	1637.7 (7.4)
98:1	19.1 (2.9)	18.5 (3.0)	–44.1 (–1.3)	344.2 (19.8)	15.7 (1.1)	–5.6 (–0.1)	1945.5 (9.3)

Notes: The values in parentheses are percentage change of fixed investment relative to actual figures.

continued throughout 1998. This is close to the 10% obtained by Motonishi and Yoshikawa.

CONCLUSION

This chapter analyzes the role of bank loans in the Japanese economy by examining the lending behavior of banks and the investment behavior of corporate borrowers.

We could successfully explain the lending behavior of Japanese banks by splitting the sample period into three: the pre-bubble (1976–86), the bubble (1987–90), and the post-bubble (1991–95). Our main findings are that the lending behavior is quite different by types of banks and of borrowers. For regional banks, loans are more sensitive to deposits. This implies that the degree of capital market imperfections is more severe for regional banks and that the shocks to the balance sheet of regional banks cannot be completely offset by adjustments to bank portfolios. For major banks, real estate plays a more vital role as collateral. We also find that real estate is more important when lending to small firms and to non-manufacturing firms. The shares of small and of non-manufacturing firms in total loans has increased constantly. Therefore real estate functioned as a device to reduce agency costs stemming from the asymmetry of information between new borrowers and banks. It is also notable that loans to small and non-manufacturing firms are more sensitive to shocks in deposits.

As for findings on the real side of the economy, expenditures on fixed investment are more sensitive to bank loans for smaller firms that do not have close substitutes for bank loans. In particular, our simulations demonstrate that reduced loans supply is largely responsible for the stagnancy of investment in the downturns after the burst of the bubble and the financial turmoil in 1997.

Our findings are quite useful in designing stabilizing policy for the real economy. Due to the inability of regional (smaller) banks to offset shocks to their balance sheets, the shocks are easily propagated into the real economy. Since the customers of small banks are also small in size, they do not have substitutes for bank loans and thus their activity is directly affected by bank lending.

Shocks to asset prices, notably land prices, also affect the supply of loans to small firms by large banks by way of changing the value of the collateral the firms can offer. Dependence on collateral also makes loans to small firms more sensitive to shocks in asset markets. In particular, small firms are more likely to be constrained in credit markets during a recession.

The effects of tight credit conditions or financial distress fall disproportionately on small firms. This distributional aspect should be borne in mind in implementing stabilization policy. Recognizing this problem, the government expanded the amount of credit insurance to small firms by ¥20 trillion in October 1998. It is expected that bank loans are channeled to small firms in need of funds in an efficient manner by this policy.

ACKNOWLEDGEMENTS

An earlier version of this chapter was presented at the Finance Forum, Kobe University, Nagoya City University and Osaka University. We thank Takeo Hoshi, Anil Kashyap, and Hugh Patrick for numerous suggestions and comments in improving the quality of the chapter. We are also grateful to Charles Calomiris, Kenya Fujiwara, Atsuo Fukuda, Yuzo Honda, Charles Yuji Horioka, Kiyoshi Kuga, Katsumi Matsuura, Eiji Nezu, Yoshiyasu Ono, Fumio Ohtake, Makoto Saito, Masaya Sakuragawa, Toshiaki Tachibanaki, Yasuhiko Tanigawa, Hideki

Toya, Yoshiro Tsutsui, Yasuharu Ukai and the conference participants for helpful comments and suggestions. This research was partially supported by grants-in-aid from Asset Management Service Industry in the Osaka School of International Public Policy of Osaka University. Any remaining errors are the sole responsibility of the authors.

NOTES

1 The lending channel is discussed by Kashyap and Stein (1994). Kashyap and Stein (1995, 1997) obtain evidence supporting the lending channel for the United States using panel data for commercial banks. For a test of the lending channel in Japan based on time-series data, see Ueda (1993), Hatakeda (1997), Hiroshima (1997), Miyagawa and Ishihara (1997), and Tanaka (1997).
2 Sui (1995) is the only study for Japan that the authors know of that estimates bank loan equations derived from a dynamic model of banking firms. Sui uses quarterly aggregated data rather than panel data. As for the United States, Elyasian et al (1995) construct a dynamic model of bank behavior and estimate the optimal conditions for loans and deposits jointly based on the panel data of US commercial banks.
3 Based on time series data, Shimizu (1995), Yamazaki and Takeda (1996), and Ogawa and Kitasaka (1998) analyze the effect of real estate as collateral on bank lending. Also see Ueda's analysis in this volume (Chapter 3).
4 The excluded banks are 4 city banks (Asahi, Sakura, Sumitomo, and Tokai) and 7 regionals (Akita Akebono, Hokuto, Iyo, Kumamoto Family, Michinoku, Nishi-Nippon, and San-in-Godo). Members of the Second Association of Regional Banks are included with regional banks.
5 In a static model, Yamazaki and Takeda (1997) include land price as a variable to affect the adjustment cost of loans and derive the optimal loan supply equation. They show that the optimal loan supply is a function of the interest differential between the loan rate and the call rate and the land price. Our model is interpreted as an extension of their model in the dynamic setting.
6 Kashyap and Stein (1995) run a similar kind of regression of the growth rate of loans on the growth rate of core deposits. If deposit growth does matter for lending, it is an indication that the bank is constrained in the capital market and does not have enough liquid assets. The testing procedure is simply to add the growth rate of deposits to the explanatory variables and test whether its coefficient is significant or not.

REFERENCES

Berger, Allen N and Gregory F Udell. 1995. "Relationship Lending and Lines of Credit in Small Firm Finance." *Journal of Business* 68(3): 351–81.

Elyasiani, Elyas, Kenneth J Kopecky, and David D Van Hoose. 1995. "Costs of Adjustment, Portfolio Separation, and the Dynamic Behavior of Bank Loans and Deposits." *Journal of Money, Credit, and Banking* 27(4): 955–74.

Hatakeda, Takashi. 1997. "Nippon ni okeru Ginko Hakyu Keiro no Jyuyosei (On Importance of Bank Lending Channel in Japan)." *Finance Kenkyu* 22: 15–31.

Hiroshima, Tetsuya. 1997. "Chushou Kigyo muke Kashidashi to Jittai Keizai Katsudo ni tsuite (Loans to Small Firms and Real Activity)." Bank of Japan, Working Paper 97-4.

Honda, Yuzo. 1997. "Some Implications of the Basle Accord: The Case of Japan." Processed.

Ito, Takatoshi and Yuri Nagataki Sasaki. 1998. "Impacts of the Basle Capital Standard on Japanese Banks' Behavior." Hitotsubashi University, Institute of Economic Research, Discussion Paper Series A-356.

Kashyap, Anil K and Jeremy C Stein. 1994. "Monetary Policy and Bank Lending." In N Gregory Mankiw, editor, *Monetary Policy*. University of Chicago Press.

Kashyap, Anil K and Jeremy C Stein. 1995. "The Impact of Monetary Policy on Bank Balance Sheets." *Carnegie-Rochester Conference Series on Public Policy* 42: 151–95.

Kashyap, Anil K and Jeremy C Stein. 1997. "What Do a Million Banks Have to Say about the Transmission of Monetary Policy?" NBER Working Paper 6056.

Miyagawa, Tsutomu and Hidehiko Ishihara. 1997. "Kin-yu Seisaku, Ginko Kodo no Henka to Macro Keizai (Monetary Policy, Change in Bank Behavior and the Macroeconomy)." In K Asako, N Yoshino, and S. Fukuda, editors, *Gendai Macro Keizai Bunseki*. University of Tokyo Press.

Motonishi, Tazio and Hiroshi Yoshikawa. 1998. "Causes of the Long Stagnation of Japan during the 1990's: Financial or Real?" Tokyo University working paper.

Ogawa, Kazuo, Shin-ichi Kitasaka, Toshio Watanabe, Tatsuya Maruyama, Hiroshi Yamaoka, and Yasuharu Iwata. 1994. "Asset Markets and Business Fluctuations in Japan." Economic Planning Agency, Economic Research Institute, *Keizai Bunseki*.

Ogawa, Kazuo and Shin-ichi Kitasaka. 1998. *Shisan Shijyo to Keiki Hendo – Gendai Nippon Keizai no Jissho Bunseki (Asset Markets and Economic Fluctuations – An Empirical Analysis of Modern Japanese Economy)*. Nippon Keizai Shinbunsha.

Ogawa, Kazuo and Shin-ichi Kitasaka. 1999. "Bank Lending in Japan: Its Determinants and Macroeconomic Implications." Osaka University, Institute of Social and Economic Research. Discussion Paper.

Ogawa, Kazuo. 1999. "Monetary Policy, Credit and Real Activity: Evidence from the Balance Sheet of Japanese Firms." Processed.

Shimizu, Yoshinori. 1995. "Ginko no Jyoho Seisan to Tochi Tanpo Tsuki Kashidashi (Production of Information by Banks and Lending Secured by Land)." *Business Review* 43(3): 52–66.

Sui, Qing-yuan. 1995. "Kin-yu Chukai Katsudo to Keiki Hendo (Financial Intermidiation and Business Fluctuations." *Nippon Keizai Kenkyu* 29: 31–49.

Tanaka, Kumiko. 1997. "Ginko Shinyo to Kin-yu Seisaku no Koka (Bank Credit and Effects of Monetary Policy)." Processed.

Ueda, Kazuo. 1993. "A Comparative Perspective on Japanese Monetary Policy: Short-Run Monetary Control and the Transmission Mechanism." In KJ Singleton, editor, *Japanese Monetary Policy*. University of Chicago Press.

Ueda, Kazuo. 1999. "Causes of Japan's Banking Problems in the 1990s." Chapter 3 in this volume.

Yamazaki, Fukujyu and Yosuke Takeda. 1997. "Tochi Tanpo no Kachi to Ginko no Kashidashi Kodo (The Collateral Value of Land and Bank Lending)." In K Asako and M. Otaki, editors, *Gendai Macro Keizai Dogaku*. University of Tokyo Press.

Chapter 8

THE POSTAL SAVINGS SYSTEM, FISCAL INVESTMENT AND LOAN PROGRAM, AND MODERNIZATION OF JAPAN'S FINANCIAL SYSTEM

Thomas F Cargill
University of Nevada, Reno

and

Naoyuki Yoshino
Keio University

The postal savings system and the Ministry of Finance's Fiscal Investment and Loan Program (FILP) represent an extensive involvement of government financial intermediation in Japan's flow of funds. As such, they constitute important parts of Japan's financial system, but they are little known and little discussed outside of Japan.

Many postal savings systems have been established and many continue in operation throughout the world. Japan's, established in 1875, is one of the oldest in continuous operation. In a few countries, other systems play a larger relative role in their country's financial system; however, the Japanese system is special. It is the largest in absolute terms and close to the largest in relative terms. Japanese post offices also sell life insurance, accounting for 31% of life insurance sold in fiscal 1998.[1]

Most of the funds collected by the postal savings system are used in FILP which provides repayable funds through various government intermediaries to local governments and private users. The receipts and disbursements of FILP are an official part of the government budget process and are determined simultaneously with the general budget. The program is over half the size of the general budget and, as a result, has earned it the designation as Japan's "second budget." The collection and distribution of FILP funds combined with receipts and expenditures in the general budget reflect the combined fiscal impact of the government on the economy.

Postal savings and FILP pose troubling and complex issues for Japan's effort to achieve a transition to the type of modern financial structure outlined in the

Big Bang proposal of November 1996, which is the operating outline for Japan's financial liberalization. Neither institution was mentioned in the proposal, nor were they part of the flurry of legislative action in 1997 following the Big Bang announcement (Cargill, Hutchison, and Ito 1998). Indeed, despite over two decades of an official policy of financial liberalization, postal savings and FILP have increased their role in Japan's financial system. There have been no meaningful reforms to either institution, although some modest reforms have occurred to postal savings beginning in October 1994 and some steps toward revamping FILP began in June 1998.

Unless Japan can develop an acceptable exit strategy for the government to significantly reduce its extensive involvement in the financial system, Japan will not achieve a modern financial system consistent with the goals of the Big Bang.

This chapter discusses the postal savings system and the FILP from an institutional, quantitative, and policy perspective. The focus is on the relationship between these institutions, the efforts to reform Japan's financial system during the past two decades, and the financial distress that has been the dominant feature of Japan's financial system in the 1990s.

First, the current structure and size of the two institutions are explained, followed by a history of their development. The early history of postal savings and FILP and the role they played in the old—pre-liberalization—financial system are outlined to provide context for later events. Development from 1976 (when the first official liberalization policy action was taken) through the end of the bubble economy in 1989 is reviewed in light of concerns raised about their growth by private financial institutions, especially banks, and the Bank of Japan. Attention then shifts to the role in the economic and financial distress of the 1990s played by government financial intermediation and its relationship to the Big Bang.

With that context, the report and recommendations of the Asset Management Council of the Trust Fund Bureau (of which Yoshino is a member since 1996) and the subsequent legislation of June 1998 that initiated fundamental reforms of government financial intermediation are taken up. These have the potential to deal seriously with this complex issue of Japanese finance. Finally, we offer a solution that, although not ideal, would significantly reduce the problems generated by the postal savings system and FILP as they existed in mid-1999. The solution, if adopted, might provide a basis for the complete withdrawal of government from the business of offering deposit services in Japan.

(In this chapter, the phrase "postal savings" includes both the postal savings system and the postal life insurance system. It is the deposit service that generates the most serious problems, but the issues raised with regard to the role of the post office as a life insurance provider are clearly nontrivial.)

SIZE AND STRUCTURE

The structure of the postal savings system and of FILP was formalized in the early 1950s, though the magnitudes and relative importance of various components has changed over time.

Postal Savings

Postal savings and insurance are administered by the Postal Savings Bureau and the Postal Life Insurance Bureau, respectively, in the Ministry of Post and Telecommunications (MPT).

The volume of deposit liabilities held by the postal savings system makes it the largest private or public financial institution in the world. As of 31 March 1998, the system held ¥240 trillion in deposits ($2 trillion at 120 yen/dollar), mostly in the form of 10-year time deposits. This represented 36% of total deposits.[2]

Although the market share of postal savings has fluctuated for a variety of reasons, it has consistently played an important role in Japan's financial structure from the very start. Figure 8.1 illustrates the market share of postal deposits to total deposits from 1888 to 1998. Table 8.1 gives absolute numbers for 1974–98 for both deposits and life insurance.

Fiscal Investment and Loan Program (FILP)

Postal deposits and life insurance receipts are placed with the Trust Fund Bureau (TFB) and the Postal Life Insurance Fund (PLIF), respectively, where they are combined with other funds that are managed by the Ministry of Finance (MOF). The Trust Fund Advisory Council, part of the Prime Minister's Office, has oversight on investment policies for these funds.

Currently about 20% of the total has been used to purchase government bonds and other assets while the remainder has been available for Fiscal Investment and Loan Program (FILP) management.

FILP is a collection of activities and institutions and not a single institution. It is sometimes considered to be the country's capital budget, although this is somewhat misleading because it funds not just infrastructure and other government capital projects but also private-sector investment. Also, while often subsidized, disbursements are loans that are expected to be repaid.

Repayment is expected because the sources of funds are postal savings deposits; surpluses in the postal insurance, welfare insurance, and national annuity programs; and minor amounts from other sources. These funds are collected

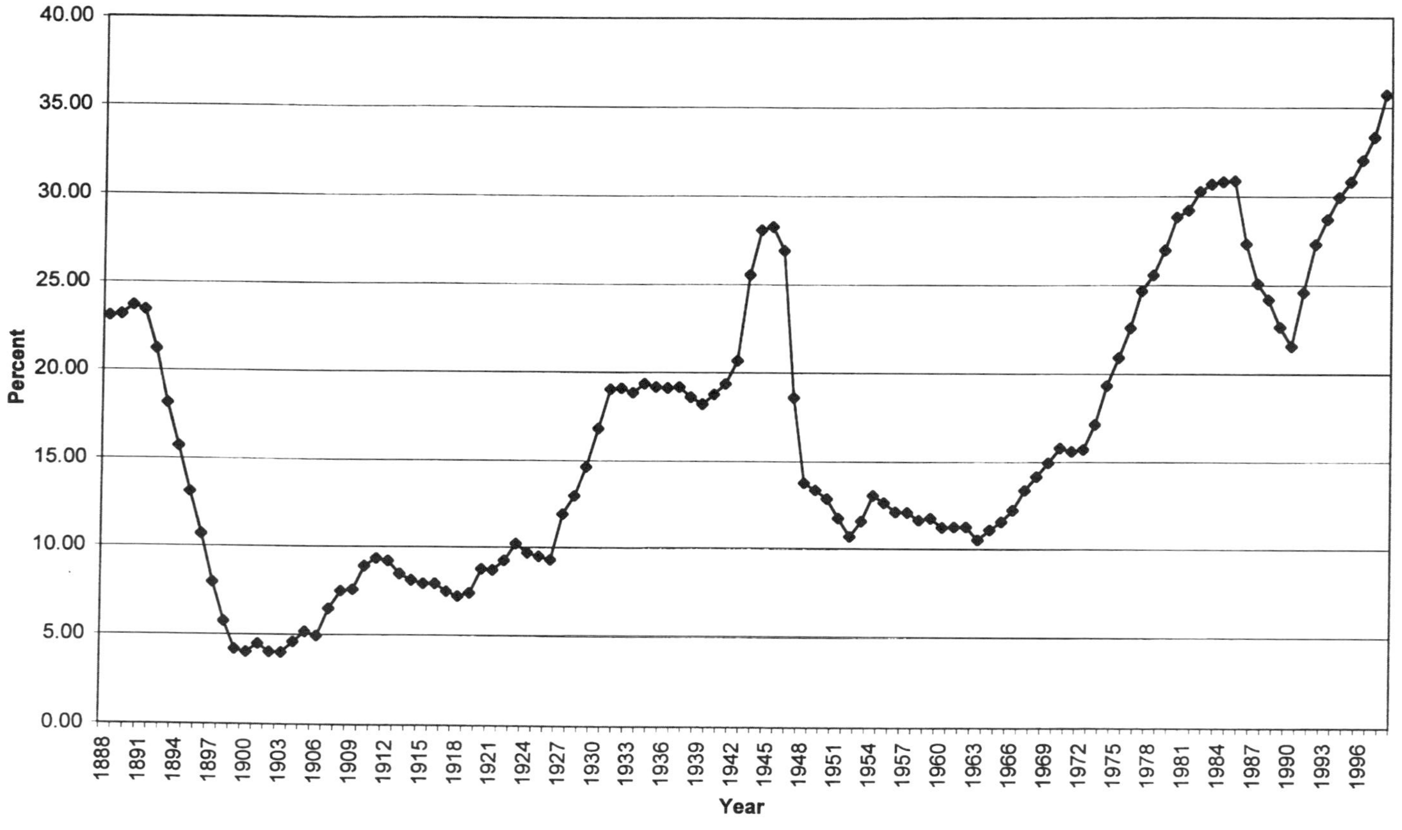

FIGURE 8.1. Postal deposits as a percent of total deposits, 1888–1998.

TABLE 8.1. Postal Savings System Share of Total Deposit and Life Insurance (in million yen)

Fiscal Year	Total Deposits	Postal as % of Total Deposits	Postal/ Total Deposits
1974	755,401	153,765	20.36
1975	899,633	194,311	21.60
1976	1,064,718	245,661	23.07
1977	1,236,588	305,248	24.68
1978	1,429,530	377,264	26.39
1979	1,647,474	449,962	27.31
1980	1,855,070	519,116	27.98
1981	2,078,724	619,543	29.80
1982	2,314,110	695,676	30.06
1983	2,525,205	781,026	30.93
1984	2,722,205	862,982	31.70
1985	2,942,360	940,421	31.96
1986	3,180,054	1,029,979	32.39
1987	3,401,636	1,103,952	32.45
1988	3,658,950	1,173,908	32.08
1989	3,937,885	1,258,691	31.96
1990	4,360,835	1,345,723	30.86
1991	4,688,454	1,362,804	29.07
1992	5,034,967	1,550,470	30.79
1993	5,280,704	1,700,906	32.21
1994	5,549,690	1,835,348	33.07
1995	5,872,459	1,975,902	33.65
1996	6,133,435	2,134,375	34.80
1997	6,397,098	2,248,872	35.15
1998	6,741,353	2,405,460	35.68

Source: Ministry of Posts and Telecommunications, *Annual Statistics*, for postal savings and life insurance. *Economic Statistics Annual*, Bank of Japan, for bank deposits and private insurance.

in the TFB, PLIF, or the Industrial Investment Special Account (funded by taxes). In addition, banks buy government-guaranteed bonds earmarked for FILP activities.

Most FILP money goes through the TFB, although some is used by the depositing institution—the PLIF in particular—to invest directly. In both situations, the collected funds are used to purchase securities issued by, and extend loans to, program implementers—government financial institutions, government agencies, and local governments. These, in turn, make loans or disbursements to the private sector. Table 8.2 shows this structure and the amounts involved for fiscal 1998, 1993, and 1997.

The use of FILP funds has evolved. In the 1950s private-sector industrial facilities and utilities were the major users, followed in the 1960s by infrastructure and declining industries. Housing has emerged as a major user in the 1990s.

TABLE 8.2. Fiscal Investment and Loan Program Fiscal 1988–98 (in billion yen and percents)

1988		1993		1998		
¥	%	¥	%	¥	%	
33,114	-	46,771	-	57,760	-	Total
Sources						
2,407	7.3	2,000	4.3	2,600	4.3	Government-guaranteed bonds
91	0.3	58	0.1	64	0.1	Industrial Investment Special Acct
4,409	13.3	7,053	15.1	7,100	12.3	Postal life & annuity premiums
26,207	79.1	37,660	80.5	48.960	83.3	Trust Fund Bureau
7,900	23.9	10,400	22.2	11,400	19.7	Postal savings
3,500	10.6	7,190	15.4	6,000	10.4	Welfare insurance & national annuities
14,807	44.7	20,070	42.9	30.096	53.1	Repayment to FILP[1]
Disbursements						
3,500	10.6	1,000	2.1	7,800	13.5	Purchase of government bonds
29,614	89.4	45,471	97.9	49.959	66.5	FILP disbursement
4,270	12.9	9,175	19.6	13,300	23.0	Fund operation service[2]
25,344	76.5	36,596	78.2	36,659	63.5	General FILP
16,477	49.8	25,026	53.5	20,237	35.0	Government financial institutions
4,745	14.3	5,700	12.2	9,345	16.2	Local governments
4,122	12.4	5,870	12.6	7,077	12.3	Public investment institutions[3]

Initial budget basis. Data for 1998 therefore exclude subsequent supplementary budget items.

[1] This item represents funds repaid to the FILP system from previous loans and thus, these funds become available in the current fiscal year to finance new loans from the Trust Fund Bureau.

[2] Funds managed directly by the Postal Savings Bureau of the Ministry of Post and Telecommunications. These are invested primarily in government bonds, foreign bonds, and bank debentures.

[3]Data for 1998 also includes ¥145 billion for the Special Account for National Forests.

Source: Ministry of Finance for all underlying data. Data 1988 and 1993 are from a similar table in Matsuoka and Rose (1994, p 160). Very detailed data are available in English on MOF's web site: www.mof.go.jp

Table 8.3 indicates the uses of FILP funds from 1955 to 1998. The government financial institutions represent a subset of the uses of funds and made loans to a variety of targeted sectors at subsidized loan rates.

The importance of postal savings as a direct competitor of private banks in the deposit market and a direct competitor of life insurance companies requires that it be considered independently of FILP. At the same time, postal savings are the principal source of funds for FILP.

TABLE 8.3. FILP Uses of Funds (Percent of Total)

Fiscal Year	Housing	Improvement of Living Standard	Welfare	Education	Small Business	Agriculture	National Land Develop-ment	Road	Transportation	Regional Develop-ment	Industry and Technology	Export and ODA	Postal Saving Own Inv
1955	13.82	7.67	2.14	4.54	8.14	8.88	7.70	3.67	12.21	8.51	15.72	6.99	0.00
1956	14.01	7.22	1.86	3.32	8.74	6.88	5.36	3.95	11.43	13.27	12.92	4.67	0.00
1957	13.79	9.27	1.71	3.13	16.94	6.20	4.21	2.67	11.37	9.63	20.21	0.88	0.00
1958	15.36	9.60	1.46	3.10	14.63	7.13	4.84	3.41	9.71	9.41	21.35	0.00	0.00
1959	13.81	8.36	1.30	2.83	14.13	8.59	6.33	3.91	12.04	7.37	15.71	5.62	0.00
1960	12.62	9.10	1.74	3.42	12.54	7.02	6.41	4.35	14.64	6.97	13.41	7.76	0.00
1961	12.42	10.96	3.18	2.51	11.35	7.24	3.81	6.51	14.49	8.74	11.43	7.37	0.00
1962	13.48	10.87	3.18	2.32	12.60	6.24	4.57	6.36	13.39	8.06	9.96	8.95	0.00
1963	13.71	11.08	3.17	2.75	11.84	6.52	3.21	8.73	13.23	8.36	10.10	7.30	0.00
1964	13.48	11.79	3.31	3.01	12.25	7.00	3.25	8.33	13.82	8.60	8.19	6.99	0.00
1965	13.94	12.40	3.61	3.04	12.62	7.21	3.12	7.92	13.88	0.70	7.79	7.52	0.00
1966	15.99	11.51	3.25	3.49	12.35	6.81	3.54	8.32	13.30	5.99	7.58	7.87	0.00
1967	15.98	11.11	3.20	2.99	13.79	5.90	2.61	9.87	13.28	4.70	6.64	9.92	0.00
1968	16.33	11.48	3.17	2.34	14.36	5.75	2.17	9.66	13.23	4.43	6.59	10.49	0.00
1969	17.29	11.25	3.11	2.38	14.93	5.54	1.74	8.74	12.72	4.28	5.89	12.13	0.00
1970	19.26	11.64	2.84	2.21	15.43	4.99	1.56	8.60	13.19	4.00	5.66	10.61	0.00
1971	20.22	12.15	2.76	2.25	15.38	5.06	1.44	8.20	13.20	4.18	5.37	9.79	0.00
1972	20.47	14.06	2.65	1.92	14.47	4.80	1.86	9.48	12.20	3.90	4.70	9.67	0.00
1973	18.06	16.37	2.92	2.04	14.80	4.57	2.27	9.44	13.11	3.92	3.55	8.94	0.00
1974	19.65	16.40	3.10	2.54	15.49	4.09	1.04	8.66	13.60	3.64	3.05	8.75	0.00
1975	21.45	16.73	3.37	2.96	15.58	4.08	1.18	8.00	12.73	3.29	2.97	7.69	0.00
1976	22.73	15.87	3.66	2.42	16.58	0.14	1.06	7.59	11.42	2.82	2.82	8.18	0.00
1977	24.27	14.65	3.29	4.22	16.74	4.92	1.12	7.10	10.30	2.79	2.77	7.84	0.00
1978	24.70	14.87	3.27	4.72	16.07	4.85	1.63	7.07	10.82	2.51	2.74	6.76	0.00
1979	25.57	14.23	3.71	4.94	17.27	5.07	1.37	5.94	10.36	2.51	2.81	6.24	0.00
1980	26.19	14.15	3.45	4.45	18.70	4.87	1.72	5.67	9.59	2.58	3.01	5.61	0.00

TABLE 8.3. FILP Uses of Funds (Percent of Total) (continued)

Fiscal Year	Housing	Improvement of Living Standard	Welfare	Education	Small Business	Agriculture	National Land Develop-ment	Road	Transportation	Regional Develop-ment	Industry and Technology	Export and ODA	Postal Saving Own Inv
1981	26.23	13.94	3.38	4.08	19.63	4.70	1.42	6.07	10.02	2.34	3.05	5.16	0.00
1982	25.29	14.11	3.46	3.76	19.25	4.47	1.53	7.26	9.61	2.65	3.13	5.49	0.00
1983	25.62	13.35	3.15	3.78	19.04	4.65	1.61	7.65	9.30	2.47	3.02	6.35	0.00
1984	25.06	14.25	3.02	3.68	18.80	4.90	1.80	8.11	8.94	2.37	2.94	6.13	0.00
1985	25.36	15.73	2.86	3.57	18.05	4.27	2.27	8.76	8.45	2.45	2.89	5.34	0.00
1986	26.43	16.68	2.83	3.06	16.70	4.07	1.91	9.14	9.10	2.56	2.87	4.67	0.00
1987	23.37	14.77	2.32	2.90	14.72	3.35	1.82	8.73	8.36	2.43	2.33	2.55	7.39
1988	23.37	15.03	2.23	2.15	13.61	3.31	1.38	8.48	7.53	2.20	2.32	3.95	8.44
1989	23.12	13.55	2.28	1.61	12.94	2.86	1.11	7.99	7.32	2.10	2.35	4.40	9.30
1990	24.20	12.21	2.46	1.60	12.55	2.53	0.95	7.81	6.66	1.97	2.30	1.74	10.12
1991	25.74	11.66	2.79	1.58	12.21	2.47	0.90	8.11	3.99	1.93	2.55	5.16	10.87
1992	24.02	12.64	2.72	1.43	11.84	2.23	0.92	8.27	5.47	2.02	2.37	5.16	13.23
1993	23.09	12.98	2.99	1.39	11.42	1.96	1.14	7.75	6.18	2.10	2.76	4.50	10.16
1994	27.59	13.53	3.01	1.72	12.31	2.08	0.99	7.26	4.65	2.23	2.74	4.22	10.45
1995	29.45	13.72	3.34	1.70	12.79	2.45	1.06	6.49	3.84	2.18	2.56	3.93	10.38
1996	35.64	17.48	4.26	2.03	13.27	2.95	1.49	8.29	5.24	2.84	2.49	4.01	12.34
1997	35.26	18.50	4.23	2.04	13.01	2.63	1.42	9.67	4.16	2.71	2.42	3.95	13.99
1998	35.56	17.49	4.02	2.07	16.75	2.41	1.50	10.44	1.73	2.87	2.42	4.10	NA

Source: *Fiscal and Monetary Statistics Monthly* (FILP Volume), Ministry of Finance

PRE-LIBERALIZATION FINANCE

Japan's modern financial system began with the Meiji Period (1868–1912) when a wide range of policies were set in motion to transfer an agrarian and feudal society into a modern industrial and military power that would first achieve, then surpass, the industrial and military power of the West. The Meiji Restoration started with a number of favorable conditions from the preceding Tokugawa era: an educated work force with a strong work ethic, accumulated capital (savings), a developed system of agricultural, and an infrastructure of roads and irrigation. Japan, however, had no experience with the institutions of industrialization, so it sent numerous missions to the United States and Europe to learn about them. In particular, the basic elements of Japan's financial system were modeled on institutions in the United States, Belgium, France, and the United Kingdom.[3]

Japan established a national banking system in 1872 based on the US system and, like the United States, found that, in the absence of a central bank, such a system did not achieve a stable financial infrastructure or price stability. As a result, the Bank of Japan was established in 1882 to serve as the sole issuer of notes and pursue other activities appropriate for a central bank. Japan turned to Belgium for a central bank model.

Japan's postal savings system was modeled after that of the United Kingdom and the management of those funds based on the French. In 1875, as part of a new postal system being established throughout Japan, post offices offered money order and deposit services. Direct transfer (giro) services transferring funds from one account to another were added in 1906 and life insurance in 1912.

Postal funds initially were deposited in the First National Bank. Because of problems with private national banks stemming from over-issuing currency, in 1878 the deposits were transferred to the MOF's Deposit Bureau. At the turn of the century, MOF began the practice of using postal deposits and life insurance receipts to provide funds to various government-related banks. This system of government financial intermediation was formalized during the war mobilization of the 1930s (Teranishi 1995).

The extent to which postal savings and FILP are basic features of the approach to financial infrastructure adopted by Japan prior to the start of financial liberalization goes beyond what even their sheer size suggests.

The postwar financial system prior to the mid-1970s was regarded as an instrument of industrial policy. This regime was designed to achieve a specific set of objectives: support re-industrialization, support domestic investment and export-led economic growth, encourage high household saving rates, ensure international isolation, and ensure that household saving was directed to the business sector rather than used to support consumer or housing expenditures. These objectives were achieved by rigid regulation and administrative control; market forces played only a small role. In fact, as of 1976, Japan had the most rigidly regulated and internationally isolated financial system among the industrial countries.

The household sector was offered only a small number of low-interest financial assets and had limited access to consumer or mortgage credit. At the same time, households were encouraged to save. Thus, as part of the *maruyu* system, interest income on certain types of savings, including postal savings, was exempt from taxation.

Reasons for Postal Savings' Success

In an effort to stimulate saving, the pre-1980s postal savings system offered a mix of saving assets, convenience, and interest rate advantages not offered by the private banks. Banks, for example, did not have permission to sell life insurance so that post offices provided a broader range of asset services than private banks. These advantages are reflected in the growth of postal deposits relative to total deposits throughout most of the postwar period (Figure 8.1).

The majority of banks were concentrated in major industrial centers and had little economic incentive (or regulatory permission) to branch outside them, away from their borrowing customers. In contrast, the ubiquitousness of post offices brought deposit services to virtually every segment of the population (Table 8.4). Yoshino (1991) and Yoshino and Sano (1997) provide empirical evidence that the number of post offices relative to the number of private bank branch offices is by far the most important determinant of the ratio of postal to bank deposits. In 1980 there were more post offices offering financial services than private bank branches in every prefecture.

The system also benefited from its attraction to tax evaders. Interest income on up to ¥3 million of combined deposits of certain types was tax exempt (the *maruya* system); later maximum deposit size was increased to ¥5 million, and now ¥10 million though the tax exemption was ended in 1987. Because of the large number of post offices in any given area, the lack of taxpayer identification, and a lack of official concern, it was relatively easy for an individual to exceed the limit by having multiple deposits. In contrast, multiple accounts were difficult at private banks, especially the large ones. Private banks were especially critical of the willingness of regulators (with occasional exceptions) to tolerate tax-avoiding deposits. Feldman (1986) discusses a failed attempt in the early 1980s to restrict multiple accounts in the postal savings system known as the "green card" program by which individuals would be assigned a unique identity number (similar to the US social security number); a similar system is currently under consideration in Japan.

The system aggressively sought deposits. Postal officials were paid commissions on their performance in securing deposits. This practice was widely criti-

TABLE 8.4. Ratio of Post Offices to Bank Branches, 1980, 1988, 1989, and 1995

Prefecture	Ratio of Post Offices to Bank Branches 1980	Ratio of Post Offices to Bank Branches 1988	Change in Ratio From 1980 to 1988
Hokkaido	5.45	4.64	–0.81
Aomori	2.24	1.84	–0.40
Iwate	3.56	3.03	–0.53
Miyagi	2.75	2.58	–0.17
Akita	3.17	2.54	–0.63
Yamagata	3.54	2.84	–0.71
Fukushima	4.63	3.90	–0.74
Ibaragi	3.18	2.46	–0.72
Tochigi	3.14	2.47	–0.67
Gunma	2.68	2.09	-0.58
Saitama	1.61	1.51	–0.10
Chiba	1.91	1.63	–0.28
Tokyo	1.03	**0.85**	–0.18
Kanagawa	1.45	1.24	–0.21
Niigata	3.17	3.00	–0.17
Toyama	2.29	2.08	–0.21
Ishikawa	2.27	1.98	–0.30
Fukui	2.25	1.83	–0.42
Yamanashi	4.25	3.56	–0.70
Nagano	5.94	4.71	–1.23
Gifu	3.14	2.38	–0.76
Shizuoka	1.82	1.81	–0.01
Aichi	2.44	2.39	–0.05
Mie	3.02	2.37	–0.65
Shiga	2.71	2.33	–0.38
Kyoto	2.51	2.29	–0.23
Osaka	1.38	1.35	–0.04
Hyogo	3.25	2.77	–0.48
Nara	2.80	2.51	–0.29
Wakayama	4.08	3.66	–0.42
Tottori	2.52	2.32	–0.19
Shimane	5.07	4.74	–0.33
Okayama	3.88	3.42	–0.46
Hiroshima	3.34	2.96	–0.39
Yamaguchi	2.93	2.74	–0.19
Tokushima	2.31	2.09	–0.22
Kagawa	1.75	1.61	–0.15
Ehime	2.94	2.66	–0.28
Kochi	4.70	4.01	–0.68
Fukuoka	2.55	1.63	–0.92
Saga	2.64	2.04	–0.59
Nagasaki	2.98	2.03	–0.95

TABLE 8.4. Ratio of Post Offices to Bank Branches, 1980, 1988, 1989, and 1995 (continued)

Prefecture	Ratio of Post Offices to Bank Branches 1980	Ratio of Post Offices to Bank Branches 1988	Change in Ratio From 1980 to 1988
Kumamoto	5.39	4.44	–0.95
Oita	3.69	3.07	–0.62
Miyazaki	3.30	2.48	–0.82
Kagoshima	6.59	5.28	–1.31
Okinawa	1.08	1.09	0.01

	Ratio of Post Offices to Bank Branches 1989	Ratio of Post Offices to Bank Branches 1995	Change in Ratio From 1989 to 1995
Hokkaido	3.07	2.90	–0.16
Aomori	1.75	1.69	–0.06
Iwate	2.20	1.97	–0.22
Miyagi	1.46	1.45	–0.01
Akita	1.84	1.83	–0.01
Yamagata	1.54	1.51	–0.03
Fukushima	2.09	1.89	–0.20
Ibaragi	1.74	1.54	–0.20
Tochigi	1.67	1.48	–0.19
Gunma	1.65	1.51	–0.14
Saitama	1.28	1.21	–0.08
Chiba	1.24	1.25	0.01
Tokyo	**0.19**	**0.73**	0.54
Kanagawa	1.08	1.08	0.00
Niigata	1.97	1.92	–0.05
Toyama	1.43	1.44	0.00
Ishikawa	1.40	1.33	–0.07
Fukui	1.30	1.35	0.05
Yamanashi	3.37	2.79	–0.58
Nagano	3.49	3.14	–0.34
Gifu	1.81	1.67	–0.14
Shizuoka	1.44	1.36	–0.08
Aichi	1.29	1.27	–0.02
Mie	1.56	1.46	–0.10
Shiga	1.50	1.37	–0.13
Kyoto	1.79	1.84	0.05
Osaka	**0.86**	**0.86**	0.00
Hyogo	1.58	1.60	0.02
Nara	1.84	1.78	–0.06
Wakayama	1.95	1.86	–0.09
Tottori	1.68	1.85	0.17

TABLE 8.4. Ratio of Post Offices to Bank Branches, 1980, 1988, 1989, and 1995 (continued)

Prefecture	Ratio of Post Offices to Bank Branches 1989	Ratio of Post Offices to Bank Branches 1995	Change in Ratio From 1989 to 1995
Shimane	3.28	3.35	0.07
Okayama	2.27	2.10	–0.17
Hiroshima	1.75	1.63	–0.12
Yamaguchi	1.92	1.87	–0.05
Tokushima	1.36	1.30	–0.05
Kagawa	1.04	1.06	0.02
Ehime	1.45	1.56	0.11
Kochi	2.11	2.02	–0.10
Fukuoka	1.09	1.06	–0.03
Saga	1.45	1.33	–0.12
Nagasaki	1.48	1.42	–0.06
Kumamoto	2.42	2.43	0.00
Oita	2.12	2.09	–0.03
Miyazaki	1.82	1.77	–0.05
Kagoshima	3.54	3.38	–0.16
Okinawa	**0.83**	**0.91**	0.07

Note: The number of bank branches increases from 1988 to 1989 because of a reclassification of sogo banks as regional banks II. Therefore, 1989 statistics on bank branches are not comparable to earlier values.

cized and as a result, was unofficially stopped about one year ago (1998). Post offices openly advertised the advantages of postal deposits over bank deposits and adopted a marketing approach to services close to what one would expect with an aggressive private bank. Deposit rates were set and changed by the MPT, independently of the Bank of Japan and MOF, in such a manner to attract private bank deposits (Suzuki 1987, p 149). Prior to 1990 the MPT frequently lagged downward interest rate adjustments on postal deposits to induce shifts of funds from banks to post offices. There was at least one instance when this was done between 1991 and 1995; however, since 1995 postal rates are set "close to" bank deposit rates.

The *teigaku* time deposit has been the most important postal savings offering since it was created in the late nineteenth century. *Teigaku* is a 10-year fixed-rate time deposit; however, the funds can be withdrawn after 6 months with no penalty. This provides the system with a significant competitive advantage over banks (Kamada 1993; Yoshino and Sano 1997). Sakakibara refers to *teigaku* as the "jewel" of the postal savings system because of its superiority to any time deposit issued by private banks (1991, p 66).

Private banks frequently pointed out that postal deposit growth was at the expense of bank deposits. They also argued that they were not able to offer *teigaku* because of the embedded interest rate risk. Unlike post offices, banks were required to meet reserve and capital-asset requirements, pay income taxes and, after 1971, pay deposit insurance premiums. Further, the banks had overhead for branches, while the MPT absorbed many branch costs as part of providing postal services, thus subsidizing postal savings.

However, the relative growth of postal savings during 1950–75 also reflected the priorities of the private banks. Through the early 1970s they focused on the business sector and were not aggressively interested in servicing the household sector, in terms of consumer and mortgage lending; however, banks were interested in attracting household deposits. Banks operated under conditions of excess demand for business loans, had easy access to (subsidized) funds at the Bank of Japan discount window, and offered essentially no loans or other financial services to the household sector. Corporate demand for funds was intense and corporations had no alternatives in the form of domestic money and capital markets or external markets. City banks in particular were continually experiencing excess demand for credit from the corporate sector. Regional banks, not subject to the same pressure for loans, could easily channel excess funds to the large banks via the interbank market. Banks also had a secured deposit base as corporations were required to maintain large compensating balances. This is not to imply that inaction on the part of the banks accounts for the increased market share of postal deposits. Banks did compete directly with post offices, but the higher priority placed on servicing the business sector and the advantages held by the post offices limited the resources banks were willing to devote to attracting household deposits.

Postal deposits are essentially government debt and, hence, have no default risk; however, this played no role in the relative growth of postal deposits during the first part of the postwar period because the financial system operated with a policy of no failures of financial institutions. Japan established a formal deposit insurance system for commercial banks in 1971.

Government Banks

The government banks have served several purposes. First, they provided subsidized loans to encourage investment, a "low interest rate effect". Second, government-bank loans had a herding effect ("cow bell" in the literature) in that they indicated which industries private banks could safely support. Third, loans supported activities such as infrastructure that had high productivity for the entire economy but which, because of long gestation periods in generating benefits or other types of market failure, could not easily be financed by private banks. This can be referred to as the "quantitative effect."

The "low interest rate effect" increases the demand for funds increasing the amount of borrowing and investment. The "cow bell effect" and "quantitative effect" both increase the supply of credit and increase the rate of investment spending over what it would be in the absence of FILP.

Evaluation

Postal savings and FILP played an important role in Japan's pre-liberalization financial structure. Postal savings was part of an overall effort to provide incentives to save and to bring deposit services to remote parts of Japan. FILP in general, and the government banks such as the Japan Development Bank in particular, were designed to provide incentives to investment to targeted sectors of the economy (Ogura and Yoshino 1988). Regulated postal deposit rates, subsidized loan rates at government banks, and government-directed credit allocation reflected a basic feature of pre-liberalization Japanese finance. The flow of funds were more sensitive to regulatory discretion and administration than to market incentives.

It is an open question whether postal savings and FILP actually made the contributions to the economy intended—and frequently claimed—for them. The provision of deposit services to all prefectures likely increased the overall saving rate; however, much of the growth of postal deposits relative to bank deposits reflected regulatory advantages provided postal savings and a greater willingness to address the needs of the household sector.

The net effect on investment of the funds provided through government banks or directly to government corporations and enterprises is debatable. Yoshino and Nakata (1997) estimated quarterly investment functions for manufacturing and non-manufacturing industries to determine the magnitude of the effects of government financial intermediation discussed above. The study shows that before 1980 all three were relatively small. The low-interest-rate effect was the largest before 1980, but still relatively small. During the period 1965–74, for example, it increased investment spending in manufacturing from about 3 to 4 percent over what investment spending would have been in the absence of FILP. Each of the effects became virtually zero after 1980. Similar results were obtained for non-manufacturing. This empirical result is not surprising in light of results obtained from a formal model of FILP. Yoshino (1987) provides a theoretical flow of funds model extended in Cargill and Yoshino (1999) that suggests the net effects on income are likely exaggerated.

1976 TO THE END OF THE BUBBLE ECONOMY

The operating environment of postal savings and FILP changed in the second half of the 1970s. The new environment rendered the past role of government intermediation finance incompatible with new economic, political, and technological forces, which require more openness and flexibility. As a result, there was more criticism of postal savings and FILP. The criticism intensified as government financial intermediation actually increased in importance even as other parts of the financial system were liberalized and became subject to market forces. Private banks and other financial institutions argued that government financial intermediation tilted the playing field against them.

Higher energy prices and completion of postwar re-industrialization in the 1970s meant a slower natural growth path for the economy than during 1950–70. That period is referred to as the High Growth Period because real GDP expanded at an annual average of around 10%. In the slower-growth environment of the 1970s, banks faced reduced corporate demand for credit. The banks were forced to reduce and eventually eliminate compensating balance requirements, and this gave them more reason to be critical of the role of government in offering deposit and loan services.

Slower growth had other consequences. Combined with other economic, technological, and political forces, it resulted in shifts in long-established flow of-funds patterns that brought pressure to initiate a policy of financial liberalization (Cargill and Royama 1988; Feldman 1986). Market and regulatory innovations began to circumvent and relax the constraints on market forces in the flow of funds that had been the hallmark of the previous financial system. While banks and other financial institutions and markets were given enhanced portfolio diversification powers, they also were subjected to increased competition both domestically and internationally. With their traditional customers having new sources of credit, banks were losing market share. The degree of government financial intermediation represented by postal savings and FILP was clearly incompatible with more open and competitive financial structures.

The new economic and financial environment also changed the operating environment of monetary policy, which led to conflicts between the Bank of Japan and the MPT (Suzuki 1987, p. 149). BOJ adopted a price stability objective after the end of the fixed exchange rate system in 1973 and viewed financial liberalization as a means to enhance the transmission of monetary policy and provide new operating instruments such as money market operations. BOJ viewed government financial intermediation as a constraint on liberalization, complicating and even limiting the effectiveness of monetary policy. However, Cargill and Yoshino (1999) find no evidence that postal savings actually did interfere with monetary policy in any significant manner.

The period 1976 to 1985 is in many ways the high point of Japanese economic and financial development. In the face of oil price shocks, adjustment to a flexible exchange rate, and structural changes, Japan achieved a degree of macroeconomic stability not equaled by most industrial economies.

The structural changes included a gradual opening of Japan's markets and a series of incremental changes in the financial system that achieved significant financial liberalization by the mid-1980s (Cargill and Royama 1992). The liberalization process appeared successful in light of the financial disruptions experienced by the United States, thereby adding support for the gradual approach adopted by Japan and seemingly justifying the decision to postpone any serious reform of government financial intermediation.

Thus, during 1976–85, neither postal savings nor FILP were the object of any meaningful reform, despite increasing criticism of their role in the financial system. Postal deposits continued to increase as a share of total deposits, while government bank credit remained an important part of intermediation credit (Table 8.5).

Declining Market Share

The second half of the 1980s was a turning point of sorts for postal savings as growth of postal deposits slowed relative to bank deposits (Figure 8.1). The Tax Reform Act of 1986, as part of a general overhaul of the tax system, abolished the *maruyu* system of tax exemption on interest income beginning with 1987, and thus eliminated a major advantage of postal deposits relative to bank

TABLE 8.5. Fiscal Investment and Loan Program System as of 31 March 1998 (in trillion yen)

Sources of funds		Used for	
23.9	Postal Savings	10.9	Government bonds
13.4	Welfare and National Pension	39.5	FILP
4.5	Other	=	
9.9	Postal Life Insurance	50.4	
=			
51.7	Total available		

Deposited in		FILP Funds used for	
41.8	Trust Fund Bureau	7.4	Local government
0.3	Special account Industrial investment	6.3	Special account
0.4	Government-guaranteed bonds	13.3	Government banks
5.9	Postal Life Insurance Fund	12.1	Government enterprises and corporations
=			
48.4		0.4	Government special companies (NTT and JNR)
		=	
		39.5	

Source: Ministry of Finance

deposits. At the same time, private banks were opening more branches and offering more competitive rates on deposits.

However, government financial intermediation still was not an object of regulatory changes to liberalize the financial system, and market forces actually reduced the political pressure to tackle the complex problem of reforming postal savings and FILP. Postal savings received authority in 1987 to manage a portion of its deposits rather than transferring all of them to the Trust Fund Bureau. This was called a "liberalization," but was really compensation to the Ministry of Post and Telecommunications for the loss of tax-free savings. These funds have been invested in government bonds, foreign bonds, and bank debentures. Also, a small fraction has been used to purchase equities.

ECONOMIC AND FINANCIAL DISTRESS IN THE 1990s

In May 1989 the Bank of Japan raised interest rates and soon the asset bubble burst. The economic and financial crisis following the collapse of equity and land prices in 1990–91 raised new concerns about postal savings and FILP. The share of postal deposits sharply increased after 1990 (Figure 8.1) as the public lost confidence in the banking system and began to doubt the ability of the government to maintain a policy of no failures of financial institutions or markets. The government took the unprecedented postwar action of officially closing 11 small credit cooperatives during 1991–95. By the end of 1994 the Deposit Insurance Corporation had exhausted its reserves and thus was technically insolvent.

The government response to the distress is discussed in Chapters 2 and 3, and in detail, in Cargill, Hutchison, and Ito (1997 and forthcoming). In most instances, government actions were inadequate and failed to resolve the growing distress. A major part of the problem was the unwillingness of the government to depart from the old financial regime, especially the policies of nontransparency, forgiveness, and forbearance in dealing with troubled institutions. Economic stagnation intensified the problems because it is more difficult to eliminate nonperforming loans in the absence of economic growth. Financial distress came close to financial panic in the wake of the November 1997 failure of Hokkaido Takushoku Bank and Yamaichi Securities Company and negative real GDP growth (which continued from the fourth quarter of 1997 to the first quarter of 1999).

Relative Growth of Postal Savings

In the early 1990s, there were several periods of disintermediation of funds from private banks to post offices, often encouraged by post office officials. This weakened banks and complicated efforts to deal with their nonperforming loan problem.

Factors other than bank problems[4] also account for the shift of funds from banks to post offices. Prior to 1990, the MPT frequently lagged adjusting interest rates downward in response to a general decline in interest to increase postal savings growth. This was done only a few occasions after 1990 and ceased in 1995; however, as interest rates declined in the early 1990s the lagged adjustment accounts for some of the increased market share of the postal savings system. More important is the factor that post offices offered a 10-year time deposit with an early withdrawal option. Until 1995 private banks could not offer a long-term deposit. Thus, in an environment of expected declining interest rates, funds will be placed in long term accounts. The option of withdrawal protects the depositor if the expectation turns out to be incorrect.

Four official actions were taken to stem the disintermediation and to restore public confidence in bank deposits. First, in 1993 the MPT issued instructions to individual post offices to cease advertising the problems of the banking system as a means of attracting deposits. Second, in October 1994 the MOF and MPT agreed that postal deposit rates would be set "close" to private-bank deposit rates. Previously the MPT had set and changed postal deposit rates to make them more attractive than private bank deposits. Third, the Deposit Insurance Corporation was reorganized, expanded, provided with new authority in dealing with troubled institutions, and re-capitalized in 1995. Fourth, in 1995 the MOF announced a complete deposit guarantee for the entire private banking system that would remain in place until 1 April 2001.

Aside from official actions to stem the disintermediation of bank deposits to postal deposits, no specific action was taken with respect to postal savings. In fact, the system may have contributed to the government's policy of forgiveness and forbearance through so-called price-keeping operations. Thus, postal life insurance funds were used on several occasions in the early 1990s to purchase equities listed on the Tokyo Stock Exchange. On numerous occasions in 1998 and 1999 members of the Liberal Democratic Party called on the system to use its liquidity to aggressively support equity and land prices in general, though these went unheeded.

Government Banks

Government banks also complicated the financial distress.

Private banks faced both a nonperforming loan problem and a weakened capital position because the adverse economy and collapse of asset prices made it difficult for many borrowers to service their debt, and declining equity prices wiped out latent capital gains. In an effort to improve the quality of their balance sheets, banks imposed a credit crunch which, by the late 1990s, has resulted in declining bank credit.

The crunch has had a significant impact on the distributions of funds from FILP. Housing and business loans (Table 8.3) became an increasingly important use of funds. Housing loans are made by the Housing Loan Corporation and business loans are made by Japan Development Bank, Small Business Finance Corporation, and People's Finance Corporation. Some have viewed this development in favorable terms because the relative growth of government funds to support housing and business activities in the 1990s has provided an offset to the credit crunch at private banks (Figure 8.2). The development, however, raises both short- and long-run concerns.

In the long run, the use of government bank credit to offset some of the effects of the credit crunch only further expands and solidifies the role of government financial intermediation and broadens public support of government banks. This makes it politically more difficult to achieve the types of reforms ultimately required to achieve the objectives of the Big Bang, namely to create a free, fair, and competitive market-based system of financial markets and institutions.

Nonperforming Loans at Government Banks

In the short run, the growth of credit to housing and business at the same time the economy experienced eight consecutive quarters of declining real GDP growth suggests that government banks may also have a nonperforming loan problem, although it remains hidden. Government banks hold relatively small reserves for bad debts, and no official estimates of nonperforming loans have been published. There are, however, a number of reasons to believe that whatever nonperforming loan problem may exist at government banks, it would be overstated if one applied bad-loan ratios from the private banking sector. Government banks, for example, have a stronger legal standing for collecting collateral compared to private banks and require some type of guarantee.

The point is that, whatever the problem, it is of unknown magnitude. Even if the bad-loan level is only half that in the private bank sector, nonperforming loans at the 10 government financial institutions would total ¥15 trillion yen at 31 March 1998. (This uses a nonperforming percentage of 5% percent applied to ¥305 trillion in their loans.) This is a nontrivial addition to the existing nonperforming loan problem.

1998 REFORMS

It is easy to be critical of the lack of reform directed toward government financial intermediation during the more than two decades since financial liberalization began. However, several related considerations need to be kept in mind.

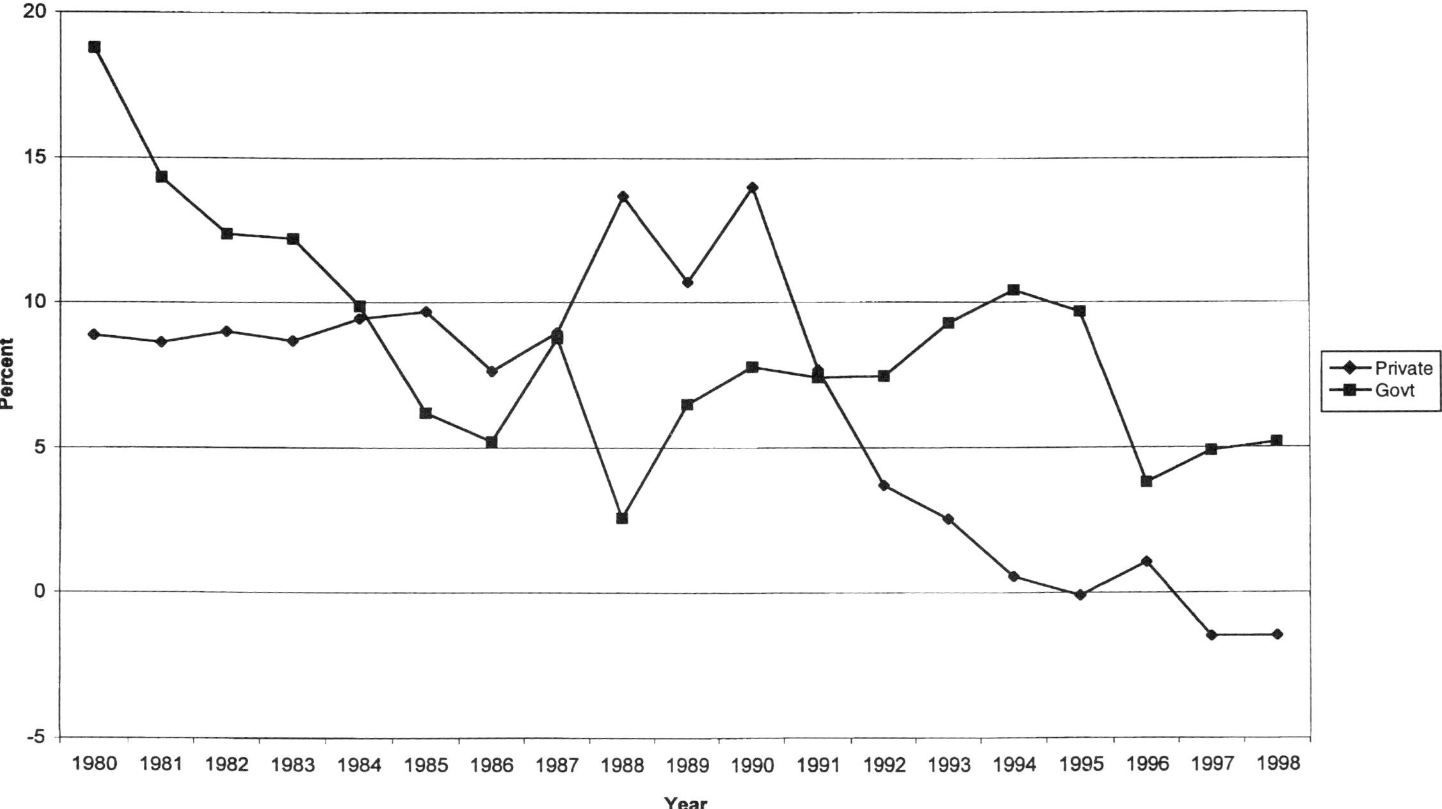

Figure 8.2. Growth Rates of Private and Govenment Bank Credit, 1980–98.

The postal savings system has been successful in terms of the objectives and structure of the pre-liberalization financial system and it remains highly popular. The same can be said for FILP, which has enhanced its public support in the 1990s by offsetting part of the private-bank credit crunch. For a long time postal savings provided deposit services to rural areas and offered services that private banks were unwilling to provide even when they possessed the ability. Only in the 1980s did banks begin to view the household sector as a profitable market. All this means that the size and popularity of postal savings, and government financial intermediation in general, present policy makers with complex economic and political challenges.

The intensification of financial problems in late 1997 and 1998 made the extent to which the old financial regime was no longer functioning much clearer to the government, and this led to changed attitudes. The steps leading to this are outlined in detail by Cargill, Hutchison, and Ito (forthcoming). It is in this context that serious reform discussions commenced in mid-1998. (This section is based directly on Cargill and Yoshino 1998.)

The June 1998 Asset Management Council Report

The Asset Management Council of MOF's Trust Fund Bureau has been in existence for many years, and in the past confined its activity to reviewing decisions by the government on how to allocate Trust funds. Starting in late 1997 the Council changed in three ways and became a catalyst for a serious reform debate about government financial intermediation.

Council membership was expanded to include a wider range of participants, some critical of the system, and involved the MPT, as well as other interested parties, as a formal part of the dialogue. The Council, charged to consider various reforms of FILP, published a major report in early June 1998.

There are three components to the report.

The first summarizes the role of FILP in Japan's financial system and economy during the postwar period and concludes that the program met its objectives and contributed to Japan's re-industrialization. The report also indicates that the new environment that emerged in the late 1970s requires reform of government financial intermediation.

The second component covers a number of current issues, focusing on the various problems of the FILP system in the new environment. The allocation principles and huge size of postal savings and FILP are deemed incompatible with a liberalized financial market. FILP in the past focused only on long-term lending; however, short-term lending and short-term government bond purchases have become a larger part of its allocation of funds. As a result, the program is moving away from its original objectives.

Deposit rates were liberalized in October 1994, which reduced the advantage postal savings enjoyed compared to private banks. Funds continue to be lent to government financial institutions and government enterprises at fixed rates, thus exposing the system to interest rate risk primarily related to differences in the maturity of assets and liabilities. Housing loans have become an increasingly important use of FILP funds, and this competes directly with the private sector. If the desire is to subsidize housing, it is felt that there are other, more efficient, means.

The basic issue raised by the Council is that the size and non-market allocation of FILP funds have become incompatible with the goal of a competitive, free, and fair financial system envisaged in the Big Bang program.

The third and most significant component outlines suggestions for reforming FILP. These are the following.

1. The entire set of subsidies contained in FILP needs to be evaluated in terms of cost-benefit analysis to determine whether a given subsidy should be continued.
2. The cost-benefit analysis should be disclosed to the public.
3. The assets and liabilities of each government financial institution and enterprise should be disclosed on a mark-to-market basis.
4. Government financial institutions should adopt the type of cash flow analysis recommended in the United States by the General Accounting Office and codified in the Credit Reform Act of 1990.
5. Lending rates offered by government financial institutions need to be market sensitive.
6. Government financial institutions and enterprises should either issue their own bonds (agency securities) or participate in Trust Fund bond issues to finance their lending activities. Government financial institutions and enterprises should not rely on either postal deposits or life insurance funds. The Council offered two options with respect to agency bonds: with or without government guarantee. Trust Fund bonds would have a government guarantee assuming the current Trust Fund structure remains in place.
7. Postal deposits, life insurance, and pension and welfare funds should no longer be deposited in the Trust Fund Bureau. This would effectively separate the MPT from the Trust Fund Bureau.

Consequences of the Report

Within weeks after the report was submitted to MOF and published,[5] the Fundamental Reform of the Central Government Industries and Agencies Law was enacted in June 1998. The new law explicitly recognizes that the FILP system is in need of reform, with the objective of making it compatible with a liberalized market. In this regard, there are two specific provisions which become effective 1 April 2001.

1. Postal savings, life insurance, and pension funds will no longer be transferred to the Trust Fund Bureau for FILP. (Point 7 in the report.)
2. Government financial institutions and enterprises will be required to raise funds in the open market. (Part of point 6 in the report.)

Given the difficulty of the problem, the Council's report and subsequent legislative action represent a bold step. The issues debated in its wake relate to what will happen to postal savings and the government financial institutions and enterprises dependent on postal and life insurance funds. The report and legislative action have set into motion a discussion that has the potential to make fundamental changes in government financial intermediation in Japan.

PRACTICAL AND SECOND-BEST SOLUTIONS

Resolution of the problems of government financial intermediation in Japan involve economic, institutional, and political factors. Resolution attempts that do not focus on all three will be counterproductive. Thus, while an efficiency argument can be made that Japan would be better served by a reduction in government financial intermediation and privatization of postal savings, the argument fails to consider the important institutional and political dimensions of government financial intermediation. The elements of government intermediation finance have been an important institutional feature of Japan for over a hundred years and, as such, are resistant to major change over short periods of time. Institutions, either as material manifestations (such as a government bank) or ways of thinking (such as dependence on government), must be considered in evaluating any potential reform. The importance of these institutions not only makes them resistant to major adjustment, it increases their political support. Ultimately it is the political institutions that formulate and execute financial reform.

There is an even more fundamental reason why reform of government financial intermediation needs to proceed in an evolutionary manner: The system is so large that any major adjustment would generate significant and uncertain effects. Japan faces many problems in the next few decades, such as absolute population decline, a rapidly aging population, and increasing levels of debt relative to GDP. In this context, prudence suggests a less than revolutionary resolution of the problems of government financial intermediation.

With this in mind, we offer suggestions for a practical, second-best resolution of the various problems identified in this chapter. The suggestions represent a middle ground between the ideal market-oriented reform and a continuation of the status quo. In the past, Cargill has argued for complete privatization of the postal savings. Yoshino (1994 and 1999) presents a less radical but more practical solution. What follows is offered as a joint solution.

Government Financial Institutions and Enterprises

Each government financial institution and enterprise should be evaluated in terms of a cost-benefit framework with methods commonly employed to evaluate public projects. This evaluation must incorporate consistent and market-oriented accounting procedures to generate realistic financial statements. Both the cost-benefit and financial statements need to be made public and generated with the objective of transparency.

The outcome of this evaluation and more transparent presentation of the activities of each government financial institution and enterprise should provide a basis for placing each into one of four categories.

The first category includes entities with insufficient justification for continued operation. This would set into motion a discussion and time table to terminate their activities. We, of course, recognize the political difficulty of this category.

The second group involves situations where there is sufficient market failure to justify government support. Bonds issued in the open market by the Trust Fund Bureau would provide the funds to support the activities of these institutions. For all practical purposes, Trust Fund bonds would be the same as general government debt and would support activities that could be justified as part of the resource allocation component of the general budget.

Some government financial institutions or enterprises cannot be justified by market-failure considerations, but that there exists a social-policy objective of providing government support of the specific activities. In these cases, the institutions would be required to offer their own debt, collateralized by their own assets, much as government-sponsored agencies in the United States issue debt. This debt would not be government guaranteed but clearly would have a subsidy element. There would need to be a transition period to full reliance on self-funding with government sponsorship.

The last category is government financial institutions and enterprises that would rely on a combination of self-funding and Trust Fund bonds.

The intent of the evaluation and cost-benefit analysis is to require self-funding with government sponsorship except in clear cases where dependence of government bonds is justified. Again, this process needs to be transparent in the hope of constraining the political log-rolling that is surely to accompany any such evaluation.

Postal Savings

Postal savings should become a separate agency, independent of the Ministry of Posts and Telecommunications. Oversight responsibility could be assigned to the Financial Supervisory Agency. Postal deposits would be invested only in government bonds. The system thus is transformed into a "narrow" government bank. The new agency will be required to reimburse the postal system for office and related expenses, as the existing branch network will still be utilized.

The enabling legislation needs to make it clear that under no circumstance is the new agency permitted to function as anything but a narrow bank. It will, however, have the authority to contract with private banks, securities companies, insurance companies, and other financial institutions to offer financial products on their behalf to depositors. These activities will not have any impact on the agency's balance sheet, but will generate revenue based on the fees charged for serving as a representative of the private entities. In this way, the benefits of the post office network of branches can be utilized to bring an improved mix of financial products to all areas of Japan.

The life insurance function of the system should be privatized, with policies sold at auction to private insurance companies.

Maturing *Teigaku* Deposits in 1999 and 2000

Some observers have raised concern over the fact that in 1999 and 2000 a large volume of 10-year time deposits will mature and possibly threaten the postal savings system with massive withdrawal of funds. We do not believe this is a serious concern for two reasons, with one caveat.

First, low interest rates on alternative investments in 1999 and projected for 2000 will provide few incentives to withdraw finds from the postal savings system. Combined with concern over the health of private financial institutions and the low levels of household confidence in the economy, it is difficult to see how large transfers of funds would take place.

Second, the government guarantee of all bank deposits announced by the Ministry of Finance in 1995 will expire April 1, 2001. It is unclear whether Japan has made the necessary attitudinal changes to move to a financial regulation and supervision regime consistent with the objectives of the Big Bang. While considerable progress has been made since 1998, much more needs to be accomplished. As a result, large shifts of funds from the postal savings system are not likely in anticipation of the complete deposit guarantee removal. There have even been suggestions by some officials that the government needs to extend the deposit guarantee. This would be a mistake, but the very fact it is discussed suggests that large shifts of funds from the postal savings system are not likely.

There is one caveat, however. Foreign banks have increased their presence in Japan's deposit market and, combined with exchange rate liberalization in 1997, there is some chance postal funds could shift to foreign banks either as yen deposits or foreign currency deposits. While more likely than a shift of funds from post offices to domestic banks, we also view this is not very likely because of the long standing relationship depositors have with the post office, the extensive branching network of the post office, and the lack of an instrument that can compete with the 10-year time deposit postal account.

CONCLUSION

Postal savings and the Fiscal Investment and Loan Program (FILP) are incompatible with a modern financial system outlined in the 1996 Big Bang program. These institutions perpetuate inefficiency in the flow of funds and, in the case of postal deposits, complicate efforts to establish a government deposit guarantee system consistent with a modern financial regulatory and supervisory framework. Despite over two decades of an official policy of financial liberalization, government financial intermediation generally has continued to expand. In the 1990s it has generated new concerns. There is evidence of disintermediation of funds from private to postal deposits, government financing of activities that further extends FILP, and a nonperforming loan problem of an unknown magnitude.

Japan still has a window of opportunity to deal with these issues but, from 1 April 2001, the blanket deposit guarantee enacted in 1995 expires. The potential for disintermediation remains a serious concern.

The solution offered here is not viewed as optimal. An optimal solution consists of privatizing both postal deposits and life insurance, perhaps through auction to domestic and foreign financial institutions. The asset side of FILP would be significantly reduced and those remaining government financial institutions and enterprises would be required to secure funding in the open market. These institutions, however, have a long and important history in Japan's financial system and economy. This makes an economically optimal solution impractical. In addition, the optimal solution still leaves unanswered the issue of how to bring a modern mix of financial services to all parts of Japan.

Resolution of the conflicts between government-intermediated finance and Japan's efforts to achieve a modern financial structure will be a significant indicator of Japan's ability and willingness to move to the type of financial system envisaged by the Big Bang program. Unless Japan can develop an acceptable exit strategy for the government to reduce its extensive involvement in the financial system significantly, Japan will not achieve a modern financial system consistent with the goals of the Big Bang.

ACKNOWLEDGEMENTS

The authors express appreciation to the Japan-US Friendship Commission for financial support in the preparation of this chapter.

NOTES

1 Japan's fiscal year ends March 31. The data presented in the tables and frequently referred to in the paper are fiscal year data, so "1998" means the year ending March 31, 1999.
2 The system is a major provider of nontransaction deposit services. However, although the system offers automatic deposits and bill paying for public utilities and similar services, only a small percentage of postal savings deposits are held as ordinary or transaction deposits because of the separate clearing mechanisms of private banks and post offices. In addition, post office cash dispensers are located only in post offices and thus are not as readily available as those operated by private banks.
The system was originally aimed at small savers and thus has had a maximum deposit size. Currently this is ¥10 million yen.
3 Discussions of the evolution of Japan's financial system in general, and government financial intermediation in particular, include: Anderson (1990); Calder (1990); Cargill, Hutchison, and Ito (1997); Hamada and Horiuchi (1987); Kuwayama (forthcoming); Patrick (1967 and 1994); and Teranishi (1995).
4 In the 1930s in the United States, the alternative of postal savings also led to funds moving from private banks to post offices. See Kuwayama (forthcoming) for discussion and evidence on this point, as well as an interesting comparison between the postal savings systems of Japan and the United States. The US system ended in 1966.
5 The Trust Fund Asset Management Council has continued its study of the FILP system. The Council has been preparing a cost analysis of each FILP agency and will be preparing a report in 2000.

REFERENCES

Anderson, Stephen J. 1990. "The Political Economy of Japanese Saving: How Postal Savings and Public Pensions Support High Rates of Household Savings in Japan." *Journal of Japanese Studies*, Winter: 61–92.

Calder, Kent E. 1990. "Linking Welfare and the Developmental State: Postal Savings in Japan." *Journal of Japanese Studies,* 16:31–59.

Cargill, Thomas F. 1993. "Deposit guarantees, nonperforming loans, and the postal savings system in Japan." FDICIA: An Appraisal. Conference on Bank Structure and Competition, Federal Reserve Bank of Chicago, pp 465–72.

Cargill, Thomas F, Michael M Hutchison, and Takatoshi Ito. 1997. *The Political Economy of Japanese Monetary Policy*. The MIT Press.

Cargill, Thomas F, Michael M Hutchison, and Takatoshi Ito. 1998. "The Banking Crisis in Japan." In G Caprio, Jr, WC Hunter, GG Kaufman, and DM Leipziger, editors, *Preventing Bank Crises: Lessons from Recent Global Bank Failures*. The World Bank.

Cargill, Thomas F, Michael M Hutchison, and Takatoshi Ito. forthcoming. *Financial Policy and Central Banking in Japan*. The MIT Press.

Cargill, Thomas F and Shoichi Royama. 1988. *The Transition of Finance in Japan and the United States*. Hoover Institution Press.

Cargill, Thomas F and Shoichi Royama. 1992. "The Evolution of Japanese Banking and Finance." In George G Kaufman, editor, *Banking Structures in Major Countries*. Kluwer Academic Publishers.

Cargill, Thomas F and Naoyuki Yoshino. 1998. "Too Big for its Boots." *The Financial Regulator* 3: 39–43 (Dec).

Cargill, Thomas F and Naoyuki Yoshino. 1999 Apr. "Japan's Postal Savings System: Financial Liberalization, Dilemmas, and Solutions." Manuscript.

Elixman, Dieter. 1992 Jun. "Current Status of Postal Banking: The Case of Europe." Korea Information Society Development Institute Conference.

Financial Times. 1998 Mar 3. "Politicians' intervention call rallies Tokyo market." Written by Gillian Tett and Bethen Hutton.

Feldman, Robert Alan. 1986. *Japanese Financial Markets: Deficits, Dilemmas, and Deregulation*. The MIT Press.

Hamada, Koichi and Akiyoshi Horiuchi. 1987. "The Political Economy of the Financial Market." In Kozo Yamamura and Yasukichi Yasuba, editors, *The Political Economy of Japan*, vol I. Stanford University Press.

Kamada, Koichiro. 1993. "The Real Value of Postal Savings Certificates." (Bank of Japan) *Monetary and Economic Studies,* 11: 59–96 (Nov).

Kuwayama, Patricia Hagan. Forthcoming. "Postal Banking in the United States and Japan: A Comparative Analysis." (Bank of Japan) *Monetary and Economic Studies*.

Matsuoka, Mikihiro and Brian Rose. 1994. The DIR Guide to Japanese Economic Statistics, p 160 t 34.6 Oxford University Press.

Ogura, Seiritso and Naoyuki Yoshino. 1988. "Tax System and the Fiscal Investment and Loan Program." In Ryutaro Komiya, Masahiro Okuno, and Kotaro Suzumura, editors, *Industrial Policy of Japan*. New York: Academic Press.

Patrick, Hugh. 1967. "Japan 1868–1914." In Cameron Rondo, editor, *Banking in the Early Stages of Industrialization*. New York: Oxford University Press.

Patrick, Hugh. 1994. "The Relevance of Japanese Finance and its Main Bank System." In Masahiko Aoki and Hugh Patrick, editors, *The Japanese Main Banking System*. Oxford: Oxford University Press.

Sakakibara, Eisuke. 1991. "The Japanese Politico-Economic System and the Public Sector." In Samuel Kernell, editor, *Parallel Politics*. The Brookings Institution.

Suzuki, Yoshio (editor). 1987. *The Japanese Financial System*. Oxford: Claredon Press.

Teranishi, Juro. 1995 Apr. "Sezenkini okeru Seisaku Kinyu-Ginko." *Keizai Kenkyu* 46.

Yoshino, Naoyuki. 1987. "Different Sources of Funds for the Fiscal Investment and Loan Program and its Impact on Macro Economy." In Shiro Yabushita and Kazumi Asako, editors, *Fiscal Policy and the Japanese Economy*. Tokyo: Keizai Shinpo-sha. In Japanese.

Yoshino, Naoyuki. 1991. "Financial Liberalization and the role of the government financing." (Economic Planning Agency) *Economic Society and Policy* (ESP)(Jan). In Japanese.

Yoshino, Naoyuki. 1994. "Five scenarios for the future direction of ¥200 trillion in Postal Savings." *Economisuto*. In Japanese.

Yoshino, Naoyuki and Masao Nakata. 1997 Sep. "Investment Promotion Effect by the Government Banks." Japan Finance Association Conference, Tokyo. In Japanese.

Yoshino, Naoyuki and Ryoko Sano. 1997. "The Relationship Between the Choice of Deposits by Households and its Convenience Factor." Japan Association of Finance Conference, Sapporo. In Japanese.

Yoshino, Naoyuki. 1999. "Big Bang of Household Asset Management." In Naoyuki Yoshino, R Asano, and M Kawakita, editors, *Financial Reform of Japanese Style*. Tokyo: Yuhikaku Shuppan. In Japanese.

PART III

Financial Structure Change and the Big Bang

Chapter 9

THE BIG BANG: IDEA AND REALITY

Akiyoshi Horiuchi
University of Tokyo

The Japanese financial system has been obsessed by the nonperforming loan problem since the beginning of the 1990s. The government failed to deal with the problem quickly, and thereby made the situation progressively worse. Ultimately, it was necessary to deal with the problem as an emergency and inject public funds into banks as additional capital in order to regain stability in the Japanese financial system. It is widely believed that regaining financial stability is a prerequisite for recovery of the Japanese economy (Horiuchi 1999a; Hoshi and Kashyap 1999).

However, we should note that a total reform of the financial system has been progressing despite the nonperforming loan problem in the banking sector. The reform has followed the "Big Bang" Reformation Plan advocated by the Hashimoto Cabinet in November 1996. In my view, this reformation implies a breakdown of the financial regime governing the Japanese economy during the last half century. The old regime was formed in the wake of the financial crisis in the late 1920s, and was strengthened both by wartime controls during the first half of the 1940s and by the reconstruction policy followed by the government immediately after the war. During the high growth era of the 1950s through the early 1970s, the old regime dominated corporate finance. Now Japan is in the process of constructing a new financial regime that will dominate the Japanese economy at least during the first decade of the 21st century. The Big Bang is the beginning of the regime change.

The 1980s was the age of financial deregulation in global capital markets. Many countries started to liberalize various regulations imposed on the financial system. In some aspects, financial deregulation is "contagious" in the sense that deregulation in one country compels others closely connected to it through capital markets to follow. Japan was not exceptional in this regard. The government started deregulation with a fundamental amendment to the Foreign Exchange Control Law in 1980, and subsequently has gradually narrowed the area of the financial system that was heavily regulated either by statute or by administrative guidance. Japanese become accustomed to ongoing, piecemeal liberalization. Thus, some view the Big Bang as a kind of culmination of Japanese financial deregulation.

However, we should recognize the important discontinuity in the story of the Big Bang plan. Most importantly, the Ministry of Finance (MOF), which used to dominate Japanese financial reform, has clearly been losing influence. This remarkable phenomenon reflects the fact that MOF resorted to traditional ways of financial administration in the face of nonperforming loans, and thereby failed to cope with the financial crisis successfully. For better or worse, the decline of the role of MOF means the disappearance of an adhesive agent that unified the separated sectors of the financial system into the old regime. This chapter explains in what sense Big Bang reforms will promote the regime change in the Japanese financial system.

In the next section, I present the background of the Big Bang plan. First, I explain how the delayed process of financial deregulation has led to an inefficient financial system in Japan. Second, I examine the traditional safety net that was an important element of the old regime. Third, I explain how MOF lost influence. I next explain some of the financial reforms that have already started. I then take up what issues remain to be settled before the goals of the Big Bang are realized. The last section discusses how the Big Bang is expected to influence the Japanese economy.

WHAT IS THE BIG BANG?

In November 1996, Prime Minister Ryutaro Hashimoto proposed a plan of financial reforms called Japan's "Big Bang." According to this policy package, the Japanese financial system is to be totally reformed following the basic principles of (1) free markets, (2) fair trade secured by transparent and reliable rules, and (3) an institutional framework satisfying international standards in such areas as legal, accounting, and supervision. Obviously, this Big Bang was produced by recognizing that both the inefficient financial system brought forth by a lack of free competition and the opaque financial administration implemented by MOF are responsible for the prolonged banking crisis. This section investigates the meaning of the Big Bang plan by explaining how the old financial regime reached an impasse.

Delayed Financial Deregulation

The conventional view is that a combination of financial deregulation and lack of effective prudential regulations can explain the bank crises observed in many countries during the 1980s and '90s (Keely 1990; Lindgren et al 1997). According to this view, financial deregulation reduced the profitability of the traditional financial services industry, particularly of banking, inducing banks and other financial institutions to take high-flying risk because of the safety net provided by deposit insurance and the like. In the absence of effective prudential regulation, it is possible for banks to extend their risk-taking activities. The consequence is a crisis in the banking and other financial sectors when the risky lending becomes nonperforming loans.

However, it is doubtful this view holds in the Japanese case. Although not totally inactive in deregulating financial and capital markets prior to 1996 (see, for example, Takeda and Turner 1992), the government (more specifically, the MOF) deliberately controlled the process of deregulation so that competition promoted by liberalization would not damage existing financial intermediaries. Deregulation of deposit interest rates was an example of the slow pace. It started with the introduction of negotiable certificates of deposits (NCDs) in 1979. However, for nearly a decade MOF permitted banks to issue NCDs only in a heavily restricted form. Full liberalization of interest rates on time deposits was not accomplished until 1994.

The government considered the stability of the financial system synonymous with absence of exit (through either liquidation or bankruptcy) of existing financial institutions. As a consequence, the pace of deregulation was kept gradual to protect inefficiently managed institutions. In particular, MOF was obsessed by the notion that preventing bank failures was the most important objective of financial administration. This induced it to bail out distressed banks under essentially any circumstances and generally using opaque measures. Somewhat ironically, this notion hindered MOF from introducing explicit rules to deal with bank failures by means of exit policy measures. The notion thus led to the notorious forbearance policy.

The government was not only rigorous in controlling new entry into the financial service industry, but also was particularly cautious in keeping the framework of compartmentalization established immediately after World War II. Institutions belonging to a specific sector of financial services have been prohibited from entering other sectors. This has protected the vested interests in each section and made the system as a whole less contestable.

The compartmentalization was to some extent effective in improving efficiency of financial intermediation. The typical example was the system of long-term credit banks. This system mitigated the difficulty of extreme maturity transformation that the banking sector was required to undertake immediately after the war, when ultimate fund raisers (firms) wanted long-term credit whereas ultimate savers (households) wanted highly liquid short-term stores of value. Long-term credit banks were created to address this problem. As the economy grew, however, the system lost its *raison d'etre*. Nevertheless, the government suppressed development of securities markets that would potentially compete with long-term credit banking.

In my view, government policy indulged the long-term credit banks by keeping the old-style lending policy despite the rapid reduction of major companies' reliance on bank borrowing. If the government had abandoned the protective policy at the beginning of the 1980s, long-term credit banks would have faced the necessity of restructuring their way of business much earlier. The fact that two of the three long-term credit banks are now nationalized because of extremely bad performance is one of the most conspicuous examples of the ultimate failure of the compartmentalization policy.

The lack of contestability produced tolerance for inefficiently managed financial institutions. The nonperforming loan problem and other difficulties that surfaced during the early 1990s immediately after the bursting of the "bubble" revealed the managerial inefficiency of Japanese financial institutions. Complaints by end-users of financial services concerning the system's inefficiency were an important factor promoting what came to be the Big Bang reform.

Too Comprehensive a Safety Net

A by-product of gradual deregulation was the ill-preparation of the government for disposing of distressed banks. The government did not want to recognize plain exit. Instead, it implemented a policy of keeping the appearance of stability through a large safety net. Not only small depositors, but also investors in bank-issued debt, were secured against bank failures. MOF guided (more precisely, ordered) the relatively strong (big) banks to absorb those on the brink of bankruptcy.

The most conspicuous example is Sumitomo Bank absorbing Heiwa Sogo in 1986. Heiwa Sogo, which was one of the largest regional banks of the mutual savings type, suffered from bad performance mainly due to inefficient management. In return for taking over Heiwa, Sumitomo obtained Heiwa's branch network in the Tokyo metropolitan area. Because MOF controlled the number and location of branches for each bank, Sumitomo otherwise would not have been able to extend its network so quickly.

As this example shows, the wide-scope safety net was supported by competition-restricting regulations such as restrictions on branching. The competition-restricting regulations conferred rents on banks and financial institutions, particularly large-scale ones. Because of the rent, large banks could afford to provide part of the safety net. This mechanism seemed rational in the sense that it did not require explicit financial support from the government using public funds. However the cost was transferred to end-users of financial services, who were provided with services of low quality at relatively high prices.

This sort of wide-scope safety net is no longer viable given the change in financial market structure that has taken place. Thus, it has been more and more difficult for MOF to persuade financial institutions to collaborate.

The opaqueness of the administration adopted by MOF undermined the safety net because it was not possible to examine whether MOF deployed the net in a cost-minimizing way. As Kane (1995) points out, the lack of effective monitoring of regulators brings forth an agency problem in the sense that the regulator does not necessarily pursue the role the public delegated to it. There exists the danger that the regulator and the regulated transfer the costs of imprudence to end-users and then to the public. Unfortunately, Japan has observed the occurrence of this agency problem in the 1990s. Thus, the full-scale competition in the financial system the Big Bang plan is promoting is closely related to the issue of how to rebuild the safety net.

Who Promoted the Big Bang?

Since the end of World War II, MOF single-handedly undertook the important decision-making regarding financial matters. But the influence of MOF in forming the Big Bang plan was not so great as might have been expected. This was because MOF has repeatedly made mistakes since the mid 1980s.

One important mistake was continuing the gradualism of reform in the face of a rapidly changing economic and technological environment. The Laws Related to Financial Reformation (LRFR, *Kinyu-Seido Kaikaku Kanren Ho*) in 1992 was epoch-making in the sense that they stipulated the possibility of cross-over entry in the form of subsidiaries between various financial sectors. However, MOF reduced the effectiveness of the Laws by restraining the scope of business newly established subsidiaries could undertake. For example, MOF did not permit subsidiaries of banks to take part in the stock brokerage business because this business was considered an important source of revenues for existing small securities companies. The subsidiaries of trust banks established by commercial banks, long-term credit banks, and securities companies were not permitted to develop full-scale trust business. This was because MOF was worried about the damage existing trust banks would suffer if they faced new competition. Thus, despite the LRFR, Japanese financial markets remained far from being contestable.

The serious nonperforming loan problem in the banking sector can also be related to MOF's traditional procedures, which failed to dispose of problem banks quickly. Rather, they produced moral hazard and a forbearance policy that made the nonperforming loan problem more and more serious. As a result of traditional MOF procedures, a huge burden was transferred to taxpayers.[1]

A direct consequence of the Big Bang was the Laws for Financial System Reformation (LFSR) enacted in June 1998. These specify various amendments of the Banking Law (*Ginko Ho*), the Law of Securities Transactions (*Shoken Torihiki Ho*), and the Law for the Insurance Industry (*Hokengyo Ho*) with a view to promoting market competition and protecting end-users (particularly individual investors) from undue risk. Formally, these amendments were based on reports submitted to MOF a year ago by prestigious advisory councils. These are the Council for the Financial System (*Kinyu Seido Chosa-kai*), the Council for Securities Transactions (*Shoken Torihiki Shingi-kai*), and the Council for the Insurance Industry (*Hoken Shingi-kai*).

The use of councils followed the procedure of previous reforms. Historically, MOF is generally believed to have almost perfectly controlled what topics are investigated by its councils and what is proposed in the reports they submit. Thus, council reports have been regarded as the policy agenda desired by MOF. This time the actual process and result have been quite different.

MOF was continuing to claim that the purpose of its administrative intervention was to provide efficiency and stability to the financial system, but it clearly had failed to achieve this. This failure fed significant outside criticism of the traditional MOF approach to administration and reform, and of the government. This outside force was the impetus for the Big Bang.

For example, in April 1995, the Deregulation Subcommittee (*Kiseikanwa Sho-iinkai*) of the Administrative Reform Committee (*Gyosei Kaikaku Iinkai*) started to list desirable deregulations in many areas of Japanese society and to demand that administrators take specific measures to realize the deregulation. The subcommittee's list included many matters related to the financial service industry, reflecting strong dissatisfaction by end-users (particularly, non-financial firms). The subcommittee was not easily ignored because it was reporting directly to a Cabinet that had promoted deregulation by statute. (The Administrative Reform Committee was formed by the Murayama Cabinet, which was a coalition of anti-LDP groups but, on coming to power, the LDP-based Hashimoto Cabinet retained the Committee.)

MOF was forced to respond specifically to the subcommittee's demands. The activities of the subcommittee contributed to MOF's change from gradualism to more positive deregulation.

Diet members have increased their influence on the process in the late 1990s by passing important laws to deal with the crisis. Considering the landscape of Japanese politics, in which the bureaucracy has been overwhelmingly influential, this is remarkable. Of course, we should refrain from being too optimistic because there remains great uncertainty about whether the legislators will be able to lead the bureaucracy to relevant decision-making regarding financial matters.

SPECIFIC REFORMS

After announcing the Big Bang in November 1996, the government has proceeded to implement reforms on many fronts. In particular, the 1998 LFSR was important in the sense that it specified reforms in various financial sectors. Other reforms have proceeded in parallel with the LFSR. This section explains reforms since November 1996 and discusses their implications for the Japanese economy.

Improvements in the Asset-Management Industry

One focus of the Big Bang is how to improve the asset-management industry. This is important because, although the Japanese households have accumulated a huge amount of financial wealth, they have not enjoyed high-quality asset management. A consequence is the continued heavy concentration of assets at banks and postal savings accounts.

Personal-sector financial assets increased by nearly four-fold from 1965 to 1996. However, the relative share of securities decreased by half, while that of deposits (at banks and in postal savings) stayed at just over 50%. Data are in Table 9.1. (For annual data since 1964, see Table 10.1 in Royama, Chapter 10.)

This means the banking sector is heavily involved in decision-making regarding the risk-sharing associated with financial intermediation. Thus, ups and downs of the banking sector influence all too vividly the whole activity of financial intermediation in Japan.

TABLE 9.1. Compositions of Financial Assets Held by the Personal Sector (billion yen and percents)

	1965 December		1996 December	
Asset	yen	%	yen	%
Cash	192	5.9	426	3.5
Deposits	1,687	52.1	6,452	53.4
Trust Accounts	144	4.4	769	6.4
Insurance	362	11.2	3,034	25.1
Securities	741	22.9	1,410	11.7
Other	111	3.4	0	0.0
Total	3,238	—	12,092	—
Securities is composed of (percentages are of total assets)				
Bank debentures	72	2.2	206	1.7
Investment trusts[1]	107	3.3	317	2.6
Stocks	515	15.9	739	6.1
Other	47	1.5	148	1.3

1. Similar to mutual funds.

Source: Bank of Japan, Research and Statistics Department, *Flow of Funds Account*, various issues.

Bank credit is one of the most important methods of risk sharing. However, the presence of other methods should be more important in the Japanese financial system. For example, many people argue that bank credit is less effective in promoting venture businesses than capital market mechanisms supported by venture capitalists (Black and Gilson 1998; Milhaupt 1997). According to their discussions, it would be desirable to change the path of the flow of funds to make direct flows from the ultimate savers to ultimate users more important. To do this, the quality of asset management services must be improved substantially.

Asset management has been primarily the province of trust banks and life insurance companies. However, they seem to have adopted strategies that are not always consistent with benefits to ultimate investors (households). For example, insurance companies reportedly collaborated with non-financial companies by holding blocks of shares in order to ward off capital market pressures on incumbent managers. In return, the companies become faithful clients for the services of the insurance companies.

It is also noteworthy that Japanese insurance companies have been deeply involved in the MOF's *ad hoc* policy to bail out distressed banks by providing the banks with capital without, at least with hindsight, reasonable returns. Sometimes, insurers have been required to purchase junior debt or preferred stock issued by banks to strengthen the banks' capital bases. But they have often experienced capital loss or default losses. Their investment practices are not justified by the standard theory of asset management.

In the wake of the bank crisis precipitated by nonperforming loans in the early 1990s, the insurance industry faces serious difficulty because of the abnormally low returns in financial markets. Most of its liabilities were issued during the "bubble" period and promise high rates of return to policy holders, so continuation of the abnormally low interest rates induced by BOJ policy to mitigate the critical situation for banks has severely hit insurers. Two have already gone bankrupt: Nissan Mutual Life in April 1997, and Toho Mutual Life in June 1999.

The entry of asset-management companies has been liberalized during the past few years. This has already been effective in fostering competition, which will improve welfare for Japanese households.

The government has started reforms intended to improve the investment trust market. For example, new types, such as the private investment trust, have been authorized by a June 1998 amendment to the Investment Trust Act.

Banks and insurance companies have been permitted to sell investment trust accounts directly to customers since June 1998. According to a survey by *Kinzai* (the periodical *Kinyu Zaisei Jijo,* 23 June 1999), as of May 1999 the outstanding amount of investment trusts sold by banks and insurance companies was ¥1.1 trillion. Although that is just 2.2% of total outstanding trust funds, it was gained in less than a year. Banks and insurance companies are expected to increase market share as they develop their services.

The development of asset management companies is expected by some observers to affect corporate governance by prodding corporate managers to be more shareholder-oriented. Some scholars expect changes in corporate governance will improve managerial efficiency (for example, Gibson, Chapter 12).

The LFSR amended the Securities Exchange Law and the Law of the Insurance Industry to establish specific organizations with the purpose of protecting investors and insurance policyholders against bankruptcies.

Reforming Corporate Finance

Internationalization of corporate finance since the mid-1980s promoted deregulation in the domestic corporate bond market even before the Big bang. In particular, the system of standards for corporate bond issue (*tekisai kijun*) which required unduly stringent financial conditions on issuing firms, and thereby, prevented development of the corporate bond market since 1954, was abolished in January 1996. Since the announcement of the Big Bang, the corporate finance system has been considerably liberalized. For example, new fund-raising methods have been introduced, including perpetual bonds (perpetual in the sense of not having to be issued at a particular time; they do in fact have maturity dates) and medium-term notes (MTNs). A firm can contract with securities companies to issue bonds repeatedly within a predetermined maximum amount under the MTNs program, which gives the issuer significant flexibility as to when to issue.

With a view to helping small-scale firms raise funds, the government has begun implementing a policy package to develop an over-the-counter market for stocks and to promote a market for unlisted stocks. A change in the law effective in May 1999 allows non-bank finance companies to lend funds raised by issuing bonds and commercial paper. It is expected that the market for personal loans and loans to small businesses will be more competitive as a result.

The merits of these reforms in corporate finance cannot be denied. However, they merely ratify for Japan improvements in corporate finance that were developed elsewhere. Many blue-chip Japanese companies have actively raised funds in international capital markets such as the Euro-bond market for almost two decades. Since they can easily overcome inconvenient domestic restrictions by going to international markets, the old rules for domestic corporate finance have promoted a hollowing out phenomenon in Japanese capital markets. If the government is to prevent a continuation of this hollowing, it must further liberalize domestic markets.

Table 9.2 shows changes in the components of fund-raising by major companies since the early 1960s. They had already started reducing reliance on bank credit in the late 1970s, before the government started deregulating. The overwhelming importance of internal funds (mainly depreciation and retained profits) during the last two decades is noteworthy. It suggests that financial deregulation has not had as significant an impact on the financing of major companies as many believe.

Probably the more important policy development is the promotion of capital markets for small-scale businesses. Traditionally, small businesses have depended heavily on bank credit and bank relationships, although their relative presence in the overall bank credit market was relatively small during the high growth era of the early 1950s to the early 1970s. Their share was only one-third in 1980, for example. However, their share increased rapidly, to over two-thirds in the late 1980s, a level it has kept during the last decade. This suggests that small businesses have found it difficult to end their dependence on bank credit. This is primarily due to the asymmetric-information problems associated with small business financing. Thus, the relationship with banks is more important for those small firms than for large ones (Petersen and Rajan 1995).

However, the bank crisis has shaken this relationship. It is necessary for even small businesses to have an alternative fund-raising method to avoid the liquidity crisis created by banks reluctant to lend. The refusal of banks to supply liquidity is a natural response to the necessity of recapitalizing, but it has fostered distrust of banks. It may take a long time for the traditional relationship between banks and firms, the so-called main bank relationship, to be rebuilt.

The traditional bank-firm relationship has not been helpful to venture businesses with high risk. We need more comprehensive mechanisms of risk sharing and technical evaluation than bank-loan methods have provided. The Japanese capital market should be more active in promoting venture businesses. However, despite its size, Japan's capital market has only started to develop this

TABLE 9.2. Components of Fund-Raising by Major Companies, 5-year Averages (in percents)

Period	Internal Funds	Bonds	Borrowing	Equity	Other
1961–65	25.4	6.5	36.1	9.7	22.3
1966–70	26.6	4.7	38.6	4.0	16.0
1961–75	33.8	7.0	42.6	4.0	12.6
1976–80	50.7	8.1	20.9	8.0	12.4
1981–85	61.2	10.5	11.7	11.4	5.2
1986–90	47.9	18.0	3.2	16.6	14.3
1991–95	102.8	9.3	3.2	2.1	–17.3

Other includes trade credit and minor items. It is negative in the 1990–95 period mainly because trade credit decreased substantially.

Source: Bank of Japan, *Financial Statements of Principal Enterprises*, various issues.

function. Japan can learn much from the venture-capital experience in the United States (see, for example, Black and Gilson 1998).

Reforms for an Efficient Capital Market

Since the liberalization of foreign exchange transactions and capital movements at the beginning of the 1980s, Japan's capital markets have become more closely intertwined with their international counterparts than have other parts of the financial system. Thus, intermediaries in the capital market have been more sensitive to competitive pressures from abroad and, relatively speaking, quicker to respond to the demand for effective liberalization of domestic markets than have domestic-oriented intermediaries.

A significant development in Japan's capital market is the strengthening of rules regarding fair and transparent transactions. The government has improved the disclosure system in two respects. First is the requiring of consolidated accounting, effective with fiscal 1998 for banks and financial companies. The old standard of consolidation was ineffective in preventing manipulation to hide bad performance by transferring losses or bad assets from a parent company's own accounts to those of subsidiaries. This was possible because subsidiaries were defined only in terms of the percentage of shares held, ignoring situations where there was effective control. In Japan, such control is common even when there is only a small holding of shares. Due to the changed rule, there was a sharp increase in the number of subsidiaries reported by banks in March 1999. (And the amount of nonperforming loans for city banks was around ¥13 trillion higher under the new rules (Nikkei Shimbun, 22 May 1999)). The new standard will be applied to non-financial companies from April 2000.

"Cash flow-based accounting" will be introduced at March 2000. Cash flow-based accounting is to evaluate the performance of companies in terms of discounted present value of cash flows. The capital market is expected to evaluate a firm's value more precisely, and to strengthen the disciplinary power of the capital market over corporate management.

Although it is not directly related to the Big Bang, the 1993 amendment to the Commercial Code that substantially lowered the cost of initiating derivative actions for shareholders seems to have been changing the landscape of corporate governance in Japan (Milhaupt 1996, p 55–57). The amendment fixed the filing fee for initiating a derivative suit at ¥82000—less than the cost of filing a case in small claims court in most US jurisdictions. Previously, shareholders needed a huge amount of money to initiate suits. Passage of the amendment was helped by the many scandals involving incumbent managers that surfaced after the bursting of the bubble at the beginning of the 1990s and the loss of faith in the traditional system of management monitoring centered on the bank-firm relationship (the so-called main-bank relationship). Only 27 suits were filed during the 40 years from 1950 to 1990. Helped by the amendment, there were 23 during the 3 years from 1991 to 1994.[2]

Reforms for Market Competition

To improve the performance of the financial service industry in Japan, we need to make the industry more contestable by allowing new entry into every segment. Competition will discipline managers by forcing inefficiently managed firms to exit. In reality, the government has undertaken a very careful (rather timid) policy of gradually reducing entry barriers.

The best-placed entrant into a specific financial service is a firm already operating in a similar segment. For example, it is easier for banks to start securities businesses than it is for non-financial companies. Mutual cross-over of intermediaries thus has been the first step in promoting contestability. Deregulation of compartmentalization started in 1993 when existing financial institutions were permitted to enter markets outside their own territories, although only by establishing subsidiaries. Insurance was an exception: it has remained segregated.

To protect existing firms, the government has not permitted new entrants to engage in the full line of services that the existing firms provide. For example, the securities subsidiaries established by the banks have not yet been allowed to take part in stock brokerage because that is the most lucrative business for existing securities companies, especially small ones. Bank subsidiaries also have been restricted in their underwriting because their parent banks are believed to be "unduly" influential in the fund-raising policy of client companies. Similarly, although the LRFR permitted commercial banks and securities companies to establish subsidiary trust banks, they are not allowed to develop full-scale trust businesses.

This restrictive approach has been criticized because it has kept the Japanese financial system far from being contestable. The Big Bang plan, through the LFSR in 1998, responded to the criticism by lifting most of the restrictions on cross-over entry within the financial service industry.

There also is some entry from outside the existing industry. For example, in March 1999 Orix Trust Bank was formed by Orix Corporation using the new approach of direct deposits: investors can deposit funds using a telephone or the internet. In April 1999 Mitsubishi Trading Company entered the securities and investment advisory businesses.

In the context of deregulating compartmentalization, the holding company system is a noteworthy issue. The Anti-trust Law used to prohibit establishing a holding company that held more than 50% of the shares in various related or unrelated businesses. In June 1997, the law was amended to permit "pure form" holding companies (see Kanda, Chapter 11).

Restrictions arising from the Commercial Code continued to limit use of holding companies until August 1999, when amendments to the Code took effect. Daiwa Securities Company has already formed a holding company. The Industrial Bank of Japan announced a plan to change its managerial structure in 2000, and its subsequent agreement to merge with Dai-ichi Kangyo and Fuji Banks will use a holding company structure.

Strengthening Prudential Regulation

The current financial crisis has belatedly forced the government to recognize the importance of prudential regulation. The crisis also forced the government to take emergency measures to reconstruct the safety net. I will not discuss the emergency measures (for which, see Horiuchi 1999 and Milhaupt 1999), but will look at some important developments in prudential regulation.

Some major reforms have been implemented since the announcement of the Big Bang in 1996. The most important is the June 1998 establishment of the Financial Supervisory Agency (FSA), which is directly under the prime minister and independent of MOF. The functions of monitoring financial markets and supervising banks and other financial institutions were transferred from MOF to FSA. In July 2000, FSA will be upgraded to being the Finance Agency (*Kinyu Cho*), responsible for wide-ranging matters related to the financial system. At that time, MOF will become the Treasury Ministry (*Zaimu Sho*) mainly in charge of budgetary and taxation matters.[3]

This reform is quite appropriate. An independent agency will be more suitable for accumulating information with respect to the financial sector than was MOF, which had acquired too widely dispersed a set of responsibilities. FSA has reportedly kept an arm's-length relationship with individual banks and financial institutions, which should reduce moral hazard.

To avoid excessive risk transfer to the Deposit Insurance Corporation, banks are required to self-assess their own capital adequacy ratios periodically, subject to external audit. The scheme, called the prompt corrective action rule (PCA) took effect in April 1998. The FSA administers the rule, which requires bank with capital ratios below certain specified levels to restructure or even cease operations. This should motivate banks with decreasing capital to restructure their balance sheets as soon as possible. PCA also is intended to prevent forbearance by regulators by having transparent rules of intervention into bank management.[4]

PCA is a preventive measure designed to reduce the severity, if not the number, of bank failures. Introduced at a time of fragility in the banking sector, it has put pressure on bank managers to adopt conservative credit policies. It is ironic that this caution has contributed to a "credit crunch" that has exacerbated Japan's economic difficulties.

Nonetheless, at present Japan needs such an emergency policy to force drastic structural changes on existing financial institutions. This is so even though the policy takes the form of an intensive government intervention that goes against the idea of the Big Bang. This is particularly applicable to the issue of how to recapitalize Japanese banks. The fact that the directions of the necessary emergency policy and the goals of the Big Bang are diametrically different complicates the process of financial reform in Japan.

WHAT ARE THE REMAINING ISSUES?

The reforms just outlined have been directed toward the goal of revitalizing the Japanese financial system through improving managerial efficiency and strengthening supervisory mechanisms. However, they are insufficient for achieving the goal. This section examines the other issues that need to be resolved in order to attain the ideal envisioned by the Big Bang.

Is Free Exit Allowable?

The dynamism of a financial system requires not only free entry but also free exit of the inefficient. However, the confusion in Japan over how to deal with distressed banks shows that we have not prepared well for outright exit. Another crisis is likely to occur immediately after the current bank crisis because of the diminished asset values and too-generous terms of the liabilities of insurance companies. There needs to be explicit rules allowing institutions to close without serious side effects.

The government has committed itself until April 2001 to a generous pay-off (deposit guarantee) procedure under the deposit insurance system. As of now, however, from April 2001 deposits will be revert to being insured only on the first ¥10 million for each depositor's accounts in each bank. This implies that holders of non-insured deposits and other bank debts will have to bear some of the burden associated with bank failures. However, under the current legal framework related to bank failure procedures, as a practical matter it will be impossible to reimburse insured depositors in a timely way.

Current law confers on the FSA the authority to initiate corporate reorganization or bankruptcy procedures with respect to banks on behalf of depositors. However, the Deposit Insurance Corporation (DIC) does not have the legal authority to serve as a receiver. Moreover, there exists no legal principle of giving priority to deposit liabilities over other debts. Thus, the pay-off procedure is expected to take longer than three weeks. To make the commitment with respect to the pay-off feasible, the government will have to substantially amend laws concerning bank failures.

Free exit is possible only if there is a clear-cut demarcation of responsibilities between the financial intermediaries (their managers and owners) and their clients. The traditional "paternalism" of financial regulators to bail out distressed intermediaries has blurred this demarcation. This issue is not yet settled.

In 1998, a committee organized by MOF finished rather general discussions about the necessity of comprehensive rules to make clear to what extent end-users of financial services should be protected from the problems of intermediaries and to what extent end-users should be responsible for protecting themselves. Many think Japan needs a unified legal framework to demarcate end-user responsibility. But we are still a long way from establishing comprehensive rules.

Will the New Supervisory Agency Work Effectively?

The Big Bang assumes the markets will work efficiently in the financial sector. However, it does not imply the government no longer plays any role. In particular, the government remains responsible for keeping the system fair and stable by supervising market transactions and monitoring the prudence of financial institutions. Those functions have been integrated into the Financial Supervisory Agency. It is required to collect relevant information from banks and other financial intermediaries and to keep an arm's-length relationship with them. Probably, administrative costs will increase substantially as a result. The FSA will also have to increase the number of its staff who are knowledgeable about details of the financial service business.

From the misbehavior of MOF, we have learned how important and difficult it is to give a supervisory agency incentives to accomplish the role delegated by taxpayers (Kane 1995 and Horiuchi and Shimizu 1998). The issue of how to motivate the agency to do good job remains to be discussed. Probably, it is necessary to require disclose of details about supervisory activities using a specified format and well-defined rules.

Although MOF now still maintains the function of financial reform planning, this will be transferred to the new Finance Agency once it is established. It will be able to use effectively the information collected by its supervisory staff. This will improve the efficiency of financial supervision and regulation.

There is still the question of whether the Deposit Insurance Corporation (DIC) should be integrated into the new Finance Agency. Due to the nonperforming loan problem, DIC has become progressively more important as the key piece of the safety net. I expect the Big Bang, by promoting free exit of financial institutions, will further increase the importance of DIC. However, DIC is not a government agency under the present legal framework; it is a special corporation with restricted authority. DIC has only limited powers to investigate bank management. Thus, it is advisable to examine the possibility of integrating DIC into the new Finance Agency.

To economize on the supervisory costs, the government should transfer some tasks to investors. Investors can be given strong incentives to monitor management of banks and other intermediaries, although it is not yet clear what form they will take.

Should Public Financial Institutions Be Kept Intact?

A big mystery about the Big Bang plan is that it did not explicitly refer to public financial institutions. Japan's financial system is characterized by a huge presence of public financial institutions—based on the postal saving and postal life insurance systems—with management that is sheltered from market discipline (see Cargill and Yoshino, Chapter 8). It seems difficult to obtain the vision of the Big Bang under such circumstances. Why was the Big Bang silent about these institutions? The major reason is political.

Postal savings is under the Ministry of Posts and Telecommunications (MPT). Bureaucratic turf battles have prevented discussion of reforms in the MPT's domain. The MPT is politically very influential because the widespread postal network has indirectly supported the electioneering of many politicians. The politicians in general do not want to abandon a convenient tool of distributing subsidies to specific areas or industries.

The public financial system has been intensively utilized to support the old financial system. For example, the government has reportedly intervened in stock trading with a view to supporting stock prices. This intervention, called the PKO (price-keeping-operation), has been regarded as important to help banks and financial institutions avoid decreases in their equity capital, which includes unrealized securities gains. Theoretically and empirically it is ambiguous whether or not the PKO has been effective. But many related to the policy believe in its effectiveness; for them, it would be unwise to abolish it.

Nowadays, there is some expectation that public financial institutions will make use of their extensive assets to mitigate the credit crunch. However, such an emergency policy should not be confused with the policy of structural reforms to construct an efficient financial system. There is a danger public involvement in an emergency policy package will transfer risk from private agents to the public sector. Such an irresponsible transfer will lead to degeneration of the financial system as a whole. In sum, the current system of public financial institutions seems to contradict the new regime the Big Bang is constructing. When and how the contradiction will be settled is an open question for Japan.

Is the Infrastructure Adaptable to Reforms?

Japan needs a more appropriate financial infrastructure if it is to achieve efficient transactions in financial markets. For example, government bonds, corporate bonds, commercial papers, and stocks have clearing and custody systems that function almost totally independent of one another. This is quite inconvenient for investors.

However, it will not be easy to establish a unified system covering the entire securities markets. Traditional compartmentalization has something to do with why there are separate systems; because each segment has sought to build a system specific to its group, combining them will not be easy. The practice of unanimous agreement has prevented a comprehensive clearing system from being realized and the government has been unable to settle the issue. It will take a considerable time to resolve this coordination failure.

Could the Tax System be Financial-Market Friendly?

Japanese taxation related to financial transactions is very comprehensive, very complex, and distorting. Although the distorting impact has been widely recognized, MOF does not seem enthusiastic about addressing the problem. Probably, it gives greater priority to collecting taxes than to whether the financial system is free from tax distortion. The taxation system should not be discussed only from the viewpoint of the financial services industry, but the system's distorting influence means it should be modified as soon as possible.

CONCLUSION

This overview of Big Bang reforms shows that the plan implies a regime change in Japan's financial system. The old regime fell into an impasse and the government has been compelled to hammer out a new policy of deregulation.

While hastening the pace of deregulation substantially, the Big Bang looks at deregulation from a long-term perspective. It restructures the safety net and the regulatory mechanism. This is a natural result of the fact that the traditional financial administration and the safety net managed by MOF were found wanting after being critically reconsidered in light of the financial crisis caused by the serious nonperforming loan problem of the 1990s.

The Big Bang plan emphasizes the importance of market competition and transparent rules of supervision. These are expected to improve the governance mechanisms in banking and at other financial institutions in the long run. However, drastic changes in the structure of the financial service industry would be required before the Big Bang's ideal is realized. For example, the number of banks and their employees will have to be reduced under the fierce competition in the financial system. This process seems to have finally gotten underway.

Obviously, Big Bang reforms tend to promote development of the securities market in comparison to banking (See Royama, Chapter 10). The theory of corporate governance predicts this tendency will change the system of corporate management control. Banks have played an overwhelmingly important role in the mechanism of corporate governance (Hoshi, Kashyap, and Sharfstein 1990 and 1991; Aoki and Patrick 1994). However, development of securities markets will decrease the importance of banks and will increase the importance of the disciplinary role of the capital market. In this sense, the Big Bang will move the Japanese system toward the Anglo-American system. This system change in corporate governance may increase the adaptability of corporate management to environmental changes. However, it is uncertain whether the system change will contribute to efficient management in the corporate sector from a long-term perspective.

ACKNOWLEDGEMENTS

The author appreciates the constructive comments and suggestions of Takeo Hoshi and Hugh Patrick; they greatly contributed to improving the quality of this paper.

NOTES

1 The Law on Emergency Measures to Revitalize the Functions of the Financial System and the Law on Emergency Measures to Promptly Restore the Function of the Financial System, both enacted in late 1998, established two special accounts, the Account for Prompt Financial Restructuring and the Financial Revitalization Account, within the Deposit Insurance Corporation (DIC). The Account for Prompt Financial Restructuring is to provide financial support for strengthening bank capital bases. The Financial Revitalization Account is to provide funds necessary for liquidation, temporary nationalization of failed banks, or transferring them temporarily to bridge banks. Both accounts are publicly supported by ¥53 trillion in the form of government guarantees. In addition, the government has provided government bonds amounting to ¥7 trillion to a special DIC account to protect depositors in the event of bank failures.

2 Reportedly the structural impediments initiative (SII) of the United States forced a substantial amendment to the Commercial Code. Besides leading to lower filing fees, the percentage of stock ownership required to inspect corporate books was reduced from 10% to 3%.
3 The Ministry of Finance has been proud of having a name (*Okura Sho*) going back in Japanese history more than 1300 years. (It is one of the eight ministries recognized in 702 by the *Taihoryo*, and existed by the time of a 689 reform of government structure. (See Samson 1958, p 67–68).) The loss of such a prestigious name is thus a powerfully symbolic punishment for the misbehavior and policy failures of the 1990s.
4 Under an amendment to the banking law (passed on 18 June 1996) which became effective on 1 April 1998, bank regulators can issue corrective orders as a bank's total risk-based capital adequacy ratio falls below each of three thresholds: 8%, 4%, and 0% for those banks with foreign branches, and 4%, 2%, and 0% for those without foreign branches, respectively. In category I (below 8%), a bank is required to create and implement a business improvement plan. For category 2 (below 4%), the bank must formulate a plan to increase capital, restrain gross asset growth, or cease expanding into new busineses, as deemed warranted. Banks falling in category 3 (below 0%) must suspend business. By June 1999 the FSA had applied the PCA to five banks.

REFERENCES

Aoki, Masahiko and Hugh Patrick. 1994. *The Japanese Main Bank System: Its Relevancy for Developing and Transforming Economies*. New York: Oxford University Press.

Black, Bernard S and Ronald J Gilson. 1998. "Venture capital and the structure of capital markets: banks versus stock markets." *Journal of Financial Economics* 47: 243–77.

Hanazaki, Masaharu and Akiyoshi Horiuchi. 1998. "A vacuum of governance in the Japanese bank management." Center for International Research on the Japanese Economy, Discussion Paper Series F-29, Faculty of Economics, University of Tokyo.

Horiuchi, Akiyoshi and Katsutoshi Shimizu. 1999. "Did amakudari undermine the effectiveness of regulator monitoring in Japan?" *Journal of Banking and Finance* (forthcoming).

Horiuchi, Akiyoshi. 1999. "Financial fragility and recent developments in the Japanese safety net." *Social Science Japan Journal* 2(1): 23–43.

Horiuchi, Akiyoshi. 1999a. "Japan's Bank Crisis: An Overview from Governance Perspectives." Paper presented at International Conference, Reform and Recovery in East Asia: The Role of the State and Economic Enterprise on 21–22 September 1999 at Australian National University, Canberra.

Hoshi, Takeo, Anil Kashyap, and David Scharfstein. 1990. "The role of banks in reducing the costs of financial distress in Japan." *Journal of Financial Economics* 27: 67–88.

Hoshi, Takeo, Anil Kashyap, and David Scharfstein. 1991. "Corporate structure, liquidity, and investment: Evidence from Japanese industrial groups." *Quarterly Journal of Economics* 106: 33–60.

Kane, Edward J. 1995. "Three paradigms for the role of capitalization requirements in insured financial institutions." *Journal of Banking and Finance* 19: 431–59.

Keeley, Michael C. 1990. "Deposit insurance, risk, and market power in banking." *American Economic Review* 80 (5): 1183–200.

Lindgren, Carl-Johan, Gillian Garcia, and Matthew I Saal. 1996. *Bank Soundness and Macroeconomic Policy*. International Monetary Fund.

Milhaupt, Curtis J. 1996. "A relational theory of Japanese corporate governance: Contract, culturE, and the rule of law." *Harvard International Law Journal* 37: 3–64.

Milhaupt, Curtis J. 1997. "Thc market for innovation in the United States and Japan: Venture capital and the comparative corporate governance debate." *Northwestern University Law Review* 91: 865–98.

Milhaupt, Curtis J. 1999. "Japan's experience with deposit insurance and failing banks: Implications for Financial Regulatory Design?" Bank of Japan. Monetary and Economic Studies 17, 2: 21–46.

Petersen, Mitchell A and Raghuran G Rajan. 1995. "The effect of credit market competition on lending relationships." *Quarterly Journal of Economics* 109: 408– 43.

Sansom, George. 1958. *A History of Japan to 1334*. Stanford University Press.

Takeda, Masahito and Philip Turner. 1992. "The liberalization of Japan's financial market: Some major themes." Economic Paper 34, Bank for International Settlement.

Chapter 10

THE BIG BANG IN JAPANESE SECURITIES MARKETS

Shoichi Royama
Takaoka National College

A process of financial disintermediation has begun in Japan. Intermediation by banks was a dominant feature of postwar Japanese finance. The bulk of funds saved were deposited in banks that, in turn, extended loans to businesses. This bank-centered system served Japan well for several decades, but now it must—and is—changing to accommodate new circumstances. Households and other ultimate lenders for the most part still make use of intermediary financial institutions, as they do in most countries. The key change is in who the intermediaries are. Increasingly the flow of funds to borrowers moves through a broader channel - one that includes securities markets as well as the conventional channel of bank lending. Table 10.1 illustrates that, although households still hold their financial assets largely in the form of bank deposits, the proportion in insurance policies, pensions, and various offerings from non-banks is on the rise.

In other words, what I call the "securities market system" is more and more important to the Japanese financial system, and it is generally recognized that its continued growth is essential for Japan. The Japanese government should promote the trend by all means, and policy measures to cope with the various issues facing the Japanese economy should be compatible with the trend.

That said, the table shows that the percentage of the total households invest invested in negotiable securities has been declining—falling in half between 1989 and 1997. This reflects the burst in the stock price bubble (1989 was the peak), but it is also a result of the low level of trust Japanese place in their country's securities market system. Neither securities firms nor regulators have tried hard enough to meet investor needs.

A process of gradual reform will not be able to change the wariness of the public. Only a drastic reform will persuade people that there has been meaningful change. A new vision of the industry must be formulated, and measures to realize it implemented quickly.

One reason for the need for change is that the risk-bearing capacity of the current bank-centered system is approaching its limit. Table 10.2 illustrates the decline in the ratio of the net worth of financial institutions as a whole relative

TABLE 10.1. Allocation of Household Financial Assets: 1964–98

End of Year	Total Financial Assets (100 Million yen)	Cash & Deposits	Trust Accounts	Insurance and Pension	Securities Investment Trust	Stocks	Other Securities
1964	267,923	59.4%	4.1%	11.5%	4.6%	17.1%	3.3%
1965	312,634	60.1%	4.6%	11.6%	3.4%	16.5%	3.8%
1966	368,622	60.8%	5.0%	11.8%	2.6%	15.1%	4.7%
1967	427,524	62.6%	5.4%	12.1%	2.0%	12.6%	5.3%
1968	511,181	61.8%	5.5%	12.2%	1.6%	13.5%	5.4%
1969	627,386	60.8%	5.3%	11.9%	1.6%	14.9%	5.5%
1970	716,600	62.6%	5.6%	12.6%	1.7%	11.8%	5.7%
1971	855,700	62.0%	5.6%	12.7%	1.7%	11.8%	6.2%
1972	1,113,458	60.1%	5.4%	11.6%	1.5%	15.5%	5.8%
1973	1,277,312	64.7%	5.6%	11.9%	1.6%	10.2%	6.0%
1974	1,482,031	65.5%	5.7%	12.2%	1.8%	8.9%	5.9%
1975	1,784,637	64.3%	5.8%	12.0%	1.7%	9.9%	6.3%
1976	2,086,751	64.2%	6.0%	12.1%	1.7%	9.0%	7.0%
1977	2,383,784	64.5%	6.2%	12.3%	1.8%	7.8%	7.4%
1978	2,761,873	64.0%	6.0%	12.3%	1.8%	8.3%	7.6%
1979	3,098,572	64.4%	6.1%	12.7%	1.7%	7.7%	7.5%
1980	3,440,324	64.3%	6.0%	13.2%	1.5%	7.4%	7.6%
1981	3,859,283	63.8%	6.3%	13.5%	1.6%	7.1%	7.8%
1982	4,277,128	62.8%	6.6%	13.9%	1.8%	6.8%	8.0%
1983	4,776,162	60.7%	6.7%	14.2%	2.5%	7.9%	8.0%
1984	5,267,657	59.2%	6.8%	14.7%	2.9%	8.5%	7.9%
1985	5,721,344	58.5%	6.9%	15.5%	3.0%	8.5%	7.6%
1986	6,422,768	56.1%	6.5%	16.3%	3.6%	10.9%	6.6%
1987	6,963,165	55.7%	6.3%	17.6%	4.7%	10.0%	5.6%
1988	7,857,442	52.7%	6.4%	18.6%	4.9%	12.6%	4.8%
1989	8,934,421	51.7%	6.3%	19.2%	4.6%	13.9%	4.3%
1990	9,246,119	53.9%	7.0%	21.0%	4.2%	9.0%	4.9%
1991	9,809,059	54.9%	7.1%	21.7%	3.5%	8.1%	4.7%
1992	10,178,181	55.4%	7.4%	23.0%	3.7%	6.2%	4.3%
1993	10,751,453	55.1%	7.3%	24.0%	3.3%	6.6%	3.7%
1994	11,309,336	55.3%	7.1%	24.7%	2.8%	6.6%	3.6%
1995	11,816,068	55.7%	6.7%	24.8%	2.8%	6.8%	3.2%
1996	12,091,513	56.9%	6.4%	25.1%	2.6%	6.1%	2.9%
1997	12,293,513	58.8%	5.9%	25.6%	2.3%	4.8%	2.5%
1998	13,056,563	55.2%	2.8%	27.8%	2.1%	7.2%	5.0%

Source: Bank of Japan, *Flow of Funds Statistics.*

Note: 1998 numbers are based on new flow of funds statistics that BOJ started to publish in 1999 and not exactly comparable to the earlier figures. For example, trust accounts held by pension funds on behalf of households were classified in "Trusts" in the old statistics and "Insurance and Pension" in the new statistics.

TABLE 10.2. Ratio of Stocks and the Net Worth of Financial Institutions to Their Financial Assets, 1969–97

At the End of Calendar Year	%
1969	12.63
1970	10.73
1971	11.63
1972	15.38
1973	12.48
1974	10.73
1975	10.49
1976	10.60
1977	9.72
1978	10.48
1979	10.15
1980	10.45
1981	10.25
1982	9.86
1983	10.87
1984	11.69
1985	12.19
1986	14.11
1987	14.93
1988	17.32
1989	19.24
1990	12.60
1991	11.80
1992	8.45
1993	8.49
1994	8.67
1995	8.38
1996	7.60
1997	5.60

Source: "Balance Sheet Table of Financial Institutions," Economic Planning Agency, *Annual Report on National Accounts*, 1999, CD-ROM version.

to the financial assets they hold. The level of 5.6% in the beginning of 1998, compared to a record 19.2% in 1989, means financial institutions have decreased risk-bearing capacity. Non-performing loans accumulated in the banking sector have made banks reluctant to take positive risks.[1]

One major set of policy measures is the financial reform package disclosed in 1997 popularly known as the Japanese Big Bang; the package is also discussed in Horiuchi (Chapter 9) It is a compilation of four separate blueprints proposed by four different advisory committees within the Japanese Ministry of Finance (MOF). Its contents are varied. However, the comprehensive reform plan regarding securities markets should be considered the core.

The reform plan is an outgrowth of the Securities and Exchange Council's 1997 report on securities market reform. This chapter provides background leading to the issuance of the report and then analyzes some of its key components.

THE SECURITIES MARKET SYSTEM

Japan's securities laws were drafted in the late 1940s and early 1950s along the lines of US laws, which strictly segregate banking and securities activities. However, unlike US law, the activities Japanese securities firms can engage in are specifically listed and, when one considers the broad range of security types, the Japanese definition is quite narrow. Defined broadly, securities are financial assets that multiple investors can hold as part of their portfolios and that, in identical units, have no variation in monetary benefits according to who the holder is. Securities of diverse types can exist. Listed and over-the-counter stocks, and publicly offered bonds are examples of what can be easily bought and sold on well-organized markets.

In exchange for accepting this constraint, securities firms have been protected against entry into their business by outside firms. (Suzuki 1987, p 260–69, provides a good overview of securities companies in the pre-liberalization environment.) Compounding the restrictive definition of securities is the fact that of the more than 200 Japanese securities firms, the great majority deal only in one type—equities. Just a handful of relatively large firms trade other types of securities.

In the following, references to "the securities market system" are to the US view of what securities are: any rights or instruments commonly referred to as securities. When I wish to limit the meaning to the subsystem by which securities as legally defined under Japan's Securities and Exchange Law are traded, I speak of the "securities market."

The main component of the securities market system is the market for stocks and bonds, but it also has markets for other types of securities. As these markets compete with one another, all need to operate as efficiently as possible. The overall system, moreover, must have the potential to develop in innovative directions. This means that rules and regulations impeding domestic, as well as global, competition need to be eliminated. This is not to say that laissez faire should prevail. An institutional foundation of laws and regulations is indispensable for competition and innovation to produce desirable results and keep problematic developments in check. Reform toward a well-founded securities market system in Japan is needed for this very reason.

In each market, price formation must accurately reflect the expected returns on securities and the risks inherent in them, and buy and sell orders must be executed efficiently. This is especially important in the stock and bond markets, which are the largest components of the securities market system and have a vast number of participants. Both these markets must have great depth and breadth.

The securities market system will function as it is meant to only when participants exercise self-discipline. It should be a system that rewards those who take responsibility for their own actions. Securities market institutions have to be based on rules that are transparent, lucid, and rational. Moreover, the trading on this institutional foundation has to be fair. Accordingly, a strict surveillance system is necessary. Monitoring is needed to deter market players from unfair practices. Strict punishment must be meted out when rules are violated. Both public officials and self-regulatory organizations should handle surveillance. Japan currently makes use of just such an arrangement, which is presided over by the Securities and Exchange Surveillance Commission (SESC, established under the Ministry of Finance, but transferred to the Financial Supervisory Authority, an agency of the Prime Minister's Office, in June 1998) as a public regulatory organization.

The securities firms in a properly structured securities market system should be able, in their capacity as agents, to provide services with a large value-added component. To this end, they should strengthen their roles as credit-raters, analysts, and financial planners. The securities industry as a whole has the potential to be one of Japan's leading industries in the 21st century. For this to happen, they must demonstrate entrepreneurial spirit and come up with innovative products. Thus far Japan's securities firms have focused too narrowly on stock brokerage. Henceforth they should not merely reinforce operations on the stock market's periphery but also expand into a broad range of financial services with a bearing on the securities market system.

THE BIG BANG

On 11 November 1996, Prime Minister Ryutaro Hashimoto instructed the Minister of Finance, Hiroshi Mitsuzuka, and the Minister of Justice, Isao Matsuura, to fundamentally restructure the financial system. In an unusual move, the decision was made public immediately in a document subtitled "Toward the Tokyo Market's Rebirth in 2001." If the reform envisioned could be accomplished by March 2001, it will truly merit the adjective "radical". Recognizing this, the media has labeled it Japan's version of the Big Bang.[2]

In several respects this plan has parted ways with earlier reforms. A specific and not-too-distant date of 2001 was set for completion; the aim was stated quite simply as the creation of a "free, fair and global" financial system; and the Prime Minister himself stepped forward as the architect of the overhaul. This reform drive should be of historic significance for the securities market system in particular. Although the securities market system is only one component of the whole financial system, inherent in Hashimoto's concept is the presumption that it ought to occupy the central place in Japanese finance. The securities market system is where the best concrete results can be achieved in reforms aimed at making the financial system free, fair, and global. In fact, all nine of the tasks listed in the document as examples are related to the securities market system directly or indirectly.

Working Out the Details

The work of drafting the Big Bang reform has followed the same traditional pattern as financial reforms in the past. That is, blue-ribbon panels have been given the task of advising what should be done.

Immediately after the instruction by the prime minister, the finance minister asked four advisory panels—the Securities and Exchange Council (SEC), the Financial Systems Research Council (FSRC), the Committee on Foreign Exchange and Other Transactions, and the Insurance Council—to study the matter and advance proposals. On 15 November, Mitsuzuka met with representatives of these bodies as well as the Business Accounting Council to reiterate Hashimoto's instructions personally.

The SEC is responsible for deliberating on matters concerning the securities market and its regulatory system. In June 1996 it created "the general committee," on which I served, and began deliberations on problems in the securities market, its industry and its regulation.[3]

Atsushi Nagano, director general of MOF's Securities Bureau, remarked when the committee held its first meeting that the panel was established because "When we look ahead to the 21st century, we can see that consolidating the securities market from a longer-term perspective is a pressing issue." After meeting nine times, the committee released a report on 29 November. This was basically an interim report on reform of the securities market to move it toward the 21st century securities market system, though it was given the low-key title "Summary of Points at Issue." The report clarifies the wide gap between the market at present and the hopes for it in the future, and it offers proposals on how the gap should be narrowed. The following paragraph is a summary of the report's first section. It shows the committee's view on the market's status and problem points.

> The Japanese financial and capital market has emphasized the role of allocating funds effectively and in concentration to key industries. The market, however, has entered a stage where the emphasis should be changed. As the percentage of elderly persons within the general population increases, indi-

vidual financial assets now total as much as ¥1200 trillion. Financial and capital markets now have to work to ensure that assets are invested more effectively. At the same time, the maturation of the economy has made it more important to provide funds to various new industries comprising positive risk burden in funding. In addition, because of the huge accumulation of financial assets in Japan, the Japanese market now has to play a greater role in the effective distribution of funds from a global point of view. Such a role cannot be fulfilled under the traditional Japanese system of indirect financing based upon bank loans and deposits. It is assumed that the securities market, which could effectively perform the functions of risk management and allocation, could satisfy financial intermediary needs of the new era. Today's Japanese securities market, however, is far from such a desirable condition. In other words, deposits and savings continue to account for far larger share of financial assets than that of the vastly smaller share accounted for by individual investors. Borrowing continues to play an important role in business funding. In addition, participation by overseas investors and companies in the Japanese market is restricted.

OTHER OFFICIAL REFORM PROPOSALS

While the SEC was examining the Japanese securities market system of the future, other MOF advisory panels also were busy responding to the Big Bang directive. The Committee on Foreign Exchange and Other Transactions report, issued on January 6, 1997, proposed that foreign exchange transactions in Japan should be entirely free, which attracted much public attention. However, the proposal was just another step in a series of liberalizations of foreign exchange controls. Many conjectured that a freed foreign exchange market would cause a drastic shift of Japanese portfolios from yen-denominated assets to dollar assets, but that did not occur.

In the Financial Systems Research Council (FSRC) and the Insurance Council, discussions were not so clear as those in the SEC. Indeed the FSRC established an ad-hoc committee to formulate a vision of the future Japanese banking system. MOF's Banking Bureau introduced bank holding companies as the key issue that should be discussed. Then the Bureau became so absorbed in the issue of how the bankruptcy of housing finance companies (*jûsen*) should be treated that it could not find any room to consider other problems seriously. Thus, the ad-hoc committee did not achieve its purpose.

The Insurance Council had to bridge the gap between MOF (the Insurance Section in the Banking Bureau) and the insurance industry that had widened in the course of the US-Japan negotiations on liberalization of the Japanese insurance industry. In May 1995 an extensive rewriting of the previous insurance law was promulgated. The industry was dissatisfied with it and with the consequences of the negotiations that MOF had with the United States. Thus, discussions within the Insurance Council focused on resolving these issues, resulting in somewhat vague proposals with later dates for proposed implementation.

PREPARING THE REFORM PROPOSAL

The November 1996 interim report of the SEC, titled "Issues for Discussion" lists five intermediate goals to achieve a "free, fair and global" financial system in accordance with the Big-Bang directive.

Make the securities market the lead actor in fund intermediation.
Improve the functioning of the Tokyo market.
Create a framework suited to the 21st century.
Open the market to everyone.
Achieve a fair, transparent, and trusted market.

The report suggests that "the deadline for completing virtually all reforms should be the start of the 21st century." The report calls for reform in 21 major areas of the market and the industry. They cover more than a restructuring of the regulatory system: everything from the Commercial Code to the tax and corporate accounting systems, and even the way companies behave, was put up for review and found in need of reconstruction.

On completing the interim report, the SEC study group set up three working parties to map out details. Their assignments were investment products, the securities market, and agents in the market. Enlisting the help of some outside experts, the various working parties met 24 times before unveiling their individual reports on 16 May 1997. These had titles referring to "Attractive Investment Instruments," "Trustworthy and Efficient Market Arrangements," and "Diversified Services for Customers' Needs."

With these reports in hand, the general committee completed its final report on 13 June 1997. Titled "Comprehensive Reform of The Japanese Securities Market For a Rich and Diverse 21st Century," the report was formally approved by the Securities and Exchange Council the same day and submitted to the Minister of Finance.

THE REFORM BLUEPRINT

The final report succeeded in answering all the questions that had been left unresolved at the stage of the interim report. Although the English version is less than 20 pages, in the report one finds a blueprint of the securities market system that Japan should have in the coming century. The document presents a truly comprehensive reform plan, even offering a schedule for implementation of each measure. If its proposals are adopted, Japan will find itself with reborn securities markets at the start of fiscal 2000.

Below I comment on what the report proposes with regard to government oversight, investment instruments, market organization, and securities market agents.

Government Oversight

Securities markets and their participants have been regulated by a system that seeks to avert all conceivable evils by intervening in the activities of securities firms in advance. This approach tends to lack transparency, as the regulators (the Securities Bureau at MOF in the case of securities firms) can use discretion regarding what to approve and what to forbid. Firms must secure a license from the MOF before they engage in businesses, but licensing has also led to instances of collusion between securities firms and bureaucratic administrators. Most fundamentally, this regulatory style has left little room for participants either to demonstrate inventiveness or to learn self-discipline. Operations in the securities market have suffered from rigidity, and changes to meet new needs have been slow to arrive. Here is a passage from the final report on what has gone wrong in the regulatory system.[4]

> In Japan, there has been a tendency to introduce new instruments and services on a one-by-one basis: typically, an instrument or a service that had been developed in overseas markets will be identified; its domestic market potential and investor protection measures studied; and, after a consensus on desirability had been reached, the new instrument or service will be introduced under a common industry standard. Such a strategy was efficient in the sense that it eliminated trial-and-error process by introducing only those instruments and services with a proven track record. However, it not only limited the scope of options available to investors and issuers, but may also have encouraged an imitative attitude among financial intermediaries and discouraged creativity. Similarly, an approach that placed emphasis on distancing investors from risk rather than making risk known to investors, may paradoxically created the misperception that those areas where restrictions had been lifted were safe areas with an official seal of approval, thereby weakening the idea that each market participant is responsible for his own judgment and must behave in the market with self-discipline. (Part II, Section 1.)

The following is also worth quoting.

> A sense of trust that fair transaction rules are universally observed is the most basic requirement for a market. Such a goal cannot be achieved through the traditional approach of ensuring the soundness of the market by regulating the business activity of intermediaries, given that the proposed reform intends to create a framework in which [the] market mechanism is to drive market development. A transition from preventive regulation to rule-based surveillance, and in particular strengthening of disclosure, fair transaction rules, and monitoring and enforcement mechanisms are essential. Although such a penalty-based system provides an underpinning for the market, it will not be enough to rely on criminal penalties alone. A system of dispute settlement whereby compensation for financial injuries from unlawful and unjust actions is quickly and reliably recovered is also important. In addition to penal and administrative penalties, the existence of such a civil procedure will also be an effective deterrent to unfair market activity. (Part II, Section 2.1)

In short, the new system should change the way investors are protected. Instead of trying to buffer them from risks and ensure that they do not suffer losses—the premise of the existing Securities and Exchange Law—efforts will be directed at familiarizing market participants with risks through thoroughgoing disclosure, and ridding the market of shady or illegal practices. Full disclosure of information and stern punishment of wrongdoing are the two principles that must serve as the foundation of market rules.

Upholding fairness will become even more important as new products and services are introduced and trading becomes more sophisticated and complicated. In expanding their range of operations, securities firms, exchanges, and over-the-counter markets are making more use of electronic trading and of new products. An improved set of rules is indispensable in such an environment in order to prevent market manipulation, insider trading, and other acts that harm investor interests. Stiffer penalties will be needed, especially for insider trading. To ensure that trading is fair, better arrangements for monitoring, auditing, and disciplining will have to be put in place.

The Financial Supervisory Agency was created under a law enacted on 16 June 1997 and the Securities and Exchange Surveillance Commission was transferred to this agency from MOF. The powers of the Commission will need to be strengthened so it can perform monitoring and auditing functions adequately in a liberalized market. The basic issue is how to keep people who fail to discipline themselves from profiting. The most realistic approach is to provide flexibility by leaving some affairs to the self-discipline of market players and to deal with unfair trading *ex post*, using civil and other procedures for assigning liability. In this regard, the role played by self-regulatory organizations is still to be clarified.

The Japan Securities Dealers Association (JSDA) and the eight securities exchanges are legally established self-regulatory organizations (SRO). The banking, life insurance, non-life insurance, and other financial service industries do not have any legally recognized self-regulatory organizations. Their industry associations, however, work as if they were SROs.

The theory is that if trading is made transparent through disclosure of pertinent information, and if investors are fully aware of the risks that products entail, their independent investment decisions will cause the market mechanism to function properly and prevent disputes from arising. For this to be realized, corporate accounting must be reformed, auditing by certified public accountants must be enhanced, and accessing disclosed information must be made easier.

It is not yet clear how far disclosure requirements will go. If the decision is to release only the minimum data currently required, the market will face trouble. One aim of the report is to encourage a corporate practice of full disclosure. The regulatory authorities are in the process of enhancing disclosure requirements.

Investment Instruments

What sorts of products should be available to investors in the securities market? The report states that:

> The basic approach should be to eliminate rules that inhibit product innovation, and to encourage free product development. By the way of example, deregulation in the bond market [since January 1996] has already resulted in numerous types of products being launched. Yet there are cases where constraints have emerged in relation to basic laws such as the Commercial Code and the Criminal Code, thereby making difficult the use of some products that are commonly seen in overseas markets. (Part IV, Section 1.2.)

Asset-backed securities are cited as an example where legal changes, including appropriate interpretations of the Commercial and Civil Codes, are needed. Medium-term notes have begun to be used more widely since such issues were resolved.

The report calls for a greater variety of derivatives, as well as further development of investment trusts. It flatly states that institutions such as banks should be allowed to sell mutual-fund products, an idea that has been highly unpopular in some quarters. It also urges the approval of privately subscribed investment trusts, as well as corporate-type investment trusts. It also recommends that securities firms be allowed to offer customers cash-management accounts. (Part IV, Sections 1.3 and 1.4).

Expanding the legal definition of securities means widening the scope of what is subject to investor protection rules. Different types of securities require different rules. One key distinction is between those that are broadly market based and those that are more bilateral (between presumably sophisticated institutions). Thus, the argument to expand the framework of investor protection under the Securities and Exchange Law simply by amending the definition in the law's Article 2 is considered "not appropriate." Rather, as wider reform proceeds "there will be a need to rethink what system of investor protection is desirable." (Part IV, Section 1.6.)

Even after a regulatory shift toward flexible approval of new products, issuers of securities will have to devote themselves to developing products that investors find attractive, and making existing securities more desirable. Equities will be the principal security most individuals will be involved with, directly or indirectly, and this means the concept of shareholder value must take root in Japan. To this end, the report observes that "the management of firms needs to be more attuned to shareholders' interests." (Part IV, Section 1.5.2.)

The tax system also will have to be reformed. The report urges elimination of the securities transaction tax and exchange tax for the purpose of strengthening the market's ability to compete internationally. In the light of the advent of derivatives and other new products and the need for supplies of risk capital, the report also calls for a review of the taxes on interest, dividends, and capital gains with a view to ensuring that their effect on financial transactions is neutral. (Part IV, Section 1.7)

Market Organization

The interim report argued that "even if the meaning of the places where deals are executed is weakening, . . . the significance of the existence of a trustworthy trading framework (trading mechanisms including rules) is growing all the greater." The final report endorses this judgment and, in response to the scandals that have been exposed at Nomura Securities and other major securities firms, begins the section on markets by noting that "Efficiency and fairness are the two most important elements in a marketplaces where transactions take place." (Part IV, Section 2.1.)

It used to be thought that the best way to ensure efficiency and fairness was to limit trading to stock exchanges and fund raising to select companies. But now, as the final report observes, advances in telecommunications technologies and innovations in financial techniques have made various new modes of trading possible, and it has become necessary to allow a broad range of companies to raise funds on the securities market, partly for the sake of fostering new industries. (Part IV, Section 2.1.)

The report calls for scrapping the requirement that trading be concentrated on stock exchanges, and upgrading the status and functions of the over-the-counter market, as well as lifting bans on the handling of unlisted and unregistered shares by securities firms. Easier access to transaction and quote information, a better transaction settlements system, and improvements to the share-lending market (to simplify short selling) are listed as measures to improve market infrastructure. (Part IV, Section 2.2.)

With regard to cross-shareholding, the report notes several sets of views. There are those who assert that there is nothing wrong in holding shares for reasons other than making money, that the shares involved are not seriously distorting rational price formation, and that the practice helps to cement long-term ties among business partners. In cases where the arrangements do not make sound business sense, they add, the shares are already being sold off. Against this is the view that cross-holding weakens corporate governance, obstructs the market mechanism, and injects a variety of company-specific investment standards into the market, thereby diminishing the incentive of pure investors to purchase shares.

The report then states that "Cross holdings of shares should not inhibit [the] market mechanism, as that will be to the detriment of optimal allocation of resources and efficient use of capital. From this standpoint, even for cross-held shares, shareholders should constantly reevaluate the return on investment and exercise governance checks on the management of firms." (Part IV, Section 2.3.)

This note of warning sets the stage for a significant passage on bank holding companies.

> In the context of banks' entry into the securities business, the question of banks' influence over firms that emanate from the banks' large holdings of shares has been a subject of intense debate. There are those who advocate that banks no longer retain such influence and that irrational cross holdings are in the process of dissolution. Whatever the truth of such statement, it seems clear that excessively large holdings of shares by banks is not desirable, from the viewpoint of maintaining safety and soundness of banks and in its effect on the stock market. The Council strongly hopes that the introduction of holding company systems into this country will act as a catalyst that triggers a rethinking of banks' share holdings strategy, towards reducing or eliminating shareholding by the bank itself. (Part IV, Section 3.5.3)

Securities Market Agents

The historical monopoly of securities firms is being ended by the reforms. Firms affiliated with banks will be able to deal in a much broader range of securities, and more foreign firms are being allowed to enter various aspects of the business. Asset management is expected to be an especially strongly contested area. Thus, the report contains an extensive section called Financial Intermediaries: Diverse Investment Services to Fulfill Client Needs. It begins by noting that:

> Innovation in the market is ultimately driven by intermediaries. As the environment becomes more conducive to innovation, the role of intermediaries becomes even more important. In particular, a framework must be built, wherein intermediaries that respond to client needs and develop products and services with high value added will flourish. As securities market reform proceeds, competition between intermediaries, including new entrants, will become the key to providing better services for the users of the market. (Part IV, Section 3.1.)

Securities firms need to play the role of financial intermediaries faithfully. As agents that consummate deals between issuers and investors, or between securities buyers and sellers, they have to secure the trust of all parties. Quite naturally, some firms cultivate close relations with issuers, others compile a wealth of information on investors, and each seeks to develop its own individuality. However, the industry as a whole should maintain the ability to function as neutral intermediaries.

Thus far Japan's securities firms have given short shrift to individual investors. This has to be corrected, especially in marketing activities. Toward this end, new entrants to the retail brokerage business must be allowed. An overhaul of the management philosophies of the existing agents will not suffice.

Two steps are needed to reform the ways of the existing companies and open the door to others, and one has been taken already. The requirement that securities firms engage in no other businesses still needs to be dropped, but the ban on holding companies has been lifted. The report sums up the situation as follows.

> In order to provide more varied services, a legal framework that allows securities companies the freedom to combine or uncouple services, or to deliver securities transaction services together with those services that do not fall into the traditional category of securities business will become necessary. It is difficult to envisage beforehand what services might provide synergy for the delivery of securities related services, so that unless there is a clear case for prohibiting a certain non-securities related activity, securities companies

should be allowed to engage in any activity. To this end, current regulation that requires security companies to engage solely in securities business needs to be abolished. (Part IV, Section 3.2.1.)

Many people see the deregulation of stock-trading commissions as the prime example of what needs to be done to revitalize the securities market and securities firms. The report contains the clearest statement yet on this question by proposing a specific, and quick, deregulation schedule that achieved complete liberalization by the end of 1999. While acknowledging that preparations may take longer than that to complete, the report urged all concerned to move as quickly as possible toward fully negotiable commissions system. (Part IV, Section 3.3.3.) The first step was to deregulate commission on transactions valued at over ¥50 million from 1 April 1998. Full deregulation is on course to be achieved slightly ahead of schedule, in October 1999.

The report considers asset-management services to be a key element of the overall system. To increase the efficiency of fund management, three measures are proposed: allowing investment trust management companies to use outside agents to manage funds; introducing private-placement of investment trusts; and including unlisted and unregistered securities in the portfolios of investment trusts. (Part IV, Section 3.4.1.)

Arguing that securities firms should become more involved in asset management, the report recommends the use of the so-called wrap account, which is popular in the United States. These are specifically recommended as a way for securities firms to enter asset management because they pose few dangers of "churning" (repeated buying and selling to generate commissions). This is because fees are based on the value of the assets in an account, rather than on the activity level. Wrap accounts can serve as a vehicle for diversifying the business of securities firms, thereby helping them remain profitable after the decontrol of commissions. However, it cautions that a good set of rules for preventing unfair trading will have to be worked out before the accounts are allowed. After all, unscrupulous behavior by securities firms in the past led to their being banned from managing investments in their own accounts without consulting the investors. (Part IV, Section 3.4.2.)

Whether the securities market and securities firms can evolve in such ways depends to a large extent on how they are regulated. To stress a main point of the report, intermediaries need to be encouraged to exercise ingenuity. This means eliminating, as far as possible, the before-the-fact type of regulation that characterizes the old system. Toward this end, license systems that, for instance, require the submission of documents on business methods should be dismantled.

The dynamism of the securities market cannot be sustained if excessive limits are imposed on the entry of those with the will and the ability to act in the securities business. New players should be allowed to enter because they "bring new ideas, technologies, and vitality" and strengthen the market's intermediation function. To this end, registration with the authorities should be, to the extent possible, the only requirement. Authorization systems are not ruled out altogether, however.

> [O]ne should not attempt to encourage new entrants . . . by merely lowering the standards . . . . Potential entrants must possess [the] minimum level of financial and human resources required to execute business in an honest and reliable manner. The standards that are required would differ between different types of activity, reflecting the degree of specialized skills and necessary risk management levels. (Part IV, Section 3.5.2.)

With respect to new entrants, the primary question is what to do about banks. In 1993 the government, responding to ongoing liberalization, globalization, and securitization in the financial sector, approved mutual entry of banks, trust banks, and securities firms into each other's territory. In the interest of preserving the health of banks and preventing conflicts of interest, however, it stipulated that banks could enter the securities field only through subsidiaries. To ensure the stability of the financial system during this reform, moreover, it decided to ease the conditions of entry by stages. At present the rule is that subsidiaries set up by banks as securities firms must be new entities, and the operations they can engage in are limited.

In March 1997 the government approved a revised deregulation plan allowing bank subsidiaries to trade equities and stock-index futures and options—but not to engage in deals that involve underwriting stocks. The question of what other businesses they will be allowed to enter awaits the final formulation of the Big Bang plan.

Reform should not only free securities firms from the obligation to stick to a single business, but enable them to diversify and cultivate niches, and free banks to develop new products, explore new fields, and reform their organizations. Holding companies have been approved through an amendment of the Antimonopoly Law, opening the door to new ways of participating in other sectors. If all goes well, the remaining restrictions on bank subsidiaries should be removed before April 2000. At that point, at the end of the reform, even subsidiaries that banks establish during the reform process should gain recognition as ordinary securities companies.

Ensuring Safety and Soundness

The creditworthiness of financial intermediaries and investor protection in general are concerns. The report repeatedly notes that markets require trust. A good regulatory framework is an aspect of building and sustaining that trust, but it goes beyond that: intermediaries "are encouraged to set standards of conduct that rise over and above those required by law." Investors should not bear "undue loss as a result of disorderly exit by intermediaries". Among other things, this affects bankruptcy laws. (Part IV, Section 3.6.1.)

As to the regulatory framework, revising capital adequacy rules to relate to the level of risk-taking and raising disclosure standards are mentioned specifically. (Part IV, Section 3.6.2.)

After the Proposal

Also on 13 June 1997, the FSRC and the Insurance Council submitted their reports to the finance minister, and MOF quickly started implementation of their suggestions. The proposals involve two types of policy measures: those that can be implemented within the existing legal framework and those that require amendments to current laws or new legislation.

Measures available within the present legal framework were implemented during fiscal 1997. For the others, in June 1998 the Diet passed a set of laws called the Financial System Reform Enactment (FSRE). It amends the Securities and Exchange Law, the Securities Investment Trust Law, the Banking Law, the Insurance Law and miscellaneous related laws in order to allow implementation of the proposals. In addition, the Special Purpose Company (SPC) Law was enacted in September 1998 to promote securitization of loans and real estates. The special-purpose company thus legally founded will work as a conduit in the process of asset-backed securitization. (See Appendix for proposals and their dates of implementation.)

SECURITIES INDUSTRY RESTRUCTURING

In response to these new government policy proposals and their implementation and to ever-increasing market pressures, the Japanese securities industry has been in the process of profound restructuring and consolidation. Small and middle-sized securities firms are merging with eachother, and some are being acquired by banks.

The most dramatic changes have occurred within the Big Four securities companies—Nomura, Nikko, Daiwa, and Yamaichi—which dominated the securities industry and securities markets for most of the postwar period. As other chapters stress, the collapse and bankruptcy of the Yamaichi Securities Company in November 1997 was a profound shock, and the sorting out of its assets, liabilities and the losses of creditors is in process. One major surprise was that the Japan operations of Merrill Lynch took over some 30 branches and hired more than 1000 of its employees, thereby entering the Japanese retail securities market in a major way.

Each of the remaining Big Four has been in the process of developing its own strategy in response to the Big Bang. Alliances of varying degrees of comprehensiveness and complexity are being negotiated and implemented. Nomura Securities Companies has developed alliance relationships with the Industrial Bank of Japan (IBJ); that has been made more complex by the August 1999 announcement that IBJ, Fuji Bank, and Daiichi Kangyo Bank plan to merge through a holding company structure. Nikko Securities has established a comprehensive alliance with Travellers/Citicorp, which has in principle purchased a 25% equity share in Nikko, and established a joint venture, Nikko Salomon Smith Barney, to engage in Japanese institutional brokerage business. Daiwa Securities has been developing an alliance with Sumitomo Bank. In April 1999 it established a holding company, Daiwa Securities Group, which includes joint ventures with Sumitomo Bank subsidiaries, such as Daiwa SC Capital Management Company. It is not yet clear whether a larger holding company including Sumitomo Bank will result from this alliance.

Another significant change is the rapid growth of new security companies set up by banks, following the Financial System Reform of 1993. Within a short period, bank-owned securities subsidiaries have become important players in the underwriting business. In 1998, for example, their collective share incorporate bond underwriting exceeded 40%. When these bank-owned subsidiaries are allowed to enter the brokerage business as a result of Big Bang deregulation, they will pose a substantial threat to the existing securities firms. The planned merger of IBJ Securities, DKB Securities and Fuji Securities, for example, is most likely to create a firm that challenges the Big Three.

These profound changes in the securities industry structure are part and parcel of the broader process of transformation of all forms of financial services businesses as rapid change is underway to develop an effective securities market system.

WHAT ELSE IS REQUIRED?

The report's reform proposals have the potential to provide Japan with a securities market on par with those in the West in terms of institutions. But even a radical reform cannot of itself guarantee that the ultimate aim will be achieved. I will make some brief observations on what else is required.

One question is how Japan's traditional value system and social arrangements are to be reconciled with international business practices. The provisions of the Commercial and Civil Codes and relevant statutes are involved here.

France, Germany, and several other countries have legal systems similar to Japan's, so Japan could profit by looking at what they have done. Much more is needed to consolidate a judicial framework that is transparent, uses lucid rules, and operates fairly and speedily.

More fundamentally, how will intermediaries, companies, and investors make use of the new freedoms? The behavior of market players will determine whether free and efficient market institutions can generate true vitality. We must pin our hopes on the ability of intermediaries to display dynamism and ingenuity and step forward as the market's star players. Discipline and accountability are concomitants of freedom. Even as market participants make maximum use of their freedom, they will need to behave as autonomous actors adhering to a highly ethical code of conduct.

The report concludes:

> The Securities and Exchange Council believes in the ability and the awareness of the Japanese people. The Council urges the Government to proceed to refine the details of this reform package, and provide the required institutional framework without delay, taking into account as wide a range of public opinion as possible. By laying the ground for the development of Japan's securities market, it is hoped that the securities market will contribute towards providing a basis for the creation of a fair and dynamic economy and society.

CONCLUSION

How successful have these institutional reforms been in the one or two years since being formally enacted? As expected, reorganization of the financial service industry is underway. Mergers and cooperations within the securities industry are occurring in greater number, and overseas financial institutions are major participants of this reorganization movement. However, banks and other financial service firms are not yet actively promoting innovative business activities.

As the Japanese population ages, the importance of the securities market system will increase, and its roles will diversify. The system should encourage healthy management of financial assets held by Japanese. It should contribute to the Japanese economy—and indeed, to the world economy—through its asset-allocation function. From this perspective, the securities market system is a precious property and deserves to be seen as a kind of public good. As this view takes root among the Japanese, they will make increasing use of securities for investment and fund-raising purposes, always listening to "the voice of the market" when buying and selling securities. If Tokyo is to serve as an international financial center like New York and London, the competitive power of the securities market system must be promoted. This is necessary not just for Japan's own sake but also for ensuring a smooth supply of capital, particularly to Japan's developing neighbors.

ACKNOWLEDGEMENTS

This chapter is a revised version of an article with the same title published in *Japan Review of International Affairs* 11 (4) (Winter 1998). The revision reflects comments by Professor Takeo Hoshi. I thank him, as well as Professor Hugh Patrick, Professor Yasushi Hamao, and Mr. Larry Meissner for their useful advice.

NOTES

1 Non-performing loans should be disposed of by utilizing functions of the market such as securitization. Even government financial intermediation cannot be outside of the trend of securitization. Many proposals for reform of the government financial intermediation system recognize the importance of making greater use of securities as its investment and funding instruments.

2 It is not clear why Hashimoto set off the Big Bang reform. The Economic Council of the Economic Planning Agency released a report on financial reform as one of the urgent structural reforms of six key areas in October 1996, just before the Prime Minister's action. It proposed introducing more competition into every area of finance by lifting regulations on new entry, liberalizing asset-market transactions to allow creation of new financial commodities and services, and transforming government administration from so-called convoy protection to being market based. However, the Report does not appear to have been the impetus for the prime minister's action.

According to a talk Hashimoto gave to the chairs of the advisory panels of MOF, Helmut Kohl, the German prime minister, advised him to introduce a radical reform of the Japanese financial system in order to make Tokyo the financial center for Asia. Atsuro Saka, a secretary of Hashimoto's dispatched from MOF, wrote the draft of the directive. It is natural that Saka would seek the counsel of his colleagues at MOF, especially Atsushi Nagano, Director of the Securities Bureau, and Eisuske Sakakibara, Director of the International Finance Bureau.

3 The general committee had 17 members: 5 university professors of law or economics, 4 economists, 2 journalists, 3 non-financial company managers, 2 representative of self-regulatory organizations, and a Bank of Japan director. In addition, it had 10specific members representing related financial-service industries.

4 This, and subsequent, quotations are from a provisional unofficial translation of the Report. The original Japanese and the English versions are available on MOF's web site: *http://www.mof.go.jp*. The English is at *.../english/tosin/ela505.htm.*

REFERENCES

Ministry of Finance, the Committee on Foreign Exchange and Other Transactions, 1997 Jan 16 *Gaikoku Kawase oyobi Gaikoku Bo'eki Kanri Ho no Kaisei nituite,* ("Concerning the Amendment of the Foreign Exchange and Foreign Trade Control Law." Unofficial English translation available at *mof.go.jp/english/e1a702.htm*

Ministry of Finance, Securities and Exchange Council, General Committee, 1996 Nov 29, *Ronten Seiri*, "Summary of Discussions." Unofficial English translation available at *mof.go.jp/english/tosin/e1a501f1.htm*

Ministry of Finance, Securities and Exchange Council, Working Group on Investment Vehicles, 1977 May 16, *Miryoku aru Toshi Taishou*, "Attractive Investment Instruments." (available only in Japanese)

Ministry of Finance, Securities and Exchange Council, Working Group on Market, 1977 May 16, *Shinrai-dekiru Koritsu-tekina Torihiki no Wakugumi*, "An Efficient and Trusted Framework for Transactions." (available only in Japanese)

Ministry of Finance, Securities and Exchange Council, Working Group on Financial Intermediaries, 1997 May 16, *Mokyaku Niizu ni taioushita Tayona Toshi Sabisu* "Divese Investment services to fulfill Client Needs." (available only in Japanese)

Ministry of Finance, Securities and Exchange Council, 1977 June 13. "Comprehensive Reform of the Securities Market: for a rich and diverse 21st century." Unofficial English translation available at *mof.go.jp/tosin/ela505.htm*

Prime Minister's Office, Wagakuni Kin'yu Shisutemu no Kaikaku: 2001nen Tokyo Shijo no Saisei ni Mukete "Structural of the Japanese Financial Market-Toward the Revival of the Tokyo Market by the Year of 2001." Unofficial English translation available at *mof.go.jp/english/big-bang/ebb7.htm*

Suzuki, Yoshio, editor, 1987. *The Japanese Financial System*, Clarendon Press, Oxford. This is the English translation of *Wagakuni no Kin'yu Seido*, 1986, Bank of Japan.

APPENDIX

Japanese Securities Market Reforms

FSRE refers to the Financial System Reform Enactment, a set of laws passed by the Diet in June 1998. Dates in parentheses refer to when enabling measures were promulgated or are scheduled to be implemented.

I Measures intended to create attractive investment instruments

A Diversification of the types of bonds
1 Perpetual bonds (July 1997)
2 Stock-price-index-linked bonds (June 1998, FSRE)

B Full liberalization of derivatives products
1 Options on individual stocks (July 1997, Tokyo Stock Exchange, Osaka Stock Exchange)
2 OTC derivatives on securities (June 1998, FSRE)

C Developing Investment Trust Products and others
1 Cash Management Accounts
a Introduced with some constraints (October 1997)
b Expansion of permitted activities (such as salary and pension payment transfer) (time not yet determined)
2 OTC sales of investment trust products by banks
a Through "separate-window service" branches by investment trust companies in bank (October 1997)
b Direct sales by banks themselves (June 1998, FSRE)
3 Private placements by investment trusts (June 1998, FSRE)
4 Investment-company type funds (June 1998, FSRE)

D Review of the Definition of Securities:
1 Inclusion of trusted beneficiary backed by loans financial institution extended (June 1997)
2 Depository Receipts (DRs), covered warrants, and Asset Backed Securities (ABS) designated by the Special Purpose Company (SPC) Law (June and September 1998, FSRE)

E Enhancement of corporate vitality and efficient use of capital
1 Introduction of more convenient asset-backed securities (June 1998, FSRE; September 1998, Special Purpose Company (SPC) Law)
2 Promotion of medium-term notes (May 1998)
3 Smoother listing and registration of equities
a Book-building method in pricing newly traded stocks (September 1998)
b Move from ex ante recognition to ex post registration of listing stocks (June 1998, FSRE)

4 Promotion of new issues (measures not yet clarified)
5 Strengthening the OTC stock market (JASDAQ)
 a Stock borrowing and lending system (July 1998)
 b Margin and other new trading (October 1997)
 c Reconsideration of legal status of the OTC market as a complement to exchange markets (June 1998, FSRE)
 d Designation of dealers in OTC registered stocks (time not yet determined)
6 Arrangements for non-listed and non-registered stocks
 a Permission given to securities firms to deal in them (July 1997)
 b Inclusion in portfolio of securities investment trusts allowed (September 1998)

II Measures to establish an efficient and trusted framework for transactions

A Improvement of the transaction system at stock exchanges
1 Lifting constraints on trade information channel (October 1997),
2 Reconsideration of exchange trading systems such as introduction of computer trading and improvement of the cross-trading system (November 1997)
3 Legal arrangements for merger of securities exchanges (June 1998, FSRE)
4 Expansion of information on trading made available by exchanges, covering volume as well as price (time not yet determined)

B Trade concentration rule abolished (June 1998, FSRE)

C Improvement to the OTC market system (See I E)

D Deregulation of dealing by securities firms of unlisted, unregistered stocks (See I E)

E Improvement in stock lending and borrowing procedures (June 1998, FSRE)

F Improvement of the clearing and settlement system for securities

1 Japan Bond Clearing Corporation established to facilitate corporate bonds settlement (December 1997)
2 Introduction of delivery versus payment (DVP) system (December 1997)
3 Improvement of the Japan Depository Corporation (June 1998, FSRE).

G Strengthening inspection surveillance and enforcement
1 Financial Surveillance Agency created (June 1998, FSRE)

H Strengthening disclosure
1 Consolidated corporate financial reports (April 1998)
2 New accounting principle *wrt* financial commodities and retirement allowance (June 1998, FSRE)

III Measures givent to financial intermediaries to diversify investment services to meet client needs

A Deregulating brokerage commissions
1 Negotiable commission rate applied to transactions of more than ¥50 million (April 1998)
2 Full abolishment of regulated commission rate system (October 1999)

B Diverse activity by intermediaries
1 Cash management accounts allowed at securities firms (October 1997)
2 Securities firms' obligation to designated principal occupations abolished (June 1998, FSRE)
3 Wrap accounts (June 1998, FSRE)
4 PTS (proprietary trading system) allowed as a securities firms' business (June 1998, FSRE)

C Employing holding company structure (December 1997).

D Strengthening asset management services
1 See I C
2 Employment of asset management services external to the securities investment trust company, review of business operation guidance toward the securities investment trust company, and introduction of ex post registration system on trust agreement (June 1998, FSRE)

E Enhancing monitoring of the soundness of securities companies
1 Reexamination of own-capital ratio regulation imposed on securities firms, in consideration of expansion firms' business lines (June 1998, FSRE)
2 Clarification of exit procedures at a time of deficient capital ratio (June 1998, FSRE)

F Entry regulations for securities firms and securities investment trust companies
1 Change from licensing to - in principle - a registration system for securities firms and investment trust companies (June 1998, FSRE)
2 Easier entry into banking, securities and trust business (June 1998 with the exception of stock-related businesses; entirely free by 2001)

G Investor protection related to the exit of an intermediary
1 Strict separation of client assets from those of the securities company (October 1997 in case of futures and options; June 1998 in general)
2 Establishment of legally authorized investors protection funds, enhancing the existing securities deposited compensation fund scheme (June 1998, FSRE)
3 Estblishement of bankruptcy procedures for securities firms (June 1998, FSRE)

IV Taxation: review of the taxation related to securities transaction

A Securities transaction tax rate cut (April 1998)

Chapter 11

JAPAN'S FINANCIAL BIG BANG: ITS IMPACT ON THE LEGAL SYSTEM AND CORPORATE GOVERNANCE

Hideki Kanda
University of Tokyo

The impact of Japan's financial Big Bang on the legal system and corporate governance in Japan is examined in this chapter. The Big Bang program moves the Japanese regulatory environment and institutional structure toward the Western model, particularly the US model, by emphasizing the role of capital markets in resource allocation. Whether it also leads to changes in the legal system and corporate governance is another matter. I argue that in some respects it already does, but in other respects it will not.

The reforms involve changes to the body of law and interpretations, but the legal system is more than these. Three distinctive features of the Japanese legal system during the period when Japan experienced high economic growth deserve special mention: solid basic laws, a strong bureaucracy, and a small judiciary. It is the changes that are and might take place to these features that is my particular concern here.

Big Bang reforms intend capital markets to be more important. In the second half of the chapter, I address how this may affect corporate governance in Japan. To assess how governance may change, I use the fruits of recent theories regarding substitutabilities and complementarities that possibly exist among the components of a system.

The effectiveness of legal rules is a function of their enforceability. This is an important aspect of both corporate governance and legal systems that is too often overlooked. It is taken up here in order to analyze the types of changes the Big Bang might engender, especially in regards convergence with practices in other countries.

To set the stage, I begin by examining the Big Bang for some of its effects on legal structures—the specifics of laws and interpretations which, by definition of reform, are changing. Horiuchi (Chapter 9) and Royama (Chapter 10) deal with overall reform in more detail. (For regulation before the Big Bang, see Kanda (1997). For an interesting overview of the Big Bang, see Craig (1998).)

THE BIG BANG PROGRAM

The Big Bang is a program that extensively overhauls the regulatory and institutional structure of Japan's financial sector. Launched on the initiative of Prime Minister Ryutaro Hashimoto in November 1996, three fundamental principles guide what the financial sector should be as a result of the program: free, fair, and global. The reform is expected to be accomplished by 2001.

The Japanese economy has suffered in the 1990s from the bursting of bubbles in its stock and real estate markets. The process of deregulation and an appropriate response to the rapidly changing environment in world financial markets have been delayed because the Diet and the government have had to spend (and are still spending) an enormous amount of time resolving the resulting banking crisis. The Big Bang program is aimed at remedying this delay, and thus has two notable characteristics: reforms are extensive in scope and the timetable is specific and quick.

Impact on the Economy

Two aspects of the postwar economy are being fundamentally changed by the reforms. They affect the legal system both broadly and more narrowly through the specifics of the contents of the reforms. These aspects are the emphasis on stability and the dominant role of bank lending.

The traditional Japanese system emphasized stability, especially employment stability. This policy contributed greatly to past growth. Stability, however, is not compatible with adaptability, and Japan has been poor at adapting rapidly to the changing environment of world financial markets. The Big Bang program includes measures to increase adaptability. The price may be some loss in stability. In any case, the legal structures that support an adaptable system of necessity differ from those supporting a stability-oriented system.

Bank lending has dominated the postwar financial sector, successfully helping Japan achieve high economic growth and become a major economy. Once the Japanese economy reached a matured stage, however, the bank-centered system began to produce costs for the national economy due to the relatively high cost of banking services. Other major countries, notably the United States, have long had well-developed capital markets, and globalization of financial markets has required an increased role for capital markets in Japan. The Big Bang program encourages drastic improvement of the Japanese capital markets, and this will require changes in legal structures.

New Regulatory Bodies

The style of financial regulation in Japan is changing from consensus-based to rule-based. To implement the new approach, a new supervisory structure has been created.

The Financial Supervisory Agency (FSA) took over the task of regulating banks, securities firms, and insurance companies from the Ministry of Finance (MOF) on 22 June 1998. In December 1998 the Financial Reconstruction Commission (FRC) began operations. (The Japanese name is *Kin'yu Saisei Iinkai*. Although "reconstruction" is used by the FRC, some sources have translated *saisei* as resuscitation or revitalization).

The FRC is responsible for licensing and has been given the power to nationalize, liquidate, or convert a bank into a "bridge bank." Reporting directly to the Prime Minister's Office, it will share responsibility with MOF in handling bank crises and failures and oversee the FSA until the end of fiscal 2000, when it is due to end its activities. In July 2000, the new Finance Agency is scheduled to be established under the FRC (see Horiuchi, chapter 9).

IMPACT ON THE LEGAL SYSTEM

Three distinctive features of the Japanese legal system during the period when Japan experienced high economic growth deserve special mention: solid basic laws, a strong bureaucracy, and a small judiciary. (These are identified by Pistor and Wellons (1998) as part of a research project of the Asian Development Bank.)

Solid Basic Laws. In the early Meiji era Japan imported basic statutes from Europe, and thus by the late 19th century had a solid set of basic statutes in such areas as civil law and procedures and commercial law. Japan also created a Western-style judicial system, including a court system. It is noteworthy that the process of importation was relatively smooth and Japan quite successfully transplanted basic components from the Western legal system into its own.

Strong Bureaucracy. A strong bureaucracy has played a significant role during the postwar high growth period. The Japanese economy, including the financial sector, was controlled, protected, and nurtured by the government. Top universities sent many of their top graduates to be civil servants in the central government. The rules made by, and developed under the initiative of, this group governed the business and financial sectors in Japan, and contributed to Japan's impressive economic success. (The success of Japan's civil service has been much-studied for lessons applicable elsewhere. See, for example, the World Bank study edited by Kim et al (1995).)

Small Judicial System. The actual role of the judicial sector has remained small. Business sectors, including the financial sector, developed rule-making and dispute resolution mechanisms within themselves. Resorting to the courts or the judicial sector was rare. Most bureaucratic rules were promulgated through joint efforts of business participants and bureaucrats, and were almost never challenged before the courts. Disputes tended to be resolved within the business sector under the influence of the bureaucracy, rather than by means of litigation. As a result, the national budget allocated to the judiciary was very small, and the number of judges and private attorneys remained minimal in Japan, especially compared to other major industrialized countries.

The Big Bang's Impact

The Big Bang reforms mean that the style of financial regulation will change from consensus-based to rule-based. On the one hand, drastic deregulation is permitting financial institutions and other private parties great freedom in creating and offering new and innovative financial products in the market place. Ex ante prohibitions against certain risk-bearing financial products have mostly been lifted. Instead, there are rules that are enforced ex post (that is, when broken). This has important consequences to the three aspects of the legal system under examination here.

The judicial system will become larger. This must take place simply to respond to the rule-based system. The increasing number of people passing the national bar examination each year is just one indication of this change. The amount of litigation in finance and business has also begun to increase and judges are finding that they need to have more knowledge of financial transactions. All this means that the government will have to allocate more resources to the judiciary. Alternative dispute resolution systems also will need to expand.

The style of bureaucratic governance will change, and this is true whether or not the power of the Japanese bureaucracy becomes weak in the future (which is something that I do not think will happen). In the past, bureaucratic rules were promulgated by means of lengthy rule-making processes (see, for example, Kanda (1991).) The Big Bang basically abandons this approach. In the future, there will be straightforward "conduct" rules for market participants.

This does not mean that regulators will become unimportant, but their role will involve less bureaucratic rule-making and more policing of compliance with conduct rules, including detecting and sanctioning rule violations. This relates to the expected increased role of the courts. To take one example, the Securities and Exchange Act has a provision allowing regulators to seek an injunctive order from the court to stop any illegal activity (section 192). This provision has never been triggered. In the future, the provision may be used (see below).

Japan will need to add more specific legal rules to its existing basic laws, with the goal of enhancing legal predictabilities (or reducing legal uncertainties) in the financial arena. Such a trend in the Japanese legislative process is already underway. To take an example, Japan enacted a special statute in June 1998 (as a part of the Big Bang program) that confirms the validity of close-out netting agreements, which are popularly used in swap transactions world-wide. This legislation was met with great enthusiasm by market participants in the United States and Europe. On a larger scale, the package of new statutes enacted in October 1998 to deal with the banking crisis includes various special provisions to the general rules on mortgages and related matters under the Civil Code and related basic statutes.

IMPACT ON CORPORATE GOVERNANCE

Big Bang reforms intend capital markets to be more important. In this section, I address how this may affect corporate governance in Japan. I use the fruits of recent theories: the ideas of substitutabilities and complementarities that possibly exist among the components of a system.

Corporate Governance as a System of Components

All social systems can be viewed as consisting of components or sub-systems. Thus, a corporate governance system consists of such elements as firm-size, management-style, financial structure, labor, and other cultural aspects, operating in a legal-framework component.

One theory providing a good analytical tool to understand corporate governance is the idea of substitutabilities. This theory—not uncommon in traditional legal scholarship—suggests that one component of a system can serve as a substitute for another component. For application in corporate governance, see Roe (1977) and Gilson (1996).

For instance, where the market for corporate control is active, as it has been the case in the United States and Great Britain, there is less need for other monitoring mechanisms. Similarly, a country having less-developed capital markets may have stronger bank monitoring or, if bank monitoring does not work, something else, such as a strong board of directors or a controlling shareholder. Thus, France and Italy, two countries where capital markets are not well developed, have a history of heavy monitoring by the government, with the state in fact being a controlling shareholder in many major corporations.

It is also possible for various components to combine to substitute for another component. In Germany, both banks and families as controlling shareholders substitute for a less developed capital market.

The theory holds even if nothing seems strong in isolation, as appears to be the case in Japanese corporate governance. In this case, one can argue that various components each serve some—though not necessarily a strong—monitoring role, so that in total the system functions.

Another interesting theory is about complementarities. The idea is that various components (sub-systems) of a given system complement one another in certain situations. (Milgrom and Roberts (1994); Gilson (1998); Aoki (1994).)

When complementarities exist, the value of the system is not equal to the simple sum of the standard values of the individual components. The integrated value of each component may vary, depending on the degree to which the component, as a whole or in part, is complementary to another component. This suggests that the same mechanism—bank monitoring, for instance—has a different effect in corporate governance when it has complementarities with other components of the system.

Where (as in Germany) firm ownership is not dispersed, bank monitoring is less costly and thus plays a more important role than where (as in the United States) firm ownership is more dispersed. Where (as in France) state influence pervades both lender and debtor decision-making, bank monitoring is all but meaningless, despite loans being the major source of financing.

Where (as in Japan) employees under a lifetime employment system are dominant in a firm's decision-making, managers (who are committed to maintaining the lifetime employment system) are relatively better at conducting daily business, and thus information provided by banks and other business partners may be more valuable to them—which increases the value of bank monitoring. But where (as in the Great Britain) managers who come from outside are relatively adept at using information supplied by outside sources, the value of monitoring by banks and other business partners is less likely to increase much when long-time employees become managers.

Thus, given the possible existence of substitutabilities or complementarities, the fact that different countries have different corporate governance systems is not a surprise.

Form of Finance and Ownership Structure

Two important determinants of corporate governance are the form of finance and the ownership structure. Japan's Big Bang may well result in changes in both. First, various reforms mean that publicly held firms will obtain easier access to capital markets, and this will continue to reduce the role of banks.

Second, reform of mutual funds and special legislation on asset securitization will increase the presence of institutional investors, who in turn may play some role in corporate governance.

Third, though not directly related to the Big Bang, banks and other financial institutions have been selling their shares in client firms, if only because holding them is costly. Similarly, cross-holdings among non-financial firms also are being reduced. This means a reduction in "stable shareholders," which suggests a change in the role of shareholders as monitors.

While it has been debated whether banks played a meaningful monitoring role in Japanese corporate governance in the past, their presence will inevitably be reduced as a result of the Big Bang. The substitutabilities theory suggests that something must substitute. Thus, the role of shareholders, or of capital markets in general, may increase.

In some sense, the wide divergence seen since the mid 1990s in the relative prices among Japanese bank shares is indicative of the importance of market forces, as are the swings in the prices of bank shares in general as perceptions of bank performance, government policies, and the like change. The case of LTCB, declared bankrupt and nationalized in October 1998, is a good extreme example. A sharp reduction in LTCB's share price in June 1998 effectively signaled that, official reassurance notwithstanding, the market had no confidence in LTCB.

The role of outside directors and auditors might become important. Here again, market pressures may force Japanese firms to use internationally accredited auditing firms to prepare their annual reports and conduct their audits, and that would place additional pressure on management, because the information will be reflected (through disclosure) in the capital markets.

Finally, the complementarities theory suggests that to the extent that bank presence is reduced, the lifetime employment system, and thus the system for recruiting senior executives, may change.

LEGAL RULES AND THE COST OF ENFORCEMENT

A vast number of studies on corporate governance has enriched our understanding of how different corporate governance systems operate.[1]

While these studies often examine the role and function of legal rules in corporate governance, one element has received almost no attention: enforcement. This is quite surprising, as the effectiveness of legal rules is a function of their enforceability. Differing historical, cultural, and legal peculiarities mean that mechanisms and levels of enforcement can be expected to vary from country to country, especially because of differences in the cost of enforcement relative to its value to enforcers.

Variations in enforcement costs do not necessarily affect the value of the legal component of a corporate governance system if the component has substitutabilities or complementarities with non-legal components. Thus, in a given corporate governance system, components such as the structure of ownership may substitute for the legal framework. So long as the structure of ownership does not change, differences in the cost of enforcement may not be relevant. Similarly, variations in enforcement cost may simply reflect different complementarities. For example, bank monitoring actually may be improved by a lower level of enforcement of legal rules, as it reduces liability disincentives to participate more actively in the supervision of firms.

On the other hand, within the legal-framework component, enforcement necessarily interacts with substantive rules. Because substantive legal rules must be enforced, the cost of enforcement affects the value of any substantive rule. In this sense, enforcement has complementarities to substantive rules. This suggests that, other things being equal, substantive rules do not converge when the cost of enforcement is different among jurisdictions. However, one expects convergence in substantive rules when the cost of enforcement is low: courts and regulators will develop substantive rules without worrying about their enforceability. Rules also change when enforcement is too costly. Indeed, there is then reason to think that market and other forces will arise to change costly rules to ones that are enforceable at lower costs.

To see these points, simple numerical examples may be helpful.

Suppose there are two countries, each with a different substantive rule for a certain situation. The value to Country A of its rule is 100 and the value to Country B of its rule is 120, defined as how efficient a rule is before considering the cost of enforcement. Now suppose that the cost of enforcement in Country A is 50 and for Country B is 80. Disregarding complementarities or the like, and other things being equal, the situation in Country B is worse because the net value of its rule (gross value minus enforcement cost) is 40 (120 – 80), compared to 50 (100 – 50) in Country A.

Now suppose that complementarities exist, and that B's are greater than A's, so that the complemented value of each country's rule is the same. In this case both countries might stay as they are, each with a different rule and different enforcement situation.

Next, suppose that the cost of enforcement is zero. Country A, if it knows Country B's situation, may change to B's rule.

If the cost of enforcement for B's rule is very high—say 500—one would hardly believe that complementarities could offset the disadvantage of Country B having a too-costly enforcement situation. Because enforcement of its rule is too costly, it may change to A's rule.

Countries may change their rules to those that are enforceable at lower costs or are self-enforcing, in which case rules may well converge across countries.

For example, rules on "hard" information such as financial statements, and disclosure and accounting rules in general, are often enforceable at low costs. Indeed, if a publicly held company keeps supplying false numbers in its financial statements, it is most likely to be uncovered and penalized in the market place. Thus, one can expect a convergence of accounting and hard-information disclosure standards at fairly high levels.

There are, however, disclosure rules that are not enforceable at low costs. Statements relating to "soft" information, particularly non-financial or forward-looking information, frequently lead to litigation. For example, claims concerning allegedly misleading projections about future profits are often filed in US courts. This means that, for that kind of disclosure, enforcement matters. Given the variety in enforcement systems and levels among major jurisdictions, one can expect that disclosure rules on soft information will continue to vary and will not converge.

How Much Will Japanese Legal Rules Change?

The cost of enforcement is the key to whether the Big Bang will serve as a force to change any substantive legal rules in Japan.

Japan's adoption of new rules on disclosure and accounting for "hard" financial data have put it in harmony with other industrial countries having well-functioning capital markets. The cost of enforcing such rules are very low, so rules are converging.

On the other hand, I suspect that complexity, coupled with differences in enforcement mechanisms across jurisdictions, implies that corporate law rules will converge only in some areas. This is so even if the Big Bang increases the role and function of capital markets. Corporate law rules simply cover too wide a range of matters—from voting rules, monitoring devices such as board systems, to shareholder litigation—to expect a general convergence.

Convergence is more likely to occur for two category of rules: those where the value does not depend on enforcement (enforcement cost is very low) and rules having no value because of the low level of enforcement in the relevant jurisdiction (enforcement cost is very high). Convergence is less likely to occur for rules having a value determined by complementarities with the applicable enforcement mechanisms.

As an example, non-use of the rule permitting injunctions against illegal activities under the Securities and Exchange Act may be attributed to the cost of enforcement. If so, unless the enforcement mechanism changes, the rule (or the current state of non-use of the rule) does not change. While the Big Bang suggests a more active role of regulators in policing compliance with legal rules ex post, it may not result in the reduction of various costs associated with enforcing rules under the Act.

Similarly, rules on management duties have a value that varies depending on rules on shareholder litigation, including derivative suits. Here, there are complementarities with enforcement mechanisms and, because of variations in enforcement levels among jurisdictions, one should expect a lack of convergence in substantive rules about management duties.

By contrast, in transition or emerging economies where there is no solid judicial system and the level of enforcement is very low, there may be a pressure toward adopting rules that have a value independent of enforcement or that are enforceable with little involvement of the courts. As a matter of fact, and quite unsurprisingly, there is an emerging dominance of voting rules and other less-costly enforceable rules in these economies. In other words, the low level of enforcement results in substantive rules tending to converge.

Again, here, it seems that unless the enforcement mechanism changes, substantive legal rules will not change or converge. Alternatively, however, if the enforcement cost is too high for a rule, the rule is meaningless, and thus may be changed to a rule that is enforceable at lower costs.

CONCLUSION

I have examined how Japan's Big Bang reform might affect the legal system and corporate governance in Japan. I have showed that the Big Bang program in some respects does, and in other respects does not, serve as a force to change the legal system and corporate governance. Japan's Big Bang will probably require an increased role for legal rules. Whether the legal system as a whole or the Japanese corporate governance system as a whole will change remain to be seen.

ACKNOWLEDGEMENTS

The author would like to thank Gérard Hertig, Takeo Hoshi, and Hugh Patrick for their insightful comments and suggestions on the earlier draft.

NOTES

1 This section draws on Hertig and Kanda (1998). Also see Hertig (1999). Among the important studies on corporate governance in the last few years are Hopt et al (1998), Hopt and Wymeersch (1997), La Porta et al (1997), Roe (1997), and Shleifer and Vishny (1997).

REFERENCES

Aoki, Masahiko. 1994. "The Japanese Firm as a System of Attributes." In Masahiko Aoki and Ronald Dore, editors, *The Japanese Firm: The Sources of Competitive Strength.*

Craig, Valentine V. 1998. "Financial Deregulation in Japan." *FDIC Banking Review* 11 (3):1.

Gilson, Ronald J. 1996. "Corporate Governance and Economic Efficiency: When Do Institutions Matter?" *Washington University Law Quarterly* 74: 327.

Gilson, Ronald J. 1998. "Reflections in a Distant Mirror: Japanese Corporate Governance through American Eyes." *Columbia Business Law Review* 1998: 203.

Hertig, Gérard. 1999. "Comparing Convergence of Substantive Rules and Convergence of Enforcement." Processed draft.

Hertig, Gérard and Hideki Kanda. 1998. "Rules, Enforcement, and Corporate Governance." Processed draft.

Hopt, Klaus J and Eddy Wymeersch, editors. 1997. *Comparative Corporate Governance: Essays and Materials.* de Gruyter.

Hopt, Klaus J, Hideki Kanda, Mark J Roe, Eddy Wymeersch, and Stefan Prigge, editors. 1998. *Comparative Corporate Governance: The State of the Art and Emerging Research.* Oxford University Press.

Kanda, Hideki. 1991. "Politics, Formalism, and the Elusive Goal of Investor Protection: Regulation of Structured Investment Funds in Japan." *University of Pennsylvania Journal of International Business Law* 12: 569.

Kanda, Hideki. 1997. "Globalization of Financial Markets and Financial Regulation in Japan." *Zeitschrift für Japanisches Recht.* 1997 (4): 9.

Kim, Hyung-Ki, Michio Muramatsu, TJ Pempel, and Kozo Yamamura. 1995. *The Japanese Civil Service and Economic Development: Catalysts of Change.* Clarendon Press Oxford.

Rafael La Porta, Florencio Lopez-de-Silanes, Andrei Shleifer, and Robert W Vishny. 1997. "Legal Determinants of External Finance." *Journal of Finance* 52: 1131.

Milgrom, Paul and John Roberts. 1994. "Complementarities and Systems: Understanding Japanese Economic Organization." *Estudios Economicos* 1: 3.

Pistor, Katharina and Philip A Wellons. 1998. *The Role of Law and Legal Institutions in Asian Economic Development 1960–1995.* Oxford University Press.

Roe, Mark J. 1997. "Comparative Corporate Governance." Columbia Law School, Center for Law and Economics Studies, Working Paper 125.

Shleifer, Andrei and Robert W Vishny. 1997. "A Survey of Corporate Governance." *Journal of Finance* 52: 737.

APPENDIX
SELECTED BIG BANG REFORMS

Lifting the ban on pure holding companies (effective, December, 1997, for non financial firms; March, 1998, for financial institutions). The Anti Monopoly Act, which prohibited "pure holding companies" per se, was amended in 1997, and relevant statutes in the financial sector were amended to respond to this change. A pure holding company is a company, more than half of whose assets are shares of other companies. Thus, a financial group may emerge with a holding company structure where banking, insurance and securities businesses are offered through subsidiaries under centralized management of a holding company. In fact, Daiwa Securities Group established a holding company structure on April 26, 1999.

Abolishment of exchange control (effective, April 1, 1998). The Foreign Exchange Act was drastically amended. For instance, anyone may open and maintain a bank account outside Japan without regulatory permission or clearance. Part of the amount of individuals' financial assets in Japan, which total US $10 trillion, may be moved outside of Japan.

Abolishment of regulation on currency exchange industry (effective, April 1, 1998). Also as the result of the Foreign Exchange Act amendments, anyone may engage in the currency exchange industry. Convenience stores and other firms have already announced their entry into this business. For instance, travelers can now buy US dollars at the airport counter of the air carrier.

Establishment of new regulatory bodies (effective, June 22, 1998). A new agency called the Financial Supervisory Agency ("FSA") was established and given power to regulate banks, securities firms, and insurance companies. This power was transferred from the Ministry of Finance to the FSA. Also, in December, 1998, a new agency called the Financial Reconstruction Commission ("FRC") was established on top of the FSA, and is responsible for licensing and other regulatory activities in the financial sector. The FSA engages in the implementation of financial regulation. The creation of this new regulatory structure suggests that the form of financial regulation in Japan will also change from consensus based regulation to rule based regulation.

Abolishment of fixed commission system of securities brokers (partly effective, April, 1998; fully effective, October 1, 1999). This will inevitably make the securities brokerage industry more competitive.

Entry into securities business: from licensing to registration system (effective, December 1, 1998). The entry level became lower for the securities industry. This change also accompanies the abolishment of the prohibition on securities firms against engaging in non-securities activity. For instance, a manufacturer will be permitted to enter the securities industry while maintaining a manufacturing business. The number of securities firms may increase drastically.

Sale of mutual funds by banks (partly effective, December, 1997; fully effective, December 1, 1998). Only 4% of the US $10 trillion in individuals' financial assets in Japan are invested in Japanese mutual funds. Sixty-five percent are invested in bank deposits and postal savings deposits. When mutual funds become marketed by banks, the picture may drastically change. Also, important reforms for the mutual fund system were made. For instance, a company type fund (which is popular in the US but was not permitted in Japan) became available (effective, December 1, 1998). Also, private funds (funds marketed to a limited number of institutions) became permitted (effective, December 1, 1998).

Asset management by securities firms (effective, December 1, 1998). Securities firms are now permitted to offer asset management services, typically by offering a product known in the United States as a "wrap account."

Improvement in accounting (effective, fiscal year 1999). Consolidated accounting with market value accounting of financial assets will be required. The new accounting rules must be consistent with the International Accounting Standards.

Defragmentation among banking, securities and insurance industries. This is an ongoing liberalization program of fragmented industry regulation in Japan. Liberalization measures include permitting mutual entry among banking, insurance and securities industries through the subsidiary or holding company structures, and reducing firewall regulations among banking, securities and insurance industries. Implementation dates vary, but the greater part will be completed on October 1, 1999.

Securitization of loans, receivables and real property. A special statute was passed in the Diet in June, 1998 (effective, September 1, 1998). This special legislation permits a low cost method of securitizing financial assets, so that financing in the capital markets will become more attractive. Also of importance in this connection is the fact that the secondary market of securities among institutions was liberalized; certain qualified institutions may trade (non equity) securities freely among themselves as under Rule 144A of the Securities Act of 1933 in the United States (effective, June, 1998).

Chapter 12

BIG BANG DEREGULATION AND JAPANESE CORPORATE GOVERNANCE: A SURVEY OF THE ISSUES

Michael S Gibson
Federal Reserve System

In November 1996, Japanese Prime Minister Hashimoto announced a Big Bang policy to deregulate Japanese financial markets. Following a period of planning, implementation of the Big Bang began in April 1998 when all remaining restrictions on foreign exchange transactions were removed. It is scheduled to continue through March 2001. A listing of the deregulation agenda is dominated by measures to remove restrictions on how banks and securities firms do business and allow cross-entry of banks, securities firms, and insurers into each others' businesses (Table 12.1).

In this chapter, I argue that such financial modernization measures are of secondary importance for improving the performance of the Japanese economy. A more important problem facing the Japanese economy is the low return earned on Japanese wealth. Raising the return on Japan's huge stock of wealth is key to Japan maintaining a high level of per capita income in light of two facts. First, the population is aging rapidly, which will slow the rate of labor force growth. Second, Japan's industrial firms are on the frontier of technology, so the rapid productivity growth of the 1960s and '70s is unlikely to be repeated. Simply as a consequence of traditional growth accounting, with labor and productivity unlikely to provide much growth, raising the return on capital appears to be an easier route to continued prosperity in Japan.

I argue that the low return on Japan's wealth reflects characteristics of the Japanese corporate governance system. Although the system played a key role in Japan's outstanding economic performance in the 1960s and '70s, times have changed and the system has not. I argue that the proper focus of Big Bang deregulation should be on measures to strengthen corporate governance. I suggest specific changes that might lead to improved corporate governance in Japan. Some of these have already begun to occur.[1]

My emphasis on corporate governance reforms does not mean that the Big Bang's financial modernization reforms are unnecessary. Both types of reform

TABLE 12.1. Deregulation Timetable

Fiscal 1997

- Securities houses will be allowed to handle consumer payments for their clients

Fiscal 1998

- Companies and individuals can handle foreign-exchange transactions without government authorization
- Banks will be allowed to sell their own investment trusts over the counter
- Ban on financial holding companies will be lifted
- Firms can become securities brokerages without government licenses
- Securities houses will be allowed to expand asset management services

Fiscal 1999

- Securities houses will be free to set their commissions on securities trading of any size
- Market-value method will be applied for marketable securities
- Barriers that restricted banks, trust banks and securities houses from entering each other's markets will be removed
- Banks will be allowed to issue straight bonds

By the end of 2001

- Banks, securities houses will be allowed to enter insurance sector

Schedule not set

- Enactment of a new financial services law that would govern banking, securities and insurance sectors

Source: Nikkei Weekly, June 16, 1997, p 1.

can help improve the performance of the Japanese economy. Further, the partial financial deregulation of the 1980s and early '90s has helped some Japanese firms reduce their funding costs and shelter themselves from the ongoing banking crisis. Financial modernization may increase competition within the financial sector, and while common sense and some empirical evidence support the idea that competition increases productivity (Nickell 1996), this is not the same as increasing the return on wealth. (For example, the productivity of US airlines has increased dramatically since domestic air travel was deregulated in the 1970s, but their profitability has not.) If raising the return on wealth is the goal, corporate governance reforms are more likely to be successful than increased competition in the financial sector.

One well-known feature of the Japanese economy is the important role of industrial groups known as *keiretsu*. The majority of large Japanese firms belong to such groups. Research has shown the corporate governance structures of *keiretsu* and non-*keiretsu* firms to be somewhat different. Prowse (1992) shows that concentrated ownership is a more important governance tool in non-*keiretsu* firms than in *keiretsu* firms. Hoshi, Kashyap, and Scharfstein (1990) show that *keiretsu* firms' closer main bank ties, compared with non-*keiretsu* firms, lower the cost of financial distress.

In addition, research has found that *keiretsu* firms have lower average profitability than non-*keiretsu* firms (Nakatani 1984). This difference in performance should not be blamed entirely on corporate governance, as there are many other ways in which the two types of firms differ. While some of the corporate governance mechanisms I discuss relate mainly to *keiretsu* firms, others apply throughout the Japanese economy.

This chapter first documents the low returns on Japanese wealth over the past two decades and discuss possible causes linked to corporate governance. I then discuss three characteristics of the Japanese corporate governance system that reduce the pressure on Japanese firms to maximize returns for shareholders. I stress the point that the Japanese corporate governance system has not prevented Japan from producing world-class firms in many industries. However, it has not been effective at producing high returns for Japanese wealth holders during the last decade. For each characteristic discussed, I then go into detail on possible changes to corporate governance, some of which have already occurred as part of the Big Bang. For each corporate governance mechanism, empirical evidence on its effectiveness, its current status in Japan, and how it is addressed, if at all, in the Big Bang are reviewed.

JAPAN'S LOW RETURN ON EQUITY: EVIDENCE AND CAUSES

Japanese households have had a high saving rate for a long time. As a result, they have accumulated a large stock of wealth. As is true of almost all countries, Japan's wealth has been invested disproportionately in domestic assets. This stock of wealth has not produced high returns for Japanese households. In particular, equity investments have not produced as high returns in Japan as in the United States, especially since the late 1980s. This is acknowledged, albeit with a different emphasis, in the literature that argues Japanese companies face a lower cost of equity capital than US companies. (See, for example, McCauley and Zimmer (1989).)

Evidence on Return on Equity in Japan

Return on equity in Japanese firms, whether measured using stock market returns or accounting returns, has been low compared with the return earned by US firms. Both stock market and accounting returns are imperfect measures of the true return on equity, but they tell the same story. Beginning with 1980, the continuously compounded annual return on Japanese stocks has been 7.3%, compared to 16.3% in the United States (Table 12.2, Panel A). The beginning of the comparison period is 1980 because that is when restrictions on foreign investment by Japanese investors were liberalized and a comparison of United States and Japanese returns begins to represent a meaningful choice facing Japanese investors.

The difference is exaggerated but not caused by the steep increases in US stock prices since 1993. Ending the sample period in 1994, returns were 9.8% in Japan and 13.5% in the United States. Measuring returns as the excess return of the stock market over a domestic risk-free interest rate does not change the conclusion that Japanese corporations have produced lower returns for shareholders, though it does narrow the gap (Table 12.2, Panel B).

Accounting returns on equity are shown in Figure 1. Again, returns of Japanese firms fall short of those of US firms.

French and Poterba (1991) examined differences in accounting standards that cause earnings of Japanese firms to be understated relative to those of US firms. They concluded that differences in accounting could not explain all of the difference in the average price-earnings ratio between Japan and the United States during the study period 1970–90. It is thus unlikely that accounting dif-

TABLE 12.2. Stock Market Return on Equity in Japan and the United States

Panel A: Average stock market returns (Continuously compounded annual stock return)

	Japan	U.S.
1980–98*	7.3	16.3
1980–94	9.8	13.5

Panel B: Average excess returns (Continuously compounded annual stock return less continuously compounded annual return on risk-free asset)

	Japan	U.S.
1980–98*	2.4	8.9
1980–94	3.8	6.0

*Data for 1998 are through June.

Notes: Stock market returns are calculated gross of dividends, before taxes, in local currency. The risk-free asset is invested at the 3-month Treasury bill rate for the US and the Gensaki rate for Japan.

Source: MSCI, Federal Reserve Board, Bank of Japan.

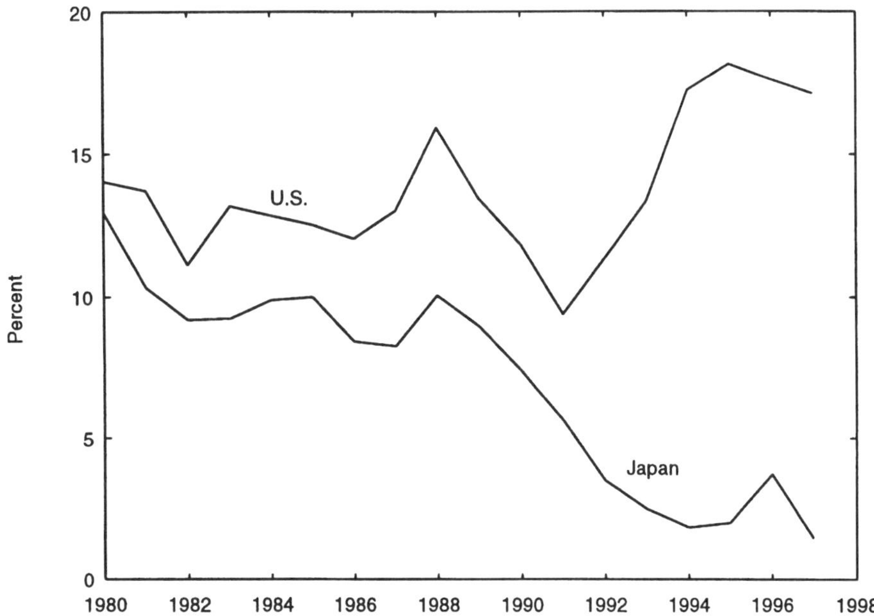

Notes: Accounting return is defined as earnings divided by book value. The accounting return for a given year uses the most recent fiscal year's data available in June of the following year (to capture data from Japanese fiscal years that end in March). The accounting return is actually computed as (P/BV) / (P/E), where both P/BV and P/E are taken from the MSCI database. The MSCI indices contain firms covering approximately 60% of a country's stock market capitalization.

FIGURE 12.1. Accounting return on equity in Japan and the US.

ferences could explain all of the difference in the average accounting rate of return between Japan and the United States.

Moreover, accounting differences lead book value to be understated at Japanese firms relative to US firms, which would tend to inflate Japanese firms' accounting rate of return relative to that of US firms. The leading example is the land and equities that Japanese companies carry on their books at acquisition cost. For many firms, acquisition costs date from the 1940s or '50s.

Accounting returns in Japan and the United States were nearly identical during 1966–79, according to Takeo Hoshi's research, so the slump shown in Figure 1 really is a striking development.

Figure 2 shows annual stock market returns. It is clear that the returns earned by Japanese shareholders have been on a downward trend. I argue below that this trend is neither an artifact of noisy data nor purely a consequence of the Japanese recession of the 1990s. Rather, it reflects real economic trends, including characteristics of the Japanese corporate governance system. The next section discusses three such characteristics.

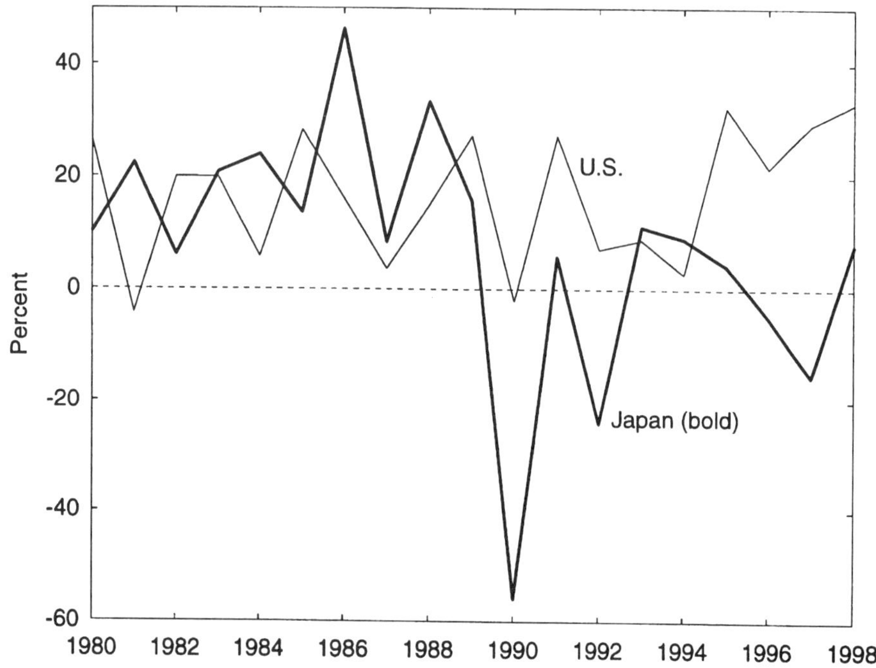

Note: Stock market returns are continuously compounded returns calculated gross of dividends, before taxes, in local currency. Data for 1998 are through June at an annual rate.
Source: MSCI.

FIGURE 12.2. Japanese and US stock market returns.

Note that regardless of what fraction of the slump in returns is due to the recession of the 1990s, the corporate governance reforms I discuss would improve the return on Japan's wealth and boost Japan's future standard of living.

Causes of Japan's Falling Return on Equity

Japanese Firms Make Poor Use of Free Cash Flow

According to Kester (1991), Japanese firms make poor use of their cash flow in excess of what is required to maintain ongoing operations. In other words, the success of Japanese firms made the lack of focus on profit by Japanese managers more costly. By virtue of their success, Japanese firms have reduced their need for outside funding and reduced the ability of the providers of external funds to monitor managers. It became easier for managers to grow their firms by taking on marginally profitable projects in a cavalier fashion. Kester notes that the managerial discretion afforded by excess cash has given rise to the expression of latent self-interests that were successfully contained during Japan's high growth period. This explanation is consistent with the declining returns on Japanese equity shown in Figures 12.1 and 12.2.

Bank Monitoring Is Increasingly Ineffective

Japanese banks and related financial institutions own substantial equity in non-financial firms. One of the characteristics of Japanese corporate governance that has been identified as an advantage is the ability of banks to be both lenders and shareholders. In support of this proposition, Prowse (1990) found evidence that the agency problem between shareholders and debtholders was diminished in Japan, reducing the distortionary effect of debtor-shareholder conflicts on a firm's capital structure decision.

However, this characteristic seems to be vanishing. With the deregulation of Japanese financial markets in recent years, alternatives to bank debt have become available to large firms. Many have replaced bank loans with direct borrowing from capital markets (bonds and commercial paper). At the same time, Japanese banks are under increasing pressure to restructure and improve performance (Fukao 1998). As a result, banks are reconsidering the wisdom of holding large equity investments. As non-financial firms gradually sell their bank shares as their reliance on bank loans falls, banks have less of an incentive to hold shares of non-financial firms for the purpose of cementing a customer relationship. Banks and firms appear to be focusing their equity holdings on a smaller range of firms. As a result, the ability of the corporate governance system to use bank monitoring to reduce the agency costs of debt have fallen and can be expected to continue falling.

Lost Profits Due to Deregulation Have Not Been Replaced

Deregulation of product markets has reduced the rents earned by Japanese companies. For example, interest rate deregulation has raised the cost of funds of Japanese banks, and some of the increase has been passed along to borrowing firms (as was some of the rent in the regulated environment). In some firms, the resulting decline in profits has not been replaced, leading to a lower return on equity. Strengthening corporate governance will not help firms find new rents, but it could give them an incentive to use resources more efficiently and thereby replace some of the profits lost due to deregulation.

CORPORATE GOVERNANCE AND THE PROBLEM OF LOW RETURNS

Three reasons Japanese firms produce low returns for shareholders are analyzed in this section. First, the Japanese corporate governance system gives primacy to insider stakeholders. Second, institutional investors, a class of shareholders that has tried to influence managers of US firms to focus on shareholder returns, are weak in Japan. Third, there is no market for corporate control in Japan.

Managers Serve Inside Stakeholders, Not Outside Shareholders

Equity ownership in Japan is dominated by insider stakeholders, a group that includes lenders, customers, and suppliers that have financial or product market relationships with the firm. According to data presented in Fukao (1998), insider stakeholders held 38% of the shares of large Japanese firms in 1996. In the Japanese system, these insiders monitor the firm's managers, and outside shareholders have little or no role in corporate governance. (The insider stakeholders often have delegated their monitoring responsibility to the firm's main bank. Another group of insiders, employees, typically have a small or no shareholding in the firm.)

Insider stakeholders profit from the return on their equity investment *and* from the return on their other relationships with the firm. A focus purely on profit maximization—which could include seeking out lower interest rates on bank loans, lower prices from suppliers, or higher prices from customers—could put managers at odds with the insider stakeholders. Because it is these stakeholders who monitor managers, it is logical for managers not to focus exclusively on maximizing profit. This is reflected in a survey of Japanese managers' goals in which "capital gains for shareholders" ranked last of 12 choices (Kojima 1997, p 20).

Given the poor performance of Japanese financial institutions in the 1990s, it is interesting that data cited in Fukao (1998) show that insider stakeholders hold 50% of the shares of financial institutions, compared with only 25% of non-financial firms. Hanazaki and Horiuchi (1998) argue that ineffective corporate governance has contributed to the depth and duration of the current Japanese banking crisis.

In the Japanese corporate governance system, outside shareholders can have only limited influence on Japanese managers. Outside shareholders are often in the minority. Also, some outside holders of large minority stakes in Japanese companies have been accused of "greenmail." Japanese greenmailers have abused the statutory rights accorded to large minority shareholders, such as the right to inspect the company books, by threatening to exercise those rights in a way that would embarrass a firm's managers (see Okumura 1989). Greenmail, or the threat of greenmail, was one of the tactics favored by the corporate extortionists known as *sokaiya*. As a result, Japanese firms have become wary of minority shareholders and the rights of such shareholders have been curtailed, de facto if not de jure.

Institutional Investors are Weak in Japan

Institutional investors, such as pension funds, mutual funds, and insurance companies, pool the assets of many households. They can more readily achieve the large shareholdings necessary to overcome the bias to inaction caused by free-rider problems. However, in Japan institutional holdings are small, just 15% of household assets, compared with 38% in the United States in 1995, the most recent year for which data are available.

There are several reasons why. Japanese corporate pensions are typically of the defined-benefit form and many plans are underfunded. In contrast, US pensions are increasingly of the defined-contribution type, which are necessarily funded in advance. Taxation of pensions favors the defined-benefit type over the defined-contribution type in Japan (Morinaga and Fukao 1997). Restrictions on pension fund asset allocation, limiting investment in equities (lifted in 1997) made it hard for pension funds to achieve high returns. Mutual funds in Japan are much less important than in the United States, primarily because their tax treatment is less favorable than the treatment of direct purchases of equities. Moreover, for a variety of factors, Japanese mutual funds have underperformed their benchmarks by large amounts (Cai, Chan and Yamada 1997).

Japanese institutional investors do not have a history of exerting pressure on companies to increase shareholder returns. (Of course, US institutional investors did not have such a history 20 years ago either.) The largest institutional investors in Japan, life insurance companies, have typically adopted a passive role in corporate governance. Often life insurers act as inside stakeholders, using their shareholdings as a way to retain the insurance business of a firm and its employees rather than pressuring managers to maximize shareholder wealth. Corporate pension funds, too, are often managed in the interest of the funding corporation rather than the interest of the pension beneficiaries. Both the small size of institutional investors and their limited appetite for shareholder-oriented governance make them weak monitors for shareholder interests, contributing to Japan's problem of low return on invested wealth.

There Is No Market for Corporate Control in Japan

Individual shareholders face a free-rider problem when considering trying to force managers to pay more attention to shareholder returns. The benefit of improved corporate performance accrues to all shareholders, even those who do not exert any effort to force change. The free-rider problem implies that individual shareholders will only take action to force managers to focus on shareholder returns when the cost of the action is small. Many governance mechanisms, such as electing candidates to the board of directors or sponsoring resolutions at the shareholders' annual meeting, are so costly that they are rarely pursued by individuals. The primary way individual shareholders contribute to effective corporate governance in the United States is by selling their shares when corporate performance is poor. This is critical when a firm is the subject of a hostile takeover.

Hostile takeovers have been rare in Japan. Indeed, so are mergers for any reason. Data for 1994–96 show that the average annual value of mergers was 0.4% of GDP in Japan, compared with 6.1% in the United States (SDP 1997, p xxii). Of course, only a fraction of this merger activity is motivated by corporate control reasons. The figure for Japan is 0.1% of GDP if the merger of Bank of Tokyo and Mitsubishi Bank is excluded.

To a greater extent than in the United States, Japanese firms depend on long-term relationships with suppliers and customers. These relationships are not based on the performance of specific contractual obligations. Rather, they depend on an unwritten understanding that both parties have made investments tailored to that relationship and both parties deserve to earn a fair return on those investments. It is unlikely that this network of relationships could have grown and prospered in an environment where hostile takeovers were common.

Moreover, equity ownership in Japan is dominated by stakeholders. This typically takes the form of "cross-shareholding"—that is, firms own each other's shares. If a majority of a target firm's shares are cross-held, a potential acquirer must convince at least some stakeholders to sell. Only if the acquirer can convince a firm's stakeholders that the overall return on their relationships with the target firm will be higher if the firm is taken over would the stakeholders agree to sell (see Ramseyer 1987.) In general, a takeover is more difficult (or expensive) when the target's shares are not widely held. According to an argument presented in Ito (1992, p 191), one motivation for the formation of cross-shareholdings in the 1960s was to prevent hostile takeovers (especially by foreigners).

The Japanese Corporate Governance System Is Not Dysfunctional

It would be wrong to say that the Japanese corporate governance system is dysfunctional. Japan's past outstanding economic performance proves that its economic structure, including corporate governance, has worked well. Most researchers agree that it does an excellent job of facilitating specific investments and information sharing among employees, suppliers, and customers. For example, Aoki (1994) argues that the system enhances a firm's ability to use more efficient team-based methods of production in place of more hierarchical and specialized ("Western") methods of production. However, most researchers also agree that it does not lead managers to seek to maximize shareholder returns.

Stakeholder monitoring substitutes to some extent for the non-existent market for corporate control in Japan. Kaplan and Minton (1994) show that stakeholders send directors to sit on a firm's board much more frequently in large Japanese firms than in large US firms. The frequency of a new stakeholder-affiliated director is 12.9 percent for Japanese firms compared with 2.3 percent in US firms in their sample. Conversely, only 0.3 percent of the Japanese firms in their data sample are taken over, compared with 2 percent of the US firms.

Thus, researchers have documented the success of the Japanese corporate governance system in imposing checks on corporate managers. Berglof and Perotti (1994) show that the *keiretsu* system of corporate groups can, in theory, prevent managers from shirking. Often the *keiretsu* monitoring is delegated to the *keiretsu* main bank, as described by Aoki and Patrick (1994).

Morck and Nakamura (1999) examine the circumstances under which Japanese banks send directors to firms and conclude that bank monitoring is more focused on a firm's liquidity position than its profitability. They conclude that bank oversight is an imperfect substitute for shareholder oversight.

Kaplan (1994, 1997a) found that turnover of the top managers of the largest Japanese firms was sensitive to the firm's stock price, earnings, and sales growth, and the sensitivities were similar in magnitude to those of the top managers of the largest US firms. He also found that turnover of Japanese executives was more sensitive to poor earnings performance, and less sensitive to stock returns, than was the turnover of US executives. If earnings are the best indicator of a firm's ability to uphold its obligations to its customers, suppliers, and lenders, then the second finding is consistent with the hypothesis that monitoring of Japanese executives is done primarily by (and in the interests of) stakeholders, not outside shareholders.

Kang and Shivdasani (1996) find that the stock price of Japanese companies goes up when top managers are forced out, and that large shareholders play a role when the new managers come from outside the firm. Kang and Stulz (1996, p 137) compare the stock market's reaction to new security issues by Japanese and US firms and find evidence "consistent with the view that Japanese managers care less about short-term shareholders than American managers." Kubo (1998) finds that Japanese managers' compensation (salary plus bonus) does not depend on shareholder return but does depend on employees' average wage and company profit.

These papers suggest that the monitoring activities of insider stakeholders are not aimed at forcing managers to pursue high returns for outside shareholders. The burden of monitoring should shift to shareholders in order to raise the return on Japan's wealth.

HOW COULD THE BIG BANG CHANGE THINGS?

I have identified the problem facing Japan as a low return on wealth. Three reasons for these low returns are the lack of focus on maximizing shareholder returns, the relative weakness of institutional investors in Japan, and the absence of a market for corporate control. If the purpose of the Big Bang is to solve the problems facing Japan's financial system, the Big Bang should include measures to address these characteristics of the Japanese economy directly.

The current Japanese corporate governance system reflects the interaction of market forces and government policies over a period of decades. The relative importance of each on the development of Japan's corporate governance system is not clear-cut. Milhaupt (1996) argues that the Japanese legal system supports, but did not create, the system. On the other hand, Weinstein (1997) argues that government policies have been the driving force. Kojima (1997, p 125) contends that the shift of control away from shareholders was the result of deliberate government policy during World War II. It may be necessary for the Big Bang only to remove legal and regulatory obstacles for change to occur.

Focusing Managers on Shareholder Returns

Six ways to focus managers on shareholder returns are discussed in this section. They are equity-based compensation, more-independent boards of directors, enhanced accountability, holding companies, share buybacks, and shareholder lawsuits. The impediments to such changes are largely organizational, not legal or regulatory.

Equity-Based Compensation

In a shareholder-oriented governance system, the incentives of corporate managers must be aligned with those of shareholders. One way this can be done is for part of managers' compensation to be linked to the firm's equity return, for example by shifting their compensation from cash to stock options. Event studies on US firms show that a firm's market value rises by 2.4% on average when it introduces a stock option plan (Brickley, Bhagat, and Lease 1985). Doubling the fraction of the CEO's pay that is equity-based is associated with a 4.3% increase in the market value (Mehran 1995). Equity-based compensation is clearly good for shareholders.

In the past, the pay of Japanese CEOs has not been linked to equity return. Kato and Rockel (1992) found no relationship between CEO pay and shareholder return in a sample of 599 large Japanese firms in 1985. In a comparable sample of large US firms, the relationship was positive and statistically significant.

One way to increase equity-based compensation is through executive stock options. A ban on stock option plans in Japan was lifted in June 1997; by September 1998 160 firms had adopted plans ("American-Style Pay Moves Abroad," New York Times, 3 September 1998), which would represent just over 10% of Tokyo Stock Exchange First Section firms. In contrast, 93% percent of a similar group of US firms had stock option plans in 1996 (Peck 1998).

In Japan, stock options obtained through corporate plans are subject to unfavorable tax treatment, with only the first ¥10 million of gains each year taxed at the low capital gains rate and the remainder taxed as ordinary income (at a higher rate). Although not a part of the Big Bang, improving the tax treatment of options would make them more attractive to firms and make it easier to align the incentives of managers with shareholders' interests.

Independent Boards of Directors

In a shareholder-oriented governance system, the board of directors is a key link between shareholders and managers. It is the responsibility of the board to focus managers on maximizing shareholder value. A major trend in the United States in the past decade has been the reorientation of boards toward shareholder interests. Boards that are too heavily populated by corporate insiders have come under fire from shareholders.

Empirical evidence on the effect of boards of directors in the United States suggests that relatively independent boards do a better job of monitoring managers at poorly performing firms. Weisbach (1988) shows that the sensitivity of CEO resignation to stock market and accounting performance is higher at firms with outsider-dominated boards. However, studies looking for broader effects of board composition on return on equity typically find no effect (for example, Bhagat and Black 1996). This suggests the positive effect of an independent board is limited to those firms where the need for monitoring is greatest. However, as I have argued, the need for monitoring to be done in the interests of shareholders is great in Japan, so the benefits of an independent board are also likely to be greater in Japan than in the United States.

Japanese boards of directors have been criticized for being too closely tied to stakeholders. On average, only 22% of Japanese directors were not employees of the firm before becoming directors, compared with 65% in the United States (Fukao 1995, p 14). Most of them represent insider shareholders, primarily banks (Kaplan and Minton 1994). In addition, Japanese boards are large, typically 20 to 25 members (Kojima 1997, p 55), compared with 12 or 13 in the United States (Kaplan 1995). Large size may inhibit effectiveness. A prominent US business group suggests that smaller boards are often more cohesive and work more effectively than larger ones (Business Roundtable 1997, p 10).

One group calling for change is the Corporate Governance Forum of Japan (1997). Their Corporate Governance Principles call for Japanese boards to have a majority of independent, non-executive directors; be clearly separate from the executive board (which is responsible for execution of business activities); and separate the positions of Chair of the Board and Chief Executive Officer.

These proposals resemble the "best practices" for boards that have been promulgated in the United States in recent years. For example, the California Public Employees' Retirement System (CalPERS) has published "Corporate Governance Core Principles and Guidelines" focusing on the organization of the board. Other groups that have published similar guidelines in the United States in recent years include the National Association of Corporate Directors and the Business Roundtable.

No laws prevent Japanese firms from making their boards more independent, and a handful of firms have done so. The Big Bang contains no measures to encourage more independent boards.

Enhance Accountability and Holding Companies

Another way to align manager and shareholder interests would be for Japanese firms to change their internal organization to enhance accountability. By moving away from an organization based on frequent personnel rotation throughout the firm toward one where managers identify with (and are identified with) an individual business unit, it would become easier to hold individual managers accountable for their performance. For example, Kokusai, a mid-sized Japanese brokerage firm, has restructured itself into three units—trading, investment banking, and private banking—which will set their own salary and personnel systems. Its stated goal is to improve its return on equity before Big Bang deregulation is complete (Nikkei Weekly, 6 Apr 1998, p 13).

Relaxation of the restrictions on holding companies in Japan would make it easier for firms to adopt sweeping organizational changes. While the ban on holding companies was removed in 1997, the lack of consolidated taxation in Japan and restrictions placed on the size of a holding company under the Anti-

Monopoly Law limit the attractiveness of the structure, limiting the beneficial effects that holding companies could have on improved accountability for corporate managers in Japan.

Share Buybacks

A share buyback allows a firm's managers to signal that future stock returns are likely to be high. It also lets a firm return capital to shareholders while avoiding the double taxation of dividends. Evidence from the United States shows that a firm's share price rises by 2.3% on average when an open market repurchase is announced. Moreover, the effect increases with the size of the announced buyback (Comment and Jarrell 1991).

Until 1995, share buybacks were prohibited in Japan. In light of the argument presented above that a weakness of the Japanese corporate governance system was its inability to monitor managers of cash-rich firms, this ban seems to have been unfortunate. Since the prohibition was lifted, more than 270 firms have announced buyback plans, representing about 20% of Tokyo Stock Exchange First Section firms. Fenn and Liang (1998) report that, in an average year during 1984–95, 41% of a similar group of US firms repurchased shares.

The future tax treatment of share buybacks in Japan is uncertain, since the Ministry of Finance has given only a temporary waiver of taxation on buybacks as implicit dividends. The Big Bang contains no provisions to encourage share buybacks.

Shareholder Lawsuits

One action shareholders can take to influence corporate managers is to file a lawsuit against managers who allegedly cause damage to the company. Evidence in Strahan (1998) supports the idea that securities class action lawsuits help police US managers. He shows that lawsuits are more common in firms more likely to need monitoring (for example, large firms and non-dividend paying firms) and that the probability of CEO turnover rises after a lawsuit is filed.

In October 1993, Japan's Commercial Code was revised to reduce the fees required to file such a lawsuit. In the three months after the change, 84 derivative suits were filed ("Shareholders turning to lawsuits to ensure executive accountability," Nikkei Weekly, 9 May 1994, p 1). In June 1996, three directors of a company that had been fined for illegally selling aviation electronics to Iran lost a shareholder derivative suit and were ordered to pay the company $11.6 million in damages.

Although facilitating derivative lawsuits gives shareholders another way to pursue redress against corporate mismanagement and may encourage managers to avoid grossly wasteful policies, it may be too much to hope for derivative lawsuits to implement the subtle change in managers' objectives from stakeholder interests to shareholder interests.

Changes to Institutional Investors

Japanese institutional investors are both small and passive. In contrast, institutional investors in the United States have taken an increasingly active role in corporate governance over the past decade, pressuring managers to improve shareholder returns. For example, the Council of Institutional Investors (CII) releases a list of poorly performing companies each year that its members are urged to target for governance-related improvements, such as increasing the number of outside directors and requiring directors to be paid in stock or stock options. Opler and Sokobin (1997) found that poorly performing firms listed on the CII target lists in 1991–94 outperformed other poorly performing firms and the market as a whole. This is consistent with the notion that pressure from institutional investors can affect corporate performance. Del Guercio and Hawkins (forthcoming) find that institutional shareholder pressure has an impact on the policies pursued at targeted firms.

On the other hand, many researchers who have studied the effect of institutional investors' pressure for changes to corporate governance on firm performance have found no effect. Black (1997, p 3) surveyed this literature and concluded that "institutional investor activism doesn't importantly affect firm performance." Karpoff's (1998) survey concludes that activism is usually successful in effecting changes in corporate governance but not in raising share prices.

It may not be surprising that the empirical literature to date has been inconclusive, because of the many problems empirical tests face. For example, it is difficult to separate the effect of institutional-investor pressure from other factors affecting a firm's performance, because the decision to target a company is not exogenous. Moreover, most of the existing literature looks for an unconditional link between institutional-investor pressure for corporate governance reforms and firm performance. It may make more sense to look for a conditional link, for corporate governance to matter more at some times—for example when business conditions are bad and change is needed—than at others.

Growth of Japanese institutional investors could have additional positive effects on Japanese capital markets, even if they do not engage in active governance. An OECD study (Blommestein 1997) cited research showing that countries with a large institutional investor sector have more liquid and more efficient financial markets, more innovative risk-transfer strategies, and more developed stock and bond markets. Simply by being large players, institutional investors that do not engage in active governance, such as mutual funds and corporate pension funds, can have a beneficial effect on financial market development, another area in which the Big Bang aims to have an effect.

Changes in Legal Framework

Many aspects of the legal framework governing institutional investors in Japan have been changed or are scheduled to be changed as part of the Big Bang. Restrictions on the asset allocation of corporate pension funds were removed in 1997. Thus, management of corporate pension funds is no longer restricted to trust banks and life insurance companies. Restrictions on investment in foreign mutual funds have largely been removed.

The response to these changes has already begun. Foreign mutual fund companies have begun to establish Japanese operations to sell investment trusts. For example, Fidelity opened an office in Tokyo in June 1997 to prepare for direct sales of investment trusts to individuals following deregulation. From 1995 to 1998, Fidelity's assets under management in Japan increased nine times ("Fidelity's experience highlights financial industry changes," Asian Wall Street Journal, 1 Mar 1999, p 7). The market share of all foreign investment trust companies rose from below 3% in 1996 to 10% by year-end 1998. Japanese and foreign banks and securities firms have set up investment advisory firms to manage pension fund investments and the funds entrusted to these firms have been growing rapidly ("A giant sucking sound," *The Economist*, 23 Aug 1997, p 53–54).

Some legal changes have not yet been undertaken, but would be necessary to fully empower the institutional investor sector to contribute to a successful Big Bang. I cite two examples. The current tax treatment of investment trusts is distortionary, because a seller's cost basis for tax purposes is set equal to the average acquisition cost of all investors in the trust, not to the seller's own acquisition cost. Cai, Chan and Yamada (1997) show that this has contributed to severe underperformance of Japanese investment trusts. Reportedly, the relevant law will be changed in the 1998 fiscal year. Currently, when pension funds switch from one investment advisor to another, all investments must be liquidated and the funds reinvested by the new advisor. This raises the cost of switching advisors, which limits competition for fund management. Reportedly, this requirement will be changed in the 1999 fiscal year.

Changes in Market Practices

Again, some of the changes that are needed are not changes in laws, but changes in market practices. For example, until recently pension fund investment advisors have not been evaluated on the performance of the investments they select. Pension fund sponsors did not mark their portfolios to market, so they did not put much emphasis on investment performance. A Ministry of Finance advisory panel on accounting has recommended that mark-to-market accounting for corporate pension funds be introduced in the fiscal year beginning 1 April 2000.

Comparative data on mutual fund performance are not widely available. However, an industry association is planning, in the second half of 1999, to propose standardized performance reporting for mutual funds and pension funds, to be implemented in 2000. More pressure from households for institutional investors to provide higher returns is a necessary complement to the Big Bang reforms.

I have argued that institutional investors are more likely to contribute to improved corporate governance without requiring the development of an active market for corporate control. Given the mixed evidence from the United States on the ability of institutional investors to improve corporate performance through active monitoring of managers, it is possible that even a large Japanese institutional investor community would not be able to effectively pressure corporate managers to focus on shareholder value. In that case, developing a market for corporate control would be a necessary step to improve the returns on Japanese wealth.[2]

Changes in the Market for Corporate Control

Hostile takeovers are rare in Japan. In the United States, they function as a last-resort means of forcing change onto managers who cannot be persuaded by other means to maximize shareholder value. The near-absence of hostile takeovers in Japan reflects the key monitoring role traditionally played by insider stakeholders and the passive role played by outside shareholders. According to Kester (1991, p 97–103), the legal impediments to an active market for corporate control in Japan appear to be no greater than in the United States.

Given the lack of legal obstacles for the Big Bang to remove, it may be sufficient for the Big Bang to shift power to outside shareholders, and a market for corporate control will develop if needed. A decline in cross-shareholding would seem to be a prerequisite. The deregulation of off-exchange block trading of shares on 1 December 1998 and a requirement that cross-shareholdings be marked-to-market beginning in fiscal year 2001 may contribute to an unwinding of cross-shareholdings (*International Financing Review*, 13 Mar 1999, p 59).

It is worth noting that use of hostile takeovers in the United States has declined in the 1990s as shareholders have used other means, such as enhancing the independence and authority of the board of directors, to focus managers attention on increasing shareholder value. Another factor behind this trend is the increasing number of legal impediments that have been placed on hostile takeovers in the United States.

Although hostile takeovers may be unlikely to flourish in Japan, a more limited market for corporate control may develop in the form of activist investors (wealthy individuals and specialized investment funds) who take minority stakes in poorly performing firms. Such activists have been successful in the United States in pressuring managers to reverse inefficient diversification and increase return on equity, according to Bethel, Liebeskind and Opler (1998). Gorton and Kahl (1998) argue that activist investors are likely to face lower agency costs of pressuring managers of poorly performing firms to restructure, compared with professional asset managers. As a result, it is efficient for activists to acquire minority stakes in poorly performing firms and pressure managers to restructure. The rights of minority shareholders in Japan are not well-protected. The Big Bang contains no measures to enhance the power of minority shareholders.

CONCLUSIONS

The challenge facing the Japanese financial system is to help improve the allocation of resources to ensure that Japan's wealth earns a high return. Big Bang deregulation could push the Japanese financial system in the right direction by focusing on strengthening corporate governance. Changes such as stock option plans, independent directors, and share buybacks could help focus managers on shareholders' interests. Liberalizing the institutional investor sector could produce "active owners." Strengthening the rights of minority shareholders could lead to the creation of a partial market for corporate control. In some of these areas, laws could be changed. In other areas, laws are not an impediment to change, but habit and the self-interest of groups that would lose from deregulation may be.

To date, only a minority of Big Bang reforms have been aimed at corporate governance, despite the fact that reforming corporate governance presents a promising opportunity for Japan to improve its future economic performance. Table 12.3 summarizes the discussion in the previous section and assesses the Big Bang's progress.

One can ask what might happen if the groups in Japan with no incentive for change—managers and bureaucrats—resist the pressure for change. Because restrictions on foreign investment have been eliminated, there is no reason why Japanese wealth holders should not place their wealth in investments that earn a risk-adjusted return commensurate with what is available in global markets. Absent changes in corporate governance that could pressure Japanese managers to increase earnings, a decline in Japanese stock prices could increase the

TABLE 12.3. Summary of the Big Bang's Progress on Corporate Governance Reforms

Focus managers on shareholder returns	Little progress
Equity-based compensation	
Independent boards of directors	
Internal accountability	
Share buybacks	
Shareholder lawsuits	
Changes to institutional investors	Some progress
Deregulate mutual fund and pension fund management industry	
Encourage mutual funds and pension funds to produce high returns	
Changes in the market for corporate control	Little progress
Reduce cross-shareholding	
Encourage activist investors	

expected return on Japanese stocks by reducing the valuation attached to an unchanged stream of corporate earnings. In either case, the risk-return trade-off of Japanese equities would be made closer to that available in the global market. Barriers to foreign investment by Japanese households have been falling for several years, so it is possible that the poor performance of the Japanese stock market in the past few years is (at least partially) due to a convergence of its valuations with those available in global markets.

Overall, I believe the changes undertaken so far will have only limited success at changing the incentives for Japanese managers to improve shareholder returns. The majority of the Big Bang reforms, aimed at financial modernization, will help make the financial sector more efficient. But financial sector efficiency will give only an indirect boost to economic performance.

ACKNOWLEDGEMENTS

I thank Takeo Hoshi, Hugh Patrick, colleagues at the Federal Reserve Board, participants in the Columbia University conference on Restructuring the Japanese Financial System, the 1998 NBER Japan Project Meeting in Cambridge MA, and participants in seminars at the University of Tokyo, Japan Development Bank Research Institute for Capital Formation, and Kobe University Research Institute for Economics and Business for helpful comments on a previous draft. I also thank Takeo Hoshi for providing me with the data on accounting returns for US and Japanese firms during 1966–79.

Remaining errors are the responsibility of the author. The views in this paper are solely the responsibility of the author and should not be interpreted as reflecting the views of the Board of Governors of the Federal Reserve System or of any other person associated with the Federal Reserve System.

NOTES

1 Fukao (1998) and a small number of other authors discussing the Big Bang also have argued for the importance of corporate governance. Also see "Japan's Ray of Hope," Financial Times, 6 May 1998.

In a similar vein, Kaplan (1997b) argued that the US corporate governance system of the 1970s was ill-suited for the economic environment of the 1980s. He argues that the takeover wave of the 1980s led to improved corporate governance and improved performance by US firms.

2 For the United States, Black (1997, p 3) argues that institutional investor activism "can't substitute for a vigorous corporate control market." Del Guercio and Hawkins (forthcoming) suggest that institutional investor activism may be effective because of its interaction with the hostile takeover market.

REFERENCES

Aoki, Masahiko. 1994. "The contingent governance of teams: An analysis of institutional complementarity." *International Economic Review* 35:3 (Aug) 657–76.

Aoki, Masahiko and Hugh Patrick. 1994. *The Japanese Main Bank System*. Oxford: Oxford University Press.

Berglof, Erik and Enrico Perotti. 1994. "The governance structure of the Japanese financial *keiretsu*." *Journal of Financial Economics* 36:2 (Oct) 259–84.

Bethel, Jennifer E, Julia Porter Liebeskind, and Tim Opler. 1998. "Block share purchases and corporate performance." *Journal of Finance* 53:2 (Apr) 605–34.

Bhagat, Sanjai and Bernard Black. 1996 Mar. "Do independent directors matter?" Working paper.

Black, Bernard S. 1997. "Shareholder activism and corporate governance in the United States." Forthcoming in Peter Newman, editor, *The New Palgrave Dictionary of Economics and the Law*. Stockton Press.

Blommestein, Hans. 1997. "The impact of institutional investors on OECD financial markets." *Financial Market Trends* 68 (Nov) 15–54.

Brickley, James A, Sanjai Bhagat, and Ronald C Lease. 1985. "The impact of long-range managerial compensation plans on shareholder wealth." *Journal of Accounting and Economics* 7:1-3 (Apr) 115–29.

Business Roundtable. 1997 Sep. *Statement on Corporate Governance*.

Cai, J, KC Chan and T Yamada. 1997. "The performance of Japanese mutual funds." *Review of Financial Studies* 10:2 (Summer) 237–74.

Comment, Robert and Gregg A Jarrell. 1991. "The relative signaling power of Dutch-auction and fixed-price self-tender offers and open-market share repurchases." *Journal of Finance* 46:4 (Sep) 1243–71.

Corporate Governance Forum of Japan. 1997. "Corporate governance principles B, A Japanese view (Interim report)." Working paper, 30 Oct 1997. (Available at http://paperhost.ssrn.com/papers/9804/98041401.pdf).

Del Guercio, Diane and Jennifer Hawkins. Forthcoming. "The motivation and impact of pension fund activism." *Journal of Financial Economics.*

Fenn, George W and Nellie Liang. 1998. "Good news and bad news about share repurchases." Finance and Economics Discussion Series Working Paper 1998–4, Federal Reserve Board.

French, Kenneth R and James M Poterba. 1991. "Were Japanese stock prices too high?" *Journal of Financial Economics* 29, 337–63.

Fukao, Mitsuhiro. 1995. *Financial Integration, Corporate Governance and the Performance of Multinational Companies.* The Brookings Institution.

Fukao, Mitsuhiro. 1998. "Japanese financial instability and weaknesses in the corporate governance structure." Conference Paper 98-2-6, Keio University.

Gorton, Gary and Matthias Kahl. 1998 Mar. "Rich investors, institutional investors, and dynamic corporate control." Working paper, Wharton School.

Hanazaki, Masaharu and Akiyoshi Horiuchi. 1998. "A vacuum of governance in the Japanese bank management." Discussion Paper CIRJE-F-29, Center for International Research on the Japanese Economy, University of Tokyo.

Hoshi, Takeo, Anil Kashyap, and David Scharfstein. 1990. "The role of banks in reducing the costs of financial distress in Japan." *Journal of Financial Economics* 27:1 (Sep) 67–88.

Ito, Takatoshi. 1992. *The Japanese Economy.* MIT Press.

Kang, Jun-Koo and Anil Shivdasani. 1996. "Does the Japanese governance system enhance shareholder wealth? Evidence from the stock-price effects of top management turnover." *Review of Financial Studies* 9:4 (Winter) 1061–95.

Kang, Jun-Koo and Rene M Stulz. 1996. "How Different Is Japanese Corporate Finance? An Investigation of the Information Content of New Security Issues." *Review of Financial Studies* 9:1 (Spring) 109–39.

Kaplan, Steven N. 1994. "Top executive rewards and firm performance: A comparison of Japan and the US." *Journal of Political Economy* 102:3 (Jun) 510–46.

Kaplan, Steven N. 1995. "The homogeneity of Japanese boards." *Directors & Boards* 19:3 (Spring) 31–2.

Kaplan, Steven N. 1997a. "Corporate governance and corporate performance: A comparison of Germany, Japan and the US." In Donald H Chew, editor, *Studies in International Corporate Finance and Governance Systems.* New York: Oxford University Press.

Kaplan, Steven N. 1997b. "The Evolution of US Corporate Governance: We Are All Henry Kravis Now." Working paper, University of Chicago Graduate School of Business.

Kaplan, Steven N and Bernadette A Minton. 1994. "Appointments of outsiders to Japanese boards: Determinants and implications for managers." *Journal of Financial Economics* 36:2 (Oct) 225–58.

Karpoff, Jonathan M. 1998. "The Impact of Shareholder Activism on Target Companies: A Survey of Empirical Findings." Working paper, University of Washington.

Kato, Takeo and Mark Rockel. 1992. "Experiences, Credentials, and Compensation in the Japanese and US Managerial Labor Markets: Evidence from New Micro Data." *Journal of the Japanese and International Economy* 6:1 (Mar) 30–51.

Kester, W Carl. 1991. *Japanese takeovers: The global contest for corporate control*, Boston: Harvard Business School Press.

Kojima, Kenji. 1997. *Japanese corporate governance: An international perspective*. Kobe, Japan: Research Institute for Economics & Business Administration, Kobe University.

Kubo, Katsuyuki. 1998. "The determinants of executive compensation and its effect on company performance in Japan and in the UK." Paper presented at the Workshop on Corporate Governance, Contracts, and Managerial Incentives, Berlin, 2–4 July 1998.

McCauley, Robert N and Steven A Zimmer. 1989. "Explaining international differences in the cost of capital." *Federal Reserve Bank of New York Quarterly Review* 14:2 (Summer) 7–28.

Mehran, Hamid. 1995. "Executive compensation structure, ownership, and firm performance". *Journal of Financial Economics* 38:2, 163–84.

Milhaupt, Curtis J. 1996 "A relational theory of Japanese corporate governance: Contract, culture, and the rule of law." *Harvard International Law Journal* 37:1 (Winter) 3–64.

Morck, Randall and Masao Nakamura. 1999. "Banks and corporate control in Japan." *Journal of Finance* 54:1 (Feb) 319–39.

Morinaga, Teruki and Mitsuhiro Fukao. 1997. "The current state of the Japanese corporate pension system and its problems." Working paper, Keio University.

Nakatani, Iwao. 1984. "The economic role of financial corporate grouping." In Masahiko Aoki, editor, *The Economic Analysis of the Japanese Firm*. North Holland.

Nickell, Stephen J. 1996. "Competition and corporate performance." *Journal of Political Economy* 104:4 (Aug) 724–746.

Okumura, Hiroshi. 1989. "Stock cornering, takeovers, and tender offers: The economics of stock acquisitions." In Yukio Yanagida et al, editors, *Law and Investment in Japan*. East Asian Legal Studies Program, Harvard Law School.

Opler, Tim C and Jonathan Sokobin. 1997. "Does coordinated institutional shareholder activism work? An analysis of the activities of the Council of Institutional Investors." Working paper, Ohio State University.

Peck, Charles. 1998. *Top Executive Compensation in 1996*. The Conference Board.

Prowse, Stephen D. 1990. "Institutional investment patterns and corporate financial behavior in the United States and Japan." *Journal of Financial Economics* 27:1 (Sep) 43–66.

Prowse, Stephen D. 1992. "The structure of corporate ownership in Japan." *Journal of Finance* 47:3 (July) 1121–40.

Ramseyer, J Mark. 1987. "Takeovers in Japan: Opportunism, ideology, and corporate control." *UCLA Law Review* 35:1, 21–5.

SDP = Securities Data Publishing. *The Merger Yearbook: US/International Edition 1997.*

Strahan, Philip E. 1998 Jun. "Securities class actions, corporate governance and managerial agency problems." Working paper, Federal Reserve Bank of New York.

Weinstein, David E. 1997. "Foreign direct investment and *keiretsu*: Rethinking U.S. and Japanese policy." In Robert C Feenstra, editor, *The Effects of U.S. Trade Protection and Promotion Policies*. University of Chicago Press for NBER.

Weisbach, Michael S. 1988. "Outside directors and CEO turnover." *Journal of Financial Economics* 20:1-2, 431–60.

SUBJECT INDEX

Accounting standards. 243, 283, 289, 294
Agency costs. 168
Agricultural credit cooperatives. 29
  and jûsen. 12–13, 14, 89, 115–16
Asian countries, parallels with Japan. 105–07
Asset Management Council. 222
Asset management. 239–41, 267, 274, 275, 288–89

Bad loans. see Nonperforming loans.
Bank lending,
  by firm size. 178–80, 179 (Table 7.10), 180 (Table 7.11)
  by industry. 180–83, 181 (Table 7.12), 182 (Table 7.13)
  characteristics (generally), late 1970s to 1990s. 161–65
  collateral, real estate as. 164–65, 165 (Table 7.4), 171
  composition of. 162–64, 163 (Table 7.2)
  determinants of. Ch 7
  effect of capital requirements on. 183–86, 184 (Table 7.14)
  effect of Big Bang on. 278
  growth rate of. 162, 162 (Table 7.1)
  growth rate of, by industry. 164 (Table 7.3)
  liquidity constraints on. 171
  macroeconomic consequences. 159–60, 186–91, 193–96
  model of. 167–70
  relation to real activity of firms. 159–60, 186–91, 193–96
  role of. 240
  supply of. 176–78, 176 (Table 7.8), 177 (Table 7.9)
  to large manufacturing firms. 10 (Figure 1.1).
Bank monitoring. 283, 297, 301
Bank of Japan.
  concern with exchange rate. 47
  governing law revised (1997). 47–48
  independence from MOF. 48
  policy failure as cause of banking problem. 38, 46–47
  Also see Monetary policy.
Bank structure.
  creation of new framework (1996–98). 116–22
  non-viability of old regime. 115–16
Banking problems,
  causes (see separate index entry)
  chronology of crisis. 61–62
  end of bail-outs. 117, 118
  government response. 38
  in the 1990s. 11–19
  politicians' involvement. 98–99, 120, 121, 132–33, 238
  private-sector response. 50, 91
  resolution of crisis. 17–18
  Also see Nonperforming loans
  Also see Regulation
Banking problems, causes. Ch 5; 38
  BOJ policy failures. 38
  conventional view of. 234
  lack of critical observers. 52–53
  MOF policy failures. 92–93, 237
  rigid financial regime. 38
  structural weaknesses. 94–99
  Also see Financial system
Bankruptcy. 246
  Inadequacy of system in Japan. 151
Banks.
  bailout packages. See Use of public money.
  balance sheets. 174–75, 174 (Table 7.7)
  credit ratings. 90–91
  deposits, growth. 172, 173 (Table 7.6)
  end of bail-outs. 117, 118

Banks *continued.*
failures of. 96; Also see Safety net, Deposit Insurance Corp.
future of. 26–28
inefficiency of. 45, 236
lack of concern with profits. 45
mergers. 26–27
risk management by. 77
security holdings of. 94
types of. 2–5, 59–62
unrealized capital gains (fukumi). 78, 94–95
Basle Accord. See Capital adequacy.
Big Bang. Ch 9, Ch 10, Ch 11, Ch 12; 122–25
components of. 255, 260–69
effect on capital adequacy rules. 269
effect on capital markets. 243–44
effect on contestability. 122–24, 244, 288
effect on corporate governance. Ch 11, Ch 12
effect on economy. 278
effect on legal system. ch 11; 279–81, 285–86
effects on regulation. 247, 279–80, 288
evaluation. 271–72
formulation of. 258, 260
goals of. 234
investment instruments under. 263–64
laws implementing. 237–38, 250 (note 1), 269
nature of. 257–59, 278, 288–89
promoted by. 237
reasons for. 272 (note 2)
regulation under. 261–63
remaining issues. 246–49, 270–71
securities industry restructuring. 269–71
specific reforms. 238–46
time table for. 292
BIS ratio. See capital adequacy.
Blame avoidance. see Bureaucratic restructuring
BOJ = Bank of Japan.
Bureaucratic restructuring
and blame avoidance. 110, 111, 125, 131–33
and interest group mobilization. 110, 131–32, 132
theories of. 110–12
Capital adequacy. (Also called BIS (Bank for International Settlements) ratio) 27–28, 62, 77–78, 78, 80 (note 2), 94–95, 173, 253–55, 255 (Table 10.2)
Big Bang rules on. 269.
effects on lending. 183–86, 184 (Table 7.14)
Capital markets.
Big Bang reform of. 243–44
Also see Financial system
CCPC = Cooperative Credit Purchasing Corp.
Collateral, real estate as. See Real estate.
Compartmentalization. See Segmentation; Contestability.
Contestability.
After Big Bang. 246–47, 267–68, 276, 288
Also see Segmentation.
Convoy system. 8, 15–16, 44
undermined by reforms. 15–16
Cooperative Credit Purchasing Corp (CCPC). Ch 6; 92
and jûsen. 148
and LTCB. 152–53
bank losses on loans sold to. 147, 148 (Table 6.3), 153
evaluation of. 155–56
income of. 146–47, 147 (Table 6.2)
loan purchases. 142–44, 143 (Table 6.1), 153
loan valuations. 144–46, 145 (Figure 6.3)
origins. 139
reform proposals. 151–54
sale of loans by. 146, 147 (Table 6.2), 151–52, 153
structure. 140 (Figure 6.2), 141
Corporate finance
components of, 1961–95. 242 (Table 9.2)
for small firms. 241, 242
post Big Bang changes. 241–42
types available. 10–11, 282–83, 289
Also see Bank lending.
Corporate governance
boards of directors. 303–04
effect of Big Bang on. Ch 11, Ch 12; 281–83, 302–09, 310 (Table 12.3), 311 (note 1)
focusing managers on shareholder returns. 302–09

Corporate governance *continued.*
nature of. 281–82, 283–84
role of inside stakeholders. 298–99
institutional investors. 299–300, 311 (note 2)
market for corporate control. 300, 308–09, 311 (note 1)
system is not dysfunctional. 300–02
Corporate Governance Forum. 304
Corporate pension funds. See Institutional investors.
Credit crunch. 220
Also see Bank lending.
Cross-shareholding. 265, 282–83, 300

Debt. see also Bank lending, Government debt.
Deposit guarantees. See Deposit Insurance Corporation (DIC).
Deposit Insurance Corp (DIC). 28, 44–45, 117, 119, 120, 246, 247
reforms. 95–98
Deregulation. 9, 15, 123, 297
as cause of bank crisis. 234–35
pace of. 235
role in bank problems. 76–77
Also see Big Bang
Also see Financial System
Also see Regulation
Derivative actions for shareholders. See Shareholder lawsuits.
DIC = Deposit Insurance Corp.
Disintermediation. 27, 219, 253

Economic conditions.
Asian economic crisis of 1997–98. 86
liquidity trap, 1997–99. 100–01
overview, 1985–98. 85–87
recession of 1997–99. 48
since 1976. 216–18
stagnation in 1990s. 11–12
also see November 1997 crisis.
Exchange rate policy (yen depreciation). 99

FILP. See Fiscal Investment and Loan Program.
Finance Agency (Kinyu-cho). 109, 127, 128, 129, 133, 247
Financial Crisis Management Committee (Kin'yu Kiki Kanri Iinkai). 17
Financial institutions
assets and deposits. 2–5 (Tables 1.1, 1.2, 1.3)
types of. 2–6
Also see specific types.
Financial market reforms. See Big Bang; Deregulation
Financial Reconstruction Act (1998). 17–18
Financial Reconstruction Commission (FRC, Kinyu Saisei Iinkai). 17, 108, 116–17, 120, 128–29, 133, 279
Financial Supervisory Agency (FSA, Kinyu Kantoku–cho). 18, 108, 116, 245, 246, 262–63, 279
deciding powers of. 126–27
effectiveness of. 247–48
Financial system. 39–46, 54–56
1940s to mid '70s. 209–10
characteristics of old regime. 40 (Table 2.1)
evolution of. 39, 228 (note 3)
historical overview. 54–56, 56 (note 1).
incompatibility of old regime with changing environment. 40–41
lack of critical observers. 53–54
liberalization. 42, 66
nontransparency. 43, 52
objectives (before liberalization). 39
perseverance of old regime. 43
prewar. 209
reforms other than Big Bang. 259
role of in economy. 31–32
since 1976. 216–18
stability of. 7, 235, 236, 278
structure of under Big Bang. 264–65, 273–76
Also see Big Bang.
Also see Convoy system.
Also see Safety net.
Also see Financial system, change in.
Financial system, change in. 8–11
impetus for change. 9
prospects and remaining problems. 26–32

Financial system, change in *continued.*
role of government debt. 9
Also see Deregulation.
Also see Big Bang.
Financial Systems Research Council (FSRC). 258, 259, 269
Financial System Reform Enactment (FSRE). 269
Fiscal Investment and Loan Program (FILP). Ch 8; 46
defined. 203
evaluation. 215
reforms (1998). 222–24
reforms, factors in. 224–25
reforms, suggesting for. 225–26
since 1976. 216–18
use of funds. 205–06, 206–08 (Table 8.2, Table 8.3), 217 (Table 8.5)
Fiscal policy. 101–03
public works reform. 104
reasons for reluctance to stimulate in 1998. 102
tax cuts, proposals for. 103–04
Also see Tax system.
Foreign financial institutions. 30
FRC = Financial Reconstruction Commission.
FSA = Financial Supervisory Agency.
FSRC = Financial Systems Research Council.
FSRE = Financial System Reform Enactment.
Fukumi (unrealized capital gains). See Banks.

Government banks. 214–15, 218, 219–20
"cow-bell effect." 214–15
Also see Government financial institutions
Government debt. 9
Government financial institutions. 31, 228 (note 3), 248–49
nonperforming loans at. 220
suggestions for reform of. 225
Also see Government banks.
Also see Postal savings.
Government financial intermediation. See Government financial institutions.
Government pension programs. 30
Government policy.
importance of financial system stability. 7
directive to reduce lending to real estate. 114
Also see Government response to banking problems
Government response to banking problems. 14–16, 38, 48–50
denial. 16, 39
forbearance. 39, 67, 77–78, 87–88, 237
Also see Use of public money.

HLAC = Housing Loan Administration Corp.
Holding companies. 244, 265, 288, 304–05
Hougacho, defined. 15
Household financial assets. 239 (Table 9.1), 254 (Table 10.1)
low return on. 291
Housing Loan Administration Corp (HLAC). 90, 154
Also see Jûsen.
Housing. 103–04

Institutional investors. 299, 306–07, 307
as monitors. 53, 308
Interest group mobilization. See Bureaucratic restructuring
Interest groups. 132–33
Investment behavior by non-financial firms. 165–67, 167 (Table 7.5), 186–91
effect of restrictions on real-estate lending. 191, 192 (Table 7.16)
effect of bank failures in November 1997. 191, 192 (Table 7.17)
Investment instruments and choices. 263–64, 273–74, 283, 288
of households 30, 240–41, 263, 267, 274, 288, 307
Investment trusts.
defined. 30
Also see Investment instrument and choices of households.

Japan premium. 14, 90, 93, 113
defined. 90

Jûsen Resolution Corp (now known as Housing Loan Administration Corp). 90
Jûsen. 12–14, 89–90, 113–16
  and CCPC. 148
  and SPC. 150–51
  defined. 12
  development of. 114
  involvement of politicians. 115–16
  liquidation of (1996). 115–16
  MOF restructuring of. 13
  major features of crisis. 113–14
  1994–96 crisis. 114–15

Keiretsu. 7, 292–93, 301
Kinyu-cho. See Finance Agency.
Kinyu Kantoku-cho. See Financial Supervisory Agency (FSA).
Kinyu Kiki Kanri Iinkai (Financial Crisis Management Committee). 17
Kinyu Saisei Iinkai. See Financial Reconstruction Commission (FRC).

Land prices. 65–66 (Figure 3.1)
Legal system. 307
  cost of enforcement. 283–85
  effect of Big bang on. ch 11; 279–81, 285–86
  features of. 277, 279–81, 283–85, 286 (note 1)
Lending channel, defined. 159, 198 (note 1)
Liberalization. See Financial system
Life insurance companies. 240
  problems of. 29
Liquidity trap. 100–01
Loan write-offs. 80 (note 3), 91
  Also see Nonperforming loans.
Loan-loss provisions. 62, 91
  Also see Nonperforming loans.
Long-term Credit Bank (LTCB). 17, 18, 98–99, 119, 120
  and CCPC. 152–53
LSRF = Laws for Financial System Reformation. See Big Bang, laws implementing.
LTCB = Long-term Credit Bank.

Macroeconomic policy. 73–76
  relation to asset price swings. 73–76
Main bank system. 6–8
  definition. 7
  problems of. 8
Managers
  compensation of. 302–03
  laxness of. 67
  Also see Corporate governance.
Maruyu system. 210, 218
Mergers. See Corporate governance
Ministry of Finance (MOF).
  advisory councils of. 222, 238
  consequences of jûsen crisis. 116
  restructured as Treasury Ministry. 245, 251 (note 3)
  policy mistakes. 92–93, 237
  Also see Government response; other specific topics.
MOF = Ministry of Finance.
MOF, reorganization of. Ch 5.
  alternative arguments for. 130–32
  chronology and reasons for. 125–29
  conventional explanations. 109
  dependence on banks for policy implementation. 121
  implications. 132–33
  internal reforms. 110, 122
  old regulatory regime. 122
Monetary policy. 46–47, 73–76, 99, 100, 216
  relation to asset price swings. 73–76
  in late 1980s. 74–76
Moral hazard. 95, 119, 237
Mutual funds. See Investment and choices of households.

Non-bank financial institutions. 28–31
Nonperforming loans,
  causes. 67–73
  definition of. 18–20 (Table 1.4), 60 (Table 3.1)
  development of crisis. 87–94
  disclosure of. 87–88, 137, 138 (Figure 6.1)
  disposal of. 151, 272 (note 1)
  extent of problem at March 1998. 62–63 (Table 3.2)

Nonperforming loans *continued.*
- extent of problem in 1999. 18–20 (Table 1.4)
- loans sold CCPC, off-balance sheet liability for. 144
- MOF attempts to address, 116–22
- provisions for losses, 1993–95. 91
- public awareness of. 88
- reasons level not reduced. 63
- written off. 63
- Also see CCPC
- Also see SPC

November 1997 crisis. 16, 93–94, 119

Oigashi, defined. 88

PCA = Prompt Corrective Action
PLIF = Postal Life Insurance Fund. See Fiscal Investment and Loan Program.
Postal Life Insurance Fund (PLIF). See Fiscal Investment and Loan Program.
Postal savings. Ch 8; 6, 31, 46, 97–98, 248
- deposits in. 203, 204 (Figure 8.1), 205 (Table 8.1), 217, 219
- evaluation. 215
- in the 1990s. 218–19
- potentially destabilizing role. 97
- reasons for success. 210–14
- reforms (1998). 222–24
- reforms, factors in. 224–25
- reforms, need for. 97–98, 225
- reforms, suggestions for. 225–26
- services of. 228 (note 2)
- since 1976. 216–18
- structure. 203

Problem loans. see Nonperforming loans.
Prompt Corrective Action (PCA) (18 Jun 1996 law). 15, 28, 62, 78, 80 (note 1), 245, 251 (note 4)
Public attitude
- comparison to US S&L case. 51–52
- toward government spending. 102–03
- Also see Use of public money.

Public works. see Fiscal policy.

Rapid Recapitalization Act (1998). 17–18
RCB = See Reorganization and Collection Bank.
RCC = Resolution and Collection Corporation.
Real estate, lending to
- as cause of banking problems. Ch 3, Ch 7; 67–73
- directive to reduce level of. 90, 114
- extent. 64–66 (Table 3.3). 66

Real estate markets. 29
Real estate as collateral. 164–65, 165 (Table 7.4), 171, 191, 192 (Table 7.16), 198 (note 3)
Regulation.
- after Big Bang. 244, 261–63, 275–76
- agency problems. 53
- role in bank problems. 76–79
- Also see Deregulation
- Also see Regulators

Regulators
- constraints on. 78–79
- credibility of. 92–93
- ineffective monitoring by. 237
- Also see Regulation

Reorganization and Collection Bank (RCB). 96, 97, 118, 120, 154
Resolution and Collection Corporation (RCC). 119, 120, 154–55
Return on equity.
- level of. 293–96, 294 (Table 12.2), 295 (Figure 12.1), 296 (Figure 12.2)
- causes for low level of. 296–97
- relation to corporate governance. 298–302

Safety net. 28, 67, 236–37, 268–69
- Also see Deposit Insurance Corp

SEC = Securities and Exchange Council.
Securities and Exchange Council (SEC). 258
- members of. 272 (note 3)
- report of 29 Nov 1996. 258, 272 (note 4)

Securities industry. 266–68
- restructuring of. 269–71, 273–76

Securities laws. 256, 273–76
Securities markets system, defined. 253, 256
- Also see Capital markets; Financial system, structure of; Big Bang.

Securities markets.
structure of. 256–57
Also see Securities industry.
Segmentation.
Big Bang effects on. 244, 289
Also see Contestability; Financial system, structure of.
Shadow Financial Regulatory Committee. 98–99
Shareholder lawsuits. 243, 251 (note 2), 305–06
SPC = Special Purpose Companies.
Special Purpose Companies (SPC). 148–51
and jûsen. 150
structure for transferring bad loans to. 150 (Figure 6.4)
SRO = self-regulatory organizations. 263

Takeovers. See Corporate governance
Tax system. 249, 264, 276, 305, 307
Also see Fiscal policy.
Tax treatment
of interest paid depositors. See Maruyu system.
of loan losses. 141–42, 151
of loans sold to CCPC. 147
of loans sold to SPCs. 149
Teigaku (time deposits). 226–27
TFB = Trust Fund Bureau. See Fiscal Investment and Loan Program.
Tokyo Kyodo Bank (now Reorganization and Collection Bank (RCB)). 96
Trust Fund Bureau. See Fiscal Investment and Loan Program.

Use of public money to address banking problems. 16, 17–18, 49, 50, 92, 94, 98–99, 116, 117, 119, 121, 139
lack of public support for. 51–52
Also see Public attitude.

Zaimu-sho = Treasury Ministry (successor to Ministry of Finance, which see).